From June to October

The Middle East between 1967 and 1973

The Shiloah Center for Middle Eastern and African Studies
Tel Aviv University

The Shiloah Center is, with the Department of Middle Eastern and African History, a part of the School of History at Tel Aviv University. Its main purpose is to contribute, by research and documentation, to the dissemination of knowledge and understanding of the modern history and current affairs of the Middle East and Africa. Emphasis is laid on fields where Israeli scholarship is in a position to make a special contribution and on subjects relevant to the needs of society and the teaching requirements of the University.

Collected Papers Series

The books published in this series consist of collections of selected papers presented mostly in seminars and conferences of the Shiloah Center. The views expressed in these papers are entirely those of the authors.

M. Confino and S. Shamir (eds.) / *The U.S.S.R. and the Middle East*

Editorial Board

From June to October

The Middle East between 1967 and 1973

Edited by

Itamar Rabinovich
Haim Shaked

TRANSACTION BOOKS

New Brunswick, New Jersey

Library of Congress Cataloging in Publication Data

Main entry under title:

From June to October.

    1. Near East—Politics and government—Congresses. 2 Jewish-Arab
relations—1967-1973—Congresses.
I. Rabinovich, Itamar, 1942-   II. Shaked, Haim.
DS63.1.F76   956'.046   76-45942
ISBN 0-87855-230-8.

Printed in the United States of America

99617

Contents

The Arab Environment

Iran and the Gulf

Introduction

Introduction

It is indeed appropriate for a research project in contemporary history that its own course be affected by the very processes it has sought to explore. The present volume originated in the Shiloah Center's Annual Seminar for the academic year 1973/74. When the seminar had originally been planned, early in 1973, it seemed that the changes that had taken place in the Middle East since the 1967 War warranted a broad review of the six years that had elapsed. It was then decided to examine the major political developments of the period in the framework of a seminar that would culminate in an international colloquium.

Among many other things the October 1973 War also interfered with this plan, not only by disrupting its schedule but also by providing a point of termination for the period which opened with the June War. A clearly defined periodization was thus established for both the Seminar and the Colloquium, but two particular problems were added to the ones inherent in any examination of recent and highly charged events. There was likely to be in the aftermath of the October War a natural tendency to view the years 1967–1973 from a rather narrow perspective, focusing on the processes which led to the war and neglecting other themes and issues of that period. It would also be tempting for a group of people interested in contemporary politics and international affairs meeting in December 1974 to discuss current and future developments in the Middle East rather than dwell on the past, recent as it may have been.

With these considerations in mind the Seminar and the Colloquium were so structured as to provide as broad an outlook as possible—given the limitations of time and budget, and the scholarly disciplines of the participants—and to reflect the major changes and developments which occurred in the Middle East between 1967 and 1973. For the same reason the published volume includes several papers (on the Iraqi Ba'th regime; the Federation of Arab Republics; Saudi Arabia, Yemen and

xiii

South Yemen; and on the Sudan and Libya) which had been read during the preceding Seminar but for lack of time could not be presented at the Colloquium.

The contemporary scene became part of the colloquium in a number of ways. Quite a few participants dwelt, either in writing or during their deliberations, on aspects and problems relating to the future. They met with Minister of Defense Shimon Peres for an informal discussion. On the eve of the Colloquium Israel's Minister of Foreign Affairs, Yigal Allon, delivered a speech titled "Directions in Israeli Foreign Policy" (the transcript of which, as well as the full proceedings of the Colloquium, are kept at the Shiloah Center's Documentation Center). Mr. Allon's lecture took a comprehensive view of Israel's diplomatic position and policy in the wake of the October War and the disengagement agreements with Egypt and Syria. Against this background he dealt specifically with the issues then discussed in the context of a second interim agreement between Israel and Egypt. The Minister of Foreign Affairs also presented a set of priorities for Israeli policy in which he defined "the achievement of real peace with all our neighbors or at least with any Arab state prepared for it," as "the central goal and the primary objective of our policy." But since he could not see that a favorable response from any Arab state would be forthcoming, he set out Israel's "secondary objectives" in the following order:

> The prevention of war. If this is impossible—its postponement in the hope of eventually avoiding its outbreak. If this cannot be achieved—limiting the war to a minimum of battle fronts. If this, too, is impossible, then preventing the multiple front from becoming a simultaneous one. Of course all these steps must be taken while doing our outmost, politically and information-wise, to gain maximum understanding and sympathy for our position and policy...

The first working session of the Colloquium dealt with the Persian Gulf. The discussion which followed the presentations by Professors Ramazani and Abir and Mr. Shmuelevitz revolved around two major issues: the linkage between the Persian Gulf and the core area of the Middle East, and the repercussions of the energy crisis on the policies of the superpowers with regard to the Persian Gulf. Prompted by questions and comments by other participants, Professor Abir elaborated on the acuteness of Arab–Iranian rivalries in the Persian Gulf. He did not rule out the possibility of Egyptian and even Syrian involvement in that area. While acknowledging "the fundamental divergency between Iran and the Arab states as a whole" and its historical and cultural dimensions, Professor Ramazani took a more conservative view of the Arab–Iranian conflict. Having outlined alternative courses for Iranian policy in the Gulf area and emphasizing its pragmatism he suggested that:

It would not be a good idea to accept the scenario or the proposition that Arab–Israeli conflict under all circumstances is a welcome omen to the Iranians. Again [since it is] a case of the [Iranian[policy being fundamentally pragmatic, it all depends if that conflict is going to have a spillover into the Gulf area in the sense of again jeopardizing what Iran considers to be its basic interest.

Prof. Ramazani pursued the same themes of caution and pragmatism when other participants pointed to the apparent incongruence of Iran's fundamental pro-Western stance and its insistence on high oil prices, which seemed harmful to the Western economic system and raised the prospects of the possibility of an armed American intervention in the Persian Gulf. In response, Prof. Ramazani explained Iran's reservations with regard to a policy of *détente* which could be effective elsewhere but harmful to Iran's interests, and described Iran's approach to the price of oil as purely economic. In this he was joined by the chairman of the session, Mr. Bitan, himself a senior oil industry executive, who thought "that in that respect Iran has not behaved differently from all the other oil-producing countries," namely, that it sought to extract the highest possible revenues from its mineral resources under the most favorable circumstances.

The repercussions of the energy crisis, the Arab oil embargo and the steep rise in oil prices were discussed in greater detail during the next session. Prof. Kanovsky and Dr. Sheffer presented two different approaches to the problems of economic development and growth in Egypt, while Professor Shwadran dealt with the dramatic changes that the Middle Eastern oil industry underwent in recent years. In the ensuing discussion and in response to statements by Prof. Ramazani, Dr. Max Singer and Mr. Larry L. Fabian, Prof. Shwadran further explained that in his opinion the Saudi Arabian government was primarily motivated in its oil prices policy by economic considerations, and that the growth in the power of OPEC and OAPEC countries was largely due to the disunity as well as the ineffectiveness of the diplomatic and political action of the industrialized West. In the same vein he disagreed with the suggestion that the Arab oil embargo had been very effective and had been lifted (in the wake of the Egyptian–Israeli Disengagement Agreement) only after the actual goals set out by its authors had been achieved. Rather, he argued:

> There was a definite dropping of demands . . . and my thesis is
> that it was primarily an economic factor and once this factor
> was achieved by Saudi Arabia, Saudi Arabia was determined
> to go back to the fold, because it was an aberration of the
> entire Saudi Arabian orientation and policy.

The discussion of the prospects of Egypt's economic development pinpointed the divergence between two theoretical outlooks, presented by Prof. Kanovsky and Dr. Sheffer. The former held that economic development and growth in Egypt were impeded by factors inherent in Egyptian society and its economy, particularly the absence of sufficient skilled manpower. Consequently, even a considerable influx of Arab capital could not radically alter the situation. The latter saw the dearth of capital available to Egypt as its major problem, and was of the opinion "that Egypt is going to acquire the necessary resources to advance rapidly on a path of sustained economic growth. Dr. Gur Ofer took an intermediate position. He thought that even if Egypt was provided with all the capital it needed it could not grow over a period of time at a nine per cent rate per annum, but he believed that:

> Capital in Egypt can make a difference and a very crucial
> difference between a three per cent increase in the GNP
> which, given the rate of growth of the population, means [a]
> zero [growth] rate and maybe five and six per cent or maybe
> seven per cent of growth . . .

The somewhat theoretical discussion could not be divorced from the political realities of the Middle East. Even from a perspective which regards capital rather than manpower as the real bottleneck to growth, several questions remained to be answered: would the oil producing Arab countries provide Egypt with sufficient funds needed for its economic development as well as with the resources necessary for arms procurements? If this were the case, would Egypt be able to maintain heavy involvement in the conflict with Israel and at the same time take off economically? The discussion offered no clearcut answers to these questions. It was agreed, though, that Egypt could not remain deeply committed to the conflict and at the same time mobilize all the energy and resources necessary for an economic breakthrough. This would mean that Egypt might let "this unique chance in her history for sustained economic growth" slip by. On the other hand, it was not unreasonable to assume that the oil-producing countries were likely to continue a massive flow of capital to Egypt only as long as Egypt continued to play a prominent role in the Arab–Israeli conflict.

Whatever Egypt's long-range economic prospects, it was suggested that the rapid expansion of the combined Arab financial resources presented a serious problem for Israel. Israel, it was noted, had been able in the past to mobilize sufficient resources so as to maintain both military preparedness and a high rate of economic growth. The massive growth of resources available to the Arabs in 1974 raised serious questions with regard to Israel's ability to keep abreast with the Arab military build-up without seriously affecting its own precarious economic condition.

The next session dealt with the Powers and the Middle East. Dr. Eran, Prof. Quandt and Dr. Büren read papers on, respectively, Soviet, American and German policies towards the Middle East during the period under survey. The discussion of Soviet policy generated a debate which vividly illustrated the difference of opinion on fundamental issues among Sovietologists and other students of Soviet foreign policy. Some, like Dr. Galia Golan, took the view that Soviet policy and conduct in the Middle East had been moderated by the policy of *détente*. This and the desire to prevent the need for an open Soviet military intervention in the Middle East governed Moscow's policy during the early phase of the October War, including the resupply of Arab armies. "Only when the Arabs were in a difficult position and there was a need or an apparent need for a Soviet intervention," Dr. Golan said, "did the Soviets in fact agree to what amounted to a risk to *détente*." It was her opinion that the USSR was interested in a settlement of the Arab–Israeli conflict and that this attitude was explained by broad considerations of *détente* policy as well as by Soviet objectives in the Middle East and the Indian Ocean. She did not think the Soviets could expect to gain much from the Palestinians and regarded their support of the PLO as "mainly tactical."

Others, Prof. Alvin Rubinstein in particular, were more skeptical of Soviet intentions. He began his analysis of the post-October 1973 Soviet position with a summation of the major Soviet goals in the Middle East and their evolvement during the 1950s and 1960s. Against that background he considered "that the Soviet dividends from the October War have been enormous but not "in terms of an increase in Soviet influence in the Middle East" which, in his opinion, was not regarded as a priority area in their eyes. Far more important for the Soviets in terms of the then anticipated consequences of the October War were the disarray in NATO, the Western economic crisis and the reinforcement of the Soviets' belief that they could promote tension in the Middle East. Prof. Rubinstein did not see a dramatic decline in Soviet influence in the Arab world as a result of the war. Nor did he think that Moscow was seriously interested in a political settlement in the Middle East. He took a serious view of the USSR's relations with the PLO— a Palestinian state would "institutionalize a condition of perpetual tension" in the Middle East and thus would facilitate the promotion or at least the preservation of Soviet influence in the area.

How did Washington view the USSR's behavior during the war? According to Prof. Quandt:

> The top level American policy makers have concluded that Soviet behaviour, while objectionable, was not outside the bounds of what *détente* has come to mean; and it is partly because we also played around a little bit that we winked a bit at their playing around.

The discussion of American policy in the Middle East, despite the apparent awareness by the participants of the crucial role of US diplomacy in the area, was less animated. Mr. Yosef Ben Aharon pointed out some of what he regarded as the counterproductive aspects of that diplomacy. Speaking mostly about the years 1969–1970, but viewing them as representing a broader pattern, he suggested that rather than having a moderating effect on Egypt, the "Rogers plan" encouraged it to step up the War of Attrition. Other participants questioned Prof. Quandt's allusion to "domestic influences" on American policy toward the Middle East. In his response he explained that he had referred to "domestic influences which are not exclusively pressure groups or lobbies" and that he did not believe "that pressure groups have helped define broad basic interests either with respect to oil or Israel." However, he thought that on two occasions, in the fall of 1968 and in the summer of 1972, electoral considerations possibly affected Administration decisions with regard to the Middle East.

The next morning was devoted to the Palestinian issue. Four panelists—Prof. Dann, Dr. Ben Dor, Mr. E. Rekhess and Mr. A. Susser—presented three papers dealing with the three major actors in Palestinian politics—the Hashemite regime in Jordan, the PLO, and the Arab population of the West Bank. Both the panelists and commentators were in agreement on the major trends of the years 1967–1974: the ups and downs in Jordan's position, the reluctance of West Bank leaders to present clearcut positions on fundamental Palestinian issues and the PLO's remarkable success in mobilizing Arab support and winning considerable international recognition. It was also agreed that the marked absence of euphoria in the PLO's ranks after Yasser 'Arafat's appearance in the United Nations was justified. The PLO, it was felt, had thereby gained an important symbolic achievement but its future remained essentially dependent on the Arab states while its actual independent power in the Middle East had not significantly increased.

Opinions were divided on other related questions. Thus, it was Prof. Quandt's assessment that King Hussein "has perhaps concluded that the West Bank is not going to be returned to Jordan, particularly after the Rabat [1974] conference," and that "despite his sense of personal commitment and involvement with that issue, over time the commitment will erode and the benefits of just building up the East Bank of Jordan will become more apparent." While reluctant to speculate on this issue, Prof. Dann felt that the immediate impact of the Rabat conference was weakening and that King Hussein was returning to his former attachment to the West Bank. He mentioned "a very good national argument" that King Hussein had against relinquishing the West Bank, "namely , that a West Bank under Jordanian rule, with all the problems that it poses, is less dangerous to Hashemite rule in the East Bank than a West Bank which becomes a separate entity."

Lebanese politics did not figure prominantly in the Colloquium but the processes which led, eventually, to the 1975/76 crisis were discussed briefly in the context of Dr. Ben Dor's paper. Lebanon, it was suggested, was the one exception to the proposition that the PLO had been unable to coerce Arab states and did not have a radicalizing influence on Arab politics. The PLO, aided by other Arab parties, had been forcing Lebanon's hand, particularly since 1968. Furthermore, the leftist components of the PLO had both encouraged and influenced the extra-parliamentary Left in Lebanon.

The meeting devoted to strategic and military developments in the Arab–Israeli conflict touched on a variety of issues. Prof. Kemp opened with a paper on global strategic developments in the years which immediately preceded the October War and their impact on the Middle East. Dr. Sela dealt with the Egyptian application of the Soviet military doctrine and Dr. Evron compared two stages of the Arab–Israeli conflict, those of 1956–1967 and 1967–1973. The discussion which followed was wide-ranging and involved diverging approaches to the past, evaluation of contemporary developments and predictions about the future of the Arab–Israeli conflict. Some of the participants took issue with the model constructed by Dr. Evron and with the merits, explicit and implicit, that he attributed to the model as against the patterns of the conflict since 1967. Thus, Mr. Chaim Herzog disagreed with the contention that there had actually occurred a demilitarization of the Sinai during these years as well as with Dr. Evron's conclusions which rested on that assumption. Prof. Shamir put the accent elsewhere. He saw the year of 1967 as a watershed in the history of the Arab–Israeli conflict. He argued that in that year, and as a result of the June War, grave new elements were introduced into the conflict—deep Israeli anxieties, loss to the Arabs of Palestinian-inhabited and other territories, the revival of the Palestinian element—and a vicious spiral was created. The dynamics of that spiral led to the October War and were reinforced by its course and outcome. The deliberations then turned to the element of deterrence in the conflict. It was evident from the discussion that in view of past experience and the overriding impact of other variables this concept should be employed with great care, but that it was nevertheless of great importance in this conflict. This was illustrated by the interpretation of Egyptian decision-making and Israeli misconceptions in the years preceding the October War that was offered by Mr. Herzog:

> The Egyptian armed forces, to the best knowledge of Israeli intelligence at the time, had come to the conclusion that they could not launch a war until they had a sufficient number of medium fighterbomber squadrons to deal with the Israeli air force and airfields as an antidote to the Israeli air force. This, Israeli intelligence evaluated, would not be available until 1975.

The Soviet Union's decision to supply Egypt with Scud missiles, Mr. Herzog added, provided the latter with what it regarded as a deterrent against the Israeli air force. The Egyptians thus felt that they could go to war two years before the expiration of what Israeli intelligence regarded as a period in which Israel had at its disposal an effective means of deterrence.

The relationship between the military and political aspects of strategic decision-making was raised in other contexts as well. Dr. Sela explained that contrary to the popular myth then prevailing both in Israel and Arab countries—the Egyptian army in 1973 did not fully apply the Soviet military doctrine. The crucial difference between Arab strategies in 1967 and 1973, as he saw it, was that in the first case the Arabs were carried away by ideological visions while in the latter "they chose their political aims within the reach of their military capability." As for Israel, said Dr. Evron:

> One of the general conclusions that one can infer from the various Arab–Israeli wars is really that Israel does not have any explicit clear political objectives or hadn't had any in former wars and I cannot really see political objectives . . . in future wars. I think therefore that the Israeli notion that the destruction of Arab armies is the only strategic objective of any war remains valid. Whether any future war serves Israeli interests is another story . . .

Other constraints on military policy in December 1974 and in the foreseeable future were mentioned as well. Professors Kanovski, Rubinstein and Kemp mentioned the growing strain on economic systems and trained manpower resources; the former affecting primarily Israel, the latter posing more of a problem for the Arab states. Dr. Dale Tahtinen suggested that the arms race in the Middle East, and American military supplies to Israel in particular, had already been affected by the growing difficulties involved in providing ever-growing quantities of increasingly sophisticated weaponry. He cautioned that future wars could see the introduction of surface-to-surface missiles and perhaps even of nuclear arms. The issue of nuclear arms was pursued by other participants as well, most notably by Prof. Kemp who suggested that changing circumstances could lead Israel:

> to think of alternative ways of achieving military deterrence at less cost, and of course that opens up the nuclear options. In other words, the rationale for an Israeli nuclear option might be based on economic as well as on strategic considerations.

A major theme of the years 1967–1973, that of the making of the October War, was addressed specifically in the Colloquium's final session titled "The emergence of the Syrian–Egyptian 'Axis'." It opened with three papers by Prof. Shamir, Mr. Dishon and Dr. Rabinovich on Egyptian, inter-Arab and Syrian politics and policies, respectively.

The questions and comments which followed the presentations revealed a marked difference between two sets of issues. The changes which took place in domestic and inter-Arab politics in the late 1960s and early 1970s seemed to lend themselves to a generally accepted interpretation of the discussants. But several of the events and decisions which did take place in the realm of the Arab–Israeli conflict as well as some policy options and decisions which did not materialize remained the subject of controversy and conflicting interpretations. Were the processes which led to the October War beyond the complete control of the participating parties? Was a settlement possible between the wars of June and October and after the 1973 war? Were there moves which could avert or at least postpone the outbreak of the October War? Could responsibility for the lack of settlement be traced and determined?

The concluding session of the Colloquium was not unique in raising questions which remained unanswered in part. The previous sessions touched briefly on such problems and processes as the relationship between center and periphery in the countries of the Middle East or recent changes in the patterns of domestic politics in the region. Hopefully, future occasions will permit these, and related issues, to be pursued more comprehensively, benefiting from a lengthened historic perspective and new, perhaps different, vantage points.

The editing in 1976 of papers read in 1974 which dealt with dynamic situations presented a particular problem. This is illustrated most strikingly by the paper which was read during the Shiloah Center's Seminar on the role of the Palestinian organizations in Lebanese politics. There was no point in publishing the original paper after a year and a half of the Lebanese civil war, and a rewriting of the paper from the perspective of 1976 was, of course, out of the question. In most other cases the changes which took place since 1974 were much less dramatic and the papers published in the volume are slightly altered versions of those presented in the course of the Seminar and the Colloquium which were held in 1974. The authors and editors alike refrained from major revisions which would have endowed this collection with the benefits and drawbacks of hindsight. Only minor editorial and other changes were introduced during the process of publication. The papers thus reflect the authors' views and perspectives in December 1974.

The organization of an annual seminar and an international colloquium entails varied efforts by a great many people. A full list of acknowledgements owed to all those who have been of invaluable assistance in the preparation of this volume would be very long indeed. Our special thanks are owed to Mrs. Yardena Bar-Yehuda, Mrs. Lydia Gareh, Mrs. Edna Liftman-Katz and Miss Amira Margalit, members of the staff of Tel Aviv University; and to a Canadian friend of the Shiloah Center whose generous assistance made the publication of this volume possible.

Itamar Rabinovich   *Haim Shaked*
Tel Aviv, December 1976

External
Powers

The Arab-Israeli Conflict in American Foreign Policy

William B. Quandt

Between the third and fourth rounds of Arab-Israeli hostilities, American foreign policy passed through several stages in a quest for a peace settlement that would ensure Israeli security while meeting minimal Arab demands for the return of occupied territory. On one level American policy makers showed considerable consistency in their views over this period. A wide consensus existed that a comprehensive peace was desirable in terms of US interest; that Soviet influence in the Middle East was a growing danger and would only be checked by progress on the diplomatic front; and that American–Arab relations were likely to deteriorate in the absence of an active American role in promoting a settlement. Beyond these simple perceptions, however, there was little agreement within the US foreign policy establishment over appropriate tactics and on the issue of the priority of the Middle East in terms of US global interest. Thus, policy shifted significantly on several occasions between June 1967 and October 1973. The primary reasons for these shifts must be sought at four levels: changes in the broad international environment; changes in the Middle East; changes in American domestic realities; changes in the individuals involved in US policy making.

THE JOHNSON ADMINISTRATION

If President Johnson was genuinely irritated, as he has claimed, at the Israeli decision to resort to pre-emptive war on 5 June 1967, his subsequent actions revealed few signs of this irritation.[1] The weeks preceding the Six Day War had been agonizing ones for the President, torn as he was between wanting to prevent an outbreak of conflict and his reluctance to become involved in another area of the world while the war in Vietnam was absorbing so much of his attention and resources. Whatever migivings he may have felt about the Israeli resort to force were quickly dissipated as it became clear that the United States would not have to become militarily involved in the conflict. Besides, the Israeli victory seemed so overwhelming, and President Abdel Nasser's culpability in provoking the crisis that led to war was so apparent, that Johnson quickly concluded that the new balance of forces in the region might be turned to good advantage. Israel, now in possession of substantial Arab territory, could use occupied land as a bargaining counter for peace. Above all, the United States should not return to the Eisenhower pattern of forcing Israel to withdraw without obtaining concessions from the Arabs. Like many Israeli leaders at the time, Johnson expected that the Arabs would soon conclude that diplomacy offered the only hope of recovering territory. This, of course, would require that Israel be kept strong and that the United States refrain from pressuring Israel for concessions at an early stage.

Insofar as American diplomacy was active following the Six Day War, it focussed on establishing a context in which a settlement could take place. The forum for this activity was the United Nations, where the US was deeply involved in the diplomacy of reaching agreeement on a resolution articulating the broad guidelines for a settlement. Early in the summer the United States was prepared to accept a Latin American draft resolution which was fairly explicit on the issue of Israeli territorial withdraw to the pre-war borders, but when this was blocked by Arab and Soviet opposition the US position changed. It was not until 22 November, 1967, that a resolution was finally voted, with deliberate ambiguities concerning withdrawal and commitments to peace.

It was widely assumed in the US Government that a final peace settlement, if it could be achieved, would involve virtually complete Israeli withdrawal from the occupied territories, some settlement of the refugee problem, demilitarization of critical areas, and explicit Arab commitments to peace. American policy makers were generally less concerned with the modalities of reaching such an agreement than the Israelis. For example, few American officials felt that direct negotiations between Israel and the Arabs were essential. They did, however, acknowledge that the US should not become party to an imposed solution, at least not at an early date.

A number of considerations dictated American policy in this period. On the international level, the fact that the Soviet Union's closest friends in the Middle East had been badly defeated by an American client led to the widely shared feeling that Soviet influence in the area had suffered. The United States was not particularly anxious to go to the rescue of those who were most closely aligned with the Soviets. Jordan, of course, was another matter, but little could be done for Jordan in isolation from Egypt and Syria. The lingering US—Soviet cold-war rivalry, kept alive by the Vietnam War was one of the most decisive reasons for the Johnson administration's immediate post-war policy of support for Israel's basic diplomatic stance of waiting for Arab concessions prior to any offer to withdraw from Sinai, the West Bank or the Golan Heights.

American public opinion, as filtered through Congress, the press and various interest groups was also strongly pro-Israeli in the aftermath of the Six Day War. Any administration which might have been tempted to pressure Israel to abandon the newly won territory against its will would have paid a significant political price. With 1968 approaching as an election year, no politician would want to be branded as anti-Israel. Even within the US bureaucracy those pockets of sentiment that were less fully supportive of Israel remained relatively quiet. After all, Abdel Nasser had few admirers within the American Government in the summer and fall of 1967. American-Egyptian relations had been broken as a result of Abdel Nasser's false accusation of American involvement in the war, and a number of other Arab countries had followed suit. The Khartoum Summit Conference also seemed to preclude Arab co-operation in a peace-making effort. Insofar as pro-Arab sentiments did exist, they tended to favor a policy of helping Jordan and protecting interests in Saudi Arabia and other oil-rich Arab States. One ironic consequence of the war seemed to be a lease on life for the conservative Arab regimes now that Abdel Nasser's prestige had dropped and he had become financially dependent on Saudi Arabia, Kuwait and Libya. In brief, the net effect of American domestic realities, both in terms of public opinion and bureaucratic politics, was to reinforce a policy generally favorable to Israeli interest.

The third factor which dictated US policy after the war was the nature of the decision makers involved. President Johnson was the most important person involved in the articulation of American policy in the Middle East. Throughout his political career he had been strongly supportive of Israel. He had extensive contacts within the American Jewish community and, according to a close associate, Kennedy had taken into account Johnson's presumed ability to bring in the "Jewish vote" when he offered him the vice-presidency. As President, Johnson surrounded himself with advisers who shared his basically sympathetic view of Israel. Within the White House he had Walt Rostow as adviser for

National Security Affairs at the time of the Six Day War. At the State Department, Eugene Rostow was very actively involved in Middle East policy as Undersecretary of State. McGeorge Bundy, who briefly returned to advise Johnson after the war, was also generally sympathetic to Israel. Abe Fortas, Arthur Goldberg, Hubert Humphrey and perhaps Clark Clifford could also be expected to accord high priority to Israeli concerns. Thus, Johnson's own predispositions, as well as those of most of his key advisers, led to a fundamentally pro-Israeli orientation in the immediate post-war period.

Given the nature of US interests in the Middle East and the dynamics of the regional situation, it is not surprising that this initial consensus on policy began to erode by 1968. First, the stability of the post-war Middle East was called into question, particularly with the emergence of the Palestinian Fidayeen as a potent political force in the Arab world. Conservative regimes, rather than profiting from Abdel Nasser's embarassment, felt themselves threatened by a new wave of radical sentiment in the Arab world. Thus, traditionally friendly Arab regimes began to press the United States to do something to offer hope of a settlement in order to blunt the revolutionary forces that were rapidly gaining ground. Second, the Soviet Union decided to throw good money after bad and began a full-scale program to rearm Egypt and Syria. Soviet influence, rather than declining, seemed to be on the rise. Third, the assumption that the Arabs would sue for peace once they realized the magnitude of their defeat was less and less viable as time passed and Soviet aid increased. Fourth, Israeli requests for aid from the United States, in addition to an apparent hardening of Israeli negotiating terms during 1968, made a US policy of unconditional support for Israel appear to be increasingly expensive. Policy, after all, cannot be considered apart from cost. After the war, the least costly policy was to accept the new *status quo*. By early 1968, however, the price of such a policy in terms of both US−Arab and US−Israeli relations was rising.

Even the most pro-Israeli of presidents has at one time or another balked at total identification of US and Israeli interest. President Truman, as is well known, resented the pressures brought to bear on him to support the creation of Israel.[2] And even after Israel's independence, the United States did not officially supply arms to Israel, despite urgent requests. Johnson, likewise, expressed some irritation at Israeli policy. While agreeing in principle to Israeli requests for Phantom F-4 jet fighters in January 1968, he held up final approval until the fall of that year, when electoral pressures began to build. On occasion Johnson would make comments in private about how the United States would not become a satellite of a little country like Israel. But even more importantly, Johnson and, more vocally, the State Department, stuck by a fairly rigid interpretation of UN Resolution 242 as requiring total Israeli withdrawal, at least on the Egyptian front, in return for peace. This position, which had frequently been conveyed to the Israelis in private, was formally confirmed by Secretary of State Dean Rusk in early November 1968 in a meeting with Egyptian Foreign Minister Mahmud Riyad. This created some strain in UN–Israeli realtions and the last months of the supposedly pro-Israeli Johnson Administration were not particularly happy ones for Israel. It was thus with some relief, and perhaps some apprehension, that Israelis welcomed the presidency of Richard Nixon.

THE NIXON PRESIDENCY

As a presidential candidate and then as president, Richard Nixon had emphasized his personal interest in foreign policy. Vietnam was clearly the most urgent problem for his new administration, but it was by no means the only issue of concern to him or to his newly appointed adviser for National Security Affairs, Henry Kissinger. Above all, there was an understandable priority given to US–Soviet relations and strategic deterrence. Nixon and Kissinger made clear that they were prepared to negotiate with the Soviet Union on the whole range of issues that had dominated the Cold War era. The concept of "linkage" become the basis of the administration's approach to negotiations. In simple terms, "linkage" meant that the United States was not prepared to talk about international issues in isolation from one another. Rather, arms limitations, Vietnam and the Middle East would all be considered, and a concession by one side on arms might be met by a comparable one on Vietnam or the Middle East by the other party.

From this perspective, it is not surprising that Nixon began to deal with the Middle East primarily in the US–Soviet context. He did, however, appear to attach intrinsic importance to the area, referring to it as a "powder-keg." The implication of this imagery was that the Arab-Israeli conflict, as long as it remained unresolved, had explosive potential that could endanger international peace. By using this analogy, Nixon appeared to be rejecting the relatively passive Middle East diplomacy of the Johnson administration.

Among the first issues considered by the Nixon foreign policy team, working through the reinvigorated National Security Council system over which Henry Kissinger presided, was the Middle East conflict. Three options were considered: to remain relatively inactive; to pursue a comprehensive settlement through multilateral diplomacy; and to try for partial agreements. The second option was chosen, in full recognition that it might fail. An important judgment was made, however, that the US position in the area would be no worse for Washington's having tried and failed to reach a settlement than it would be if no effort were made at all.

Somewhat surprisingly, President Nixon authorized the State Department to take the lead in the conduct of Middle East diplomacy. In other areas, such as US–Soviet relations and Vietnam, it was Kissinger, not the State Department, who took charge.

Phase One

In the spring of 1969 American diplomacy in the Middle East moved into high gear. At the United Nations, four-power talks were begun. More significantly, Assistant Secretary of State Joseph Sisco and Soviet Ambassador Dobrynin held nine exploratory talks on possibilities for a Middle East settlement between 18 March and 22 April. During this period the United States tabled a working paper in the Four-Power talks which set forth a number of basic points that should govern any peace agreement. First, agreement was to be reached on the full "package" before implementation of any of the parts. Second, there were to be contractual commitments to peace. Third, final boundaries were not to reflect the weight of conquest. In addition, then, several vague formulations were advanced which addressed the special issues of Gaza, Jerusalem, refugees, navigation and Sharm ash-Shaykh. By spring, then, most of the elements that eventually became part of the "Rogers Plan" had been conveyed to the Israelis, Arabs and Soviets. The subsequent strain in US–Israeli relations was caused as much by disagreement over procedure as over substance.

On 24 April, the National Security Council met and authorized a further elaboration of these points, which were then transmitted to the Soviet Union. Soviet Foreign Minister Gromyko then visited Cairo on 10 June and on 17 June the Soviets made a counter proposal. During this stage of US–Soviet talks the objective was to reach agreement on a set of principles which would govern an Arab-Israeli settlement. The

United States hoped that the Soviets would use their influence in Cairo to bring about modifications in the Egyptian position on commitment to peace with Israel, while the Soviets tried to get the United States to pressure Israel to accept the idea of full withdrawal. Needless to say, the Israeli leadership, which was generally kept well informed of these deliberations, was extremely unhappy with the US—Soviet talks, since they undermined the principle of direct negotiations between Israel and the Arabs and raised the spectre of a US—Soviet imposed settlement.

During the summer the superpower dialogue was resumed when Sisco visited Moscow from 15 to 17 July. The Soviets pressed for an American commitment to full Israeli withdrawal, while Sisco held out for a stronger position from the Soviets on Arab commitments to peace. The official US policy on territory at this point was that the pre-war boundaries were "not necessarily excluded," a view that was increasingly at variance with stated Israeli objectives. Little further progress was made in the US—USSR talks until the UN General Assembly session in September, where Rogers and Sisco met with Gromyko and Dobrynin to discuss the Middle East. There the Soviets appeared to make a concession on the form in which negotiations between the belligerents might take place. The so-called "Rhodes formula" was reportedly agreeable to Egypt; this implied formal indirect negotiations, with the prospect of informal direct talks, as had occurred at Rhodes in 1949.

During September and October the United States Government debated whether to reveal its fallback position on territory in order to reach agreement on a US—Soviet draft of principles. It was widely felt that the Soviets had manged to modify the Egyptian position in several respects, especially during Gromyko's June visit and with the acceptance of the Rhodes formula, and now the ball appeared to be in the US court. While recognizing that Israel would object to any public American position calling for full withdrawal, the Administration nonetheless decided to go on record with such a position, making it clear that withdrawal was conditional on a full peace agreement. On 28 October, 1969, the new US position was given to the Soviets in the form of a draft joint US–Soviet Statement of Principles. The key change in the US position was support for the old international frontier between Egypt and Israel, provided that the final status of Gaza and security arrangements in Sinai and at Sharm ash-Shaykh could be negotiated. In a major speech on 9 December, Secretary of State Rogers revealed the general lines of the new US proposal, which was immediately dubbed the

"Rogers Plan." The following day Israel rejected the new proposal.[3] On 18 December a set of principles was advanced for a Jordan-Israel settlement which was modelled on the document of 28 October. This was tabled in the Four-Power context at the UN, since the Soviet Union was not acknowledged by Washington to have a special role to play in the case of Jordan, as it clearly did with Egypt. The timing of the release of this document was dictated by the upcoming Rabat summit, where it was hoped that Jordan could play a moderating role once the US had demonstrated its support for a settlement which included Israeli withdrawal from the West Bank. Thus, by the third week of December only the Syrian front had not been dealt with by the United States. The Egyptians were not prepared, however, to endorse the new American proposal, and their refusal was translated into formal Soviet rejection of the 28 October document on 23 December. This brought an angry reaction from Washington and put an end to the first phase of the Nixon administration's search for a settlement in the Middle East. Phase one was characterized by primary reliance on US−Soviet talks and the nebulous concept of "linkage" to establish a broad context for agreement. The lesson of the year-long diplomacy was that the Soviet Union could not be pried loose from virtually complete identification with the Egyptian diplomatic position.

Behind the US effort in 1969 was a faulty assumption concerning Soviet-Egyptian relations. It was widely believed by the policy makers that it might be possible to persuade the Soviets to pressure Egypt into modifying its policy on a peace settlement, provided the United States was prepared to use its influence with Israel on the territorial issue. Policy makers recognized that such behavior would strain Soviet-Egyptian relations, which was seen as an added benefit for the United States since Soviet influence in the area was the overriding concern of Nixon and Kissinger. As events demonstrated, however, the Soviets saw all too clearly the implications of the US proposals and in the end decided to avoid risking their Middle East investment in favor of an agreement with the United States.

During 1969 Nixon was hardly influenced at all by domestic politics as he formulated a strategy for the Middle East. Arms that had been promised to Israel by the Johnson administration were delivered on time, and the first Phantom jets reached Israel in September 1969. But no new major arms agreements were concluded despite heavy Congressional pressure. Arms, it seemed, were to be used as an element in influencing Israeli policy. If domestic politics had little to do with the shaping of US Middle East policy during 1969, however, regional changes did play a significant role in its formulation. There was widespread concern over the "erosion" of American influence in the Middle East, the growing militancy and appeal of the Palestinian Fidayeen movement, and the apparent rise in Soviet power throughout the region. In the spring of 1969 Abdel Nasser had begun the War of Attrition along the Suez Canal, and these limited hostilities reinforced the belief that the Middle East situation was explosive. They also added to the urgency of Israeli arms request. Single-minded backing of Israeli objectives was not, however, viewed as the key to reversing these trends. On the contrary, it was widely argued within the US foreign affairs bureaucracy that US identification with Israel was precisely the cause of the increased radicalism and polarization underway in the area. Once Nixon gave the State Department the go-ahead signal to pursue talks with the Soviets, this bureaucratically rooted view began to be translated into policy. The 28 October document was the most important result of this "anti-polarization" strategy. Kissinger appeared to be sceptical of the entire process, but his own power position was not yet what it was to become later, and he resisted the temptation to challenge the State Department on this issue. Bureaucratic politics, as is often the case, played an important part in shaping the contours of policy.

Phase Two

By any standard, 1970 was an extraordinary year in American relations with the Middle East. Dramatic changes in the regional setting provoked a fundamental revision in the American approach to the area and shifted the locus of decision making from the State Department to the White House, but only after another intensive diplomaatic effort to reach a peace settlement.

Following the Soviet rejection of the 28 October proposal, the Nixon Administration decided against further concessions in an effort to lure the Soviets and Egyptians back into the diplomatic process. Instead, Nixon began to come under sustained domestic pressure to reject the "Rogers Plan" and to provide arms to Israel. Whereas such pressures had little effect in 1969, in an election year the Administration might be expected to be more attentive, particularly in the absence of any evidence that the "Rogers Plan" held out hope of easing the mounting tensions in the Middle East.

The military conflict along the Suez Canal intensified in December 1969 and early January 1970 as the Israelis began to use their newly acquired Phantom jets to try to deter further escalation in the War of Attrition by carrying out "deep penetration raids" within Egypt. The consequence of this shift toward a more aggressive Israeli policy was that Abdel Nasser turned to the Soviets for additional help. During a secret trip to Moscow on 20 January, 1970, he asked for direct Soviet assistance in providing air defense, including an increase in surface-to-air missiles and Soviet aircraft and combat pilots. Meanwhile, Israel was pressing its own case for additional arms from the United States. In reply to a question at a press conference on 29 January, President Nixon stated that he would announce his decision on Israeli requests for more Phantoms within one month. This surprising news threw the US bureaucracy, the Israelis and the Arabs into a frenzy, and pressures mounted on the administration from all quarters. Finally, well after the self-imposed deadline had passed, Secretary of State Rogers announced that the US had decided to hold Israeli requests for more arms in abeyance. As consolation, substantial economic aid was offered.

During the spring, while the United States was resisting the pressures to arm Israel in the hope that this would improve the prospects for dealing with Nasser, the level of conflict on the Egyptian-Israeli front mounted sharply, as did Fidayeen activity within Jordan. Soviet equipment was being rushed into Egypt and moved toward the Canal. In April Soviet pilots were observed for the first time flying operational missions over Egypt. As early as February Middle East analysts within the US Government had urged a comprehensive review of policy in light of the growing Soviet involvement in the conflict. Other issues, however, had higher priority that spring, as the situation in Vietnam appeared to be badly deteriorating, particularly following the overthrow of the "neutralist" regime of Prince Norodom Sihanouk in Cambodia. As North Vietnamese use of sanctuaries in Cambodia grew in March and April, Nixon made the fateful decision to authorize the invasion of Cambodia, which set off massive public demonstrations in the United States against the widening of the war. With these problems dominating the top levels of the administration, it was not until 21 May that a subcommittee of the National Security Council finally met to consider developments in the Middle East. A full National Security Council meeting followed on 10 June.

Apart from the mounting Soviet involvement in the fighting, the other notable development during this period was President Abdel Nasser's 1 May speech, which was widely interpreted as a signal to the United States that Egypt was once again interested in diplomacy. The Soviets had tried to renew a dialogue with the United States in early March, but to no avail. After the experience of 1969, and with the Egyptian President's May bid in mind, the Nixon administration decided to launch its own initiative to resolve the conflict, bypassing the Soviets and dealing instead directly with Abdel Nasser, who had hinted through the Soviets that he was prepared to make further important concessions.

At the National Security Council meeting of 10 June Secretary of State Rogers presented the case for a renewed initiative which, simply stated, would aim at getting the parties to "stop shooting and start talking." On 18 June the Rogers recommendation was formally approved by the President and the following day the new initiative was launched. Prior to the adoption of the second "Rogers Plan" President Nixon had taken steps to ensure that Israeli reaction would not be automatically negative. On 21 May the President had met with Israeli Foreign Minister Abba Eban to assure him that some arms deliveries would be quietly resumed. Egyptian negative reaction was not particularly feared, since Abdel Nasser had made it known that he would not object to new deliveries of Phantoms to Israel, provided the US used its influence on behalf of a political settlement. In addition, the Phantom was beginning to lose some of its terror and mystique as new Soviet air defense equipment succeeded in shooting down a number of the high-priced F-4s that the Israelis used as "flying artillery" in the continuing War of Attrition.

The Israeli response to the new American arms decision came on 26 May in a speech by Prime Minister Golda Meir in which a softer Israeli line on Resolution 242 and the "Rhodes formula" was articulated. This did not, however, ensure a positive response to the "Rogers initiative." On the contrary, Prime Minister Meir's initial reaction was to oppose the plan, particularly after she was assured that the decision on arms was not conditional on its acceptance. On 21 June the Israeli Cabinet decided to reject the new proposal, but Washington was reportedly not immediately informed, on the advice of Ambassador Rabin, who took the line that Israel should not be the first party to reject the plan.[4]

Over the next month a very tense diplomatic-military game ensued.

Israeli intelligence began to report the forward movement of SAM equipment toward the Canal and more aggressive activity by Soviet pilots. Toward the end of July, in fact, as Israeli losses to the SAMs were rising, four Soviets pilots were shot down in an encounter with the Israeli air force. Against this backdrop of military escalation, the United States, through its highest officials, went on record with statements that might have served to reassure the Israelis. At a background briefing of the press at San Clemente on 26 June, Kissinger spoke of the need to "expel" the Soviets from the Middle East. In remarks on 1 July President Nixon referred to Israel's need for "defensible " borders. A few days later Israel received word that military equipment that could be used against the rapidly growing SAM network on the west bank of the Canal would be delivered. On 20 July, Nixon, speaking at a press conference, referred to the need to retain the military balance in the Middle East.

Despite these pro-Israel statements, Egypt accepted the Rogers proposal for a ceasefire on 22 July. Two days later President Nixon sent a letter to Prime Minister Meir urging her to take advantage of Egyptian acceptance, while promising that the US would not force Israel to agree to the Arab interpretaion of Resolution 242. On 26 July Jordan added its acceptance to Egypt's. Finally, on 31 July, after considerable dissension within the Israeli Cabinet, Israel also accepted, although a more detailed reply on 6 August stated some Israeli reservations. These were essentially ignored by the United States, as UN Secretary General U Thant was requested to announce on 7 August that all three parties had accepted the proposal for a ceasefire and a resumption of Ambassador Jarring's mission. Mrs. Meir was furious at the handling of the announcement, and she was to become even more irate in subsequent days.

The ceasefire of 7 August marked the end of the second stage of the Nixon administration's diplomacy in the Middle East. It seemed to reflect well on the patient efforts of the State Department, and there was near jubilation in the corridors of its Near East Bureau. Somehow the United States seemed to have maneuvered itself into that much-sought "evenhanded" position where it enjoyed confidence on the part of both Arabs and Israelis to play the role of mediator. At this point it was enough that the dangerous escalation seemed to have been halted. No one was asking what the next substantive steps would be to move the stalemate toward resolution.

During phase two American domestic politics played a more important role than during the preceding period, particularly in ending the freeze on new arms shipments to Israel. Kissinger was unhappy with such a policy in any event, especially at a time when the Soviets were hardly showing restraint, and in late May President Nixon came to share his view. Even more important in explaining the American initiative, however, were regional developments and in particular the growing Soviet involvement in the War of Attrition. This raised the danger of superpower confrontation, and to avoid this a ceasefire seemed eminently desirable. Abdel Nasser's 1 May speech was also an encouraging sign that the door was not shut to diplomacy. Thus, the State Department began to line up Arab acceptance, while the White House determined to reassure the Israelis. Once again, bureaucratic politics played an important role in the formulation of policy, but on this occasion Kissinger, whose stature was rising, was a less passive figure. The outcome in June and July of a dual policy of seeking a ceasefire while sending new arms to Israel reflected this shifting bureaucratic balance within the US foreign policy establishment.

Phase Three

It was not until 10 August, 1970, that the United States carried out aerial reconnaissance of the Suez Canal area, thereby providing data against which to check subsequent charges of violations of the standstill provisions of the ceasefire agreement. For several weeks the inability of the United States to confirm Israeli charges of Egyptian violations created a serious crisis of confidence between Washington and Jerusalem. Kissinger was appalled at the poor performance of the US intelligence community, believing as he did that the American "bureaucracy" was less reliable than Israeli sources of information. To assuage Israeli anger, Nixon authorized the Defense Department to offer the Israelis a small arms package for possible use against the SAM sites in the event of a renewal of hostilities. By the third week of August, however, the United States acknowledged that there had been some forward movement of SAMs by the Egyptians. During September the Egyptians ended all pretense of observing the limitations imposed by the ceasefire agreement, and this led to a US decision on 15 October to supply an additional US $ 90 million worth of arms to Israel immediately, and to request US $ 500 million from Congress for arms to Israel in the following year. Increasingly, arms were flowing to Israel in response to Egyptian and Soviet actions rather than as part of a diplomatic process or in response to domestic pressures.

During the crisis over the Egyptian violations, Israel withdrew from the proposed Jarring talks, thereby nullifying the second point of the Rogers June initiative. All that remained was the observance of the ceasefire, and even that became an open issue as tensions mounted in Jordan during the early part of September. The Fidayeen, fearing the consequences of forward movement on a peace settlement in the aftermath of the Rogers proposals, had adopted a militant posture toward King Hussein's regime in Amman. The most radical wing of the Palestine Liberation Organization (PLO) sparked a crisis by hijacking four international aircraft and diverting three to Jordan and one to Egypt. In mid-September Hussein decided to unleash his army against the Fidayeen, and in the following few days a full-scale international crisis erupted which threatened to engulf the Middle East in another large-scale war. As the Fidayeen were placed on the defensive, Syrian military units intervened in the fighting, temporarily raising the prospect of a massive Syrian invasion of Jordan. During the most critical moments of the crisis, Jordan, the United States and Israel concerted policy to deal with what appeared to be a Syrian-Soviet challenge to the *status quo*.[5] Israeli power, visibly mobilized on the Syrian front, seemed to play a role in limiting the scope of Syrian intervention, and as the crisis came to an end a new balance of power appeared to have emerged in the Middle East.

The events of August and September had a decisive influence on US policy in the Middle East. The Soviets were viewed by Nixon and Kissinger as responsible for both the violations of the ceasefire and the Syrian intervention in Jordan. In respose to these perceptions, the administration decided to adopt a "tough" policy, one element of which was the arming of Israel.

President Abdel Nasser of Egypt spent his last days trying to arrange a ceasefire in Jordan. The day after success of his efforts, he died of a heart attack. Egypt without him was unlikely to be as potent a political force in the Arab world. Likewise, Syria, after its setback in Jordan, was likely to be quiescent for a period. Finally, the Fidayeen appeared to have been eliminated as a political force. Thus, in a few short weeks the regimes and movements friendly to the Soviets had been badly weakened, whereas the pro-American forces in the area, namely Israel, Jordan, Saudi Arabia and Iran, seemed to be pillars of strength. For the first time, one began to hear American policy makers reflect the Israeli view that US–Israeli relations had a strategic dimension that was more important than the sentimental ties so frequently alluded to in the past as the basis for American support of Israel. Ironically, this image of Israel as an element in the US strategic approach to the Middle East corresponded quite closely to the Soviet and radical Arab view of Israel as the "cat's paw of Imperialism" in the Middle East. This view was enhanced, of course, by the growing arms flow from the United States to Israel.

For the next three years the United States, in its policy toward the Middle East, acted as if the regional *status quo* could be kept generally stable, provided that Israel remained strong. This view seemed to fit Kissinger's balance-of-power perspective and his desire to limit Soviet influence in the area. Israel, sensing a greater congruence of views between Washington and Jerusalem than ever before, tried hard to tie the hands of the Nixon administration by bargaining away such marginal concessions as a willingness to return to the Jarring talks in exchange for assurances on arms supply and support for Israel in future negotiations. Nixon never quite met all of Mrs Meir's requests for assurances, but in messages of 3 and 17 December, 1970, he went fairly far in Israel's direction. Israel, always anxious for 100% backing, professed disappointment in the arms promises contained in the 17 December message—one of the "greatest blows" to Israel, in Mrs. Meir's words—but by 28 December Israel had nonetheless agreed to return to the Jarring talks.

The Interim Settlement Approach of 1971

In an effort to test the prospects for some diplomatic progress between the new Sadat regime and Israel, the United States went to considerable lengths to get Jarring to stimulate movement toward some kind of agreement between Egypt and Israel. This resulted in the "Jarring Memorandum" of 8 February, which aimed at pinning down Egypt on commitments to peace and Israel on full withdrawal, the two key stumbling blocks of the past. Rather surprisingly, the Egyptians, on 14 February, conveyed a positive reply to Jarring, only to be followed on February 26 by a negative Israeli response which included the flat statement that there would be no Israeli withdrawal to the pre-5 June 1967 borders.

On 1–2 March, Sadat made a secret trip to Moscow in search of arms and diplomatic support. Within a few days of Sadat's return from Moscow, he sent a long letter to Nixon asking for an active US diplomatic role. This stimulated considerable interest in Washington particularly in the "interim agreement" deal which had first appeared as early as mid-September 1970, when Israeli officials had floated the idea of a mutual thinning out of forces along the Suez Canal. By January 1971 Egypt was indirectly hinting to the US that it might also be interested in such an idea. Thus a new diplomatic approach was conceived—an "interim agreement"—which represented a substantial break with the concept of a "package settlement." As usual, the State Department displayed the most enthusiasm for the idea, while Kissinger remained sceptical of the chances of success.

Sadat's initiative on an interim step was that it should include a reopening of the Suez Canal in return for a modest Israeli pullback from the waterway. Diplomacy moved slowly, as the US tried to elicit a favorable Israeli response. The best that could be achieved was a fairly tough Israeli proposal on 19 April which was not formally conveyed by the United States to Egypt. Contacts with Sadat had revealed his continuing interest in a Canal agreement, but it was clear that he would insist that Egyptian troops be allowed to cross the Canal, which the Israelis were not prepared to accept. By early May the White House had essentially withdrawn its support from the "interim settlement" idea as there seemed to be no prospect of agreement. Nonetheless, in May, Rogers and Sisco visited Cairo and Jerusalem, and by early June a new Egyptian position had been elicited, in part as a result of the "Bergus Memorandum." When no response was forthcoming from the US side, Sadat began to suspect that he was being set up to look like a fool. A salvage effort by Sisco in August simply confirmed that Israel was not prepared to budge. This was the last round of State Department diplomacy in the Middle East for two years. It left a bad aftertaste in Cairo, Jerusalem and the White House.

Priority to Domestic Politics–1972

Following the collapse of the "interim settlement" effort in 1971, the United States adopted a relatively passive role toward the Arab-Israeli conflict, reminiscent in some respects of the policy of the Johnson administration. In February 1972 Nixon agreed to a large Israeli arms request (including 42 F-4s and 82 A-4s). That same month, the United States formally committed itself to consultations with Israel prior to any future diplomatic initiatives. In essence, Rogers and Sisco found their hands tied, at White House directives, and the US—Israeli relationship took on an unusually warm tone. Nixon was obviously aware of the political benefits to be gained in an election year from appearing in the role of Israel's supporter, although even he may have been surprised by what appeared to be an open endorsement of his candidacy by Israeli Ambassador Rabin.

The consequence of domestic realities and regional developments served to ensure that 1972 would be a year in which the United States abstained from major Middle East initiatives. Sadat's "year of decision" had passed, making him appear ineffectual and the Middle East relatively stable. Bigger issues now came to the fore. In February Nixon made his historic trip to China. This was followed by an intensification of the fighting in Vietnam and the eventual mining of the port of Haiphong just prior to the Moscow Summit in May. When Brezhnev received Nixon despite the US moves in Vietnam, it appeared as if US—Soviet *détente* had reached the point where it was immune to the tensions generated by regional conflicts. With the signing of the Strategic Arms Limitation agreement and the US—Soviet Joint Declaration of Basic Principle, the French no longer seemed quite so absurd in speaking of superpower condominium for the policing of the world.

President Sadat, among others, clearly drew some bitter lessons from the Moscow Summit. In his view, US—Soviet *détente* amounted to a conspiracy to freeze the Middle East situation in a "no-war, no peace" mode. If Moscow was unwilling to help him unfreeze the situation, there was little point in putting up with the irritating presence of over 15,000 Soviet military advisers and combat personnel. In mid-July Sadat surprised the Soviets and the US by ordering the Russians out of Egypt on short notice. This proved to be a particularly welcome move in the Egyptian army, where the popular General Sadiq had made his anti-Soviet views widely known.

Whatever blinders Nixon and Kissinger may have worn regarding the Middle East, they did not miss the significance of the expulsion of the Soviets from Egypt. This move was bound to impress such vintage cold warriors, although its timing was perplexing. A few months before elections, Nixon could hardly be expected to respond to Sadat's move publicly. In addition, the Vietnam conflict was receiving Kissinger's priority attention, as Nixon clearly hoped that a Vietnam settlement would crown his first term. Despite these preoccupations, a "back-channel" line of communication was opened between Nixon and Sadat through which the Egyptians were reassured that the United States would soon turn its attention to the Arab-Israeli conflict,—this time with the White House directly in charge. On the eve of elections Nixon publicly reiterated this promise.

AMERICAN DIPLOMACY IN 1973

Vietnam took somewhat longer to settle than had been anticipated, but by February 1973 Kissinger was finally free of the burdens of negotiating with the intransigent leaders of Hanoi and Saigon. Seemingly a glutton for punishment, Kissinger immediately began talks with high-level Egyptians, Jordanians and Israelis. In February Sadat's adviser for National Security, Hafiz Isma'il, was the first high-ranking Egyptian to talk with Kissinger and Nixon in the post-Vietnam era. That same month King Hussein and Prime Minister Meir made the long journey to the White House. Kissinger's message to the Egyptians was a simple one: the United States was prepared to make a serious effort to help the parties negotiate an end to their conflict, but progress could only be made after the Israeli elections in October. Prior to that time some of the groundwork could be laid to find a balance between Israeli needs for security and Egyptian demands for sovereignty.[6] The net result of the first talks with Hafiz Isma'il was encouraging to the Americans and an early resumption of the dialogue was envisaged. Meanwhile, the Israelis were urged to begin thinking seriously about a step-by-step process of agreement on the Egyptian front after the fall elections.

The initial burst of US diplomatic activity early in 1973 was not sustained for long. Talks were held with the Egyptians, although the atmosphere had changed and seemed to mark a step backwards. US intentions, and perhaps even capabilities, were obviously uppermost in Egyptian thinking, with the deepening of the Watergate crisis in the spring of 1973 adding a note of concern. Instead of diplomacy, the Egyptians seemed interested in testing the United States, first with a serious war scare in April; a forced UN debate on the Middle East in the summer which resulted in a US veto of a pro-Arab resolution; and then with further signs of military activity in the fall. The US response was not encouraging to Sadat, particularly as Israeli intentions to create "facts" in the territories captured in 1967 seemed to be enshrined in the controversial Galili plan.

The US—Soviet talks in June 1973 were likewise not very promising for Sadat. Brezhnev did warn Nixon in uncertain terms that the Middle East conflict was explosive and that war could occur at any time. This was read as a pressure tactic, however, rather than as a genuine expression of concern, and by the fall the United States was only mildly alarmed by increasing signs of tension in the region. Among other things, Kissinger had just been confirmed as Secretary of State, and one of his first efforts had been to talk to Arab foreign munisters at the UN General Assembly to renew the US pledge to play an active role after the Israeli elections. The Egyptian and Jordanian representatives appeared to agree to a time schedule for indirect talks, as did the Israelis, and with this agreement in hand Kissinger took relatively little notice of the military maneuvers underway in Egypt and Syria. After all, every year there had been large fall maneuvers, and the Israelis, normally so jumpy, seemed relaxed this time. Thus, not until the morning of 6 October did Kissinger realize that war, not negotiations, was uppermost in Sadat's mind, and by then it proved impossible to prevent the outbreak of hostilities. With the October War, the political and military balance of power in the Middle East once more shifted decisively, bringing to a dramatic close the brief era opened by the Jordanian civil war. US policy seemed to lie in ruins, but it was not long before Kissinger had developed a new approach to the Arab-Israeli conflict.[7]

CONCLUSION

From this brief survey of American foreign policy toward the Arab-Israeli conflict in the period 1967–1973, it is clear that no single cause can be found for the shifts and turns characteristic of Washington's approach to the Middle East. Any attempt to trace policy exclusively to domestic factors—the influence of pro-Israeli groups or the oil lobby—will obviously fail for lack of evidence.[8] Likewise, primary emphasis on the personalities involved will miss the point that the same individuals adopted quite different stances in response to changes in the regional and international context. Yet, it would be a mistake to dismiss either domestic politics or personality entirely, for these factors often do influence short-term policy and account for important nuances which otherwise cannot be explained. The same is true of bureaucratic politics. While not the key to understanding policy in the Middle East, the bureaucratic environment structures the possible responses and adds an element of unpredictability and fluidity to the policy making process.

American foreign policy in the Middle East must be seen as the product of several elements: the priority accorded the Middle East compared to other parts of the world; the perceived threat to American interest in the region; and opportunities for a constructive American role in the peace making process. If any one of these points is viewed as unimportant or absent, the American approach to the area will be relatively passive, despite the efforts of lobbyists and the compulsions of an otherwise activist president or secretary of state. The driving force in US Middle East policy, from this perspective, is clearly to be sought in the developments within the region itself, as filtered through the lenses formed by the US—Soviet global relationship. Developments within the Middle East itself can be seen as the key to most of the shifts in US policy between 1967 and the October War. The 1973 war, of course, stands out as the most impressive example of how regional changes produced a basic reappraisal on the part of US policy makers.

Despite Johnson's initial preference for a relatively passive approach to the Middle East, which resulted from his preoccupations elsewhere, his generally pro-Israeli orientation, and his perception that the Soviet Union had lost influence in the region as a result of the Six Day War—toward the end of his administration pressures were building toward a more active US diplomatic role. The key to this change came from the region: growing radicalism in the Arab world, stimulated by the dynamism of the Fidayeen movement and the resultant weakening of Jordan; Soviet rearming of Egypt and Syria; and a hardening of the Israeli bargaining position.

Against this regional background, Nixon brought to Middle East policy a US—Soviet dimension with his interest in "linkages." This concern, and the growing tensions in the Middle East stemming from the War of Attrition, led to an active US role in pursuing an agreement with the Soviet Union on the terms of a peace settlement. This culminated in the "Rogers Plan" of October 1969. Soviet rejection of this approach in December brought the US back to seeing the issues more directly in regional terms, with fewer illusions that superpower collaboration could serve as a substitute for agreement among the parties to the conflict. Throughout 1969 domestic politics were comparatively unimportant in shaping US policy, although bureaucratic rivalries did serve to structure the specific elements of the "Rogers Plan."

Israeli opposition to the "Rogers Plan" and to Nixon's refusal to agree to new arms request, ensured that the early part of 1970 would witness serious efforts by pro-Israeli groups to bring about a change in

US policy. For nearly six months Nixon was unresponsive, in part out of a desire to keep a line open to President Abdel Nasser and in part because of preoccupations elsewhere, especially Vietnam. President Nasser's 1 May 1970 speech served to draw top-level American attention back to the Middle East, this time with a sense of real urgency. Not only was Soviet involvement in the conflict along the Canal rapidly increasing, but also the Egyptian President seemed prepared for a round of diplomacy. The US response was to press for a ceasefire and talks, while meeting Soviet arms to Egypt with American arms to Israel. Once again, changes in the region were the immediate stimulus for a new initiative, with domestic and bureaucratic politics coloring the specific nature of the US response.

The most decisive impact on the perceptions of US policy makers during this six-year period of 1967 to 1973 stemmed from the regional developments of August–September 1970. The events of these two months induced a shift in the locus of Middle East decision making in the US Government from the State Department to the White House; cast the regional conflict into Cold-War terms; and brought about the perception of an overlap in US and Israeli interest which had hitherto been less apparent. The net effect of the Egyptian violations of the ceasefire of August 1970, the Syrian intervention in the Jordan civil war, and Abdel Nasser's death was to bring the US and Israel together in defense of the *status quo*. The deceptive stability of the regional situation, combined with the realities of domestic politics, led Nixon and Kissinger first to undercut the State Department initiative on the "interim settlement" in 1971 and then to abstain from any publicly visible response to Sadat's expulsion of the Soviet advisers in July 1972.

During the 1971–1972 period other international issues dominated the attention of US policy makers. Vietnam was a continuing problem, but increasingly it was the new US–China relationship and its consequences for US–Soviet talks that preoccupied Nixon and Kissinger. A quiet Middle East could hardly compete for attention, even when Egypt's President Sadat went to remarkable lengths to open the way to a political settlement, first with his February–March 1971 initiative and then with his expulsion of the Soviets in July 1972. Unfortunately, the United States and Israel were both unresponsive to these important bids, which suggests that only regional developments which threaten conflict or instability are likely to receive much attention.

By 1973 the US was prepared to resume an active diplomatic role, but only half-heartedly, and with diminishing vigor once the Watergate crisis began to make itself felt in the spring of 1973. President Sadat clearly understood what it would take to change American policy. He could not rely on soft-spoken diplomacy or his Soviet friends. Nor was the oil lobby in the United States likely to be of much help, despite the onset of popular awareness of an impending energy crisis. From past experience Sadat could easily have concluded that the United States was most likely to play a positive diplomatic role when the Middle East situation seemed explosive and when an opportunity for effective action presented itself. Sadat's gamble was that the October War would provide the necessary stimulus to bring the United States out of its passivity and, through a combination of luck and admirable skill, he was proved essentially correct. By holding the key to regional developments, Sadat also held a major, if not the only, key to American foreign policy in the Middle East.

NOTES

1. Lyndon B. Johnson, *The Vantage Point* (New York 1971), p. 303.

2. Harry S. Truman, *Years of Trial and Hope* (Garden City 1956), p. 158.

3. See Michael Brecher, "Israel and the Rogers Peace Initiatives," *Orbis*, 18 1974, pp. 403-405.

4. *Ibid.*, pp. 411-413.

5. See William B. Quandt, *et al.*, *The Politics of Palestinian Nationalism* (Berkeley 1973), and the *New York Times*, 8 Oct., 1970.

6. Kissinger consciously tried to avoid referring to Resolution 242—with its "peace for withdrawal" connotations—the "Rogers Plan" and the "Jarring Memorandum." This accounted for his emphasis on "sovereignty" and "security" and even his reference to the need to take into account the "legitimate interests of the Palestinians." See *U.S. Foreign Policy for the 1970s: Shaping a Durable Peace*, A Report to the U.S. Congress by Richard Nixon, President of the United States, 3 May, 1973, pp. 137-138.

7. The US role after October 1973 is covered in my article, "Kissinger and the Arab-Israeli Disengagement Negotiations," *Journal of International Affairs*, Spring 1975.

8. For the impact of domestic considerations on US Middle East policy, see Quandt, "Domestic Influences on US Foreign Policy in the Middle East: The View from Washington," in Willard A. Beling (ed.), *The Middle East: Quest for an American Policy* (Albany 1973), pp. 263-285.

Soviet Middle East Policy
1967–1973

Oded Eran

The purpose of this paper is to report on some observations concerning Soviet conduct in the Middle East between two Arab–Israeli wars, namely those of June 1967 and October 1973. Since in terms of intensity and risks the regional rivalry between the superpowers had reached an unprecedented level in the period between the Six Day War and the October War, the Arab–Israeli conflict of this period may be considered as a case of a non-European cold war.

One should remember that the beginning of Soviet–American competition for influence over the Middle East coincided with the beginning of Soviet–American rivalry in Europe following World War II. For various—and changing—reasons, the Soviet Union since the defeat of Nazi

Germany has shown an unmistakable desire to become a well established and formally recognized Middle Eastern power. Toward the end of the war Stalin apparently became convinced that the Soviet Union's glorious contribution to the victory entitled it to a share in the reallocated territorial assets of the vanquished powers. In the context of the Middle East, Stalin's thinking seemingly concentrated for a while on the former Italian colonial possessions such as Tripoli and the Dodecanese Islands.[1] However, unlike the case of Eastern Europe or the Far East, the winning coalition was not agreeable with Soviet demands in the Middle East. Having encountered a firm British refusal to allow the Soviet Union any access to that part of the globe, Stalin initiated in 1946 what one might call a "war of attrition" against the British Empire in the Middle East. Stalin seemed to have believed that Britain's general weakness and impotence as a result of the war had generated some power vacuum, and that with due pressure Britain might be forced to compromise with the Soviet Union over some of its Middle Eastern assets. The Soviet refusal to withdraw from Iran in

25

1946, the military pressures on Turkey, as well as the resumption of the Greek civil war in that year, were however all counterproductive from a Soviet point of view; they introduced into the area, in partial replacement of the old and declining British Empire, an enormously virile contender in the form of the United States.

Though the initial post-World War II Soviet attempt to gain a foothold in the Middle East had been contained, Stalin remained alert and within his limits responsive to opportunities presenting themselves in that area (as shown in the case of Israel in 1947–1948) until his death in 1953. The great opportunity in the Middle East developed, however, subsequent to Stalin's death and thus the East–West struggle for mastery in the Middle East became real and intense simultaneously with the decline of the cold war in Europe and the Far East. Consequently, for many years after its initial breakthrough into the Arab world in 1955, Moscow was reluctant to allow trends of stabilization and reconciliation prevailing on the European scene to kill the political momentum in the Middle East. The first Egyptian–Czech arms deal occurred in September 1955, less than two months after the four power summit meeting in Geneva allegedly terminated the cold war; it demonstrated well the Soviet attempt to isolate the Middle Eastern question from European matters. So long as opportunities presented themselves in that part of the world Moscow could not afford to miss them.

Whoever comes to draw up the balance sheet of Soviet Middle Eastern policy in the first dozen years following 1955, that is from the Soviet sponsored break up of the Tripartite arms rationing system up to the Six Day War, must conclude that the Kremlin's achievements were outstanding. In the mid-1950s the Khrushchev leadership started practically at zero, pressing for the relatively minimal objective of frustrating the reconsolidation of Western influence over the Middle East in the form of the Baghdad Pact. By the mid-1960s the Brezhnev-Kosygin leadership was already thinking in terms of some form of alliance between the socialist commonwealth and a bloc of progressive Arab regimes,[2] and preparing for the extension of the Soviet naval presence into the Mediterranean.

To be sure, Soviet policy did occasionally suffer serious setbacks in these years: for instance, the succession of events from 1955 through 1958, such as the Suez crisis and the fall of Nuri as-Said, which produced extremely beneficial results from a Soviet point of view, was followed in the years 1959 to 1961 by a series of developments which were far from favorable to Soviet interests; Nasser's hostilities against the Egyptian and Syrian Communists and, later in this period, Qassem's anti-Communist campaign caused grave misgivings in Moscow. In the same way the trend toward further domestic radicalization which manifested itself in some Arab countries starting from early in the 1960s was counterbalanced, in the Soviet perspective, by the emergence of the Western-oriented Islamic alliance, headed jointly by King Faisal and the Shah. Nevertheless, Soviet Middle Eastern setbacks up to 1967 were clearly and unambiguously outnumbered and outweighed by Soviet gains. The general instability of the area had played directly into Soviet hands and the tactic of crisis-promotion, through the massive supply of sophisticated arms, had paid handsomely and became a central feature of Soviet policy in the region. Furthermore, fortunately for Moscow, the appearance of opportunities in the Middle East coincided with the emerging Soviet strategic needs. Thus the Egyptian opening toward Moscow occurred at a time when the Soviet Government was seeking to frustrate the deployment of Western air bases for strategic bombing along the southern border of the USSR. In the same way the radical trends in Egypt and Syria, starting in 1961 and 1963 respectively, coincided with the Soviet search for port facilities along the eastern shores of the Mediterranean, which were planned to serve as an infrastructure for the development of a Soviet naval presence in the area.

However, the impressive gains of the Soviet Union in the Middle East between 1955 and 1967 were to some extent misleading. There could be no comparison between Soviet penetration into the area which lay in proximity with the southern border of the USSR[3] and the Sovietization of Eastern Europe a decade before, let alone the historical Czarist expansion to east and south. Three basic factors, which made Soviet advances in Eastern Europe irreversible, were absent in the case of the Middle East: the Soviet military presence on the spot, the political supremacy of the indigenous Communist parties and the reluctant acceptance by other powers of Soviet influence in the area. To be sure, the Soviet Government apparently had been seeking partial compensation for the absence of Soviet military might in the Middle East; the Soviet naval build-up in the Mediterranean, starting after the mid-1960s, was clearly intended, in addition to its strategic role, to give a psychological boost to the pro-Soviet oriented local forces in their respective policies. In the same way, after despairing of Communist take-overs in the Arab nationalist movements, the Kremlin attempted to cultivate revolutionary democratic[4] parties which were expected, in ruling their countries, to ensure a permanent pro-Soviet stance. However, with no ultimate sanction available to Moscow, and in face of resistance on the part of the Western powers to recognition of the legitimacy of a Soviet Middle Eastern presence, Moscow's regional achievements remained fluid and reversible; no iron curtain could be drawn across the Middle East and no Soviet claim could long remain immune to challenge. The Soviet leadership, or at least some sectors within it, were not blind to the vulnerability of Soviet gains in the Middle East. There is clear evidence of an intense debate in the Kremlin throughout the late 1950s and early 1960s over the political reliability of Arab nationalist leaders, as well as over the desirability of Soviet material support to them.[5] Nevertheless, contemporary military and political imperatives apparently persuaded the Kremlin to continue its offensive and deepen its commitments, albeit within the terms existing in the region. Also, the extremely favorable trend, from a Soviet point of view, which culminated in February 1966 in the leftist-oriented coup in Damascus, helped at least until June 1967 to silence the waverers. The overall picture was one of Soviet influence steadily on the rise while Western influence continued to decline.

The Six Day War initiated a new phase in Soviet-American rivalry over the Middle East. In the six years which followed June 1967 the nature of that rivalry was considerably transformed in such a way as to make the regional course of events no longer unambiguously favorable to Soviet interests. During this period the central issue in the Middle East was the fate of the territories gained by Israel in the Six Day War; the regional positions of the Soviet Union and the United States were affected throughout the period by their respective ability to contribute to the solution of this problem; it all came down to the question of which of the two superpowers was capable of returning to Arab hands all or part of the territories, and at what cost to the Arab world. On this score, the Soviet position was clearly inferior to that of the Americans, and the Soviet effort to prevent the United States from exploiting the issue for the purpose of reversing the political trend in the Middle East is the key to understanding of Soviet conduct toward the Arab–Israeli conflict during these years.

TOOTHLESS DIPLOMATIC EFFORTS 1967–1968

Despite its undeniable role in encouraging and backing Arab militancy against Israel on the Syrian and Egyptian borders, the Soviet Government appeared to have no prior accurate assessment of the Arab–Israeli military ratio, nor a clear idea of the potentiality of a full-scale war, let alone knowledge of the timing of the eruption.

Up until the Six Day War significant segments of the Soviet policy-making community had been inclined to underestimate the military capability of Israel and its willingness to fight. Therefore, while never accepting in principle the objective of the elimination of Israel as a sovereign state, the Soviet leadership had not regarded the military resolution of the Arab–Israeli conflict in favor of the Arab countries as completely unrealistic or out of the question. There is evidence that, shortly before the Six Day War, a study group within the USSR Academy of Sciences was asked by the Central Committee to prepare a report evaluating the power ratio between Israel and the Arabs in case of an overall military flare-up. The study group reported its conclusions back to the International Department of the Central Committee, saying that under the circumstances any military confrontation between Israel and the Arabs would most probably result in a clear-cut Israeli victory. Reportedly, this account was overlooked and disregarded by those in the Central Committee who were responsible for making Soviet Middle Eastern policy at the time.[6] A sense of optimism regarding Arab military strength, which had been built up with Soviet help, had prevailed before the war in many Soviet circles,[7] probably including the intelligence community.

To all appearances the swift Israeli victory over Egypt, Jordan and Syria in June 1967 was traumatic to the Soviet leadership; it ruined existing Soviet evaluations with respect to the regional play and disrupted the regional timetable as perceived by the Kremlin. The intensity of domestic political activity in Moscow shortly after the war, of which the 20 June convening of the plenum of the Central Committee was the foremost manifestation, as well as official Soviet pronouncements, indicated that the leading group felt at the time somewhat apologetic regarding the decisions taken by the Politburo during the height of the crisis, and needed them to be retroactively ratified.[8] The embarrassment of Soviet Government leadership stemmed apparently from the inability of the Soviet Government in any way to influence the course of the war or prevent its disastrous consequences from a Soviet point of view.

The total defeat of its Arab clients using Soviet weapon systems was particularly painful to the Kremlin, because it came at the very moment when the Soviet Union was embarking on an intensive effort to gain credibility for its claims to a constructive influence in the region. The build-up of the Soviet naval presence in the Mediterranean, which had begun rather modestly in 1964, assumed a significant pace in 1967 shortly before the outbreak of the war.[9]

As mentioned, in addition to the counterbalancing of the American naval presence in the area and the outflanking of NATO from the south, the regional psycho-political effects of the Soviet naval presence have counted as well. Generating among the neighboring countries an awareness of the immediacy and availability of Soviet power and encouraging regional political forces to adopt a pro-Soviet orientation was an aim in itself as well as a practical short-range interest of the Soviet Union in view of the need for land facilities to maintain its growing naval presence.

Thus, the inability of the Soviet Government to effectually use its power and control events taking place under its nose had an unfavorable bearing on Soviet credibility. Neither can one escape the conclusion that the cumulative effect of the Kremlin's inability at the time to project its power in South East Asia, and save North Vietnam from American bombing, made the discomfort of the leadership, in view of developments in the Middle East, even greater. A question-mark hung over the Soviet claim to be a Middle Eastern power capable of influencing regional developments.

The Six Day War was thus the first major regional development since 1955 of an unfavorable or at least ambiguous nature from the Soviet point of view. The historical course of Soviet achievements in the Middle East appeared threatened. No wonder the Soviet leadership took emergency measures aimed at minimizing the effects of the setback on Soviet prestige and at a speedy reversal of Israeli territorial gains. Podgorny's arrival in Cairo on 20 June, shortly after the termination of the Plenum of the Central Committee in Moscow, heading a large military delegation including the Soviet Chief of Staff, was intended to symbolize dramatically the Soviet role as protector of the Arabs. Podgorny was apparently authorized to offer Egypt as well as Syria a resupply of all their material losses in the war, and available evidence indicates that up to the end of 1967 the Kremlin fulfilled 80% of its promises.[10] The frequent visits of Soviet warships to Egyptian ports, as well as of fighter bombers to Egyptian airports, during the year of the defeat also served as a symbol of Moscow's extension of its protecting wings over its beaten Arab clients.

Undoubtedly, in addition to its defensive position vis-à-vis Arab criticism, the Soviet leadership was also aware of the opportunities inherent in a situation of complete Arab dependence on Soviet material support. At the time Podgorny is reported to have raised with Nasser the demand for a Soviet naval base in Alexandria.[11] Nevertheless, it appears that in the immediate post-war period the need to cover up for Soviet impotence during the war predominated. Podgorny refused, for instance, an Egyptian request at the time to sign a mutual defense pact which would have become much more meaningful than the Treaty of Friendship and Collaboration which he himself extracted from Sadat in 1971.[12] Such a pact must have looked to Moscow a highly risky commitment under the prevailing circumstances.

Moscow did not believe at that point, nor for a long time to come, that the massive resupply of arms to Egypt and Syria would reconstruct the military option of these countries in the conflict. It was obvious to any military expert that quite a few years would be required for that purpose. However, the imperative to achieve an Israeli pullback from the territories gained during the war was very pressing. Apart from the closure of the Suez Canal, which had a disruptive effect on the Soviet global strategic naval planning and build-up, the continued presence of Israeli forces in the Sinai peninsula, the West Bank of the Jordan River and the Golan Heights, constituted a living monument to Soviet regional impotence. But any reversal of the situation could only be brought about by diplomacy.

Kosygin headed the diplomatic effort of the Soviet Government. He left for New York before the convening of the Central Committee Plenum to participate in the special session of the UN General Assembly and to seek a Soviet–American accord on the need to return to the *status quo ante bellum*. Kosygin's objectives clearly revealed Soviet thinking on the subject. At no point did the Soviet Government seem to have considered itself capable of achieving an Israeli withdrawal without the cooperation of the United States. In fact, American material support of Israel (mainly economic, because at that point Israel did not yet depend so heavily on American arms) was seen by Moscow as the most vital asset in the effort to drive Israeli forces back to the 4 June, 1967 borders.

The clear edge which Washington had over Moscow in terms of its ability to contribute to the achievement of an Israeli pullback was certainly unpleasant to the Soviet leadership, and tarnished the Soviet claim to the status of a Middle Eastern power. Nonetheless, because the necessity to undo Israeli territorial achievements was so pressing, and because no other alternative was admissible, the Kremlin was willing to pay the price. The only hope for Moscow was to cosmeticize American pressure on Israel as a Soviet–American coordinated effort authorized by the international community. The Soviet leadership was probably thinking in terms of the events of 1956–1957, in which American instrumentality in obtaining an Israeli withdrawal from the Sinai peninsula did not impress Arab nationalist leaders sufficiently to even affect, let alone reverse, the historical trend in the area toward further political radicalization. An immediate Israeli withdrawal would have enabled the Soviet Government to present the entire event as a passing episode, a mere historical accident; the Middle East would return to its regular agenda and with it the Soviet Government to its pre-1967 timetable.

This Soviet conception of a speedy resolution of the crisis was reflected in Kosygin's insistence on an imposed Soviet–American solution during his summit talks with President Johnson in Glassboro on 23–25 June, 1967. Unfortunately from the Soviet point of view the United States was reluctant to deliver an Israeli withdrawal on Soviet terms. Under these circumstances the urgent need to achieve some sort of a general framework of international consensus constituting a guide for action, no matter how vague, led the Soviet Government to endorse Security Council Resolution 242 of 22 November, 1967 which was purposely ambiguous on the subject of a total Israeli pullback.

The inability of the Soviet Government quickly to deliver an Israeli withdrawal by diplomatic means further increased Soviet troubles with the restless Arab world, and placed in doubt the future of Soviet influence in the region. Judging by Soviet official publications pertinent to the subject at the time, one can conclude that Soviet anxieties regarding political trends in the Arab world were on two grounds. On the one hand, American advantage over the Soviet Union in terms of leverage over Israel led the Kremlin to worry about rightist tendencies in Arab political circles; on the other hand, Arab impatience with the deadlock increased Soviet concern over manifestations of extremely leftist Chinese-oriented political trends.[13]

The threat of leftist deviation seems to have been much more serious in the Soviet view at the time. Unlike Nasser—who, in the absence of other alternatives, accepted the Soviet emphasis on diplomacy—Syria, Algeria and the Palestinian organizations expressed strong and vocal disbelief in political methods and rejected Resolution 242 of the Security Council. The Arab summit conference in Khartoum in August 1967 brought the inter-Arab rift into the open. The rejection of diplomacy was a fertile ground for Chinese ideology and influence, because popular war was at that point the only practical alternative available. The ideas of Chairman Mao thus appeared applicable to this stage of the Arab–Israeli conflict and Mao's appeal worried the Kremlin. It is little wonder that Soviet propaganda at this stage assumed an openly hostile attitude toward the Palestinian organizations, and a more hidden hostility toward the Syrians.[14]

During 1968 Arab restlessness produced a significant revision in Soviet conduct toward the conflict. The Soviet leadership became more favorably disposed toward the idea of exerting limited military pressures which would give more credibility to the diplomatic effort. Indications of a reassessment taking place in the Kremlin had been in the air since the spring of 1968. Soviet publications showed a more favorable line toward Palestinian terror operations in Israel; the Soviet media began to report extensively on these operations, employing positive terms, such as partisans, guerrilla fighters, etc.[15] It seems that this revised line was agreed between Nasser and the Politburo in July 1968, during the former's visit to Moscow secretly accompanied by Yasir Arafat.[16] The new arms contracts signed between Egypt and the Soviet Union during this visit, which included considerable numbers of T-54 and T-55 tanks, MiG 21s and Sokhoi 7s, constituted Soviet approval[17] for constant Egyptian military harrassment of Israeli forces along the Suez Canal. This policy was inaugurated by Nasser in the fall of 1968 under the label "active defense" and, from April 1969, as the "War of Attrition."

MOSCOW ON THE WAY TO WASHINGTON

The inauguration of the new administration in Washington in January 1969 raised some hopes in the Kremlin concerning the possibility of US–Soviet cooperation in moving forward on the issue of the Arab–Israeli conflict. Despite President Richard Nixon's record in the

Soviet memory as a Cold Warrior, the statements made by the leader of the new administration, particularly the one which spoke of replacing the "era of confrontation" by the "era of negotiation," led Moscow to believe that Washington might consider favorably a coordinated Soviet–American effort to impose an arrangement on the parties to the conflict. After all Nixon was the Vice President in the Eisenhower Administration which forced Israel out of the Sinai peninsula in 1957. The negotiations between the interested powers in 1969 regarding the Arab–Israeli conflict were channeled into two parallel forums: The two power talks between Assistant Secretary of State Joseph Sisco and Soviet Ambassador to Washington Anatoly Dobrynin, and the four power talks between the UN representatives of the US, USSR, Britain and France. The Kremlin leaders must have taken a great pleasure at the exclusion of Britain and France from the former and more meaningful forum, and probably regarded their participation in that forum and the degrading of Paris and London to the secondary forum as a sort of American recognition of Soviet Middle Eastern achievements in the past 14 years, and of the historical decline of Britain and France. Such recognition had been a time-honoured Soviet aspiration.

Unfortunately, from the Soviet point of view, the Nixon Administration proved no less determined than its predecessor to contribute to a settlement of the problem only on terms beneficial to the US; that is, to make sure that any movement toward arrangement, including an Israeli pullback from the territories gained in June 1967, would be clearly recognized and credited by the Arab world as American-sponsored. In other words, the Soviet leadership came to realize that Israeli withdrawal under American pressure might become instrumental in reversing the historical political trend in the area in favor of the United States. Thus, during 1969 several signs indicated that the Kremlin was reassessing its attitude toward the question of the price which it had been willing to pay in return for American delivery of an Israeli evacuation of the territories. The Soviet stand on the Palestinian issue was instructive of the prevailing mood in Moscow in that year. Up until 1969, despite the change for the positive in the Soviet attitude toward the terror operations of the Palestinian organizations in the spring of 1968, the Soviet media had not regarded the Palestinian question in terms of a "national problem," but rather in terms of a refugee problem. Furthermore, eager to get a quick Israeli withdrawal, the Soviet leadership pleaded with the Arab countries, particularly the extreme ones, to distinguish between the issue of occupied territories and that of the Palestinians. The Soviet point had been that tying the two issues together would complicate the task of achieving a broad international consensus and would help Israel to maintain the *status quo*. "Don't put the cart before the horse" had been the Soviet message to the Arabs on this issue until 1969.[18] Subsequent to February 1969, when Arafat was elected Chairman of the Executive Committee of the Palestine Liberation Organization, Soviet spokesmen began to relate themselves cautiously to the Palestinian problem, employing the formula, "the lawful rights of the Arab *people* of Palestine."[19] By so doing Moscow demonstrated that Israeli withdrawal alone might no longer be satisfactory from a Soviet point of view. To the Arab world Moscow was eager to show that it was at least one step ahead of the US in support of the Arab cause.

There were, however, other reasons which made the objective of an Israeli withdrawal a little less urgent from the Soviet point of view. The Kremlin's anxiety about the possibility of a wave of anti-Soviet reorientations among several Arab regimes as a result of Soviet inaction during the Six Day War was diminishing two years later. Domestic eruptions in some of the Arab countries, such as the Communist–supported installation of Jafar Numeiri in the Sudan in May 1969 and the ouster of the monarchy of King Idris in Libya in September 1969, indicated to Moscow that the radical trend had not been reversed following the June 1967 debacle. Furthermore, radical regimes, such as that of the Syrian Ba'th or South Yemen, which for a while flirted with Peking, seemed to have realized around 1969 that China could offer very little in material terms and they were therefore forced to climb back on the Soviet bandwagon.[20] The Soviet leadership also began to appreciate increasingly the benefits which stemmed from Arab dependence on Soviet military assistance. Though the Suez Canal remained closed, the Soviet Government took a great step forward in implementing its strategic plans with regard to this part of the world with the building of a deep water port in Marsa Matruh, which was begun secretly in 1969.[21] Port facilities for Soviet ships in Port Said, Alexandria and Ladhiqiyya were considerably developed at the time and Soviet naval and air reconnaissance activities intensified.[22]

Once reassured of its position in the Arab world Moscow apparently decided that it did not need to pay too expensively for all American-sponsored Israeli withdrawal. As far as Moscow was now concerned only an arrangement which would be clearly credited as Soviet–American would be satisfactory. This was exactly the point which the Soviet leadership had tried to make to the Egyptians during the height of the War of Attrition in 1970. As long as the War of Attrition had continued along the Suez Canal without a decision in favor of either side it served its purpose in the Soviet view, because it constituted a considerable military pressure as a background to the diplomatic effort. The Soviet contribution would necessarily be recognized in any arrangement which might result from the combined diplomatic and military pressures. Nonetheless, as soon as the Israeli air force in July 1969 began its deep penetration bombing, in an effort to extend the war to the Egyptian rear, and Egyptian defeat seemed unavoidable, the value of the War of Attrition became rather doubtful. The Kremlin seems to have suspected that the Israeli military effort was sponsored by the United States with the intention of demonstrating to Egypt that it did not have a credible military option, and that its salvation lay exclusively in the hands of Washington. The enunciation in October 1969 of the "Rogers Plan," which insisted on an Israeli withdrawal to the old armistice line in Sinai, looked to the Kremlin like the other side of the American effort to prove to Nasser that the answer to his troubles lay in the hands of the White House alone.

The Soviet leadership hesitated before deciding to deepen its direct involvement on the Suez front. The first initiative for this move came from Nasser who secretly travelled to Moscow in January 1970. Following Nasser's urging Brezhnev to prove that the Soviet Union was not afraid of the Americans, and that the Americans were not the only true rulers of the world, the Politburo took its decision to send Soviet pilots on combat missions over Egypt and Soviet personnel in to man the SAM-3 missile batteries.[23] The stream of thousands of Soviet personnel into Egypt, as a result of the January 1970 decision, was intended to reassure Egypt of its military credibility, and to counter the thesis that diplomacy alone could save Egypt or, for that matter, any other Arab country. To be sure, Moscow did not argue against the thesis that the key to an Israeli withdrawal was in the hands of the President of the United States, but it presented this thesis in a somewhat revised form; namely, without the military credibility provided to the Arabs by the Kremlin, nothing favorable to the Arab countries would be gained from Washington. In other words, unless the Soviet Union, through its military aid, were a main contributor to the process of producing an arrangement—Arab demands would not be met.

WITHOUT SECURITY MARGINS

In the short run, the Soviet decision to enter into far-reaching commitments to defend Egypt from another crushing defeat proved itself. Israel was no longer free to bomb the heartland of Egypt, and the War of Attrition could no longer be won. Nevertheless, the deeper Soviet involvement in the Egyptian military machine created a new situation from the Kremlin's point of view which required a reassessment of the immediate Soviet interest. The risks to the Kremlin now became very high. As long as active warfare was going on along the Canal there was the danger of a military escalation which might get beyond Moscow's control and would involve the Soviet Union in a direct confrontation with Israel and—what was more serious—with the United States. Either Israel or the United States, or even Egypt, could at this point have taken decisions which would have dragged the Soviet Union into an unnecessary, costly and terribly dangerous military engagement. The incident of 30 July, 1970, when Israeli planes shot down four Soviet planes, demonstrated to the Kremlin the risks inherent in the new situation. The Soviet leadership therefore came to the conclusion that once Egyptian military credibility had been reestablished by the Soviet physical presence, a speedy end to the War of Attrition was imperative.

The new Soviet concern for an immediate end to all military operations was so urgent and intense that it made Moscow willing to buy it even at the cost of one-sided American action. It appears that the Egyptian acceptance of the Rogers Initiative of 19 June for a cease-fire and negotiations under the auspices of the UN had been agreed between Nasser and the Kremlin during the former's visit to Moscow in July. However, in order to take some of the credit for the achievement from the United States, the Soviet mass media preferred to present the new arrangement as the Nasser Initiative.[24] This was neither the first nor the last time in the Arab–Israeli conflict when Moscow was reluctantly forced to seek or accept an American initiative in order to lessen risks which stemmed from earlier Soviet conduct. The blatant Soviet–Egyptian violation of the cease-fire agreement, by moving forward missile batteries shortly after it went into force on 7 August, 1970, was probably intended, at least on the part of the Kremlin, to inhibit any

Egyptian–American *rapprochement*, and to demonstrate that *Pax Americana* was not on the agenda.

Events in the Middle East during that summer of 1970 further dampened the Soviet appetite for a resumption of hostilities. The civil war in Jordan between King Hussein and the PLO, which culminated in September 1970 with the abortive Syrian attempt to invade Jordan and rescue the Palestinians, deepened the inter-Arab rift and put in doubt the ability of the Arab world to unite against Israel. More serious, however, was the sudden death of President Nasser, the most faithful Soviet client in the region over the previous 15 years. Moscow now found itself heavily committed to a new regime whose political nature and orientation were not yet clear.

The political fog which descended on Egypt in September 1970 was particularly embarrassing to the Soviet leadership at home. Scattered evidence, extending from the mid-1960s to 1975, indicates that the Soviet aid programs to Third World allies were not very popular among various branches of the party and government bureaucracies in Moscow, and were regarded in fact as a burden the value and benefits of which were rather doubtful.[25] The Soviet leadership must thus have been under a certain amount of pressure to justify before the Soviet establishment the extremely heavy commitments in material and risk terms which the Soviet Government undertook to bear, particularly from 1970 on. The clearest manifestation of the effort to legitimize the growing commitment was the special terminology which the Soviet mass media employed in broadcasts to the Soviet public on Soviet relations with radical Arab regimes. For instance, Egyptian delegations to Moscow were labeled "party–government" delegations in order to emphasize the party-level relations between the Arab Socialist Union and the CPSU. During his visits to Moscow in 1971–1972 Sadat was mentioned in the Soviet press both as Chairman of the Arab Socialist Union and President of Egypt, so as to indicate that relations between the two countries resembled relations between two Communist states.

The employment of this jargon by the Soviet media revealed just how eager Moscow had been to demonstrate to its own public, and particularly to its own establishment, the great achievements and fruits of Soviet Middle Eastern policy. The ouster in May 1971 of Vice President Ali Sabri and other pro-Soviet oriented figures in Cairo was thus extremely unpleasant to the Soviet leadership, particularly in its domestic context, and Podgorny was rushed to Cairo that same month to extract from Sadat the Treaty of Friendship and Collaboration which constituted the first formal pact between the two countries. This document was intended by the Kremlin to serve, for domestic as well as external consumption, as the legal framework formalizing the recently achieved Soviet status in Egypt.

Whatever domestic constraints influenced Soviet conduct the main issue remained Arab frustration at the continuance of the *status quo* and the increasing pressure on the Soviet Union to do something about it. Because the Soviet stakes in Egypt were so big after 1970, a high level of coordination between Cairo and Moscow was thought imperative. Kosygin, who attended Nasser's funeral, was very generous in offering material support to the new regime hoping to make the new leaders attentive to Soviet advice.[26] However, the new regime in Cairo seemed to have increasing doubts about Moscow's claims that Arab military credibility was enhanced simply by the Soviet presence in Egypt. The Soviet leadership soon came to realize that Cairo was seriously considering a full-scale war aimed at undermining the *status quo*. The period between the fall of 1970 and July 1972 is characterized therefore by a continuous Soviet effort of a dual nature: to postpone an Egyptian decision to go to war under the prevailing circumstances but at the same time maintain Cairo's faith in Moscow as the chief genuine supporter of the Arab cause.

The nature of the mutual understanding which the Kremlin tried to reach with Sadat was considerably different from those it had reached with Nasser in 1967 or a little later. Nasser agreed with Moscow that, with the absence of any other alternative in the short run, the diplomatic effort, first exclusively and later backed by limited military pressures, might produce desirable results. Sadat was already four years wiser with the experience of the War of Attrition in his mind. He was apparently convinced, as demonstrated in October 1973, that only full-scale war, even for limited objectives, might push forward the diplomatic effort. From 1971 on, the Soviet leadership was prepared to agree with Sadat that war was almost inevitable; it argued with him not on the principle but on the timing. The main Soviet argument, as reflected in a classified Communist document, was as follows: "We are not against war as such, we are against war because we are realistic."[27] That is to say, Egypt and Syria were not yet prepared to confront Israel on the battlefield, and any such attempt on their part would probably wind up in a new crushing defeat. While the deep and direct Soviet involvement in the war machine was probably the true and most significant consideration behind the Soviet opposition to an immediate war, there is also good reason to believe that the Soviet assessment of the military ratio between Israel and the Arabs was this time correct.

Delaying an Egyptian-Syrian tactical decision to go to war while supporting the idea in principle became the basic guideline of Soviet policy up to July 1972. Any event or development which delayed an Egyptian decision was now welcome to the Kremlin. During 1971 and 1972, first the idea of the "interim agreement" for the reopening of the Suez Canal, under American sponsorship, and later the initiative of Sisco for "proximity talks" between Egypt and Israel, served the Soviet interest, though they involved a considerable cost in terms of the effects of a successful one-sided American action. Moscow was therefore ambiguous, rather than wholly negative, toward these American efforts. On the other hand, in March 1971, during his visit to Moscow, Sadat had received the Soviet leadership's blessing for the Egyptian unilateral abrogation of the cease-fire agreement of August 1970. At the time, the decision was no more than a ceremonial move; nonetheless, the time bomb began to tick and the moment of truth between Cairo and Moscow was no longer far off. When Podgorny came to Cairo in May 1971, to extract from Sadat the Treaty of Friendship and Collaboration, he promised him MiG-23s in return.[28] Unlike the Kremlin, Sadat regarded the treaty as an exchange deal in which Egypt gave some formal recognition to Soviet status in return for a deeper Soviet commitment to prepare it for the coming war.

The Soviet leadership did not fulfill Podgorny's promise and used any pretext to stop the Egyptians. In July 1971 arms shipments to Egypt were temporarily halted as a result of Sadat's support for the suppression of the abortive Communist coup in the Sudan.[29] In December 1971, during the Indo–Pakistani war, considerable amounts of Soviet weapons and technicians were flown from Egypt to India,[30] disrupting operational plans of the Egyptian army. Moscow thus gained further time, but for how long? It seems that from the Soviet point of view, once Moscow became convinced that Sadat was determined to launch a full-scale war, the lowering of the Soviet profile in Egypt became essential. The Kremlin now needed security margins in order to reduce its risks in case of a new war.

It is thus not unlikely that sometime before July 1972 some sort of an understanding emerged between Moscow and Cairo, according to which a certain degree of Soviet disengagement from the Egyptian military machine was accepted as necessary.[31] Thus the exodus of Soviet personnel from Egypt, announced by Sadat in July 1972, was not entirely antithetic to the Soviet interest at the time. However, Sadat probably went far beyond what was understood between the two governments; he insisted on a much larger scale of Soviet withdrawal and made the exodus look and taste very unpleasant to Moscow; in order to gain American sympathy he made the entire event appear a tremendous prestige blow to the Soviet Union, above and beyond the damage caused to Soviet strategic installations, and he infuriated leaders in the Kremlin, who disliked him anyway for his removal of Ali Sabri a year earlier.

AID AND SUPPORT BUT NO RESPONSIBILITY

Between July and October 1972 Soviet–Egyptian relations reached their lowest ebb since 1955. The clearly anti-Soviet tone of the Egyptian media highlighting the departure of Soviet personnel was very embarrassing to the Soviet leadership, which had done its best to convince its own establishment that Egypt was irreversibly on the way to socialism. To some extent this embarrassment was counterbalanced by a considerable improvement in Soviet relations with Syria and Iraq during the year. As early as February 1972 the Soviet Union had concluded an impressive series of agreements with Syria, including one between the CPSU and the Ba'th Party which resulted in the formation of a "national progressive front" in Damascus between the Syrian Communist Party and the Ba'th. A month later a Treaty of Friendship and Collaboration, almost identical with the Soviet–Egyptian treaty, was signed between Moscow and Baghdad. Nevertheless, the bitter taste of Sadat's move increased Soviet anxieties that Egypt might drift away from the Soviet sphere of influence altogether, and embark on a one-sided pro-American course. The lesser the Soviet risks in the area after the withdrawal, the less Moscow was inclined to pay for an American initiative. Thus, the summer of 1972 witnessed a significant hardening in the Soviet terms for an Arab–Israeli settlement, which manifested itself mainly in the Soviet stand on the Palestinian issue. In July Arafat was in Moscow to receive concrete promises of direct Soviet arms shipments to the PLO.[32] It was a clear Soviet move to put obstacles on any Egyptian inclination toward one–sided American arrangement.

The Soviet–Egyptian quarrel did not last long. It soon became clear to both sides that the evacuation of Soviet personnel had created a basis for a new understanding between the two capitals. Nonetheless, the Soviet leadership did not become enthusiastic about full-scale war even after July. Although statements emanating from Washington (such as "the US will defend Israel but not Israel's conquests") made it clear to the Kremlin that Arab military operations were still possible as long as they were limited to the occupied territories—the Soviet estimate that Israel was militarily far superior to the Arabs led the Kremlin to fear that, in the event of any full-scale war, Israel might decide to cross Soviet red lines such as the Suez Canal or Damascus. Such a possibility was too dangerous from the Soviet point of view. Nevertheless, with the absence of a massive Soviet presence in Egypt, Moscow became more tolerant toward Egyptian thinking and preparations for the crossing of the Canal. It should be stressed that *détente per se* did not seem to constitute any major constraint on Soviet conduct over this issue because there was no agreement whatsoever between the two superpowers, neither in the Moscow summit of 1972, nor in the Washington summit of 1973, to terminate regional competition short of direct confrontation. As far as the Soviet Union was concerned *détente* was irrelevant to the Middle East, particularly if the initiative for a new war were to appear on the surface to be exclusively Arab, without the prior knowledge of the Kremlin.

The Kremlin probably articulated its new stand on the issue of another Arab–Israeli war in October 1972, during the visit to Moscow of Aziz Sidqi, the Egyptian Premier, the first such visit since the rift of July that year. He was told that the Soviet Government did not advise Egypt to go to war but that if Sadat so wished that was Egypt's responsibility; the Soviets would help Egypt to purchase the necessary capability, but war would be the Egyptian Government's responsibility and it would have to be prepared to bear the risk. Judging by Sadat's remarks later he was pleased with Soviet arms deliveries, such as the MiG-23s, during the winter and spring of 1973.[33] It is also possible that even the Scud missiles were promised to the Egyptians as early as February 1973, but were not delivered before September, in order to prevent Egypt from going to war at the time of the summit in Washington. Whatever the exact dates, it is clear that Soviet conduct during this period can be summed up as giving the capability without assuming the responsibility. The evacuation of families of Soviet advisors from Cairo and Damascus three days before the outbreak of the October War can be interpreted as a Soviet attempt to inform the US of the forthcoming battle, or even as a signal given to alert the Israelis to mobilize and by so doing to force Sadat to call of the entire operation. No matter what the real reason, the Soviet leadership remains strategically responsible for having enabled the Syrians and Egyptians to resume the war.

The assessment of the ratio of forces between the Arab and Israeli armies continued to dominate Soviet considerations even during the war. In the first two days after the Syrian–Egyptian attack in October 1973, being convinced that an Israeli counterattack was a matter of hours away, the Soviet envoys in Damascus and Cairo pressed for an immediate cease-fire and the consolidation of the initial territorial gains. Only after it had become clear that Israel was not responding as quickly as expected, did Soviet messages to Sadat and Asad become more milit-ant, encouraging and aggressive.[34] It was not until 16 October, ten days after the Arab attack and the very day that Israeli Prime Minister Golda Meir announced in the Knesset (Israeli Parliament) the presence of an Israeli task force on the west bank of the Suez Canal, that Kosygin flew to Cairo to resume Soviet pressures on Egypt to accept a cease-fire. It can thus be argued that Soviet restraint on the issue of the Arab–Israeli conflict since 1967 has been directly related to the Kremlin's recogni-tion of Israel's military superiority.

THE IMPACT OF THE OCTOBER WAR ON SOVIET PERSPECTIVE

The October War between Egypt, Syria and Israel does not seem in any way to have changed the Soviet assessment of the military balance of forces in the conflict. In fact, no one knows better than the Soviet political and military leadership what would have been the fate of the Egyptian army had the fighting not been stopped by outside interven-tion on 24 October. Therefore, thus far, Moscow has no ground what-soever for a reevaluation of its current view of the military solution and its perils.

Moreover, the October War and its consequences may have provided further evidence to support those in the Soviet leadership who were already wary of involvement in regional military flare-ups. The war did not reverse Egypt's already two-year-old drift away from the Soviet Union. On the contrary, despite massive Soviet material support for Egypt and Syria during the fighting, and despite the Soviet Govern-ment's display of brinkmanship in order to save the Egyptian Third Army from total defeat, the war wound up with a further decline of

Soviet influence in the region and with the accelerated recovery of the influence of the arch rival of the USSR for local hegemony—the United States. Whoever believes that the Soviet leaders engineered the October War with the intention of rejuvenating Soviet–Egyptian relations must certainly conclude that they miscalculated. Of all Arab–Israeli military crises since the mid-1950s the one of October 1973 produced the poorest results from a Soviet point of view. Consequently, Moscow can no longer be certain that crisis situations will necessarily play into its hands in the future. The tactic of crisis promotion which had so handsomely paid off for the Kremlin in the past may prove to have exausted itself because the danger to world peace inherent in an Arab–Israeli military clash is bound to generate the need for a third power competent to mediate between the adversaries. No power is more capable of accomplishing this mission than the government of the United States.

While no Soviet change of mind on the question of a military solution to the Arab–Israeli conflict has been detectable subsequent to the October War, Soviet perception of how to bring about an Arab–Israeli settlement has not changed either. In the Soviet view an Arab–Israeli settlement has never been a matter involving compromise, consensus or genuine negotiations between the parties concerned but a forceful act of rape. As a consequence, Soviet thinking has remained unsophisticated regarding the technicalities of negotiations between the parties and the vast amount of detail involved in the process. The Kremlin's belief that a settlement can indeed be imposed derives from its assumption that Israel would be incapable of resisting American pressure. Thus, in contrast to the Six Day War, which had destroyed contemporary Soviet perceptions and convinced the Kremlin that Israel was militarily indestructible, the October War has deepened Moscow's belief in the validity of its previous approach, which assumed the likelihood of a superpower-imposed solution.

The Soviet Government's current conduct in the Arab–Israeli conflict reflects well its accumulated experience from 1967 through 1973. The main goal appears to be the convening of a Soviet–American sponsored conference in Geneva for the purpose of executing a very specific type of settlemment. There are two guiding principles in the Soviet conception of this settlement: one, the maximization of Arab satisfaction and; two, the guarantee of a future Soviet role in the Middle East. In Soviet thinking, a major political victory for the Arabs would enhance the credibility of the Soviet Union as a superpower and ensure the continued survival of its client regimes in the area. In the absence of political achievements on the Israeli front, these pro-Soviet regimes might either collapse or drift away from the Soviet sphere of influence.[35] Enhancing the prestige of the "progressive regimes," and providing them with political momentum is thus a constant consideration of Soviet policy makers, and invariably influences their decisions. Consequently, a high degree of coordination, if not identity, between the Soviet and Arab positions on the principles of a settlement (as distinguished from the techniques of achieving it) is an imperative of Soviet regional conduct. In fact, the specifics of the arrangement have not worried the Soviet leadership as much as the necessity of harmonizing Soviet and Arab positions.

This contention is well demonstrated by the fact that where Arab consensus has been static, the Soviet position has been static as well; but where Arab consensus has continuously developed the Soviet position has also undergone frequent adjustments. On the issue of an Israeli pullback from the occupied territories the Kremlin's position has been absolutely inflexible since 1967. No Soviet depiction of an Arab–Israeli settlement has fallen short of a full and total withdrawal from all the territories occupied in 1967. This has not been the case with the Soviet view of the "legitimate national rights of the Arab people of Palestine," which has been periodically revised to fit in with the continuously developing Arab consensus.

The Soviet concept of the desired settlement does not contain Arab components only. It is clear that a great deal of thought is being given to Soviet interests proper involved in the formation of a new order in the Middle East. This concern has grown with the increasing prospect of an Arab–Israeli settlement following October 1973. All Soviet official references to the Geneva Conference, without exception, insist that in addition to the achievement of a peace settlement on Arab terms, the question of "international guarantees" must be discussed. The Soviet sources emphasize, time and again, that the Soviet Union is willing to contribute to and participate in the system of guarantees.[36] It appears that Soviet policy makers intend to make the Soviet Government a co-guarantor of any settlement with the United States. More specifically Moscow intends that any Arab–Israeli settlement be tied to the establishment of an international regime—one may call it Soviet–American Condominium—which from time to time would require international policing; Moscow wishes to become co-gendarme of any Arab–Israeli settlement with the United States. The achievement of such a status in the region by the Soviet Union would mean, at long last, the formalization and legitimization of Soviet Middle Eastern involvement by the international community.

This objective, one has to admit, constitues a considerable diminution of Soviet hopes concerning the future of the area. Formalizing the Soviet position at the price of co-formalizing the American position is not an excellent deal from the Soviet point of view, particularly in a region which, to use Soviet terms, lies in proximity to the southern border of the USSR. It will give the Soviet Union more than it has now, but will still fall far short of the original aspirations of the Kremlin leaders to achieve supremacy in the area. Nevertheless, Moscow seems to regard this arrangement as teh best that it can obtain under the circumstances and for the time being. This trend in Soviet policy seems to be the product of a growing recognition among Soviet leaders that there has been no necessary correlation between their aid policy and the extent of their influence, and that the historical process in the region might indeed be reversible. Long before October 1973 the Soviet Government had come to realize that in the Arab world, as elsewhere in the Third World, the politics of influence has been a highly fluid game; that influence can be neither bought nor assured, and that massive aid may indeed produce very poor results in terms of influence. Moscow found that in the final analysis it was influential only to the extent that its client actually desired to be influenced.

Furthermore, these lessons may have undermined some of the Marxist–Leninist convictions of the Soviet leadership that "time is on our side." Such confidence that the historical process (a euphemism for whatever is pro-Soviet) in the area is irreversible was expressed in Soviet writings on the Arab East throughout the 1960s.[37] The mood which is reflected in recent Soviet articles on the same subject, and particularly in relation to Egypt, is characterized by an unprecedented sense of pessimism and a high degree of uncertainty regarding the question "on whose side is time?"[38] (What sweetens the Soviet pill somewhat is the fact that neither the United States nor any other power can be sure that time is on its side in this part of the world.) Prior to October 1973 the conclusion of Soviet treaties of Friendship and Collaboration with Egypt and Iraq (as well as with India), and the long-applied Soviet pressure on Syria to sign such a treaty, indicated optimism in Soviet thinking on the subject. The sharp decline of Soviet influence in the

Arab–Israeli conflict after the October War has aggravated the Kremlin's anxiety about the endurance of its influence. The prospect of forming an international regime presents the Soviet leadership with an opportunity to consolidate its assets to date. Since the Soviet position in the Arab world is analogous to the case of a man who has invested a fortune in real estate, and has not managed to record his ownership in the registry of deeds, the Geneva Conference is analogous in Soviet thinking to the act of registration of the Middle East in the Soviet name in the international real estate register.

There are those who argue, of course, that an Arab–Israeli settlement is incompatible with Soviet regional interests. According to this argument, with the absence of tension and high war risks there would be no arms race, and consequently no need for Soviet military assistance. Under such circumstances the Soviet Union would be deprived of its only pretext for involvement in the region. In view of this, the declared Soviet position in favor of a settlement should not be taken seriously. This argument, which has been part of the conventional wisdom concerning the Kremlin's perception of its Middle Eastern interests oversimplifies not only Soviet perspectives of the Arab–Israeli conflict, but also the objective conditions which govern that conflict. Soviet Middle Eastern experts are no less aware than anyone else who is acquainted with the problems of the region, that no settlement in the world will completely erase the sources of frustration and bitterness in the Arab–Israeli conflict. The Soviet Government does not have to worry about keeping the conflict on a low fire because low fire is a given actuality of the region. Thus, any arrangement would be, almost by definition, an armed peace requiring the superpowers permanently to maintain a balance between the forces. Furthermore, an arrangement governed by a Soviet–American condominium is far more promising and preferable to the Soviet Union than the continuation of the present situation; it would promote the Kremlin's role as recognized Middle Eastern arbiter and would make the Soviet Union less dependent on unstable regimees in the Arab world by providing it with an additional, more solid and secure means of participating in the politics of region. Moscow has every reason in the world to promote this particular type of settlement.

Nevertheless, any settlement which did not satisfy most of the Arabs' demands or formalize Soviet responsibility in its preservation, such as, a separate Israeli–Egyptian arrangement under American sponsorship, would be less acceptable to the Soviet Union than the existing situation.[39] Maintaining high war risks in the form of massive weapon supplies to the Syrian army, as well as the prospect of the resumption of supplies to the Egyptian army, has been and still is the chief Soviet means of ensuring that no progress be made in this part of the world except in the direction desired by Moscow. The Soviet Government seems to be convinced that the availability of the military option to the Arab countries is the only guarantee of the feasibility of a settlement of the proper type. Any Arab–Israeli arrangement achieved without a background of high war risks is likely to be of a type inimical to Soviet interests. The insoluble Soviet dilemma is, of course, how to control a potentially explosive situation, how to prevent the risks from actually being realized. The Soviet Government does not seem to have any practical solution to this dilemma and it appears to be one of the main constraints on Soviet policy making in the area. At the same time the Soviet Government is not likely to reassess its current Middle Eastern conduct as long as it remains convinced that the type of settlement most favorable to it is achievable, and that the pressure for it is bound eventually to be fruitful.

Nor are the poor results of Soviet arms policy, in terms of the Kremlin's ability to influence major decisions of the Arab countries concerned, likely to change the Kremlin's mind on the matter, because the available Soviet choice is not between a policy producing high political profit and one producing smaller political profit, but between a poor profit making policy and the total elimination of Soviet influence from the Middle East. Reconstructing and maintaining the Arab military option is the only method by which the Kremlin can hope to maintain its influence in the region.

Against this background of Soviet short-range objectives in the Middle East, it is difficult to interpret Soviet intentions toward Israel, particularly following the cease-fire of August 1970. Despite the extremely hostile tone taken by the Soviet mass media in relation to Israel, reports on the forthcoming resumption of diplomatic relations between Moscow and Jerusalem are deliberately circulated about every six months, mostly by various Soviet sources. Furthermore, some official Soviet statements, particularly after October 1973, were worded as if with the intention of pleasing the Israeli Government. For instance, on the occasion of the opening session of the Geneva Conference in December 1973 Gromyko's speech contained a reference to Soviet willingness to recognize the 4 June, 1967 armistice lines as the legal borders of the State of Israel.[40] This is supposed to be a Soviet bonus to Israel in return for a total troop withdrawal from the Arab lands occupied since 1967. Apparently, Israel is expected to clutch at this opportunity since thus far the 1947 partition lines are the only ones which have the status of legal borders. The apparent Soviet interest in occasionally generating the impression of a balanced approach to the Arab–Israeli dispute is to be understood in the context of the Soviet desire to become a co-guarantor of a settlement. The Kremlin's policy makers seem to realize that the image of a responsible Soviet approach may be instrumental in promoting their chances of success. No wonder that the timing of each rumor concerning the reestablishment of diplomatic relations with Israel in the last three years has been coordinated, either with imminent diplomatic progress in the conflict, or with an overaccumulation of one-sided, pro-Arab moves by the Soviet Government.

Nevertheless, the Soviet Government is likely to be genuinely interested in resuming formal relations with Israel, even prior to the formation of a new international order in the region. Soviet Middle Eastern diplomacy suffers from tactical inferiority vis-à-vis the United States just because it is incapable of communicating with both sides in the negotiations. Soviet anxiety about the possibility of an undesirable arrangement are largely related to this tactical inferiority. At the same time, the probability of a Soviet–Israeli *rapprochment* before any substantial progress toward a settlement has been made is not very high, and on this at least Soviet spokesmen should be trusted. It is unlikely that the Soviet Union, having at long last manufactured the grand coalition isolating Israel, would itself constitute the weak link which breaks it. If such a development were to occur it might be a sign of a reconsideration by the Kremlin of the feasiblity of its most favored type of settlement. Any genuine *rapprochement* between Moscow and Jerusalem will not be possible, however, without some demonstration by the Kremlin of greater sensitivity to, and understanding of, Israel's security problems.

NOTES

1. See D. Dallin, *Soviet Foreign Policy After Stalin*, Methuen 1960, pp. 104-107.

2. See Kosygin's speech before the Egyptian National Assembly, 17 May, 1966.

3. See Y. Roi, *From Encroachment To Involvement*, (statement of the Soviet Foreign Ministry on the situation in the Middle East), p. 139. Israel Universities Press, Jerusalem 1974.

4. See, for example, Akademiia Nank SSSR, Institut Mirovoi Ekonamiki, *Mezhdunarodnoe Revolutsionoe Dvizhenie Rabochevo Klassa*, Moskva 1964, 1965.

5. See O. Eran, "Soviet Perception of Arab Communism and its Political Role," in M. Confino and S. Shamir (eds.), *The USSR and the Middle East*, Israel Universities Press, Jerusalem 1973.

6. This tone was manifest in Brezhnev's speech before graduates of the Military Academy on July 5, 1967, when he claimed, "In retrospect we can confidently say that our actions during the critical days of the crisis in the Middle East were correct"; three official forums of the CPSU and the Soviet bloc were convened to give *post factum* support to the policy pursued during the crisis: Central Committee plenum as well as two meetings of East European communist leaders and heads of states, on June 9 and July 11-12.

7. The escalation of the Soviet naval build-up in the Mediterranean took place suddenly in 1967, after slow going for almost four years; 60 Soviet warships passed through the straits into the Mediterranean in the period from January through May 1967. The first large-scale movement of Soviet naval units into the Mediterranean took place in February 1967. See *Middle East Record*, Vol III, 1967, p.10.

8. See John Dornberg, *Brezhnev; The Masks Of Power*, Andre Deutsch 1974, p. 212-214.

9. See O. Eran, *Soviet Area Studies and Foreign Policy Making*, Tempo, Center For Advanced Studies, Washington D.C., 1974, Ch.C, n. 2C; the absence from Moscow of Brezhnev, Podgorny and Kosygin in the few days before the war points to their ignorance of the timing as well as misjudgment of events.

10. See *MER*, Vol III 1967, p. 17.

11. *Ibid*, p. 11.

12. See H. Heikal, *The Road to Ramadan*, 1975.

13. See N. Safran, *From War To War*, N.Y. Pegasus 1965, p.411.

14. See A. Iskenderov in *Literaturnaia Gazeta*, No. 33, 16 August, 1967, as well as Selem and Babiker in *World Marxist Review*, No. 01, October 1967.

15 See O. Eran, *The Soviet Union and the Palestinian Guerrilla Organizations*, Occasional Papers, The Shiloah Center For Middle Eastern and African Studies, June 1971, Tel Aviv.

16. *Ibid*.

17. See Heikal, *ibid*.

18. See *Mer*, Vol IV 1968, p.36.

19. *Sovetskesia Rossiia*, April 6, 1969 (reported in RLR, February 13, 1970), also: E. Ya'ari, *Fatah*, Levin Epstein, 1970 (Heb.) pp. 227-228.

20. The first Communist ceremonial declaration to use this term was the "Statement of the International Conference of Communist and Workers Parties," Moscow, June 7, 1969.

21. In May 1969 the Syrian Chief of Staff was sent on a mission to Peking to verify possibilities of Chinese aid to Syria. Disappointed and disillusioned with these possibilities, President Nur ad-Din
Attasi and Hafiz al-Asad went to the Soviet Union in July 1969 in an effort to mend the Syrian-Soviet rift.

22. See *MER*, Vol V, pp. 450, 466, 467.

23. *Ibid*.

24. See H. Heikal, *op. cit*.

25. See *Pravda*, July 30.

26. I. Balyaev is reported to have said to an Israeli communist correspondent present in Moscow in September 1964, in reference to Soviet commitments in Egypt: "We have taken on ourselves a burden which is too heavy to carry" (interview with B. Balti, Tel Aviv, 30 May, 1975. The latest evidence concerning this mood in Moscow appeared in the Egyptian paper *Ruz Al-Yusuf*, 28 April, 1975, p. 3, reporting on Foreign Minister Fahmi's visit to Moscow that month. The report attested to the existence in the Party and the military of a group opposing the aid programs.

27. See Y. Roi and I. Dimant Kass, *The Soviet military Involvement in Egypt, January 1970-July 1972*, Research Paper No. 6, The Soviet and East European Research Center, Hebrew University, Jerusalem 1974.

28. *Opinions and Comments of Soviet Leaders and Ideologists on the Political Program of the Syrian Communist Party–May 1971*, published in *Al Raya*, Lebanon, 26 June, 1972 (Heb. translation, p.31).

29. See Y. Roi and I. Dimant, *op. cit*., p. 34n.

30. *Ibid*, pp. 39, 58n., 59n.

31. *Ibid*, p. 40.

32. This is verified by reports in the Soviet press concerning the reasons for the departure of Soviet personnel from Egypt. See *Pravda*, 20 July, 1973.

33. Until then Soviet arms reached the PLO only through East European countries (see O. Eran, *The Soviet Union and Egyptian Syrian Preparations for the Arab Israeli War of 1973*, Stanford Research Institute, Washington D.C., p. 55n.

34. *Newsweek*, April 9, 1973.

35. See Heikal, *op. cit.*

36. *Pravda*, "International Week," 23 June, 1974, as well as Kirilenke's speech on the ocasion of the November 7 celebration, *Pravda*, 7 November, 1973, p. 2.

37. *Opinions and Comments, op. cit.*, pp. 15, 31.

38. See Gromyko's speech at the opening session of the Geneva Conference, December 21, 1973, *Pravda*, 22 December, 1973.

39. See, for example, U. Kisselev, "Arabskii Proletariat Nabiraet Sile," *Azia i Afrika Sevodniia*, No. 6, June 1962, pp. 20-21.

40. See Tolkunov, "Dve Tendentsi," *Izvestiia*, 25 July, 1974, p. 4.

41. See Gromyko's speech on the occasion of the November 7 celebration *Pravda*, 7 November, 1974, p. 3.

42. See Gromyko's speech, 21 December, 1973, *ibid.*

West German Policy
Towards the Arab States

Rainer Büren

HISTORICAL BACKGROUND

German policy toward the Middle East was governed until the early 1960s by broad considerations that had little to do with the Arab countries. The initial control by the three Western allies and the later integration into the Western system of alliances called for a coordination with Western policies. The striving for rehabilitation and acceptance led to the Luxemburg Reparation Agreement of 10 September, 1952 with the State of Israel as a major party. The policy of non-recognition pursued toward the German Democratic Republic led to the Federal Republic's formulating a code of behavior known as the Hallstein Doctrine, which characterized the strengthening of relations with the German Democratic Republic by a third party as an unfriendly act which would give the Federal Republic the right to resort to sanctions including the severance of diplomatic relations.

The Arab states played only a subsidiary role in these considerations. Their importance in the foreign policy of the Federal Republic was determined by the extent to which they could either hinder or support Bonn in the realization of its objectives.

By recognizing Israel as the main recipient of compensation, according to Luxemburg Agreement, Chancellor Adenauer had taken a deliberate step against the Arab policy of non-recognition of Israel, the more so as the funds were specifically allocated for the integration of immigrants. The Arab states presented their objections to the Chancellor's decision both bilaterally and collectively (through the Arab League). However, as it turned out, they were unable to obtain satisfaction in this matter.

There were, nevertheless, tentative moves by the Federal Republic toward an autonomous Arab policy. The Bonn Foreign Ministry rightly

53

considered that Egypt held the leading position in the Arab world and therefore attempted to win influence with the other Arab states via Cairo. In spite of the pro-Israel decision at Luxemburg, diplomatic relations were established in 1952 with Syria and Egypt.

Otherwise, the Middle East policy of the three Western powers limited West Germany's political room to maneuver in relation to the Arab states. The Federal Republic took no direct part in the various attempts to incorporate the Arab states in the Western containment policy towards the Soviet Union in the context of the East–West confrontation as a whole. The Soviet action in Hungary in 1956 led Chancellor Adenauer to emphasize even more strongly than before the conformity of his Middle East policy to that of the West. Therefore, the Federal government adopted an extremely tentative position towards the simultaneous action of Israeli, French and British forces against Nasser's Egypt.

The Federal Republic's non-recognition policy towards the German Democratic Republic was met with understanding by most of the Arab states mainly because of the economic significance of the Federal Republic.

THE 1965 CRISIS

In the mid-1960s it became apparent that the basic approach of the Federal Republic to its main foreign policy goals was no longer the same as in the initial phase of the West German state. Rather, there arose in 1964–65 a conflict of priorities between the need for conformity with the West, the non-recognition policy and the striving for rehabilitation. This conflict also resulted in a crisis in relation to the Arab states.

At the initiative of the US president, Chancellor Adenauer concluded in 1960 a secret arms delivery agreement with Israel. In spite of initial objections, Adenauer had shown himself ready to oblige the leading power of the Western alliance. Moreover, the Chancellor was able once more to act in accordance with Germany's goal of rehabilitation. When, in 1964, press articles about the West German arms deliveries to Israel appeared, the President of the Federal Parliament, Gerstenmaier, went in November to Cairo to explain the affair to President Nasser. Gerstenmaier's statement, that the deliveries would immediately stop was, however, not observed in practice. Pres. Nasser invited the President of the State Council of the German Democratic Republic, Walter Ulbricht, to visit Egypt. Although there was no formal recognition of the German

Democratic Republic by Egypt and no establishment of diplomatic relations, the Federal Government nevertheless felt that the effectiveness of its non-recognition policy had been called in question. Chancellor Erhard, however, did not break off diplomatic relations with Egypt, thus neither applying nor invalidating the Hallstein Doctrine. On the contrary, he switched the field of confrontation by establishing diplomatic relations with Israel, thereby calling into question the Arab non-recognition policy. Nasser recommended that the Arab states respond to the West German step by establishing diplomatic relations with the German Democratic Republic but was unable to secure implementation of this policy. Instead, the Arab states, with the exception of Morocco, Tunisia and Libya, withdrew their ambassadors from Bonn and severed diplomatic relations.

This crisis in the German–Arab relationship made apparent the fact that the Federal Government, essentially on the recommendation of the three Western powers, had renounced the consistent observance of its non-recognition policy. The Federal Republic achieved a notable success in its striving for rehabilitation when Israel agreed to establish diplomatic relations. This success, however, turned out to be at the expense of the Federal Republic's claim to be the sole representative of the German people, since the Federal Republic now had to withdraw her official presence from most Arab states, and this at a time when the German Democratic Republic had just achieved a notable advance in her international position as a result of Ulbricht's visit to Cairo.

The contradictions and inconsistencies which were brought to light in this crisis demanded an assessment of the Federal Republic's position and a new conception of foreign policy.

THE NEW FRAME OF REFERENCE
FOR WEST GERMANY'S FOREIGN POLICY

The new foreign policy conception began to develop under the so-called "Grand Coalition" between the Christian Democratic Union and the Social Democratic Party (1966–1969), but reached its full development only under the so-called "Social Liberal Coalition" between the Social Democratic Party and the Free Democratic Party (since 1969).

Particularly noteworthy in this context was the gradual change in the policy of non-recogniton towards the German Democratic Republic. On 30 May, 1969, the Federal Government openly declared its modification of the so-called "Hallstein Doctrine": while the recognition of the

German Democratic Republic by a third party was still to be considered an unfriendly act, the Government would henceforth avoid automatic retaliation through the severance of diplomatic relations. The Federal Government adopted a flexible position, declaring that instead of severing relations "in such a case, it would make its attitude and its measures dependent on the given circumstances in accordance with the interest of the whole German people." In a government declaration on 28 October, 1969, Chancellor Brandt spoke of the existence of two states in Germany, although with the reservation that neither state could be a foreign state for the other on account of the unity of the German nation.

This modified view of internal German relations, as well as the approval by the three Western allies, and the Soviet Union as the fourth occupying power in Germany, made possible the acceptance both of the Federal Republic and the German Democratic Republic in the United Nations with full membership status. Its UN membership status obliged the Federal Republic to observe UN resolutions and in particular with respect to the Middle East, Security Council Resolution 242 of 22 November, 1967. This resolution reflected a compromise suggested by Great Britain, and its deliberate vagueness allowed the maximum possible scope for nations to read into it their own interpretations. Its consideration of the legitimate security requirements both of Israel and her Arab neighbors and its mention of the refugee question—albeit only from a humanitarian and not from a political point of view—constituted an approach towards a balanced attitude.

The Federal Republic's new foreign policy conception is additionally distinguished by this fact: the desire for rehabilitation still persists, but its repeated demonstration is no longer considered a primary requirement to the same extent as in the initial phase. The Federal Republic had already given concrete evidence of its desire to dissociate itself from the Nazi past in its attitude towards Israel. We can cite here the faithful fulfilment of the Luxemburg Compensation Agreement, the extension in 1965 of the statute of limitations for Nazi crimes, the establishment of diplomatic relations with Israel and the almost unanimous support for Israel by public opinion in the Federal Republic during the Six Day War in June 1967. The *Ostpolitik* was the expression of a rehabilitation process primarily involving the Soviet Union, Poland and Czechoslovakia. Therefore the Federal Republic now felt free to conduct a more balanced Middle Eastern policy.

In some fields, such as in its monetary policy of *Ostpolitik*, the Federal Republic had definitely achieved a certain consciousness of its emancipation. Nevertheless, integration with and loyalty to the West are still the most important imperatives of Bonn's foreign policy. Despite this, the Federal Republic's position within the Western alliance was complicated by the fact that the United States and her European partners no longer had completely congruent opinions on vital questions. The United States favored the idea of an Atlantic Community and a close interdependence between security questions on the one hand, and economic, monetary and foreign policy issues, on the other. Certain Western European states, however, preferred a divergent conception: they generally favored—albeit with a few exceptions—close cooperation with the United States in the military and security field, but advocated in other areas an active Western European regionalism which would pursue its own interests.

Since the Federal Republic considers that its security interest is in a sufficient American presence in the Republic and Western Europe, close ties with the United States are an obvious priority for West Germany. Furthermore, the European Community has as yet made little progress towards political union beyond the existing customs union and the economic and incipient monetary union. American dominance of the world monetary system presents an additional argument for the Federal Republic's integration into the American network of interests.

Finally, differences within the Western alliance are accentuated by the distinctive points of departure regarding the supply of energy, in particular oil. Here the United States benefits from a relative self-sufficiency. Its position is further safeguarded by its dominant share in the multinational oil concerns. But the member states of the European Community, as is well known, are highly dependent on supplies from the petroleum exporting countries in North Africa and the Middle East. The Federal Republic's dependence on the Arab states and Iran, for example, amounts to roughly 80 percent. This advantageous position has helped the Middle Eastern oil-producing states in the past to achieve an increasing self-confidence which, it must be said, found direct expression only in the economic field as exemplified by the successful demands for higher income at the conferences of Tehran and Tripoli in 1970 and 1971. Since the Six Day War, however, the energy question has become intertwined with the Arab–Israeli confrontation.

The development of the Palestinians as an independent political force led to a further complication. While in the 1950s and early 1960s one could speak only of a refugee question, since 1965 one can observe the manifestation in an organizational form of Palestinian nationalism. This Palestinian nationalism adopted a distinct attitude toward both the Arab states and Israel. Thus the question of future treatment of Palestinians had, in the interests of a durable solution, to be regarded no longer as solely a technical or humanitarian question but as a political one as well.

For some years there had been voices in Arab states calling for the use of petroleum as a political weapon in the confrontation with Israel, but this did not normally prove feasible before October 1973.

On account of the altered frame of reference it was more necessary than previously for the Federal Republic to have a balanced basis for its Middle East policy and a reactivation of its partially neglected Arab policy. As a result of the largely similar interests of the European Community member states, the Federal Republic had to safeguard its Arab policy in the context of a balanced European Middle East policy in which contradictory positions had to be removed, or at least relativized.

These developments had implications also for the Federal Republic's non-recognition policy toward the German Democratic Republic, the modification of which was influenced by Bonn's relationship with the Arab states. When Iraq, Sudan and South Yemen announced their diplomatic recognition of the German Democratic Republic in 1969, the Federal Government did not hide its disapproval. However, its reaction was only a declaration that it did not wish to enter into any new economic commitments. When Egypt likewise recognized the German Democratic Republic in the same year, the Federal Republic replied merely by cancelling the German share of European Community wheat deliveries to Egypt for one year. In the case of Algeria, which recognized the German Democratic Republic in 1970, Bonn declared that it would only enter into new economic commitments according to Germany's interest. This measured and flexible reaction enabled the Federal Republic to recoup political influence leading to the eventual re-establishment of diplomatic relations with important Arab states.

The Federal Republic's integration into the UN gave Resolution 242 and its balanced formulation an increased significance for Bonn. Even before its formal acceptance in the United Nations, Chancellor Brandt, in his first policy statement, on 28 October, 1969, declared the resolution "to be in the interest of the peoples concerned," and expressed his desire for good relations with all states in the area. This desire for balance was made concrete in an internal circular from the Foreign Ministry dated 5 June, 1970 concerning the basis of the Federal Republic's Middle East policy. The following guiding principles were expounded: "the preservation and, where necessary the restoration of friendship with the Arab peoples"; only then does there follow "the respecting of our tragic relationship to the Jewish people." In order to show the compatibility of the two guiding principles, the circular contined: "Our excellent relations with Jordan—the land which has suffered most from the Middle East conflict—and with other Arab countries, demonstrate that good relations with Israel do not exclude a friendly relationship with Arab countries." It concluded: "The Federal Government does not take sides in the Middle East conflict... It considers Resolution 242 to be a suitable basis for a peaceful solution of the conflict."

On 1 April, 1971, a West German government spokesman confirmed this position publicly. The progressive shift towards the Arab position also showed itself on the level of definition: the Federal Republic's relations with Israel were characterized as "special relations," but the interpretation of these "special relations" in the sense of a privileged status was denied.

After the European Community's foreign ministers had decided on a unification of their consultation mechanisms in November 1970, it was the Arab–Israeli conflict itself which gave cause for the first common approach in foreign policy. In the so-called "Middle East Paper" of the European Community of July 1971, the foreign ministers developed a balanced approach to the conflict. This paper was based on Resolution 242, but in reality stemmed from the European Community's own political conception. In places it went beyond the resolution, particularly in mentioning the Palestine question as such.

The conception indicated in the Middle East Paper was developed further in the Middle East Resolution of the European Community of November 1973. This development came when the October War had destroyed the state of immobility of the Arab–Israeli confrontation; only then did the Arab states under the leadership of Egypt and Saudi Arabia demand that the United States and the members of the European Community induce Israel to observe Resolution 242 as they interpreted it. The Arab request centered upon that element in the resolution prescribing "withdrawal from occupied territories," but also went beyond the resolution calling for a political solution to the question of the Palestinians. Arab governments emphasized that the Western states would receive oil supplies from the Arab countries (which had previously joined together to form OAPEC) to the extent to which they complied with these demands. This situation in particular—in conjunction with factors above—influenced the Federal Republic's Middle East policy. Together with the other eight members of the EEC it stated its readiness to contribute toward the implementation of Resolution 242 in all its parts. But furthermore they all emphasized the responsibility of the UN Security Council and the UN Secretary General. In this European resolution, they expressed their view even more clearly:

> The nine governments of the European Community consider that a peace treaty has to be founded above all on the following points:
> 1. The unacceptability of territorial acquisition by force;
> 2. The necessity for Israel to end the territorial occupation which it has maintained since the 1967 conflict;
> 3. The respecting of the sovereignty, territorial integrity and independence of each state in this area as well as its right to live within secure and recognized borders;
> 4. The acknowledgement that it is necessary, in creating a just and durable peace, to take into account also the legitimate rights of the Palestinians.

With this formulation the European Community declaration went considerably beyond UN Resolution 242 and adopted the Arab point-of-view in two important aspects: the acceptance of the Arab demand for an Israeli withdrawal from *all* territories occupied in 1967 (point 2, above), and by taking the position that the Palestinians are a national minority and consequently present a *political* problem (point 4).

Chancellor Brandt, in his visit to Israel, Algeria and Egypt in April 1974, when he was holding the post of President of the European Community Council of Ministers, acknowledged that the Federal Republic was attempting to achieve a new, balanced Middle East policy, and was also trying to attain at the European level an active pro-Arab policy. The occasional ultimative position taken by the Arab states in particular showed the Europeans the necessity of harmonizing their foreign policies.

CONCLUSION

In conclusion, one can observe a continuous reassessment and upgrading of the importance of the Arab states in the Federal Republic's Middle Eastern policy. Alongside this development, agreement to a considerable extent was reached between West German, European and Arab views on important questions such as the *political* assessment of the question of the Palestinians. It would thus seem that the way to a mutually advantageous European–Arab dialogue been opened. With due consideration to the United States' dominant position in Bonn and suitable regard for the existing ties with Israel, German–Arab policy will contribute an important input into this dialogue.

Strategic
Aspects

Strategic Changes in the Middle Eastern Arena

Geoffrey Kemp

The purpose of this paper is to examine the recent historical background of the current strategic situation in the Middle East. The period 1967 to 1974 witnessed major changes in the international strategic environment. These changes have been accelerated during 1974 and are likely to continue for several years to come. It is not possible to analyze the specific strategic changes that have occurred in the Middle Eastern arena unless these broader geo-political trends are fully appreciated. The first part of the paper is a review, in very general terms, of these major trends at the international level. Then, certain specific features of these trends, namely, changes in the overall US–USSR global military balance and the evolution of new military technologies, are highlighted. Finally, certain quantitative and qualitative features of the Middle East environment that have emerged since the mid-1960s are analyzed.

MAJOR TRENDS AT THE INTERNATIONAL LEVEL

A very simple proposition sums up my interpretation of the international events of the past six or so years. These years have seen the gradual erosion of worldwide US strategic power and the parallel, though not symmetrical, increase in Soviet military power. At the same time a more general worldwide diffusion of power has begun which may eventually erode Soviet as well as American capabilities to intervene physically in certain regional conflicts. In the case of the Arab-Israeli conflict, Israel's dependence on the United States as its sole credible supporter has increased while overall US power has diminished and both superpowers are more deeply involved in the Arab-Israeli conflict than at any time in the past. However, in the context of the Persian Gulf, the emergence of new major powers, especially Iran and to a lesser extent Saudi Arabia, has taken place because of the diminished presence and influence of external powers. Insofar as these two Middle East issues can be regarded as a sample of regional international political trends, the events that have occurred in the Persian Gulf are the more typical.

At the most general level, the changes in the global system which affect the geo-strategic environment can be summarized under seven related headings. First, the worldwide economic balance of power has been changed as a result of the energy crisis and inflation in the economies of the industrialized and developing countries and the worldwide increases in the demand for raw materials and food. This led to further price increases and balance of payments deficits and the emergence of two very distinct economic groups in the "old" Third World—the rich or potentially rich producer countries and the poor and superpoor consumer countries that have little hope of adequately feeding their populations let alone raising their living standards over the next decade. Although the economic crisis has amply demonstrated the importance of global interdependence in the modern world, the practical effect has generally been to create more divisiveness than cooperation.

Second, and clearly related to the first change, the continued rapid population growth in the less industrialized countries has exceeded the supply of scarce resources, especially food. Rapid population growth, in turn, will make today's shortages more acute and potentially even less tractable in the near future.

Third, relationships between Moscow, Washington, and Peking have altered, even though major practical political differences remain. The effect has been to play down the role of ideology in determining relationships among powerful states and, instead, to emphasize more traditional or classical concepts of the balance of power.

Fourth, the emergence of reasonably strong regional powers such as Iran, India, Nigeria and Brazil, has begun to influence the military balance in major regions in much the same way that American and Soviet policies have shaped regional power balances over the past generation.

Fifth, increasing use of international terrorism by irregular, criminal and political, groups points to the highly vulnerable nature of many institutions of advanced countries, and the distinct possiblity that rich industrial consumer and major producer nations may be held increasingly to ransom by dissidents equipped with modern technology.

Sixth, the development of new military technologies in both the nuclear and the non-nuclear fields have had and are likely to have a major influence on future military tactics and strategy as well as on the nature of revolutionary warfare.

Seventh, the first Law of the Sea Conference has made it evident that the 12-mile national territorial limits and 200-mile economic zones are likely to be codified within the next five to ten years. This can only increase the growing closure of the world's oceans and thereby diminish traditional concepts of the freedom of the sea.

The likelihood of increased conflict stemming from these changes in the international environment is based in part on the record to date—military force has already been used in recent years to protect or lay claims to various scarce resources. The brief but important conflict between China and South Vietnam over the ownership of the Paracell islands in 1973 and the "Cod War" between Britain and Iceland may be a sign of things to come.

CHANGES IN THE US–USSR GLOBAL BALANCE

With this background in mind three specific issues that relate to changes in the US–Soviet global balance should be discussed. First, in spite of the improved relations between the superpowers codified by the Strategic Arms Limitation Talks (SALT), the Mutual Balanced Force Reduction negotiations (MBFR), and increased US–Soviet trade, both superpowers have continued to deploy increasingly sophisticated strategic nuclear forces over the past 7 years. However, no matter what criteria are used to measure the US–Soviet balance over this period, the Soviet Union has spent more money, deployed more basic forces and at a greater rate than the United States. In terms of launchers for nuclear weapons, the Soviet Union now has a lead. For instance, in 1967, the balance of launchers was: United States—2,310 while the Soviet Union had 800. By 1973 the figures had changed to: United States—2,152; Soviet Union—2,275. These trends have led to the belief that the Soviet Union can achieve superiority in most but not all categories of nuclear capabilities by the mid-1980s if the SALT talks fail to limit the throw-weight of missiles. While many would say that such Soviet superiority would be meaningless given the invulnerability of US strategic systems, especially the sea-based systems, others point to the political advantages that would accrue to the Soviet Union and may already be accruing if it, rather than the United States, can demonstrate that it is the world's number one nuclear power.

The second issue relates to the post-Vietnam syndrome in the United States and the high cost of maintaining modern military forces in Western societies. These trends have placed great pressures on the United

States and its allies, particularly the European allies, to cut defense budgets at a time when Soviet military expenditure is at an all time high and shows no sign of slackening. Thus, there is an increasing fear that the West may also be falling behind the Soviet Union in terms of non-nuclear as well as nuclear capabilities. These fears, in turn, have begun to erode the confidence of the Europeans and other allies in the credibility of American guarantees, and there is increased speculation that the United States is becoming a more isolationist power, whose role as a military protector can no longer be taken for granted.

The third issue is the emergence of the Soviet Union as a major naval power increasingly capable of challenging the United States in certain key sea areas, especially the Mediterranean. This development has coincided with improvements in Soviet air and sea lift capabilities which increase the potential for rapid intervention in overseas conflicts in close geographical proximity to the Soviet land mass. For instance, if one compares US and Soviet capabilities in the eastern Mediterranean, in the context of the 1956 Sinai Campaign, the 1958 US landings in the Lebanon, the 1967 Six Day War, the Jordan crisis of 1970 and the 1973 October War, the point is obvious—the Soviet capacity to deter unilateral action by the United States Sixth Fleet has grown proportionally year by year and shows no sign of slackening. Thus, it is somewhat ironic that the United States will soon have strategic nuclear warheads sufficiently accurate to target with a high probability of destroying individual power stations 6,000 miles away in eastern Siberia, yet it is becoming increasingly difficult for the United States to fly subsonic transport aircraft into the Middle East or to deploy its fleet wherever it likes.

Soviet interest in the role of naval power, of course, also coincides with the growing importance of the oceans. Over the period under consideration, the oceans have become more important, essentially for three reasons: (1) as a source of resources, of which oil, minerals and food are particularly important; (2) as world trade increases, the sea has become more important as a means of transportation; (3) it has also become more important as a medium for deploying military forces, in particular the strategic forces of the two superpowers and of the medium nuclear powers, in particular Britain and France. The importance of the oceans has stimulated demand in many countries other than the United States and the Soviet Union for better military maritime capabilities, both surface ships and air power. An examination of the inventories of a growing number of countries shows increasing emphasis on maritime capabilities. This is especially so in the case of Norway, Britain and Brazil, all of which are worried about protecting offshore resources in the future.

THE EVOLUTION OF NEW MILITARY TECHNOLOGIES

In the nuclear field, the major developments in technology have been very great over the period under discussion. The most important changes have been the increasing sophistication in the design of warheads and the deployment of Multiple Independently Targeted Reentry Vehicles (MIRVs) in the United States and the beginnings of deployment in the Soviet Union. There have been great improvements in the accuracy of these warheads, especially in the case of US missiles, and there is every indication that the Soviets will be able to develop good accuracies in the future. Other developments have been the increasing yield-to-weight ratios of warheads which permits the use of higher yield warheads for a given payload; the growing range of sea-based missile systems; the improved ability to retarget strategic delivery systems (which has implications for the conduct of nuclear war); and the major improvements in command, control, and communications as well as reconnaissance for nuclear forces.

These trends have led to a new debate in the United States about basic nuclear strategy and the forces that will be required to make that strategy possible. There have also been improvements in the nuclear forces of Britain, China and France, the detonation of an Indian nuclear device and the enhanced possiblity that India, Israel and South Africa will become nuclear powers in the years to come. The Soviet Union now has to take account of third nuclear forces when considering its own nuclear requirements. If the trends toward nuclear proliferation continue we will soon be living in a truly multi-polar and multi-nuclear world. There is every indication that in this type of world the old rules of nuclear diplomacy, which have conditioned so much of our thinking in the past, will have to change, though no one, to my knowledge, has yet speculated on how they will change.

In terms of non-nuclear technologies, the Vietnam War and the 1973 October War in the Middle East provide us with the most up-to-date data we have concerning the implications of new weapon systems for non-nuclear conflict. However, precisely because the conditions that existed in these two wars were in many ways unique, it is not easy to make sweeping generalizations about future battlefield environments.

In the case of South East Asia, the United States' use of "smart" bombs in the closing stages of the air war against North Vietnam has commanded most attention. Had these precision guided munitions, or PGM's, as they are now known, been available during the first major Vietnam air campaign in the mid-1960s, there is a high probability that the effectiveness of aerial bombing would have been much greater and this, in turn, *might* have had an important impact on the course of the whole war. By 1972 the United States was able to use air power to destroy targets that had persistently escaped direct hits in the earlier campaign. The "smart" bomb and the generation of weapons to follow from it, therefore represents a major breakthrough for air-delivered munitions and—based on the Vietnam experience—can be said to enhance the effectiveness of offensive air power. In contrast, however, the October War resulted in wide publicity for the effectiveness of anti-aircraft missiles, especially the Soviet SA-6 missiles. At the time of the 1973 war some observers were claiming that since the current generations of anti-air and anti-tank missiles were so effective, the next generations of these weapons would herald a new era in warfare in which major military offensives involving the combined use of air and armor would be limited. However, as the actual data of the war was made available, it became clear that the offensive uses of air and armor were in no sense restricted in that war. Nevertheless, despite the ambiguous data, new technologies *are* likely to influence expectations, at least about the conduct of future conventional warfare, which in turn will help to shape the future security environment.

Some of the other more important non-nuclear technologies include weaponized lasers, surface-to-surface missiles for both maritime and land application, remotely piloted vehicles (RPVs) and rocket-propelled grenades. Similarly, technologies are, or will soon be available for major advances in tactical command and control and communications as well as real-time reconnaissance and surveillance. These new developments together with the greater capability for dispersing forces, will help to determine the future tactics in non-nuclear warfare. Although many new weapon systems will be highly complex and expensive on a per unit basis, large numbers of them will be relatively cheap, relatively easy to operate, and available in large quantities. They will be available, it should be added, not only to the major powers, but to small states as well as to non-state actors such as terrorists and criminals.

THE MIDDLE EAST STRATEGIC ENVIRONMENT

Quantitative Dimensions

Since 1967 the quantity of military equipment transferred to the Middle East, or negotiated for transfer, has reached what can only be described as staggering proportions. The estimated values of transfers and orders is well over US $ 20 billion. Of this total, by far the largest proportions have resulted from US aid and sales to Israel, Iran and Saudi Arabia, and Soviet transfers to Egypt and Syria. The magnitude of these transactions can be explained by two separate and somewhat obvious phenomena. The 1967 and 1973 wars between Israel and the Arabs drastically depleted weapons inventories and required major US and Soviet replenishment programs. The decision by the oil producing nations, especially Iran, Saudi Arabia and Kuwait to embark on major programs—designed in part to bolster their security in regions beset with political conflict—accounts for at least half the orders that have gone in.

In terms of defense expenditure, the proposed outlays for 1974 by the Gulf States now equal, if not exceed, the proposed outlays for those countries most directly involved in the Arab-Israeli conflict. For instance, Iran now ranks ninth in the "world defense expenditure league," while as late as 1966 it ranked twenty-ninth. This is not to belittle the cost of defense expenditure in Israel and Egypt. Prior to the Six Day War, Israel's defense expenditure was about US $ 500 million or about 11-12% of its GNP; Egypt's was about US $ 650 million, or about 12-13% of its GNP. By June 1973 these figures had tripled—Israel was planning to spend about US $ 1.5 billion or about 20% of its GNP, while Egypt's plans called for expenditures of about US $ 1.7 billion or about 27%. The October War caused another spectacular rise in defense expenditures. The estimates for June 1974 suggest that Israel's defense budget has risen to about US $ 3.7 billion (based on the old pre-1974 exchange rate). Egypt's budget has risen almost as much, to US $ 3.1 billion. These budget figures make Israel and Egypt, respectively, the seventh and tenth highest consumers of defense expenditure in the world. Simple percentages of GNP are very superficial measures of the relative defense burden. However, it seems to be only single statistic that indicates the general defense burden. The manpower burden in Israel, the Arab countries and Iran can only get worse as the levels of weapons increase. Small Arab countries will have to rely on mercenaries for the next decade to operate a lot of their equipment.

Israel is certainly much more dependent on the United States than Egypt and Syria are on the Soviet Union, because of the vast flow of Arab money to the latter from Saudi Arabia and Kuwait. As the United States defense budget comes under greater pressure, supplies to Israel may not be as forthcoming in the future as they are now. If this happens there are various options open to the Israelis. One is negotiation, but should negotiations with the Arab states fail, another, more horrendous option, is to develop alternative ways of achieving military deterrence at less cost. This raises the question of the nuclear option, since one rationale for an Israeli nuclear program might be based on economic grounds. It is true that Egypt and Syria are in a better position. However, they are becoming increasingly dependent, not only on the Soviet Union, but on Saudi Arabia and the other Arab oil producers. This dependency has costs in the sense that they are dependent on the whims of the oil shaykhs. It is doubtful whether President Sadat would want to live with this situation indefinitely since the shaykhs can cut off the flow of money any time they want to. The problem in the Persian Gulf is somewhat different. Here there is not only a lot of money, but there are alternative arms suppliers. If the United States will not sell, the Shah can go to Britain, France and West Germany which would be only too delighted to sell him billions of dollars worth of equipment. However, Iran and to a greater extent Saudi Arabia, Kuwait and the smaller Arab states, face real problems in absorbing all the military hardware, given their limited manpower. We may have seen the peak arms orders to the smaller Arab countries.

The Qualitative Aspects

The quality of the equipment that has come into the Middle East or has been requested by the major consumers, parallels the quantitative aspects of this build-up. Iran has ordered the very latest generation of US air superiority fighters (80 F-14 Tomcats) and the very sophisticated Phoenix missile system. The Iranian airforce already has in service or on order over 150 F-4 Phantoms, 250 F-5s as well as six Boeing 707 air tankers and many of the latest US avionic systems. It will soon have one of the largest inventories of helicopters, with over 550 US helicopters on order including 200 Sea Cobra gunships. Iran will soon have one of the world's largest inventories of modern tanks; 800 Chieftain tanks are on order from Britain. In terms of naval forces, the Shah will soon possess the world's largest hovercraft fleet, as well as two of the very latest British frigates. The proposed Saudi Arabian and Kuwaiti programs, although less spectacular, are replete with extremely modern weapons, including the US F-5 (and possible future orders for Phantoms), as well as the French Mirage.

Israel has reached an agreement in principle for the most advanced US air systems including the F-14 Tomcat, the Lance surface-to-surface missiles, many more Phantoms plus dozens of sophisticated armaments of the type mentioned before, and support systems, including air and surface launched precision guided munitions and electronic counter-measures aircraft. Egypt and Syria are believed to have in their arsenals Soviet Scud surface-to-surface missiles as well as some of the latest generations of Soviet fighters, including the MiG-23. However, it is important to make a distinction here between these groups of countries. Unlike the oil-rich countries, Israel and its immediate Arab adversaries—Egypt, Syria, Jordan and Lebanon—cannot afford to be very selective about their suppliers since none of them has the foreign exchange to buy their weaponry on the open market. Thus, while the quantitative and qualitative dimensions of the build-up are impressive throughout the Middle East, there is an important difference between those recipients who are operating in what can only be described as a buyers' market and those—like Israel and Egypt—who are becoming increasingly dependent on their friends and allies to provide them with weapons or the money to buy weapons at subsidized rates.

In the case of the Arab-Israeli conflict the quantitative and qualitative aspects of the arms race reflect the perceived need by both sides to keep abreast of modern technology. Israel has consistently stressed its requirements for extremely modern equipment, especially for the crucial air superiority mission. The Arabs have learned from bitter experience the importance of air superiority. Therefore, one of the most intense aspects of the arms race is the struggle for air supremacy. Without this supremacy Israel's military position would be greatly weakened. Nevertheless, given the new technologies mentioned earlier, it is becoming increasingly difficult to estimate the balance of air power based on simple aggregate calculations of total numbers of combat aircraft in either side's inventory. Some systems such as air-to-surface missiles, and growing investments in the electronic battlefield make aggregate comparisons of strength relatively meaningless.

The question of the ever-growing sophistication of the weapons coming into the Middle East and whether or not this might work to Israel's benefit given the types of computer technologies and the skills that are required to operate them, is an important point. Certainly, if one looks at the history of technology, when new technologies first appear they are in the first stage of growth, are complicated to operate, and require skilled technicians. However, as technologies improve they usually become easier to operate and often cheaper. Classic examples of this are transistor radios, pocket calculators which perform sophisticated calculations, and a camera such as the Polaroid X-70, which is a remarkable feat of engineering and technology and can be operated by anybody. Similarly, new military technologies are expected to become less difficult to operate and, to that extent, the trend would work against Israel, which up to now has counted on its skills to overcome its manpower deficiencies.

Under the present circumstances superpower initiatives for arms control options in the Middle East are highly unlikely. For the future there are some possibilities that there might be a MALT—Mid-East Arms Limitation Talks. The most we can expect, however, are informal US–Soviet agreements to put limits on the transfer of certain types of equipment over certain time frames, perhaps starting with surface-to-surface missiles. That would not mean banning them, but agreeing to hold the numbers down to the hundreds rather than the thousands.

As for nuclear deterrence, not only does deterrence relate to questions of rational calculus concerning costs and benefits of alternative actions, but it is also a psychological phenomenon. We should be very careful in attributing to deterrent models universal application. A deterrence model is very sensitive to the particular political leadership and particular circumstances at any juncture in time. Probably, Adolf Hitler would not have been deterred from using nuclear weapons even if the allies could have destroyed every single German city and every single German. In contrast, at this moment in time the Soviet leaders are probably deterred by a very small embryonic Chinese nuclear force that is nothing like as sophisticated as the Soviet force, but which in a second strike could probably destroy one or two Soviet cities. Therefore, to be effective, deterrence does not have to involve mutual assured destruction. Given some of the emerging non-nuclear technologies, it is possible to think of counter-value targeting options open to the Arabs and the Israelis that would pose great threats and might make leaders on both sides think very carefully before engaging in counter-value military strikes.

CONCLUSION

To summarize then, strategic developments in the Middle East over the past seven years have been influenced by more general changes in the international environment, especially in the context of superpower relations and in the realm of non-nuclear technologies. However, insofar as the Middle East has been and remains an important strategic area, local developments, in particular rearmament programs and the experience of two wars have, in turn, influenced external perceptions of new geopolitical relationships that are seen to be emerging in many regions of the world today.

The 1967 and 1973 Arab-Israeli wars have suggested that the outcome of a conflict can still decisively change the balance of political-military power, at least in the short run. Another lesson is that key ingredients of effectiveness in war are deception, speed and surprise. These lessons have ominous implications not only in the Middle East but elsewhere.

Soviet Military Doctrine and Arab War aims

Amnon Sella

The purpose of this paper is to examine the way in which Soviet military doctrine, hardware and political constraints worked in conjuction with Egyptian and Syrian capabilities and thereby shaped the strategy and tactics of the 1973 October War.

The Six Day War of June 1967 seemed to have all but shattered Arab defiance. Little was left of the arrogance expressed in explicit threats to "throw the Jews into the sea," and not much of what used to be the pride of the Arab world, namely, the fine Egyptian army with its modern planes and tanks, which were strewn over the desolate peninsula of Sinai. Yet, it did not prove too difficult for the Soviet Government to replenish the lost material. The Kremlin actually had no alternative, for the Soviet Union's reputation as a superpower and as a manufacturer of the very latest in weapons was at stake. Efficiently, and with amazing speed, the Egyptian and Syrian armies were reequipped and restored to their former combat strengths. Soviet advisers, instructors and technicians were sent to train the Egyptian and Syrian armies and prepare them for future wars.

The difficulties confronting this Soviet-Arab undertaking were not clear at the outset. It was easy to fall back into the rut of past routine and to shape the future war machine in the mould of the previous one. Military systems, in their rigid discipline and traditional training methods, tend to suffer from inertia; President Abdel Nasser apparently found it easier to keep to well-trodden ways. The Soviet advisers were also constrained both by their habitual military thinking and by political considerations. The results were manifold. The ties between the Soviet Union and Egypt and Syria after 1967 seemed stronger than ever, while the two countries received much the same hardware that they had had before the Six Day War. This is how Egypt plunged into the "War of

77

Attrition," which brought no great victories to either side but which did teach several important lessons. These lessons were not lost on Egypt and Syria and were apparently thoroughly analyzed by Soviet experts. Perhaps the most important lesson was the efficacy of anti-aircraft missiles. The rate at which Israeli planes were being lost toward the end of the War of Attrition, though not prohibitive, was nevertheless costly. This rate could only be kept within reasonable bounds on two conditions: continual US replenishment of the aircraft lost, and relentless attacks on the missile launching-sites. But even granted these conditions, there were still problems of manpower and of the cost of an airplane as compared with the cost of the missiles used against it. However, these and other lessons could not be applied until Abdel Nasser's death—and then only with the greatest difficulty.

By the time President Sadat felt secure enough to turn his attention to plans for a war to recover the lost territories, the political world around him had changed considerably. The USSR was still the champion of the Arab national liberation movement, but was mostly taken up with the new-found formulae of *détente* and *rapprochement* with the US. The energy crisis created an opportune moment for military action, but beyond the blocked Suez Canal lay Israel, as yet impregnable. The recovery of the Golan Heights, which were to be the target of the second operational front with Israel, seemed an even more impossible objective.

The Soviet Union was inching its way toward Sadat's point of view, and that in spite of tremendous complications. In the first place, the Soviet military advisers and instructors assigned to rebuild the wrecked Egyptian and Syrian armies were true adepts of their own reliable, well-worn military doctrine. Soviet weapon systems, moreover, were designed to meet the needs of a militry machine with this particular doctrine as its guideline. When Sadat finally came to the decision that he must break the Middle East deadlock, he had to define his war aims. Egypt and Syria had the choice between a total war against Israel on the pattern of previous wars but with better equipment and improved training, or a limited war. Each of these possible strategies called for different preparations and a modified program of training. Theoretically, all that the Egyptians and Syrians had to do was to assess the pros and cons of each and every past Arab-Israeli encounter, and produce new tactics, in order to outclass the Israeli Defense Forces. However, at the outset the Arabs had to decide whether to adopt an outright offensive strategy or a partially defensive one. They had also to take into consideration the Soviet pattern of arms delivery. It is well-nigh impossible to say at what point in time the Arabs decided that they would have to make do with whatever weapons they had. But, in fact, whatever they had at that particular moment was the result of Soviet supply policy.

Indeed, if the Soviet government wanted to see an exact model of its own armed forces reproduced in the Arab countries, it should have changed its policy on arms delivery. The fact that it did not do so is another proof of Soviet–Arab technological and political constraints. Although the Soviet government was more generous in its arms deliveries to the Arab countries than had been its predecessors, Great Britain and France, it could hardly hand out everything it had, on demand. In the first place, the time-lag between the appearance of a new weapon system in the Soviet arsenal and demands for it from Arab countries contracted in the course of the years after 1955. Secondly, the Soviet Union has never consented to confine its relations with the Arab countries to the supply of armaments. Both these considerations were sources of endless friction and tension between the Kremlin and Cairo and also to a lesser extent with Damascus. There were four major problems in Soviet–Arab relationships: how large Arab weapon inventories should be, how advanced, how much Soviet control should be there over the use made of them and, finally, what the Soviet Union was to receive in return. In order to close the technological gap between the Arab and the Israeli armies, the Arabs demanded colossal quantities of weapons. As early as the crisis that preceded the 1967 war, Egypt had proved that the Soviet Government had little if any control over its foreign or military policy. Sadat began gradually to change the face of Egypt, first in name, when in 1971 he changed this from the "United Arab Republic" to the "Egyptian Arab Republic," and then in deed, when he dismissed 'Ali Sabri. The year 1971 put Soviet–Egyptian relations to a severe test. American Secretary of State William Rogers was attempting to apply his "even-handed policy" and was welcome in Egypt, while Sadat reshuffled his government, clearing out diehard followers. It is instructive to note that in the high-powered Soviet delegation that visited Egypt in May 1971 there were both political and military personalities.[1] The nature of the Egyptian–Soviet difficulties can also be inferred from Sadat's visit to Moscow (11–13 October, 1971), where Podgorny praised "the constructive attitude of the Arab Republic of Egypt, directed toward the speediest attainment of a political settlement of the

Middle East conflict," while Sadat said: "We proceed from the conviction that force, only force, is the way to bring pressure on Israel and to liquidate the aggression against our lands."[2] In July 1972 Sadat showed the Kremlin that the latter would receive very little in return for increased commitments to supply Egypt with more and more advanced armaments. Between July 1972 and October 1973, the Soviet leadership was faced with a bitter dilemma: either to help the Arabs in their preparations for a war or else to see most of its investment lost. Moscow still managed to deny the Arabs the most advanced airplanes, the most sophisticated command and control systems, some important radar items, the capacity for full mobility and large quantities of medium-range ground-to-ground missiles. The Russians were also very careful not to commit themselves on the ground. Even so, Egyptian–Soviet relations were patched up somehow. Each side was in dire need of the other: the Soviet Union was apprehensive at the possibility of losing the influence it had so painstakingly built up, and Egypt could not prepare for war without Soviet help.

During the war itself, elements of Soviet military doctrine applied to the Egyptian and Syrian armies on the tactical and operational levels, while performance on the strategic level was ably effected by Soviet naval and air forces. In retrospect it seems that Egypt and Syria, in fact, had only vague ideas about the strategy of the war they were planning to conduct in October 1973. Their ideas were somewhat clearer as far as operational plans were concerned, and on the tactical level they were precise. What linked up the three levels, however, was the degree of likelihood of success at each state: that is, a brilliant tactical success could have enlarged the scope of operational aims, and full-fledged operational success could have affected the strategic aims. During the October War, Egypt and Syria achieved initial tactical success and operational coordination, but after the Syrian army was badly mauled there was only a marginal effort to maintain operational momentum, and most of the moves on the Egyptian side were tactical in character, aimed at retaining the territorial gains of the first 24 hours of the war.

To discover which of the elements of Soviet military doctrine were applied in action by the Egyptian and Syrian armies requires a brief analysis of Soviet military doctrine as a whole. The principal source of this doctrine is the legacy of World War II, although experience in conflicts between the World Wars, and even Czarist military traditions, are also important factors.[3] This doctrine is founded on three basic tenets—a mass army, offensive spirit and "battle in depth."[4] After World War II, the traditional idea of infantry was discarded in favor of mechanized infantry. The tank emerged as king of the battlefield, mobile, heavily armored and armed. Bitter combat lessons taught the Russians that the rifleman must not lag far behind fast-moving armored columns. Eventually, Soviet industry became capable of producing armored personnel carriers and trucks for its infantry. The long-sought solution for bold thrusts of mass armored formations was found. Once this problem was solved, the infantry could fight both aboard their APCs, the fire power of which was increased, and on foot to engage any target as the need might arise.[5] The offensive spirit matured when practice caught up with theory. Speed, maneuverability and mobility, both on land and in the air, opened new vistas for the concept of fighting in the entire "depth of the battlefield." While armored and mechanized divisions push forward from their starting points as deeply as possible into enemy defense systems, airborne divisions and paratroopers attack the enemy's rear. The air force's task is to isolate the battlefield, preventing the approach of reinforcements and disrupting communications.

The nuclear era introduced novel ideas in strategy, operations and tactics. Strategic Soviet doctrine gained in sophistication as a result of the numerous variations introduced by the concepts of "deterrence," "first strike," "second strike," "massive retaliation" and "flexible response." Although ideas about the "class character" of future war were not altogether discarded, some Soviet writers now realized that the first nuclear strike, whether Soviet or American, might also be the last.[6] On the one hand, this notion accelerated missile production and the quest for multiple independently targeted reentry vehicle (MIRV);[7] on the other, it allowed for *détente* and for further sophistication of deterrence on land, in the air and at sea.[8] Consequently the operational concept also changed. Instead of the former concentration of forces around the starting areas, which risked too much from tactical nuclear strikes, the Soviet Army introduced a "spread" concept of concentrations of highly mobile forces. Thus, the breakthrough force is divided into several sub-units, which are supposed to join up by means of helicopters after the enemy has launched all its tactical nuclear missiles.[9] Operationally this means that every sub-unit must be highly mobile, with every commander capable of calculating many more variables than previously. It also assumes greater coordination between units, namely, better signals and more initiative on the side of both commanders and soldiers.[10] On the tactical level, the new doctrine emphasizes collaboration between men and machine, that is, "engineering" the human factor on the battlefield. In other words, today's Soviet soldier, while being part of a group, must also be highly individualistic in his education and proficiency, highly capable of initiative in action and technically-minded.

To carry out its tactical obligations within an operational program under a strategic plan, a mechanized Soviet division of 10,000 men has in its inventory 260 tanks, 190 APCs and 1300 trucks. It includes tactical missiles and a number of helicopters. Its pace of advance is rated at about 40 kms. a day. It is not supposed to stop in order to engage minor targets, which it is assumed are to be left behind to succumb eventually to air raids, artillery barrages, or the pressure of isolation and lack of contact with other units.[11]

Egyptian and Syrian soldiers were trained by Soviet advisers to use weapon systems, both individual and crew-manned, and to operate highly sophisticated missiles. After arduous and thoroughgoing tactical preparations, the Egyptian and Syrian soldier was able to give of his best, and this was sufficient to achieve the operational aim of the October War. This aim, as it unfolded during the war, was to involve a massive number of troops on two fronts to compensate for their deficiencies in coordination and sophistication. The Syrians threw into battle three mechanized divisions, about 28,000 men and two armored divisions (over 15,000 men) with more than 1000 tanks. The Egyptians crossed the canal with three mechanized divisions in about six hours, and these were reinforced in the first 24 hours by about 30,000 troops and 500 tanks. Two armoured divisions joined battle on the following day.[12] On the face of it, it looked as if the Egyptian and Syrian armies were following Soviet prescripts to the letter. They concentrated their forces along a sector of a front and launched a surprise attack in a coordinated thrust, but there the similarity ends. As far as the Syrians were concerned, their initial tactical success began to peter out just when their tanks reached a point beyond which they might have turned a tactical advantage into an operational one. It is worth noting that the T-62 main battle tank's range is 600 kms., and even the older T-55 tank's range is 350 kms. (and 500 kms. with jettisonable fuel tanks mounted over rear track guards), while the width of the Golan Heights is only 30 kms. at most. Although they were fiercely attacked by Israeli aircraft these tanks were moving along the few good roads in the region and did not have to deviate and expend fuel in wide maneuvers. On the Syrian front there was no need to move forward ground-to-air missiles, as these could conveniently cover the airspace above the battlefield from where they were stationed before the battle started. Indeed, the heavy toll of Israeli aircraft over the Golan Heights during the first afternoon of the war is proof both of the accuracy of Soviet weapon systems and of the unpreparedness of the Israeli Defense Forces for such a war.[13] But the sharpest deviation from Soviet military doctrine was the scarcity of Syrian aircraft. No attempt at all was made by the Syrians to gain supremacy in the air.[14]

Having crossed the thinly-defended Suez Canal, the Egyptians spent three days clearing the Bar Lev Line. The bulk of the Egyptian armored forces crossed the canal only after the bridgehead on the eastern bank had been made relatively secure.[15] Although the Egyptians made more use of their air force during the first hours of the attack than the Syrians, there was no concerted effort to gain air supremacy, but rather a move to confuse the IDF and to hit command and communications centers.[16] The Egyptian commando raids at several points behind the front lines were of the same nature, striking so far out that these units could hardly expect ever to be joined by the main body of their forces.[17]

Apparently not much was left of Soviet military doctrine. The Syrians and the Egyptians deployed mass armies on wide but shallow fronts in order to achieve limited aims. When these aims had been achieved the Syrian advance became hesitant (largely because of the Israeli Air Force), and the Egyptians entrenched themselves on the narrow strip they had seized on the eastern bank of the canal. It is now clear that the key to the initial success on both the Syrian and Egyptian fronts was the heavy ground-to-air missile belts. As the Egyptian and Syrian armies hardly attempted to advance beyond the range of their missile sites, and did not try to move these missiles forward, it follows that they had only limited war aims.

Soviet military doctrine did not envisage this type of offensive. It is not surprising that the Soviet army newspaper, *Red Star*, informing its professional readers about the war, referred to an Egyptian advance of about 40 kms.[18] The average Soviet military expert might not comprehend the brilliant idea of using masses of troops under a heavy anti-aircraft umbrella for the sake of limited political aims. He might have been equally puzzled by the explanation given by General Ahmad Ismail, the Egyptian Minister of War and Commander-in-Chief, for the decision not to capture the Gidi and Mitla Passes. Speaking in late November 1973, General Ismail said that the anti-aircraft missile umbrella was "the key to the army's success in crossing the canal, but could not be moved forward quickly enough to allow immediate capture of the passes."[19] Anti-aircraft defense systems of a Soviet division, on the other hand, are all mounted and they move with the advancing armored column, while the air force task is to secure air supremacy.[20]

To all intents and purposes, by the end of the first week of the war the Syrian Army had ceased to exist as an offensive war machine.[21] The span of its intensive activity was altogether too short for any definite conclusions about its merits as a fighting system. The question as to what would have happened had the Syrian Army been very successful all along, or had the impact of the surprise been greater, remains an open one. Under the circumstances, analysis may safely concentrate on the performance of the Egyptian Army. As explained above, the entire approach of this army to the conflict with Israel had changed tremendously since the Six Day War. Although it was trained by Soviet advisers (who were possibly absent from Egypt for several months after July 1972) and used Soviet weapon systems, its war aims were defined by the Egyptian High Command. The result was an effective combination of Egyptian war aims and performance with Soviet technology and training.[22]

Quite a few of the residual shortcomings of the pre-July 1972 Soviet–Arab military collaboration were still evident in the October War. The language problem in 1973 was still a barrier, both in direct contact and in the understanding of technical instructions, which were either in Russian or in English. The more sophisticated the weapon systems the greater the difficulties. The main victim of this short circuit in communications was, obviously, the air force, the most dynamic and sophisticated of all the services. Egyptian and Syrian pilots were still deficient in night flying, instrument flying and in the fine art of low flying over water. One reason for this might be the restrictions on flight hours in peace-time because of the high rate of accidents.[23] According to Soviet military doctrine, the task of the tactical air force is to gain air supremacy over the battlefield, but this was not attempted during the October War. Soviet technology worked in conjunction with Arab war aims to find a solution that would avoid complete reliance on the air force as a major offensive arm. The Arabs assigned their mighty air force only a minor role in the October War, intending to exhaust the

IAF in futile or very expensive attacks on the anti-aircraft defense before they committed their own air forces. It was the Israeli reliance on a highly sophisticated, very expensive—and therefore quantitatively limited—air force that the Soviet advisers and the Arab tacticians set out to counter, by relying on relatively simple, inexpensive and quantitatively much less restricted anti-aircraft defense systems.[24] The Soviet doctrine of the battle for air supremacy was adapted to the Arab war aims in reverse. Suffice it to say that about half a million men serve in the Soviet Air Force as against about 250,000 in the Air Defense (PVO), whereas in the Egyptian Armed Forces 75,000 men serve in the Air Defense and only 25,000 in the Air Force.[25] In the air battle, as well as on the ground, the offensive was a limited one, using a mainly defensive configuration. Compared to the Soviet anti-aircraft tactical system, the Arab one fell short in several respects. The Egyptian and Syrian AA systems were far more static than the Soviet, being confined to a passive role both by war aims and by technological deficiencies. The lethal SA-6 system, for instance, was limited in its search capacity and altitude-discrimination because the Arab armies did not have the Long Track surveillance radar of the SA-4 system, which is part and parcel of a coordinated air defense system in the Soviet Armed Forces.[26]

In conclusion, none of the Soviet basic tenets—a mass army, offensive spirit and the "battle in depth"—was simply imitated by the Arab armies, while some elements were partially adapted and then not for the same purposes. The task assigned by the Soviet High Command to huge formations of armored forces and highly mobile infantry is to cover vast stretches of territory in a very short time. The concept is to feed in more and more reserves after the advanced forces have carried out the breakthrough and the enemy is paralyzed, broken, or in retreat. The second wave assignment is to pursue the retreating enemy relentlessly. As has been demonstrated, only some elements of the Soviet doctrine of mass armies were applied by the Arab armies. The offensive spirit was soon spent and the idea of battle in the entire "depth of the battlefield" was unceremoniously forgotten.

Despite many shortcomings in the Egyptian and Syrian fighting systems, and regardless of whether they did or did not imitate Soviet doctrines, they nevertheless managed to upset the balance of power in the Middle East. The strategic level and the roles played by the superpowers are beyond the scope of this paper, but even on the operational and tactical levels, the Arab war machine posed several problems which are of regional and general interest. Before October 1973 there was reason to believe in the existence of a quality gap between the IDF and any Arab army. Exponents of this argument put up a strong case, based on all the previous Arab–Israeli wars, to the effect that Israeli pilots and tankmen are superior to their Arab counterparts. Past experience was based on air encounters and armor-against-armor clashes when Israel generally had the advantage of surprise and initiative. Nevertheless, even under the impact of the surprise Arab attack, Israel managed to snatch the initiative, although the price in human lives and in war material strained its resources to the limit. The reasons for the initial Arab success were the combination of modern technology, surprise attack, clearcut war aims and better coordination of fighting systems than previously, superior to anything the Egyptians or Syrians had either been capable of, or been given the opportunity to deploy in the past. To put it somewhat paradoxically, the Arab armies demonstrated that given the right conditions they can make a sophisticated use of crude capability; whereas in the initial stages of the war, under the impact of surprise, the Israeli war machine demonstrated a clumsy deployment of sophisticated capability.[27] However, since most of the sophisticated Soviet weapon systems are readily available, and can indeed be bought, and since there is no reason to believe that the Arab soldier will not improve still further, Israel will have to find different answers to the problem of future wars in the Middle East.

Egyptian and Syrian achievement in the war for air supremacy should be analyzed as a whole, including AA missiles, conventional fire and the use of the air forces.[28] It should also be remembered that in the Soviet Union, as well as in Syria, the defense has its own organic Air Force units. While detailed analyses of the war in the air show that in dogfights the Israeli pilots were far better than either the Egyptians or the Syrians, and that many more Israeli planes were lost to conventional ground fire than to missiles, one must not overlook the most significant point: at the beginning of the war it looked as if the IAF was in a crisis. The surprise of the attack must have caught several air units unprepared for the kind of warfare they were, in fact, to face, while the level of operational coordination between the Syrians and Egyptians strained the IAF to the utmost. As losses kept mounting, it became increasingly difficult to keep air force priorities in the right order.[29] Since the essence of a surprise attack is that its victim is denied the time needed for a reasonable choice of priorities, the IAF had to gain time on the Golan Heights while mobilization proceeded, and concurrently to change its target priorities on the Egyptian front. During this initial period in particular the agile sophistication of the IAF, which had been caught unawares, encountered the (far from perfect) deployment of sophisticated systems. The need to contain the Syrian tank columns made the IAF vulnerable to defense belts, which it had no time and not enough resources to deal with at that stage[30]; and at the same time, guided by the philosophy that the Egyptians must be stopped at the Canal, the IAF attacked the bridges and exposed its aircraft to defense systems designed precisely for this situation.[31] In carrying out these attacks, the IAF tried as best it could to avoid missiles, but the accuracy of the SA-6 was a little-known phenomenon, as was the sheer abundance of all the types of missiles engaged and the extensive use made of them. Thus, in trying to avoid the missiles the planes fell victim to the ZSU-23 mm. guns. In short, the IAF was fighting a system of which the dog-fight was only one component.

In armored warfare, too, it is the system that must be examined, rather than one or another of its components. The Sagger anti-tank missiles were indeed lethal, and so was the profuse use of RPGs (Soviet bazooka) by masses of infantry. Yet, it was neither of these, but rather the combination of both with anti-tank gun emplacements and tank-gun fire, which led several tank specialists to conclude that the tanks as a weapon system had no future.[32] The first analysis of the war led some people to believe that the anti-tank missile had succeeded in driving the tank off the battlefield. Later analyses revealed that tank-guns and conventional anti-tank fire had also taken their toll, and qualified the first assumptions as well as the evaluation of Egyptian gunnery. It is true that new materials and new designs will have to be found to cure the vulnerability of tanks in an anti-tank missile environment, but it is equally important to find a solution for future armored warfare on a battlefield where missile-targeted areas restrict the movement of armored vehicles and expose them to other means of destruction.[33] The limited war aims of the Egyptians also put at a disadvantage Israeli armored forces faced with entrenched masses of RPG-armed infantry, but once the Israeli tanks were free to maneuver they could bring their superior tactics to bear. However, political considerations are part and parcel of warfare: since Israel is fighting an Arab capability that is improving and is combined with Soviet military philosophy, it follows that political considerations may become an integral part of future wars on the tactical and operational levels no less than on the strategic level.

The October War throws new light on superpower-client relationships. On the one hand, it became evident that a superpower can hardly refuse its clients increasingly advanced weapon systems; on the other hand, the availability of certain types of weapon systems is instrumental in shaping military philosophy. Technology and fighting capability dictate the nature of the military doctrine and this in turn qualifies war aims. The war also brought out an aspect of the quality gap that had not been sufficiently analyzed before. It has become apparent that modern technology can be bought, and even sophisticated weapons can be operated to some exent in simple ways, as long as the battlefield is reasonably limited. Consequently, there is a greater incentive for the superpowers to sell modern weapon systems, when the only obligation on the seller in the new commercial relationship is to send advisers and technicians, without the heavy commitment that former relationships involved. However, closing the quality gap and approaching a new balance of power in which the quantity of easily-operated, sophisticated, weapon systems makes quality more and more expensive, may open the way to a new generation of weapon systems. Last, but not least, the attempt of the Arab countries to improve their system performance may lead to a certain stability in the area, but may also lead to highly developed means of first strike capability and to territory-circumventing weapon systems.

If there is to be a settlement in the Middle East, the superpowers will have to work out a plan that may ultimately lead to less uncertainty over zones of influence in this troubled region. Such a plan must cover the arms race, nuclear energy for peace and war, and eventually also recognized zones of influence over the different countries. So far, it seems that the USSR has adopted a policy of "sanctuaries"—to use Brodie's phrase (B. Brodie, *War and Politics*, New York, Macmillan, 1973, p. 66)—delimited by "red lines." A "sanctuary" can be a country, a town or some prestigious project. On several occasions the "red lines" were symbolized by the presence of Soviet personnel, in others they were actually defended by Soviet pilots. "Sanctuaries" may have salutary and stabilizing effects if they are sensible and well-defined by "red lines," the demarcation of which has been signaled well in advance of a crisis. It is, of course, impossible to turn a whole regime into a "sanctuary" without backing that pledge to the hilt, meaning a full superpower commitment to defend its client come what may, but it is quite possible to make a sanctuary of a capital city, a harbor, or a given area, in order to restrict but not prevent enemy raids. The Soviet Union apparently made clear in the past that it would not allow Israel to cause the removal of what were termed "progressive regimes" in either Egypt or Syria and also that Cairo, Damascus and the Aswan Dam were "sanctuaries." However, since the Israeli government has never harbored any desire to occupy or destroy any of these, it was an easy commitment to undertake. There seems to be a tacit understanding between the United States and the USSR that Israel should not be destroyed and that the US would not allow its destruction. The vital questions, such as: what actually denotes a mortal danger to Israel's existence, how far its sovereignty should reach and what the exact contour of its borders should be—have never been openly discussed. However, developments brought to the fore by the October War may force the United States to delimit its own "sanctuaries" and draw its own "red lines." One such new development is the energy crisis. By hidden threats and open denials, the US has made it uncertain whether it might not use military force to prevent another oil boycott. But even if there is no such crisis, the fact that Iran has emerged as the best equipped military force along the Persian Gulf, and that other countries in the same area show a lively interest in purchasing weapon systems, may itself result in spheres of influence being delineated or the the declaration of US Presidential, or Soviet, doctrines to define pledges and commitments.

The October 1973 crisis may have been admirably managed by the superpowers—up to a point—but the future looks grim and menacing in the Mediterranean, in the Red Sea, the Persian Gulf and the Indian Ocean.

NOTES

1. *BBC Summary of World Broadcasts: The Middle East and Africa*, 28 August 1971.

2. Yaacov Ro'i, *From Encroachment to Involvement*, (Jerusalem, 1974), p. 558-59.

3. See V. D. Sokolovsky, (ed.), *Voennaya strategiya*, (Moscow, 1963), pp. 28-36; *Melikov, "Kritika i bibliografiya," Voina i revolutsiya*, No. 8, 1929,

pp. 137-46; G. Isserson, *"Razvitie teorii sovetskogo operativnogo iskusstva v 30-e gody,"* *Voenno istoricheskii zhurnal (VIZ)*, No. 1, 1965, pp. 34-46, and *VIZ*, No. 3, 1965, pp. 47-61; A. M. Vasilevskii, *"K voprosu o rukovodstve vooruzhennoi bor'boi v velikoi otechestvennoi voine,"* *Voprosyi istorii*, No. 5, 1970, pp. 49-71.

4. See V. E. Savkin, *Osnovnie printsipy operativnogo iskusstva i taktiki*, (Moscow, 1972), pp. 57-61; K. Malan'in, *"Razvitie organizatsionnikh form sukhoputnykh voisk v Velikoi Otechestvennoi voine,"* *VIZ*, No. 8, 1967, pp. 28-39, but mainly p. 29; *Polevoi ustav rkka 1936*, (PU-36, Moscow, 1937), pp. 9-10.

5. Lt. Colonel A. Zheltokhov, *"Vzaimodestvie osnova uspekha v voiyu,"* *Voenniy vestnik*, No. 9, 1973, pp. 46-50; also, General of the Army S. L. Sokolov, *"Vsegda na strazhe v Boevoi gotovnosti,"* *Krasnaya zvezda*, 23 February 1974, p. 2. For tactical exercises in the Soviet Armed Forces according to the doctrine, see, for instance, Major L. Orlov, *"Taktika i ogon nerazelimy,"* *Voennyi vestnik*, January, 1973, p. 95.

6. V. E. Savkin, *op. cit.*, p. 73. For Soviet ideas about US nuclear policy, see, for instance, L. N. Ignat'ev, *"Yadernde oruzhie i amerikanskaya vneshnyaya politika,"* *Voprosi Istorii*, No. 5, 1970, pp. 81-90.

7. For Soviet tests of MIRV and achievement in new ICBMs, see *Aviation Week and Space Technology*, 21 January, p. 14, and 25 February, 1974, p. 20.

8. See *Vneshnyaya politika sovetskogo soyuza, 1972, Sbornik dokumentov*, (Moscow, 1973), pp. 77-86. See also Elizabeth Young, *A Farewell to Arms Control*, (Penguin Books 1972), Chapter II; J. Erickson, "Soviet Military Power," *Strategic Review*, Spring, 1973, pp. ix-xv. For further sophistication of deterrence see (USAF), General George S. Brown, "Technology: The Mold for Future Strategy," *ibid.*, pp. 23-28.

9. For the Soviet idea of approaching separately and striking together (*khodit vroze, a dratsya vmeste*), see V. E. Savkin, *op. cit.*, p. 17.

10. For the "new" Soviet commander see Major General A. Dzhizha, *"Komandir tvorets boya,"* *Krasnaya zvezda*, September, 1972, p. 2; Colonel I. Vorobyov, "Role and Place of the Commander in Battle," *Soviet Military Review*, February, 1972; Lt.-General I. Yershov, *"Informatsiya i upravlenie v boyu,"* *Voennyi vestnik*, No. 9, 1972, p. 2 (for signals in modern battle).

11. For several aspects of modern attack, see, for instance, Colonel I. Kirin, *"Povyshat tempy nastupleniya,"* *Voennyi vestnik*, No. 7, 1973, pp. 36, 38, 39. For many of the ideas in this part of my paper I am indebted to J. Erickson's deep analysis in his "Soviet Military Power," *Strategic Review*, Spring, 1973, Special supplement, pp. 1-127.

12. S. L. A. Marshall, "Egypt's Two-Week Military Myth," *The New Leader*, 12 November, 1973, p. 11; *The Sunday Times*, 14 October, 1973; Henry Stanhope, "Text-book Invaders Dither Towards Disaster," *The Times*, 26 October, 1973. For different accounts regarding the number of Syrian tanks in the first attack, see "The Syrian Army Planned to Take the Golan Heights in 24 Hours," *Ha'aretz*, 19 April, 1974. "An Interview with General Khofi," *Ma'ariv*, 19 April, 1974.

13. For a breakdown of IAF losses, see *Aviation Week*, 3 December, 1973, p. 19. See also Dayan's press conference on 9 October, 1973, *Ma'ariv*, 15 February, 1974.

14. Insight Team of the Sunday Times, *Insight on the Middle East War*, (London 1974), p. 62.

15. S. L. A. Marshall, *op. cit.*; *Insight on the Middle East War*, p. 69.

16. *Insight on the Middle East War*, p. 84; *The Sunday Times*, 14 October, 1973.

17. *Insight on the Middle East War*, p. 86.

18. *Kransnaya zvezda*, 11 October, 1973.

19. *Aviation Week*, 17 December, 1973, p. 17.

20. See, for instance, *Posobie dlya ofitserov zapasa motostrelkovyikh i tankovykh voisk*, (Moscow 1971), p. 69; "SA-6—Arab Ace in the 20-Day War," *International Defense Review*, Vol. vi, December 1973, p. 779.

21. *Insight on the Middle East War*, pp. 101-103; *Observer*, 14 October, 1973.

22. For the Egyptian war aims see Haykal's article, as translated by *Yediyoth Aharonoth*, 21 October, 1973. See also, "Anwar Sadat's Uncertain Trumpet," *Newsweek*, 9 April, 1973.

23. *Aviation Week*, 17 December, 1973, pp. 14-17.

24. For the Soviet assessment of Arab achievement in anti-aircraft defense, see, for instance, *Krasnaya zvezda*, 4 November, 1973. For the effect of the Arab system, see *Ma'ariv*, 15, 17 February, 1974; *International Defense Review*, Vol. vi, December 1973, pp. 699-700; *Aviation Week*, 3 December, 1973, p. 19.

25. *Aviation Week*, 17 December, 1973, p. 16. For data on the Soviet Air Force, see J. Erickson, *op. cit.*, pp. 61-69.

26. For the performance of Soviet AA units, see, for instance, Colonel I. Polyakov, *"Boesposobnost zenitnykh podrazdelenii,"* *Voennyi vestnik*, February 1973, pp. 82-84. For a short survey of the Soviet Air defense troops (PVO), see Colonel-General P. Levchenko, *"Voiska PVO na novom etape,"* *Voennyi vestnik*, August 1973, pp. 57-61; J. Erickson, *op. cit.*, p. 69. For

deficiencies in the Arab AA system, see "SA-6—Arab Ace in the 20-War," *International Defense Review*, Vol. vi, December, 1973, p. 779.

27. Ilan Kfir, "The Battle of Armor Against Missiles," *Yediyoth Aharonoth* (weekly supplement), p. 20 (in Hebrew). See also, N. Dunevitz, "Sinai: Heroism During the First Days," *Ha'aretz*, 10 October, 1973 (Heb.); A. Dolev, "Bama'oz shelo nafal," *Ma'ariv*, 14 December, 1973; U. Benzion, "Nesurim bama'ozim," *Ha'aretz*, (weekly supplement), 30 November, 1973; A. Dolev, "68 Hours," *Ma'ariv*, 9 November, 1973 (Heb.); Z. Schiff, *Ha'aretz*, 2 November, 1973.

28. See *International Defense Review*, Vol. vi, December 1973, pp. 699, 701, 779-81; *Aviation Week*, 3 December, pp. 17-19, 11; *Insight on the Middle East War*, pp. 93-97.

29. *Insight on the Middle East War*, p. 85; *The Sunday Times*, 14 October, 1973, (comment about the scarcity of Israeli air cover in Sinai on 9 October; US House of Representatives, *Report of the Special Subcommittee on the Middle East of the Committee on Armed Services*, 13 December, 1973, p. 5; *Ma'ariv*, 10 October, 1973 (quoting the BBC to the effect that Israel asked the US for an immediate supply of airplanes).

30. *Insight on the Middle East War*, pp. 82-83.

31. *Ibid.*, pp. 84-85.

32. For a short and interesting discussion of the tank in modern warfare, see Brigadier V. Thompson, "Lessons of the Yom Kippur War," *Ma'ariv*, 18 February, 1974 (in Heb.); Z. Schiff, "Men Against Tanks," *Ha'aretz*, 4 November, 1973, (Heb.).

33. R. M. Ogorkiewica, "The next generation of battle tanks," *International Defense Review*, Vol. vi, December 1973, pp. 754-58. For some more technical and tactical comments, see *Ha'aretz*, 11 February 1974; *Ma'ariv*, 19 March 1974. For the effect of missiles on targeted area and the combination of anti-tank missiles with conventional fire, see, for instance, Ilan Kfir, *Yediyoth Aharonoth*, 24 April, 1974.

Two Periods in the
Arab-Israeli Strategic Relations
1957–1967; 1967–1973

Yair Evron

The purpose of this article is twofold: first, to point out very briefly the central variables which determine the *dynamics* of the Arab–Israeli conflict and to establish the relationships among them in a somewhat schematic fashion[1]; second, to analyze two periods in Arab–Israeli relations, the first following the 1956 Egyptian–Israeli war (1957–1967) and the second from the 1967 Six Day War to the 1973 October War (1967–1973), emphasizing the strategic factors in these relations. The interactions between the central variables mentioned serve as a basis for the comparative analysis of the two periods.

The emphasis on the dynamics of the conflict is crucial. No attempt is made here to discuss the remote roots of the conflict or the possible political solutions to it. Instead, the emphasis is on analyzing changing patterns of interactions between the parties to the conflict.

The approach used here stresses interstate relations and intentionally ignores several approaches and models in the study of international relations and foreign policy: discussion of the domestic political structures[2] and political elites[3] of the national actors involved and the linkages between these structures and conflict behavior; various "decision-making" schools, such as the bureaucratic and governmental models[4] and the detailed analyses of the process of decision-making based on studies of the behavior of individual or groups of decision-makers.[5] There is, therefore, in this study, an emphasis on the macro-level[6] and on "interaction" approaches.[7] Implicitly, however, there is some reference to the rational decision-making model when we deal with the problem of deterrence in Israel's strategies vis-à-vis its Arab opponents.[8] In this article even the macro-approach is not fully comprehensive since there is only partial discussion of, for example, the effects of the *structure* of the Middle Eastern subsystems[9] on the Arab–Israeli conflict.

DELINEATION OF HISTORICAL PERIODS

One of the preliminary questions is whether one can indeed identify the two periods 1957–1967 and 1967–1973 as separate and distinct historically.[10]

To begin with, is the starting point of the first period (1957) a valid turning point in the history of the conflict? Did it mark a major change which could be described as the beginning of a different period in Arab–Israeli relations? Needless to say, the delineation of historical periods is always a hazardous venture. The fixing of turning points is quite arbitrary and there is usually some continuity in some factors from one delinated period to the next. In a number of ways the 1967 war was the watershed in the history of the conflict.[11] According to this line of argument, then, one would consider the whole history of the conflict (once it became an international one) as being divided into two periods: from the end of the Israeli War of Independence in 1949 until June 1967 and from then until the present or until October 1973.

Four changes have occurred since the 1967 war, as compared to the entire preceding period. First, the growth in particularist nationalism and the differentiation in the declared ideological and political postures of the Arab side (see below). Second, the volume of diplomatic activity increased in comparison to the preceding decade and even to the pre-1956 period.[12] Third, a major process of self-examination began in the Arab world, with Arab intellectuals severely criticizing the malaise which had been endemic in Arab society.[13] Finally, the Palestinian organizations made their real appearance and attained undreamt of political power only after 1967.[14] For their part, the Israelis developed fundamental misperceptions after 1967 about their political power and behaved as if they were operating in a vacuum.

Saying all that, it seems too that there are several marked differences between the 1957–1967 period and the preceding one in the Arab–Israeli strategic dialogue, differences which justify regarding 1957 as a beginning of a new period in the conflict. The central change is that, in terms of *violence along the borders* and the *expectations*[15] of war, there was a marked difference between the two periods. While the first was characterized by a relatively high level of violence and expectation of war, the second was relatively calm.

The comparative discussion of the two periods, 1957–1967 and 1967–1973, will be oriented toward the question of what determines the *intensity* of the conflict. The most important indicator of this intensity is the level of violence.[16] In its most extreme form this means full-scale war; in a more moderate form—violence along the borders short of war.

CENTRAL VARIABLES OF THE CONFLICT

The central variables are: the "ideological" dimension of the conflict; the national interests of the various states; the patterns of Arab coalitions and the level of the Arab states' commitments to each other; superpower involvement (not dealt with here); arms races; and violence short of war along the borders. The dependent variable in the various interaction patterns among these variables is war. In their relationship to war, all the variables are independent. At the same time, some of them at different times and in varying degrees, act as intervening variables between the others and the dependent variable—war. Although the literature on the conflict is rather extensive, still not all of these variables have been studied in depth nor have the causal interactions among them been sufficiently examined. The following discussion is thus based on incomplete evidence and some of the inferences must be regarded as tentative.

The emphasis on the dynamics of the conflict means that we shall consider changes in the central variables. Causal relationships, changes over time between the variables and the outcome, violence in general and war in particular are, therefore, a central theme.

The "ideological dimension" has at times been described as the major variable affecting developments in the Arab–Israeli conflict. In this context, "ideology" refers to the basic clash of attitudes between Arabs and Israelis which, over the years, has developed into a somewhat systematic hostility toward Israel on the part of the Arabs. These Arab attitudes relate both to the Palestinian problem and to basic perceptions of the nature of the Israelis and of the State of Israel. This "ideology" entails a certain set of conclusions, the crucial one being that the Arabs cannot and should not accept the existence of the State of Israel and should, indeed, seek to destroy it. In any case, Arab hostility toward Israel, as formulated in ideological terms, is very intense and springs from the political and human suffering of the Palestinians, from strong rejection of outside intrusion into the Arab world (and Israel is considered as such an intrusion) which amounts sometimes to xenophobia, from an emphasis on exclusive Arabism and the desire to keep the Middle East made up of exclusively Arab political units. Many of these attitudes and positions spring from deep-rooted factors inherent in the structure of Arab society, culture and in Islam.[17]

Because of the apparent centrality of the ideological dimension of the conflict, it is advisable to look first into its possible impact on the intensity of the conflict. The basic images of "Israel," the "Israelis" and of their objectives had begun to be formulated by the late 1940s and early 1950s.[18] The acute form of the "Palestine problem" had already taken shape immediately after the creation of the State of Israel. The image of the Israelis as an aggressive people, intent on further expansion, and who are simultaneously devilishly clever and, having demeaning characteristics, has been there from the start.[19] These elements were all eventually joined together into a more coherent and detailed Arab attitude.

There has been a lack of studies of qualitative changes in Arab attitudes toward Israel over time, based on more sophisticated methodologies. Thus, for example, the methodology of contents analysis using quantitative approaches has not been applied to the analysis of Arab leaders' (or Arab political elites) utterances over time. Such studies may have given us a better instrument to measure changes in attitudes or changes in the intensity of attitudes. There are several important works, of which Harkabi's are the better known, which analyze Arab attitudes but most of them do not study variations in these over time (during the period 1949–1967)[20] or their interactions with political developments. Notwithstanding these obvious deficiencies which make very hazardous any analysis of political strategic developments dependent on the ideological factor, studies of Arab attitudes and ideology still offer many insights into the possible correlation or lack of it between ideological developments and the politico-strategic developments.

Several developments after 1957 turned Arab perceptions and images of Israel into an apparently more potent ideological force. Though the basic images remained constant, the growth of pan-Arabism in both its Nasserist and Ba'thist forms in the latter part of the 1950s and in the 1960s up to 1967, if anything brought about a hardening of the Arab position vis-à-vis Israel.[21] The struggle against "imperialism" and "reaction" was linked throughout this period with the struggle against Israel. Zionism was perceived as the catspaw of imperialism trying to reestablish the Western presence in the Arab world.

Thus, during the period 1957–1967, though the Arabs' basic images and perceptions of the Israelis remained constant, the ideological position was elaborated somewhat. If the "ideological" variable is taken as the most important one, then one would expect a marked escalation of the Arab–Israeli conflict during this period. As we shall see below, this was not the case.

After the 1967 war, Arab attitudes and ideology underwent several changes and became more diversified. Several schools of thought concerning the conflict have emerged in the Arab world during this period; according to Harkabi's categorization[22] four such schools have emerged. First, there is the traditional, intransigent one which remains attached to the old axioms, thus denying the possibility of any compromise at all with Israel and maintaining that the Arabs must sooner or later resort to force of arms in order to destroy Israel and thus resolve the Palestinian problem. The existence of Israel is held to threaten the very fiber of Arab society. A second school of thought endorsed the same ultimate objective but argued that Israel's disappearance sould be achieved by means other than war, though this might take a very long time. For some the period involved could be measured in decades, for others in hundreds of years. This approach by "stages" thus, at least in some of its manifestations, relegated the final desired outcome to either a closer or more remote future.[23] The operational conclusion was that some political compromise with Israel could and even should be reached, while the final outcome was kept in mind. This then entailed the acceptance of Security Council Resolution 242. If Israel accepted the resolution it would in time be weakened and, eventually, eliminated. This meant then that the Arabs should devote their energies to bringing about changes in their own societies, or to accomplishing other more immediate foreign policy objectives besides the resolution of the Palestine problem. A third school argued in favor of a "tactical" acceptance of Resolution 242, arguing that Israel would reject the resolution in any case, and that the Arabs would therefore score a net gain in support in world public opinion. The fourth school of thought, expounded by some groups of Arab intellectuals[24] and by the Jordanian Hashemite regime, reformulated the entire Arab position vis-à-vis Israel. It maintained that the time had come to make peace with Israel on the basis of the 1967 territorial position. In general, then, it could be argued that on the attitudinal and political planes there has been some serious shift in the position of some sections of the Arab elites. Instead of a unified ideological and political total rejection of Israel one could discern a search for alternatives and even contending approaches.

Despite this change, the intensity of the conflict has increased greatly as compared to the 1957–1967 period, as will be shown below. Thus, the only conclusion one can draw is that there is no direct correlation between the basic ideological Arab–Israeli confrontation and the intensity of the conflict. Therefore, in order to analyze the dynamics of the conflict one must consider the other variables. This consideration will now be made with an emphasis on the "strategic" variables—including violence along the borders and arms races. In addition, I shall consider the role of demilitarized zones and strategic doctrines. Overlapping with strategic doctrines and of central importance is the question of the Israeli deterrent posture. My basic contention is that the most important independent variable in the intensification of the conflict in the period 1967–1973 was the specific state interests of three Arab states—Egypt, Syria and Jordan—resulting from the continued occupation by Israel of the territories conquered in 1967.[24]

INTENSITY OF THE CONFLICT

The two main indicators for the intensity of the conflict are number and frequency of wars and other acts of violence, and the number of casualties. During the first period under discussion, 1957–1967, for almost eleven years, no war occurred, and the level of violence along the borders and the number of casualties was low (see Table 1). During the second period, 1967–1973, a period of only six years, one war—the War of Attrition—raged, and the period ended with another very intensive war. Moreover, the level of violence along the borders and number of casualties was very high (see Table 1).

THE ROLE OF DETERRENCE

The notion of Israeli deterrence is central to an understanding of the distinctions between the two periods 1957–1967 and 1967–1973. Deterrence is a complex psychological process which contains, as is widely understood, the following elements: the relative military capabilities of the deterring party and the deterred one as perceived by both; the nature of the threat of the deterring party against the deterred one; the credibility of the threat; and finally, the cost–benefit balance of military action as evaluated by the deterred party.[25] This last element is crucial. If the deterred party is planning an action which the deterring party does not want him to pursue, the latter must threaten to punish the former in such a way that the losses will certainly outweigh the expected gains. If, however, a certain *status quo* which the deterred party considers intolerable continues (so that the ongoing losses are in any case very heavy), then his motivation to change the situation will increase significantly. To deter an action based on desperation will require a very high level of anticipated punishment. In other words, the punishment threatened must be enormous.

Alexander George[26] has suggested that in coercive diplomacy, one must combine the "stick" approach with the "carrot" approach. Coercive diplomacy, according to George, can have several variants: first, forcing the opponent to stop a certain action he has already begun; second, forcing him to undo the part of the action already implemented. Both these modes of coercion are "defensive"; and the first one is close to deterrence though not identical with it. (According to Thomas Schelling it is included in it.) The third variant is the offensive one, namely, to force the other to do something he had not planned on doing at all. The level of threatened violence should rise as one moves from deterrence through the two variants of defensive (or negative) coercive actions and up to the offensive (or positive) mode. George also argues that the need to combine positive inducements (bribes) with threats should increase as one moves from one type of action to the next, with the offensive mode requiring more positive inducements. It seems that the combination of inducements and threats is essential also in situations of pure deterrence, in which the deterred side feels that the continuation of the *status quo* is politically unbearable. More positive elements are essential in such a situation. Deterrence is thus connected with a more dynamic political element. The elements of "political grievance" (see below) must in a more articulated way form part of the pure model of deterrence, or alternatively should be connected with the deterrence models as an extraneous variable.[27]

THE 1957–1967 PERIOD

Ideology and the Formation of Arab Coalitions

This period was characterized by a strong and uncompromising ideological commitment to the destruction of the State of Israel, and by the rapid development of Egyptian identification with the Arab world. This identification, though always an undercurrent in Egyptian national attitudes, was greatly reinforced after the Sinai Campaign. This was linked with a strong drive toward Arab unity under Egyptian leadership and hegemony (although the creation of the United Arab Republic was more the result of Syrian, primarily Ba'thist prompting

Table 1

Israeli Dead by Arab Actions
(as indicator of intensity of conflict)

	Soldiers	Civilians	Total
1949–1956 War	222	264	486
1956 War	190	—	190
Between 1956 War and 1967 War	64	71	135
1967 War	777	26	803
Between 1967 War and 1973 War	651	219	870
1973 War	2527	19	2546

than of Egyptian machinations). The latter part of this period, after the dissolution of the United Arab Republic in 1961, was characterized by a growing feud between different groupings in the Arab world, and by the continuous shifting of Arab coalitions.

During this period no fewer than 16 Arab coalitions (formal or informal) were formed. Out of these, five arose partly out of issues to do with the Arab–Israeli conflict. However, the most important causes of the formation of Arab coalitions were related to inter-Arab developments.[28]

The Israeli Deterrent Posture

In 1956 Israel emerged victorious from its campaign against Egypt. Nevertheless, there were a number of snags to this victory. First, in one of the crucial battles—at Abu-Ageila, the Egyptians fought very well and for three days succeeded in repulsing the Israeli attacks. Furthermore, they withdrew of their own volition under orders issued by the Egyptian High Command, partly because it was felt that the collapse of the whole front was imminent, and partly because of the threat they faced as a result of the British–French ultimatum and operations.[29] Then again, Egypt stood alone against three opponents, two of them international military powers. It is not important in this context that in fact only a very small part of the military forces of these two middle powers were actually deployed on the field of battle, that only part of the Israeli reserves were mobilized for the fighting, or that an analysis of the campaign indicates that, in any case, the Israeli forces by themselves would have succeeded in overcoming the Egyptian forces. What is important is that the Egyptians could have consoled themselves by saying that the Israeli victory was not, in fact, so overwhelming after all. Nasser's eventual political success also contributed to dullingng after all. Nasser's eventual political success also contributed to dulling the feeling of defeat. Thus, the Israeli victory was far from being so elegant and devastating as is sometimes suggested in the literature, and the Egyptian perception of the Israeli success was even more sceptical.

Nevertheless, Israel's victory was sufficient to deter Egypt for more than ten years from pursuing lines of action which could lead to crisis and war. Even the 1967 crisis began not with a deliberate Egyptian decision to go to war, but rather as a result of several other factors. Primary among these were inter-Arab politics and, related to it, the process of escalation along the Syrian–Israeli border. The Egyptians did not intend to go to war, but to deter Israel from attacking Syria and possibly to remove UN forces from the Egyptian–Israeli border permanently.[30] Up until the crisis itself began to unfold, the chief Egyptian decision maker, President Nasser, considered the military punishment likely to be meted out by Israel as a major inhibition on his activity. The crisis, however, assumed an internal logic of its own, and eventually Nasser's readiness to "accept" war if Israel struck increased. The crisis itself should be treated as an independent unit of analysis, where the rules of behavior of the two sides were analytically distinct from those operating in the Arab–Israeli conflict until then.[31] But even then, the side that actually launched a military attack was Israel and not Egypt, which showed that the residual effect of Israeli deterrence posture did operate as an inhibition on Egypt's behavior throughout the crisis.

In terms of an intents/capabilities equation, Egyptian intent (motivation) to attack Israel was checked by Egyptian assessment of the relative capabilities of Egypt/Israel. The intensity of the Egyptian motivation was less than the punishment the Egyptians envisaged themselves suffering in the case of a war with Israel. As we shall see, when Egyptian motivation reached a high level of intensity (during the period 1967–1973) because of the grievance felt, its assessment of the level of punishment it was ready to suffer at the hands of Israel changed. Egypt was ready to suffer a much higher level of punishment. Thus, the level of deterrence Israel succeeded in securing during the period 1957–1967 was high both because of the military successes gained in 1956 and because the intensity of Egyptian (and Syrian) motivation to start war was relatively low.

Tacit Understandings and Partial Demilitarization

The relationship between the two most important military powers in the heart of the Middle East—Israel and Egypt—was characterized by a set of tacit understandings, primarily on the strategic level. The most important of all these was the tacit partial and limited demilitarization of the Sinai Peninsula (particularly of its eastern part).[32] To be sure, Egyptian forces were deployed in the Sinai but their size was limited, and most were in the vicinity of the Suez Canal. Moreover they comprised, according to varying estimates, from one to one-and-a-half of a total of about five to six Egyptian divisions.[33] The proportion of the Egyptian armored forces which were in Sinai was even smaller. Thus, the majority of the Egyptian forces were not in the Sinai Peninsula at all. On the other hand, the Egyptians maintained a strategic infrastructure composed of military installations, fortifications, airfields, stocks of ammunition and a network of roads and water pipelines, which could serve the Egyptian forces once they decided to march into Sinai.

One of the probable reasons for this partial demilitarization was the possibility of an Israeli reaction to a concentration of Egyptian forces in the eastern part of the Sinai. Thus, there was an implied perception of *casus belli* involved in such a move. Second, there were logistical reasons: the maintenance of a large concentration of Egyptian forces in the Sinai desert, far from its regular bases, would have involved great expense. Third, the defense of the Canal remained one of the most important objectives of the Egyptian forces. The Canal had to be defended against both Israel and external powers (this was the lesson learnt from the 1956 British–French intervention).

Even this very partial demilitarization had several important further loopholes. It was not formally recognized by the international community, and consequently the violation of the demilitarization was not perceived as a legitimate Israeli *casus belli*. Second, even Israel did not officially maintain that it considered a concentration of Egyptian forces in eastern Sinai a *casus belli*. Thus, the deterrent effect of Israel against such infringements was somewhat blunted. Nevertheless, it was sufficient for more than ten years. The only exception was Operation

"Rotem"—the code name given to it by Israel—when Egyptian forces were moved up to the Israeli border in 1960, and a diplomatic crisis ensued.[34] The crisis was resolved with the help of intervening external powers. But, before that, some mobilization took place in Israel and some of the units of the Israeli standing army which were not ordinarily deployed along the Sinai border were rushed there.

The "Rotem" operation only proved, first, that in ordinary times most of the Egyptian forces were *not* deployed along the Israeli border, or in the Sinai, and were moved there only in *extremis*; second, that such a move indeed immediately causes a crisis; third, that there was room for some doubt as to Israel's interpretation of such action and its possible reaction. On the one hand, therefore, the "Rotem" episode proved that Israel would react—and must react, according to the logic of its strategic doctrine—to a massing of Egyptian forces along its border. On the other hand, however, the very fact that Israel had not reacted immediately by taking military action, weakened the tacit assumption that such a massing of Egyptian forces would constitute a *casus belli* for Israel.

The lack of a formal *casus belli* under these circumstances provided more freedom of maneuver for the Israeli Government. It also enabled Israel not to "lose face" when it did not immediately declare war on Egypt at that juncture, and resorted instead to diplomatic action. Be that as it may, there was a lack of formal *casus belli* in case of major Egyptian moves toward the Israeli border.[35]

Yet another tacit understanding between Israel and Egypt during this period was related to small-scale violence along the border. In previous years (up to the 1956 war) such clashes were the rule of the day and occurred very frequently. They were originally caused by Arab infiltration into Israel but were critically aggravated by massive Israeli counteractions—the reprisal attacks. Between 1957–1967 no such activities took place. Egypt recognized tacitly that such activities would probably lead to escalation and war. There were several added tacit understandings. One important example, which persisted throughout the period, was that no foreign Arab forces were allowed to enter Jordan. In this case Israel formulated a clear *casus belli* which created that tacit understanding. The *casus belli* was primarily related to the West Bank but somewhat more ambiguously extended to the eastern side of the river as well. This *casus belli* which resulted in the said tacit understanding led to

Israel becoming also a tacit guarantor of the independence of Jordan against any Arab intervention or attack on it.[36]

The Arms Race

The arms race between Israel and Egypt has been one of the most important characteristics of the Arab–Israeli relationship. The arms race signified, on the one hand, limited continued expectation of possible war between the two sides in the medium run. In terms of defense expenditures there have been significant rises, but in terms of percentages of GNP, the race accelerated only slightly, from around 9% in the case of Israel in 1957 to 11–12% for the same country in the period 1965–1967 (up to the war). The corresponding rise in Egypt was also slow. Thus, although there was a "race" or at least a "walking race," still it was—to use Richardson's model—tending to become a "stable" one.[37] In fact, during the period 1965–1967 (again up to the war), the expenditures in terms of percentages of GNP of both sides levelled off.

In terms of weapon systems actually delivered to Israel and its Arab neighbors, there had been a significant growth in quantities coupled with qualitative changes throughout this period. Soviet–Egyptian arms deals were signed in 1957, 1959, 1961, 1963 and 1965.[38] The most elaborate one was that of 1963 which, apart from increasing considerably the quantities of Egyptian arms, also introduced new weapon systems. The 1965 agreement increased, for example, the number of MiG 21s in the hands of the Egyptians, but overall consideration of the arms transfers to Egypt will show a quantitative increase in the airforce spread over the whole period 1962–1967 without a sudden jump in the period immediately prior to the war.[39] The 1965 agreement was probably connected at least in part with the war in the Yemen.

The arms race of 1957–1967 did not destabilize the Israeli–Egyptian (Syrian) strategic relationship. Both sides—Egypt and Syria on the one hand and Israel on the other—acquired weapon systems of the same characteristics. Also the quantitative ratio in the more important weapon systems (aircraft and armor) remained, on the whole, constant during the years with some annual variations. Indeed, the Israeli estimates were that if war occurred, it would break out only in 1969 or 1970. This estimate was based on an analysis of Egyptian capabilities. The crisis that ensued in 1967 was not related to the arms acquisition process but to a completely different set of factors.

Israeli Strategy

The Israeli strategic doctrine during the period was based on assumptions of the strong deterrent effect of the Israeli victory of 1956 and the continued increase in Israeli capabilities; indeed—as has been pointed out—this deterrent effect was potent and was consistently acknowledged by the Egyptian leadership. The formulation of deterrence as the main posture of the Israeli forces became more explicit during the period 1963–1967 but had certainly been a salient feature of the Israeli position since 1957.[40] It had two levels, the conventional one and the one aimed at the development of a nuclear option. The emphasis on deterrence also included an element of "deterrence by frustration," namely, the periodic need to prove to the Arab states that they are incapable of launching a successful attack on Israel. One of the forms which this deterrent posture assumed was counter blows to Arab countries from which armed infiltrators penetrated into Israel.

The actual absence of large concentrations of Egyptian forces along the border, coupled with the fact that, by tacit understanding, the majority of Jordanian armor was never stationed in the West Bank, enabled Israel to maintain its reserve system. There was no need for Israeli intelligence to base all its estimates on an assessment of Arab intentions. If the Arabs moved their forces with offensive intent, this could be detected in "real time," and a long enough warning period for the mobilization of the reserves could be secured.

For several reasons, the Israeli doctrine had to rely on carrying the war into enemy territory.[41] This was also connected with the growing emphasis on armor and aircraft as the two principal instruments in Israel's operational capability. This reliance was partly connected with the need to "carry the war into enemy territory," but also with the realization that the Israeli forces were superior to the enemy in fast mobile operations. Important considerations too were the international constraints, which imposed a limitation on the duration of a war and the reserve system. Thus, Israel had to be prepared to take military initiatives. In this context there have been three types of such military initiatives: preventive war, anticipatory strike, and preemptive strike.

The Israeli posture also contained a strong emphasis on counterforce strategy; this was evident among other things from the weapon systems acquired by Israel (an emphasis on interceptors with a capability for close support of ground forces).[42] The main objective was the destruction of the armies which threatened Israel, in Clausewitzian terms: "disarming" the enemy's army.[43] No political objectives for a war had been formulated and, in that sense, it was a non-Clausewitzian approach. During this period, despite the notion of "deterrence by frustration," there was no doctrine of large-scale destruction of the enemy's population and economic infrastructure. The punishment of the civilian populations by strategic bombing was considered unnecessary for the purpose of deterrence. The 1967 Israeli attack was thus aimed at the destruction of the Arab armies but had no political objectives.

These strategic and operational postures were well suited to Israel's main political objective up to 1967: maintaining the territorial *status quo* and bringing the Arabs around to the—preferably formal—acceptance of this *status quo*.

In terms of expectations of an outbreak of hostilities, the Israeli–Egyptian relationship between 1957 and 1967 could be defined as "stable armistice," on a continuum running from "general war" to "formal peace with active cooperation." From 1964 to 1967 some elements of another situation were introduced, namely that of "dormant war"[44] side by side with the elements of "stable armistice." However, the "stable armistice" was the predominant state of affairs between the two sides. The situation was different as far as the Israeli–Syrian relationship was concerned. There, from 1964–1967, the elements of "dormant war" were much more significant.

In comparison, the situation during the 1950s and primarily during 1954–1956, could be defined as "partial sporadic war" along all of Israel's borders and especially the Egyptian and Syrian ones.

The element of a specific Egyptian and Jordanian grievance (as opposed to all-Arab) was rather limited, and thus Egypt was preoccupied with other foreign policy activities, apart from the Arab–Israel conflict. Without the participation of Egypt in a war, the other Arab countries (and primarily Syria) would not have dared to start hostilities.

The net result was a rather stable system between Israel, on the one hand, and Egypt and Jordan on the other. The elements of stability were based on lack of a very high level of operational motivation on the part of the Egyptians and Jordanians to change the *status quo*; a credible Israeli deterrence posture; *de facto* partial demilitarization of Sinai coupled with tacit agreements concerning lack of violence along the borders; and an arms race which did not destabilize the military balance. Instability in this relationship could have been affected by the unstable relationship between Israel and Syria; Egyptian inter-Arab commitments and Israeli overreaction to limited violence initiated by Arabs.

Destabilizing pressure began to develop by 1963, as Israel's Jordan Waters Project neared completion. Tension started to build up and Syria's activities in trying to divert the water led to a series of clashes between Israel and Syria.[45] The situation deteriorated further after al-Fath began its operations on 1 January, 1965. Yet a word of caution must be added here: al-Fath's activities from 1965 through May 1967 had a negligible impact, resulting in only 11 Israelis killed during the entire period and in only slight damage to property.

Inter-Arab Politics

The escalation along the Israeli–Syrian border coincided with a deterioration in inter-Arab relations. To be sure, this deterioration had already begun soon after the dissolution of the UAR in 1961 but continued throughout the period Malcolm Kerr has called "The Arab Cold War,"[46] right up to 1967. Partly because of the border tension and partly becasuse of Soviet prompting, Egypt agreed to sign the 1966 defense pact with Syria. Thus, high inter-Arab tension persisted during most of the period of relative stability between Israel and Egypt and Jordan. There are two crucial questions to be asked here. First, does a high level of conflict behavior between Arab states contribute to escalation in the Arab–Israeli conflict?[47] Second, if so, what are the time ranges involved, namely, at what point in time does inter-Arab conflict behavior translate itself into Israeli–Arab conflict?

It appears that there is no general answer to the first question. The 1956 and 1967 wars came after high levels of inter-Arab conflict behavior. The War of Attrition, and especially the 1973 October War came after relatively low levels of inter-Arab conflict behavior. It seems, therefore, that there are other variables to be taken into account. These have to do with both inter-Arab politics and with Arab–Israeli relations. All the Arab–Israeli wars were preceded by some Israeli–Arab military escalations or a high level of political grievance on the part of the Arab states. In 1967 there was also the defense agreement between Egypt and Syria. Thus, it appears that inter-Arab conflict behavior can be considered a cause of Arab–Israeli war only when combined with some escalation in the conflict between Israel and one Arab country, which is involved on its part in intensive conflict with one or more Arab countries within the framework of general deterioration in inter-Arab relations. The mechanism which actually transferred inter-Arab tension into escalation in the Arab–Israeli conflict in 1967 was the Egyptian–Syrian defense agreement of November 1966. The crisis would not have occurred however, had there not been further escalation in the Syrian–Israeli conflict.

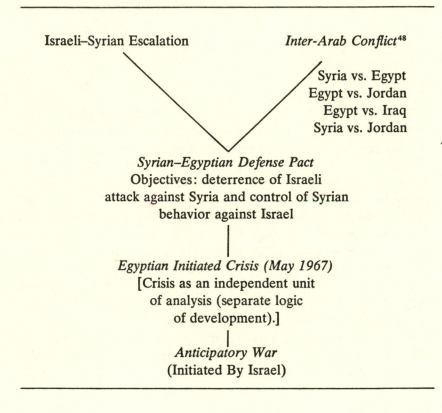

Israeli–Syrian Escalation   *Inter-Arab Conflict*[48]

Syria vs. Egypt
Egypt vs. Jordan
Egypt vs. Iraq
Syria vs. Jordan

Syrian–Egyptian Defense Pact
Objectives: deterrence of Israeli
attack against Syria and control of Syrian
behavior against Israel

Egyptian Initiated Crisis (May 1967)
[Crisis as an independent unit
of analysis (separate logic
of development).]

Anticipatory War
(Initiated By Israel)

THE 1967–1973 PERIOD

The 1967 war was an immeasurably greater victory for Israel than the 1956 war had been.[49] Israel faced three Arab armies instead of one, in addition to contingents from yet another army. No other external powers, such as France and Britain, collaborated in the operation, and the war was won with a comparatively very small number of casualties. It was indeed an elegant victory. If anything, the deterrent effect of the war should have been very considerable. But in fact, as noted above, the period from 1967–1973 was characterized by a very high conflict intensity level. It appears, therefore, that a new element was created here, namely that of specifically Egyptian, Jordanian and Syrian "grievances," quite distinct from their attachment to the ideological dimension of the conflict.[50] These "grievances" were, of course, provoked by the presence of Israeli forces in large parts of Egypt and Syria. Thus, the deterrent effect of the 1967 war was more than outbalanced by this new provocation. All this does not mean that deterrence ceased to exert a major influence in Israeli–Arab relations, but the factor of political "grievance" must be considered as modifying the deterrence equation. The outcome seems clear. While there was one war—the Six Day War—after a period of almost eleven years of calm, there were two major Arab–Israeli wars during the short span of six years following the victory of 1967. Moreover, between 1967 and 1970, when the War of Attrition finally ended, the level of violence along the Eastern Front was again very high. After the end of the War of Attrition, military activity switched over to the northern Israeli–Lebanese border, where clashes alternated with intermediate truces almost until the outbreak of the 1973 war.

Inter-Arab Politics and the Formation of Arab Coalitions

It was precisely the escalation of the Arab–Israeli conflict, which characterized the period—which led to an increase in the number of meaningful partial coalitions in the Arab world, whose main objective lay in the political and military campaign against Israel. All other foreign policy objectives assumed lower priority compared with that one. Competition in the Arab world for positions of hegemony has not ceased, but the amount of energy that the confrontation states were able to divert to rivalry among themselves became much more limited. The confrontation countries were able to divert much less attention to the formation of partial coalitions whose aims lay within the inter-Arab arena, and instead strove to create coalitions which could assist them in their campaign against Israel. Thus, out of 22 formal or informal partial coalitions among Arab states, or between an Arab state and an external power (the Soviet Union), at least ten were oriented primarily to the conflict.

Moreover, some of the others were more symbolic demonstrations of ideological commitment rather than meaningful coalitions.[51]

Israeli Strategic Doctrine

Israel's victory in 1967 led to some changes in the strategic relationship between the two sides. Israel's large territorial gains led its military leadership to consider a possible change in its basic strategic doctrine.

First, the attainment of more territory eventually led to the concept of strategic depth.[52] In the Israeli context, this meant that should the Arabs launch an attack against Israel, the standing army would be able to hold it off until the reserves were mobilized. As noted above, this was also part of the Israeli doctrine before the 1967 war, only then the basic notion was that of a preemptive Israeli strike. The maintenance of an "absorptive" posture until the reserves were mobilized had been only a "second best" option. A concomitant change after 1967 concerned the notion of "carrying the war into enemy's territory."[53] This was a basic principle of Israeli doctrine up to the 1967 war. Afterwards, the approach was modified and the possibility of a "pure" defensive war surfaced. In Israeli strategic doctrine, "strategic depth" was therefore perceived as potentially allowing for a major change. The lessons of the War of Attrition were, in this respect, multi-dimensional and contradictory. On the one hand they could only serve to bear out this doctrinal change; although the War of Attrition imposed a great strain on Israel, and proved that in such a war Israel's superiority in mobile fighting is undercut, Israel demonstrated that it could withstand such a long, static war along its new borders in Sinai without resorting to major mobilization. This capability was, of course, partly due to the extensive use of the Israeli air force along the Suez Canal, which cancelled out the overwhelming Egyptian superiority in artillery. It should be stressed in this context that the deep penetration bombing of Egypt from January 1970 did not necessarily have only that purpose, but was also aimed at achieving wider objectives beyond the requirements of the actual fighting along the Canal.

At the same time, though, the War of Attrition proved that Egypt too is capable of sustaining a long, static war. Moreover, if the Egyptians could neutralize at least part of the effectiveness of the Israeli aircraft, the outcome might be more favorable to Egypt.

Probably unrelated to these lessons of the War of Attrition was Israel's continued concentration on the development of its mobile forces. Thus, although the basic strategic doctrine moved gradually toward a more defensive posture (or alternatively to an "absorption-of-first-strike-without-preempting" posture), the actual build-up and operational training of the bulk of the Israeli ground forces continued to be primarily based on armor and the offensive mode.[54] In this respect, the Israel Defense Forces continued their pre-1967 approach, in its post-1970 phase. The emphasis in the order and structure of forces was on mobility and on the factor of shock (created by a rapid concentration of armor) rather than on static fire power. One of the results was the relative neglect of artillery.

This emphasis on mobility and the shock effect was more in tune with the offensive theme which was still maintained on a different level in the Israeli doctrine. It found some expression, for example, in the plans for crossing the Suez Canal. But the main contingency plan for battle in the south—*Shovech Yonim* or "Dovecot"—was primarily a defensive one.[55]

Another basic change took place after 1970. Instead of relying on a counter-force strategy, Israel gradually began to develop a countervalue strategy as the basis for its deterrent posture. This doctrinal change was apparently the result of the deployment of the Phantoms in Israel, coupled with the increased influence of the air force in the defense establishment. It also stemmed from another "ideological-political" factor. The new borders were perceived as securing the country's defense much more effectively than the old ones. They were seen as a defense against a major war aimed at completely overrunning the country. There was, however, always the possibility of another variation of the War of Attrition, or another static war. How does one deter the other side from such a war? Here, the notion of deterrence by punishment surfaced. If the Arabs were to know that their attack would be followed by a terrible punishment of their economic infrastructure, they would be deterred from an attack on Israel. Thus, the notion of secure borders and a defensive strategy had to be linked to some variant of deterrence-by-punishment if Israel wanted not only to defend itself in the event of war, but also to deter such war from actually happening.

The deterrence of war became essential for Israel not only because Israel did not want war, but also because the whole Israeli political position from 1970 on was based on the assumption that the *status quo* created after 1967 was stable, and that the United States should not pressure Israel to change it. This position became more and more credible with the passage of time after the end of the War of Attrition. The major pillar of this *status quo* became more and more the Israel air force, and primarily its Phantom component.

The 1973 war proved, of course, that this posture of deterrence by punishment was completely untenable, and that at a certain point of political grievance, Egypt and Syria would not be deterred, even if there were a high likelihood of severe punishment. Furthermore, once even a small number of Scud missiles had been brought to Egypt, that country was in a position to threaten Israel with counter-strikes at Israeli population centers. To be sure, the Egyptian reprisal—if Israel had indeed attacked the Egyptian heartland during the 1973 war—would have been negligible compared to the havoc that Israel could have wrought. Nevertheless, Israel refrained from resorting to the strategic bombing of Egypt during this war. Syria, on the other hand, was bombed. The economic infrastructure of Syria was heavily bombed[56] and indeed, it was within the capability of Israel even to extend this bombing and cause much more damage to Syria. Israel chose to refrain from it. It is, however, important to point out that the rate of recovery of the Syrian infrastructure was very rapid.

The IDF had always emphasized the importance of different variants of the indirect approach. The element of surprise, particularly a surprise first strike, as one possible mode of the indirect approach, assumed great saliency and importance in the military thinking of both sides, after the successful 1956 Sinai Campaign, and even more so after the great success of the 1967 war. However, because of the illusion of greater

---

Table 2

Defense Expenditures of Israel
(in millions of US dollars at 1970 prices

	1957	1958	1959	1960	1961	1962	1963	1964
Egypt	259	[242]	[246[	[264]	[292]	[330]	369	463
Israel	97	109	121	144	144	162	201	262
Jordan	(50)	(59)	(73)	(68)	(67)	(71)	(72)	(71)
Syria	44	[79]	77	78	79	90	94	103

[Rough estimates]
(For military expenditure: estimates based on budget figures or using an estimated consumer price index, or both.)

---

security created by the new borders, and the mixture of defensive strategy and deterrence-by-punishment posture, the premium attached to both strategic and tactical surprise lost some of its importance in the Israeli strategic approach and gained in Egyptian and Syrian military thinking. In passsing, it should be noted however, that the Egyptian and Syrian attack in October 1973 would have been carried out even if Israel had found out about it beforehand. Of course, the Arabs did whatever they could to cover their preparations and to achieve as much surprise as possible.

Tacit Understandings

The militarization of Sinai by Israel following the 1967 war eliminated one of the most important restraining factors in the strategic relationship between Israel and Egypt. The conquest of the West Bank also pushed aside another restraining factor, namely, the inadmissibility of the introduction of foreign troops into Jordan. As noted above, Israel formulated a *casus belli* related to precisely this issue. The war, and the continued state of semi-crisis which ensued, changed the context of Israeli–Jordanian relations. One of the severest punishments which Jordan could suffer at the hands of Israel for allowing foreign troops to enter has already been applied. Now, foreign troops (the Palestinian organizations and Iraqi troops) were already positioned in Jordan. Yet, a related element in the Israeli–Jordanian relationship remained as it was before 1967, namely, Israel continued to act as the tacit guarantor of the independence of Jordan against intervention from other Arab

---

and Arab Confrontation States 1957–1973
and 1970 exchange rates)

1965	1966	1967	1968	1969	1970	1971	1972	1973
501	516	718	740	836	1263	1450	1420	2327
288	365	562	730	955	1278	1370	1375	2415
(71)	(85)	115	136	135	105	109	109	95
113	93	102	159	164	162	156	180	289

Source: SIPRI Yearbook 1975, *World Armaments and Disarmament* (The MIT Press, Cambridge and London 1975) p. 126. Part of Soviet arms deliveries to Egypt and Syria are probably not included in the defense budgets.

countries. This was amply demonstrated during the 1970 Jordanian Civil War. It was the threat of Israeli military intervention which was the main reason for Syria's reluctance to send more armor and aircraft against the Jordanian army. Israel deterred Syria from doing that, and thus decided the outcome of the war.[57] To be sure, the Jordanians themselves were able to destroy the initial Syrian tank thrust. It is not clear, however, whether the Jordanians would have been able to withstand a concerted full-scale Syrian attack on Jordan.

Another basic rule of the strategic game which persisted into the period 1967–1973 was the readiness of Israelis and Arabs often to limit their military actions, and to allow peaceful operations and even intensive peaceful contact to go on side by side with military operations. Thus, while the War of Attrition raged, both Israel and Egypt continued to produce oil in the oilfields on both sides of the Gulf of Suez. Similarly, while military encounters between Israeli units and Jordanian and Palestinian guerrilla forces took place along the Jordan River, the volume of civilian transport across the river kept growing. Mortars were firing at one point, and several kilometers away lorries and taxis were calmly being checked by Jordanian military guards and Israeli military police at either end of a bridge only a few yards long. The limited and restrained use of force along Israeli borders was the result of either tacit bargaining or of explicit contacts. It seems reasonable to assume that as far as Israeli–Egyptian relations were concerned, this was done pri-

Table 3

Defense Expenditures of Israel
as percentage

	1957	1958	1959	1960	1961	1962	1963	1964
Egypt	5.5	6.1	5.9	6.9	7.0	8.4	10.9	12.2
Israel	8.6	8.2	9.5	9.4	9.2	10.4	10.8	11.5
Jordan	17.6	17.8	20.2	18.0	14.6	14.5	14.9	13.0
Syria	5.7	12.1	12.3	9.7	8.7	8.5	9.5	10.4

Sources: For the years 1957-1970 Yair Evron, "Arms Races in the Middle East and Some Arms Control Measures related to them," in ed. Gabriel Sheffer, *Dynamics of a Conflict*, Humanities Press, 1975, p.103.
For the years 1971-1973 see IISS, *The Military Balance 1975-1976*, pp. 76-77.

marily by tacit bargaining, based on rational evaluation by each side of the interest of the other. This assessment was coupled with signals sent primarily through actions or withholding of otherwise expected action.

The Arms Race

The arms race in the Middle East has undergone a major quantitative and qualitative change since 1967. In sheer quantities of arms and the size of armed forces, both sides have increased their armed forces considerably. Indeed, the arms race after 1967 became—side by side with violence along the borders—the most prominent feature of the strategic relationship. In sheer terms of quantities, the ratio between Israel and its adversaries has not changed considerably over the whole period, although there were fluctuations from year to year. What has changed is the overall quantities of forces and arms on both sides, and also the level of sophistication. Also, Egypt and Syria concentrated—from 1970 onward—more and more on the deployment of weapon systems which could cancel the effectiveness of the offensive systems (armor and aircraft), in the use of which Israel had (and still has) such a marked superiority. By greater reliance on surface-to-air systems and anti-tank missiles, Egypt especially was able to develop a strategy for limited offense, a strategy which was successfully put to the test in 1973.

The Egyptian–Syrian decision to go to war, taken probably in April 1973, was motivated primarily by the continued Israeli presence in the

---

and Arab Confrontation States 1957—1973
of GNP

1965	1966	1967	1968	1969	1970	1971	1972	1973
12.5	11.7	11.5	12.9	16.7	19.1	21.1	19.9	31.0
11.8	10.6	16.1	18.0	21.7	25.3	23.6	21.1	46.3
11.1	11.9	11.1	13.9	16.5	20.0	14.8	16.0	16.4
10.9	8.8	8.5	12.4	10.3	9.3	11.8	12.1	16.0

For the Israeli defense expenditures (excl. direct imports) as percentage of GNP, see Yaacov Lifshitz, "Defense Expenditure and the Allocation of Resources," in Nadav Halevi and Yaacov Kop, *Issues in the Economy of Israel*, Jerusalem, Falk Foundation, 1975).

---

territories conquered in 1967. However, it was the great influx of arms sent by the Soviet Union that enabled Egypt and Syria to launch the actual attack. Indeed, it appears that Syria was helped much more by the arms transfers as compared to Egypt. Syria received $ 724 million in 1973 in arms as compared to Egypt's $ 480 million. This, and the nature of the defensive systems (anti-air and anti-tank) were important factors in the actual decision to go to war. In summary, the war was not *caused* by the arms race, but the transfer of some specific weapon systems enabled the Arabs to launch an offensive, to which they were committed in any case.

Model of Causes of War 1973

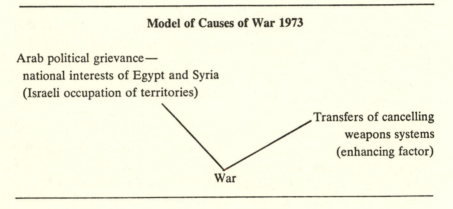

Arab political grievance—
national interests of Egypt and Syria
(Israeli occupation of territories)

Transfers of cancelling
weapons systems
(enhancing factor)

War

CONCLUDING REMARKS

The evidence available suggests that the intensification of the ideological factor in Arab animosity toward Israel is not necessarily correlated with the intensification of violence or the frequency of wars. Secondly, intensive diplomatic activity and actual expectations of a settlement do not exclude the possibility of the intensification of violence and greater frequency of wars. Thirdly, the escalation of the arms race is correlated with the intensification of violence and the frequency of wars. This, however, does not mean that the arms race is an independent cause of war. Still, while the political grievance of specific Arab states motivates them to go to war (as in 1973), a speedy accumulation of arms is a necessary condition. Fourthly, the formation of meaningful Arab coalitions directed against Israel is correlated with the intensifications of the Arab–Israeli conflict and probably is precipitated by it. Fifthly, fierce inter-Arab conflict, coinciding with escalation in the Arab–Israeli conflict, is a strong indication of the likely outbreak of war. Sixthly, Israel's deterrent posture is enhanced by superior Israeli military capabilities coupled with the diminution of Arab political grievances.

A comparison of the two periods under discussion, 1957–1967 and 1967–1973, indicates that during the second period all the central variables of the conflict (except perhaps for the ideological one) have tended increasingly to interact so as to make war increasingly likely.

NOTES

1. For dynamics of conflicts, see *inter-alia* R. Warren Phillips, *Dynamic Patterns of International Relations: A Dyadic Research Design,*" University of Hawaii, 1968; Paul Smoker, "A Time-Series Analysis of Sino-Indian Relations," *Journal of Conflict Resolution*, XIII, 2 (June 1969) 172-191.

2. For some discussions of the relations between domestic politics and foreign policy in general, see: Henry A. Kissinger, "Domestic Structure and Foreign Policy," *Daedalus*, LXXXXV, 2 (Spring 1966) pp. 503-529; R. Barry Farrell, "Foreign Policies in Open and Closed Political Societies," *Approaches to Comparative and International Politics*, ed., R. Barry Farrell (Evanston, Ill., Northwestern University Press, 1966) pp. 167-208; James N. Rosenau, ed., *Linkage Politics* (New York, Free Press, 1969); Jonathan Wilkenfeld, ed., *Conflict Behavior and Linkage Politics* (New York, McKay, 1973).

3. See for example; P. M. Burgess, *Elite Images and Foreign Policy Outcomes: A Study of Norway*, (Columbus, Ohio State University Press, 1968); J. N. Rosenau, "Private Preferences and Political Responsibilities: The Relative Potency of Individual and Role Variables in the Behavior of US Senators," *Quantitative International Politics*, ed., J. David Singer (New York, Free Press, 1968) pp. 17-50; Alexander George, "The 'Operational Code': A Neglected Approach to the Study of Political Leaders and Decision-Making," *International Studies Quarterly*, XIII, No. 2 (June 1969).

4. G. T. Allison, *Essence of Decision: Explaining the Cuban Missile Crisis* (Boston, Little Brown, 1971); G. T. Allison and M. Halperin, "Bureaucratic Politics: A Paradigm and Some Policy Implication," *Theory and Policy in International Relations*, eds., R. Tanter and R. Ullman (Princeton, N.J., Princeton University Press, 1972) pp. 40-79; M. Halperin, *Bureaucratic Politics and Foreign Policy* (Washington D.C., Brookings Institute, March 1974).

5. For some important examples, see R. C. Snyder, H. W. Bruck and B. Sapin, eds., *Foreign Policy Decision Making* (New York, Free Press, 1962); G. D. Paige, *The Korean Decision* (New York, Free Press, 1968); M. Brecher, B. Steinberg and J. Stein, "A Framework for Research on Foreign Policy

Journal of Conflict Resolution, XIII, 1 (March 1969) 75-101. An outstanding and definitive contribution to the study of decision making in Israel are the two volumes by Michael Brecher, *The Foreign Policy System of Israel*, (Oxford University Press, 1972) and *Decisions in Israel's Foreign Policy* (London, Oxford University Press, 1974).

6. J. D. Singer, "The Level of Analysis Problem in International Politics," *International Politics and Foreign Policy*, ed., J. N. Rosenau (rev. ed., (New York, Free Press, 1961) pp. 20-29; B. Moul, "The Level of Analysis Problem: Spatial and Temporal Aggregation in International Relations," paper presented at the 44th Annual Meeting of the Canadian Political Science Association (Montreal, June 1972).

7. W. R. Phillips, "The Conflict Environment of Nations: A Study of Conflict Inputs to Nations in 1963," *Conflict Behavior and Linkage Politics, op. cit.* pp. 124-147; W. R. Phillips, "The Dynamics of Behavioral Action and Reaction in International Conflict," *Peace Research Society Papers*, XVII (1971) 31-46; I. K. Feierabend and R. Feierabend, "Level of Development and International Behavior," *Foreign Policy and the Developing Nations*, ed., R. Butwell (Lexington, University of Kentucky Press, 1969) pp. 135-188, see especially p. 146; C. A. McClelland, "International Interaction Analysis: Basic Research and Some Practical Uses," University of Southern California, World Event/Interaction Survey Technical Report 2 (November 1968); C. A. McClelland, "Access to Berlin: The Quantity and Variety of Events, 1948-1963," *Quantitative International Politics, op. cit.*, pp. 159-186.

8. This model serves as a basis for various strategic models. See: T. Schelling, *Arms and Influence*, (New Haven, Yale University Press, 1966), and *Strategy of Conflict* (Cambridge, Mass., Harvard University Press, 1960); Herman Kahn, *On Escalation*, (New York, Praeger, 1965); K. W. Deutsch, *The Analysis of International Relations*, (Englewood Cliffs, N.J., Prentice Hall, 1968).

9. For some discussions of the structure of the Middle East subsystem, see: M. Brecher, *The Foreign Policy System of Israel: Settings, Images, Processes*, (London, Oxford University Press, 1972) pp. 47-64; Leonard Binder, "The Middle East Subordinate International System," *World Politics*, X, (April 1968) pp. 408-429; Yair Evron, *The Middle East: Nations, Super-Powers and Wars*, (London, Elek, 1973) pp. 192-207.

10. Historians generally introduce studies of periods with only short justifications for the delimitation of these periods; there seem to be no general criteria for such delimitation and differences over definition are not uncommon. See, for example, H. M. Gwatkin, "Constantine and His City," *The Cambridge Medieval History*, Vol. I, eds., H. M. Gwatkin and J. P. Whitney (Cambridge University Press, 1936) pp. 1-2; "Introduction," *The Cambridge Modern History*, Vol. I,

ed. G. R. Potter (Cambridge University Press, 1967) pp. 1-19; J. P. Cooper, "General Introduction," *Ibid*, Vol. II, pp. 1-2.

11. The 1967 war affected Israel and the Arab states in many ways, politically, socially, and in policy terms. The references are manifold. For a penetrating assessment of the changes in the Arab side noting the growth in particularist nationalism as opposed to pan-Arabism, following the Six Day War, see Shimon Shamir, "Some Arab Attitudes Toward the Conflict with Israel between 1967 and 1973," in Gabriel Sheffer (ed.) *Dynamics of a Conflict: Re-examination of the Arab-Israeli Conflict*, (Humanities Press, 1975). To briefly mention just one more example: Jean Lacouture argues that following the 1967 war, Nasser came to the conclusion that war was not a feasible way to solve the Arab-Israeli conflict; see his *Nasser*, (New York, Knopf, 1973).

12. No quantitative analysis has been conducted on the volume of diplomatic activity after 1967 or comparisons made with the previous period. But even on a more superficial impressionistic plane, it is abundantly clear that the volume of activity increased manifold. It was conducted in different modes and on different levels. There have been several direct secret meetings with King Hussein and leading Jordanian officials. There has been very intensive, though fruitless, activity by the United Nations special representative, Gunnar Jarring. The more meaningful diplomatic contacts were pursued by the United States and the Soviet Union in their bilateral talks. The United States launched three major diplomatic plans: Roger's Plan A (October-December 1969), Roger's Plan B (the cease-fire and standstill proposal in 1970), and Roger's Plan C (the various ideas for interim agreement). Apart from that, there have been the Four Powers negotiations and many unilateral efforts. The volume of diplomatic activity between Israel and the United States on the one hand, and Egypt (and other Arab countries) with the Soviet Union and the United States, on the other, also was very considerable. The number of books and articles on all these efforts keeps growing. For some books, see: L. Whetten, *The Canal War*, (Cambridge, Mass., MIT Press, 1974); and Evron, *op.cit.*

13. See brief reference to this in Shimon Shamir, "Some Arab Attitudes Toward the Conflict with Israel between 1967 and 1973," in Gabriel Sheffer, (ed.) *Dynamics of a Conflict, op. cit.*, p. 187. A comprehensive anthology of Arab writings, including self criticism, is included in Yehoshafat Harkabi, *Lekah Ha'aravim Mitvusatam*, (Arab Lessons from Their Defeat), (Tel Aviv, Dvir, 1969).

14. Bernard Lewis, "The Palestinians and the PLO: A Historical Approach," *Commentary*, LIX, 1 (January 1975) 36; Gerard Chaliand, *La resistance palestinienne*, (Paris, Editions du Seuil, 1970) pp. 7-8, 69-71, 149-150; Yehoshafat Harkabi, *Aravim, Palestinim Ve'Israel*, (Arabs, Palestinians and Israel), (Jerusalem, The Van Leer Jerusalem Foundation, 1975) pp. 38-39 (Heb.);

M. H. Kerr, "Regional Arab Politics and the Conflict with Israel," *Political Dynamics in the Middle East*, eds., Paul Y. Hammond and Sidney S. Alexander (New York, Elsevier, 1972) pp. 63-64.

15. The distinction between three periods: 1949-1956; 1956-1967; 1967-1973, is quite widely held. See, for example, Brecher, *The Foreign Policy System of Israel, op. cit.*, pp. 47-64, for such a distinction (with the last period designated as from 1967 on). These two differences are related, the first to the operational environment, the second to the images held by Arabs, but perhaps most especially by Israelis. Israeli security thinking from the early 1950s took into consideration a high likelihood of an Arab second round. The expectation of war intensified in the period 1954-1956. On Israeli images during that period see M. Brecher, *Decisions in Israel's Foreign Policy op. cit.*, pp. 225-317.

16. See for example, R. S. Rummel, "Dimensions of Conflict Behavior Within and Between Nations," *Conflict Behavior and Linkage Politics, op. cit.*, pp. 59-106; L. A. Hazlewood, "Externalizing Systemic Stresses: International Conflict as Adaptive Behavior," *Ibid*, pp. 148-190.

17. The most comprehensive discussion of Arab attitudes toward Israel is Y. Harkabi's *Emdat Ha'aravim Besichsuch Israel-Arav*, (The Arab Attitudes toward Israel), (Tel Aviv, Dvir 1968) (Heb.). For a discussion of the cultural and psychological factors affecting the Arab attitudes, see H. W. Glidden, "The Arab World," *American Journal of Psychiatry*, CXXVIII, 8 (February 1972) 984-988. For a recent essay on the ways in which Islam determines modern Arab politics, primarily in its rejection of non-Moslem political aspirations in the Middle East, see Bernard Lewis, "The Return of Islam," *Commentary* Vol. 61, No. 1 (January 1976), 39-49.

18. Some of these attitudes were surely there even before the creation of Israel, but were further developed after the 1948 War. The more profound articulation of their attitudes took place even later.

19. See for example Harkabi, *The Arab Attitudes Toward Israel*, (Eng. edit.), *op. cit.* pp. 244-245, 240, 241, 293.

20. For an analysis of changes in Arab attitudes following the 1967 war, see Shimon Shamir, "Some Arab Attitudes Toward the Conflict," *op. cit.*

21. See Nadav Safran, *From War to War*, (Pegasus, 1969), pp. 83-88. Harkabi *op. cit.* does not differentiate between intensity of attitudes according to time, but a reading of his account of Arab attitudes will show that most of the quotations from Arab literature representing the hard attitude toward Israel are from the late 1950s and the 1960s.

22. See his "Obstacles in the Way of a Settlement," in *Dynamics of Conflict: Re-examination of the Arab-Israeli Conflict, op. cit.*, and "The Israel-Arab

Conflict on the 25th Anniversary of the State of Israel," *Gesher*, XVIII, 3-4 (December 1972) pp. 138-196 (Heb.). The conclusions from the *Gesher* article are, however, multidimensional. Harkabi differentiates between the different schools in the Arab positon. However, he points out that Arab *hatred* of Israel intensified as a result of their defeat in the 1967 war (see pp. 163-165). For a different differentiation of Arab positions, see Shamir *op. cit.*

23. According to Harkabi, the Egyptian regime endorsed the step-by-step approach.

24. For an elaboration of the position of this school of thought, see Shamir, *op. cit.*

25. For a somewhat different analysis of the structure of deterrence, see A. George and R. L. Smoke, *Deterrence in American Foreign Policy: Theory and Practice*, (New York, Columbia University Press, 1974).

26. A. George, D. Hall, and W. Simons, *The Limits of Coercive Diplomacy*, (Boston, Little Brown, 1971).

27. For attempts to formulate a wider theory of influence which places deterrence as one element within a wider context of political influence considering political grievance and political positive inducements as extraenous variables to deterrence, see George and Smoke, *op. cit.*, R. Rosencrance, *Strategic Deterrence Reconsidered*, Adelphi Papers, No. 116, IISS, London 1975.

28. See on this, Y. Evron and Y. Bar Siman-Tov, "Coalitions in the Arab World," *The Jerusalem Journal of International Relations*, I, 2. (January 1976).

29. On this, see M. Dayan, *Yoman Ma'arechet Sinai*, (Diary of the Sinai Campaign), (Tel Aviv, Am Hasefer, 1965), p. 111, (in Heb.). For analyses of the military operations in Sinai during that operation, see *inter alia*, Dayan, *ibid*; R. D. Q. Henriques, *One Hundred Hours to Sucz*, (London, Collins, 1957); S. L. Marshall, *Sinai Victory*, (New York, W. Morrow, 1958); E. O'Ballance, *The Sinai Campaign 1956*, (London, Faber & Faber, 1959).

30. On this, see M. H. Heikal, *The Cairo Documents*, (New York, Garden City, 1973) pp. 240-241. On the basis of a very well documented and comprehensive study, this is also the conclusion reached by B. Geist and is also the accepted view of most observers. For a contrary approach, see T. Draper, "From 1967 to 1973: The Arab-Israeli Wars," *Commentary*, LVI, 6 (December 1973) pp. 31-45.

31. For crisis as an independent variable influencing the behavior of decision makers, see C. F. Hermann, "International Crisis as a Situational Variable," *International Politics and Foreign Policy, op. cit.*, pp. 409-421. The literature on crisis behavior is already considerable. For one well known collection, mainly from the decision making approach, see C. Hermann, *International Crisis:*

Insight from Behavioral Research, (New York, Free Press, 1972); for an example of a study of crisis behavior on the macro-level, see O. Young, *The Politics of Force*, (Princeton, N.J., Princeton University Press, 1968).

32. For a study of the partial demilitarization of Sinai during 1957-1967, see Y. Evron, *The Demilitarization of Sinai*, Jerusalem Papers on Peace Problems, (Jerusalem, Davis Institute, February 1975).

33. See *ibid.*, note 6.

34. For the political backround to the crisis that led to the Rotem operation, see M. Gilboa, *Shesh Shanim, Shishah Yamim* (Six Years, Six Days), (Tel Aviv, Am Oved, 1969) (Heb.); *Middle East Record, 1960*, I, pp. 197-204.

35. There have been several Israeli *casi belli*. Only two of these were stated explicity as formal *casus belli*: the closure of the Straits of Tiran and the concentration of large formations of foreign Arab troops in Jordan. An Israeli official once elaborated in private on four *casi belli*, including "the concentration of Egyptian military power in the Sinai Desert" (see M. Brecher, *The Foreign Policy System of Israel, op. cit.*, p. 67). For the unofficial elaborations of alternative Israeli *casi belli* by Yigal Allon and Shimon Peres, see D. Horowitz, *Hatfisah Ha'israelit Shel Bitahon Leumi*, (Israel's Concept of National Security), (Jerusalem, The Eshkol Institute, the Hebrew University, 1973) p. 25 (Heb.).

36. This was explicitly proved during the Syrian attack on Jordan in September 1970. It also served as a further inhibition to an Egyptian takeover of Jordan in earlier periods.

37. See L. F. Richardson, *Arms and Insecurity*, (London, Stevens, 1960). For an elaborate and comprehensive review and critique of Richardson's work on both the arms race and on other causes of wars, see A. Rapoport, "Lewis F. Richardson's Mathematical Theory of War," *Journal of Conflict Resolution*, I, 3., (1957). For Rapoport's discussion of Richardson's stable arms relationship, see especially pp. 278-280.

38. See G. Lenczowski, *Soviet Advances in the Middle East*, (Washington, D.C., American Enterprise Institute for Public Policy Research, 1971) pp. 145-149. The 1965 arms deal was negotiated and possibly agreed by late 1964.

39. See "Register 10. Arms Supplies to Egypt," *The Arms Trade with the Third World*, (Stockholm and New York, SIPRI, 1971), pp. 838-839.

40. See M. Handel, *Israel's Political-Military Doctrine*, Harvard University, Center for International Affairs, Occasional Papers No. 20 (July 1973) p. 67. Handel's is a fine analysis of Israel's strategic doctrines. His mentioning of deterrence as a "central peacetime goal" of the IDF does not refer to a specific peiod. It seems, however, that compared to the period 1949-1957, the period 1957-1967 was much more colored by the emphasis on deterrence.

41. *Ibid*, p. 66. There are many other references to this in Israeli writings and in various interviews with reserve officers.

42. The concept of counter-force was probably not known at the time. But the actual strategy was included in the Israeli military behavior. Even the air-force, which usually in other countries emphasized notions such as strategic bombing, defined its two operational objectives as denial of enemy's attacks on Israel's ground forces, close support to ground forces and striking at enemy's ground forces; see on that E. Weizman, *Lecha Shamaim Lecha Eretz*, (Yours the Sky, Yours the Country), (Tel Aviv, Sifriat Ma'ariv, 1975) p. 175 (Heb.). There had of course been variations, but the essential objective of destruction of the enemy's armed forces remained the main objective.

43. See, for example, S. Tevet, *Moshe Dayan*, (Jerusalem and Tel Aviv, Schocken, 1973) p. 574 (Heb.).

44. This phrase was coined by Rabin in a lecture given in Tel Aviv on 21 September, 1967, to describe the situation existing during 1949-1967 (except for the 1956 war). See Horowitz *op. cit.*, p. 9.

45. On this see *inter alia* N. Bar-Yaacov, *The Israel-Syrian Armistice: Problems of Implementation, 1949-1966*, (Jerusalem, Magnes Press, 1967) especially pp. 145-151; Brecher, *Decisions in Israel's Foreign Policy, op. cit.*, pp. 173-224.

46. See his *The Arab Cold War* (3rd ed., Oxford University Press, 1971).

47. There is no systematic study devoted primarily to this highly important point. Many of the traditional studies of conflicts in the Middle East refer to this point. For attempts at a quantitative study of patterns of conflicts in the Middle East see J. Eilkenfeld, V. L. Lussier and D. Tahtinen, "Conflict Interactions in the Middle East, 1949-1967," *Journal of Conflict Resolution*, XVI, 2 (June 1972) 135-154; R. Burrows and D. Muzzio, "The Road to the Six Day War: Aspects of an Enumerative History of Four Arab States and Israel, 1965-1967," *ibid*, pp. 211-225.

48. That inter-Arab conflict was the main (or one of the two main) causes of the escalation and crisis of 1967 is amply proved by B. Geist, *The Six Day War: A Study on the Setting and the Process of Foreign Policy Decision Making under Crisis Conditions*, (Unpublished Doctoral Thesis, the Hebrew University of Jerusalem, 1974), see especially Chapter 13. On the Israeli process of decision making in the crisis of 1967, see *ibid* and Brecher, *Decisions in Israel's Foreign Policy, op. cit.*, pp. 318-453.

49. There have been several accounts of the military operations in 1967. For books in English, see *inter alia* R. and W. Churchill, *The Six Day War*, (London, Heinemann, 1967); N. Safran, *From War to War: The Arab-Israeli Confrontation, 1948-1967* (New York, Pegasus, 1969); S. Tevet, *The Tanks of Tammuz*,

(New York, Viking Press, 1969); E. Luttwak and D. Horowitz, *The Israeli Army*, (New York, Harper & Row, 1975), ch. 7. Several in-depth analyses of specific battles appeared in different issues of *Maarachot*, (the IDF journal).

50. These grievances were probably responsible for the growth of state nationalism in different Arab countries as distinct from the general Arab national feeling. See on this, S. Shamir, "Some Arab Attitudes," *op. cit.*

51. See on this, Y. Evron and Y. Bar Siman-Tov, "Coalitions in the Arab World," *op. cit.*

52. The notion of strategic depth in the context of Israeli strategic thinking became paramount after 1967. For a discussion of the changes in the Israeli strategic doctrine after 1967 as a result of the attainment of strategic depth, see Herzog, *The War of Atonement, op. cit.*, pp. 12-13.

53. See, Handel, *op. cit.*, p. 66.

54. During the six years that elapsed since the 1967 war, Israel has considerably enlarged its tank force. According to some estimates, the size of the tank force has increased by at least 50%, and probably more than that. Moreover, many of the new tanks were of better quality than the older types. As far as APCs are concerned, Israel absorbed a certain amount of M-113s from the United States. Until then, Israel relied only on various models based on the M-4 half track. According to Safran, *From War to War, op. cit.*, Israel had 11 armored brigades in the Six Day War. An analysis of the various accounts of the 1973 war would show that Israel had at least, and probably more than 17 armored brigades in that last war. See, *The War of Atonement, op. cit.*; Z. Schiff, *October Earthquake*, (Tel Aviv, University Publishing Projects, 1974); E. Luttwak and D. Horowitz, *The Israeli Army, op. cit.*

55. According to this plan, two-thirds of the standing tank force deployed in Sinai were to be in preplanned positions along the Suez Canal in order to frustrate any Egyptian attempt to cross. To be sure, other plans covered possibilities such as counter-attack to the other side of the Canal (one of those was actually put into action) or destruction of those Egyptian units which might, in part, succeed in overcoming the Israeli defenses. But, basically, *Shovach Yonim* served as the main contingency plan.

56. For brief accounts of these bombings, see *The War of Atonement, op. cit.*, p. 130; and *October Earthquake, op. cit*, pp. 119, 132, 212.

57. For one account of the 1970 Jordanian crisis, see H. Brandon, "Jordan: The Forgotten Crisis (1) Were We Masterful...," *Foreign Policy*, No. 10, 1973, pp. 158-170.

Economic
Aspects

Does the Expansion
of Arab Financial Resources
Imply Economic Development?

Eliyahu Kanovsky

One of the editors of the *Middle East Economic Digest* of London, who had returned from a trip to Egypt in April 1974, stated that "Egypt has almost all the resources for sustained industrial development, except money. It has a large pool of labour, skilled manpower, mineral resources and a reasonably developed infrastructure." He reported that many Western businessmen were flocking to Egypt, and that Egypt was likely to receive capital, in significant amounts, from the oil-rich Arab countries.[1]

Anyone specializing in the Middle East, and even the general public, has read or heard, similar reports during the past year. That the financial resources of the oil-rich Arab countries have expanded very rapidly is well-known. The extent to which they will share this wealth with the poorer Arab countries is not so clear. According to the International Monetary Fund, foreign grants to Egypt were $ 250–300 million annually between 1968 and 1972.[2] There was no tendency toward any increase in Arab aid during this period. Saudi Arabian financial grants to *all* other Arab countries amounted from $ 50–100 million annually between 1968 and 1972, though its central bank foreign exchange reserves had risen very sharply from $ 520 million (1970) to $ 2,347 m. in 1972, as a result of the large increase in oil prices during this period, as well as increased oil production. In 1973 Saudi Arabia increased its financial grants to $ 378 million, while its foreign exchange reserves had risen to $ 3,707 million. By October 1974 these reserves had risen to $ 10,105 million.[3] There have been many reports in the press to the effect that Saudi Arabia and other oil-rich Arab countries have paid very large sums to the Soviet Union, and to Western European countries, directly, for arms deliveries to Egypt, and to other Arab countries. These, apparently, do not appear in the balance of payments reports. Our concern here is with financial aid for *economic* development, and the question to which we should address ourselves is: assuming a far greater flow of financial resources to Egypt, and to other poorer Arab countries, in the form of grants, concessionary loans, etc., does this necessarily imply a significant increase in the pace of economic development? If we accept the thesis that the constraint in Egypt, with respect to economic development, has been financial, then the removal of this constraint, would, *ipso facto*, imply that Egypt is about to enter into a phase of sustained rapid economic growth and development. My own thesis is that in Egypt, there have been other serious constraints which have hindered economic growth in the past. The removal, or attenuation, of these obstacles, can only be effectuated, if at all, over a very long period of time. I shall begin with Egypt, as the most important of the Arab countries, and then deal briefly with some of the other Arab states.

A good starting point might be the Five Year Plan for 1960–1965. This was the period during which Egypt initiated its major Aswan Dam project, designed to provide a large increase in argricultural land and irrigation, as well as electric power for the economy as whole. The main focus of the Plan was on a rapid expansion of the industrial sector. During this period investment was to be on a scale almost double that of the previous five years. Industrial production was to increase by almost 15% annually, agricultural production by 5% annually, and gross domestic product by 7%. Since Egypt had exhausted its sterling balances (accumulated during World War II) by the end of the 1950s, investment was dependent, in large measure, on major increases in foreign aid. During the first half of the 1960s, Egypt was the beneficiary of large-scale foreign aid. The United States provided over one billion dollars, mainly in food shipments; the Soviet Union about $ 800 million in economic aid; other Eastern European countries, and Communist China, an additional $ 500 million; and other Western countries plus the World Bank, about the same amount. "Loans" from Kuwait were another important source of capital. In terms of today's prices of food, raw materials, and capital equipment, and in relation to Egypt's gross national product at that time, foreign aid was very large. This is *aside* from military aid from the Soviet Union. Expectations ran high, not only in terms of anticipated large increases in production, but that the "big push" would bring Egypt into an era of rapid sustained economic growth, and by 1965, the last year of the Plan, Egypt would begin to have surpluses in its (basic) balance of payments, and would begin to reduce its foreign debts. An Egyptian economist stated in a 1966 publication that during the second half of the 1960s "food production will nearly catch up with demand, and a much bigger surplus will be available for export...largely brought about by the construction of the Aswan Dam."[4]

An assessment of the Egyptian economy is made difficult by the tendency of the regime to exaggerate its economic achievements, as has been noted by such economic research organizations as The Economist Intelligence Unit of London.[5] Economists have serious doubts with respect to the accuracy of the price indices used for correcting production data in order to arrive at real changes.[6]

According to the US Department of Agriculture, Egyptian agricultural production increased by an annual average of 2.9% between 1952–1954 and 1962–1964. Since the growth rate of the population was about 2.5%, agricultural production per capita increased by less than one half of one per cent per annum. Between 1962–1964 and 1970–1972 the rate of growth of agricultural production was 1.5%, about one half of that in the earlier period. Since the population growth rate was about the same it meant, in effect, that per capita agricultural production in 1970–1972 was 7% lower than in 1962–1964.[7]

Throughout this period agriculture accounted directly for about 30% of gross domestic product, and indirectly for a greater share of the national product, since much of industry (textiles), trade, transport, and other sectors are dependent on the farm sector. The retrogression in the agricultural sector has been a major factor in the stagnancy of the Egyptian economy as a whole. The explanation is often offered that this is due to the worsening land–population ratio. The Aswan High Dam and other reclamation projects were supposed to alter this ratio. According to official sources, the cropped area increased by about one million feddans (a feddan is somewhat larger than an acre) between 1952 and 1960; i.e., an increase of 11%. Between 1960 and 1970, reclaimed areas amounted to 884,000 feddans. However, the cropped area in 1971 was but 372,000 feddans greater than in 1960. In fact, the 1971 cropped area was lower than in 1965.[8] It is sometimes argued that yields have reached their natural limits, but a recent study of Middle Eastern agriculture by the Rand Corporation indicated that even in Egypt there was considerable room for much larger yields within the existing constraints of land and water, providing that inhibiting institutional restrictions are removed, and improvements take place in management, farm practices, etc.[9]

The major push and the largest allocations within the context of the 1960–1965 Plan were to the industrial sector. According to the official reports 96% of the planned targets for investment were realized; 800 new factories were established. However, the rate of growth of industrial production was, according to the official report, 8.5%, as compared with the planned goal of 14.6% annually.[10] As noted earlier, there are serious doubts with respect to the price indices used to estimate real growth rates, and there is reason to believe that the actual growth rate was lower. In other words, despite the massive investment in a host of industrial projects, the rate of growth of industrial production in 1960–1965 was probably not much higher, if at all, than in 1952–1959, or in 1945–1951.[11] *A priori* one might have expected that as the new industrial projects were being completed, and experience was being acquired in production, the trend should have been toward *higher* growth rates of industrial production. However, the official reports indicate that during the three years *preceding* the Six Day War of June 1967, there was a steady *decline* in the rate of growth of industrial production from 11.7% in 1963/64 to 4.9% in 1964/65; 2.6% in 1965/66 and 0.9% in 1966/67.[12]

Officially the gross domestic product increased by an annual average rate of 6.5% during the Five Year Plan. Professor Hansen, after making *some* corrections, concluded that it was really 5.5%.[13] His corrections were, in my view, incomplete, and the real growth rate was probably less than 5%; i.e., about the same as in the previous five-year period. Here, too, there was a marked decline in the rate of growth after 1962/1963, according to the official reports. The decline continued *after* the completion of the Plan, and during the last year preceding the Six Day War, there was virtually no economic growth.

The question that arises is why the large infusion of capital resources failed to generate a period of sustained economic development. There were undoubtedly many factors involved, including: the nationalization measures of 1960–1961; the lack of adequate incentives for farmers as well as in other sectors; the Yemen war which diverted large resources; the policy of compelling government administration as well as public enterprises to employ unneeded workers; and the poor selection of investment projects. However, in the final analysis it boils down to poor management, both macro and micro;, i.e., in terms of the economy as a whole, as well as in the multitude of individual enterprises. There is a lack of a large cadre of technical personnel, and I am not referring only or primarily to so-called high level manpower, but to the middle levels, those in the technician categories. There is a serious imbalance within the educational system, and between the educational system and the needs of the economy. It is easy enough, if one has the requisite capital resources, to build various enterprises, industrial as well as others, often by, or with the aid of foreign companies or experts. The problems that arise are the management of these enterprises *after* they have been completed. Professor Fuad El Taher of the State University of New York, in an article published in 1969, concludes that "Egypt has suffered from critical shortages of competent administrators, experienced specialist staff in different fields, and trained supervisors...the management of industrial enterprises suffered from the overlapping of various managerial functions, and from a shortage of skills at all levels...Training is still urgently needed to promote work efficiency so that productivity may be increased...the government has made little progress in overcoming the problem of inadequate training. It is fairly easy to build a new plant and bring in new equipment; ordinarily this can be accomplished in one or two years. (However) the training of an efficient manager may require fifteen to twenty years."[14] Professor El Taher does not address himself directly to the overall management of the economy and the efficiency of the governmental administration, where the problems are often even more acute.[15]

In line with Professor El Taher's evaluation there was a report in July 1973 that a high Soviet official, the Deputy Chairman of the Committee for Foreign Economic Relations, who had headed the Soviet delegation to the inauguration of the central pumping station on the Nubariya Canal, was highly critical of Egyptian maintenance of equipment.[16]

During the year following the Six Day War the Egyptian economy continued to decline, but this was, apparently, followed by a revival during the next two years. During the three years between the cease-fire of August 1970 and the war of October 1973, the rate of growth of the economy was again declining steadily. Officially, the rate of growth of the economy was about 4% per annum, but in view of the unreliable price indices, it seems probable that it was much lower, in real terms. It was reported that President Sadat stated in the fall of 1974 that before the October War, the economy was in a situation of a "zero growth" rate.[17] Our information on the economy since the October War is even more meager. Press reports published recently speak of severe shortages of basic commodities, of very sharp price increases, and of burgeoning black markets.[18] The *Economist* of London reported, in November 1974, a serious breakdown in public transportation and in other facets of the infrastructure.[19] All this is not to imply that the large infusions of capital expected by Egypt from Arab and Western sources cannot or will not improve matters. There have been indications, even before the October War, that President Sadat was making serious attempts to open up the economy to private enterprise, both local and foreign, and that he was moving in the direction of greater incentives for the producers. These changes, plus the capital imports, may well raise the growth rate of the economy from its low levels. However, a longer period of *sustained rapid* economic development would require a more basic and fundamental restructuring of the economy, and the training of a large and more effecient cadre of managerial and technical personnel—in its broadest context. Such institutional changes are necessarily slow and *may* possibly take place over a far longer time span. However, so long as the Egyptian leadership accepts the thesis—as they did during the period of the 1960–1965 Plan—that capital investment is the basic solution to its economic problems, there is not much likelihood that the far more fundamental, and far more difficult, structural, institutional, and manpower problems will be dealt with.

One must always be wary of making too-broad generalizations about all the Arab countries, in the economic as well as political spheres. My reference is not only to the differences between those oil-rich Arab countries with small populations and the others. The conclusions with respect to Egypt are applicable, though to a lesser extent, to Syria as well. Syria *did* have an extended period of rapid economic growth. Between 1950 and 1957 its national income increased by an annual average rate of 8–10%.[20] There are clear indications that this high growth rate was a continuation of a trend that had begun before World War II.[21] This period of rapid economic development came to an almost abrupt halt between 1957 and 1969. During the latter period the growth rate of the economy was 4.6%, or about 1.2% per capita, as compared with 5-6% per capita in the earlier period.[22] Between 1969 and 1972 a reversal seems to have set in and Syria's rate of economic growth increased significantly to 6.2% or 2.9% per capita. The Syrian Minister of Economy stated that in 1973—prior to the war in October—the growth rate of the economy was 7–8%.[23]

What factors accounted for the rapid growth during the two decades preceding 1957, the stagnancy of the 1957–1969 period, and the relative buoyancy of more recent years? Space does not permit a detailed analysis.[24] The public policies adopted by the regime during the period of the merger with Egypt in 1958–1961, and even more so during the 1963–1969 period, were major deterrents to private enterprise, which had been the mainspring of Syria's rapid growth until 1957. The Syrian merchant classes—in sharp contrast with the experience in many other underdeveloped countries—provided the entrepreneurship and capital for the development of both industry and agriculture.[25] The policies adopted by the regimes after 1958 brought about a major flight of capital—and what is even more important—of large numbers of skilled and managerial personnel. The results were predictable. Agriculture, which continues to be private, but far more subject to governmental controls, was in a state of absolute decline. According to US Department of Agriculture estimates, agricultural production in Syria between 1952–1954 and 1962–1964 had increased by an annual average rate of 4.9%, or about 1.5% per capita. In 1970–1972 agricultural production was 6% lower than in 1962–1964, and on a per capita basis, the decline was 27%.[26] The cultivated, cropped, and irrigated areas, were significantly lower in the 1970–1972 period than a decade earlier.[27] Private investment in agriculture dropped sharply during the 1960s, compensated only, in part, by public investment. There was a significant change in public policies with respect to agriculture—as well as other sectors—beginning with the later 1960s, which together with the completion of the major Euphrates Dam project, may reverse the decline in this major sector of the Syrian economy, which employs about one half of the population.

The take-over of most of Syrian industry by the State, or the fears of nationalization, were similarly responsible for a major reversal in the growth rate of the industrial sector. During the 1950s—until 1958—the growth rate was about 9% annually. During the following decade it fell to about 4%; i.e., barely exceeding the rate of population increase. Since 1967, and especially since the development of its crude petroleum resources in 1968, there has been a marked uptrend. Crude oil production is of minor proportions, in the context of Middle East output, but accounts for about a third of the increment in the industrial sector between 1968 and 1972. The loss of large numbers of technical and managerial personnel during the period of nationalization—as well as the capital flight—were the main factors accounting for the stagnancy of this sector during the 1960–1968 period. Both labor productivity and efficiency (total factor productivity) were declining. The reversal of public policies, since the later 1960s, accounts, in no small measure, for the uptrend evident since that time.

Would the greater availability of capital from the oil-rich Arab countries have significantly increased Syria's rate of economic growth during the 1960s? The evidence for the pre-1958 period indicates that Syria has the potential for more rapid sustained growth. No doubt the larger allocations to military expenditures restricted public investment. However, the major deterrent seems to have been, again, the human factor, namely, the availability of sufficient technical and managerial personnel, in its broadest context, and the lack of sufficient incentives. The economic liberalization measures of the present regime have apparently succeeded, in part, in reversing the downtrend. However, recent reports from Syria indicate that the inefficencies of the public sector—which dominates most of industry—are not readily amenable to correction. In July 1974, the deputy premier spoke of the "manifest insufficiency" of production by the state economic organizations affecting both industry and agriculture, adding to inflationary pressures. No less noteworthy is the announcement, also in July 1974, of stringent measures and severe penalties to be applied against those government employees leaving Syria without permission.[28] We have no precise information regarding the dimensions of the "brain drain" but the announcement of severe penalties would seem to indicate that it continues to be significant. The increased aid from the oil-rich Arab countries can compensate only in part for this loss.

I have recently, completed a study of the Jordanian economy.[29] During the pre-1967 period the Jordanian economy was making very rapid progress—unlike the situation in Egypt and Syria. Though Jordan was far less developed than both countries in the late 1940s, by 1966 its per capita income was higher than in all the other Arab countries, with the exception of the three richest oil states, and Lebanon. It put greater emphasis on developing its human resources. Agriculture, industry, as well as other economic sectors, showed rapid advances. Public policies were designed to stimulate private enterprise. The Six Day War proved to be a short-lived setback, and the gross national product of the East

Bank (Transjordan) in 1969 was significantly higher than in 1966, and unemployment rates were lower—despite the large influx of refugees. The severe civil war between the Fidayeen groups and the Government of Jordan was followed by a boycott and the closing of the borders by Syria, with very disruptive effects on the Transjordanian economy. However, the gradual relaxation of the Syrian restrictions in 1971, and their complete abolition in 1972, were instrumental in permitting a reversal of the 1970 decline. Toward the end of 1972 the Government announced a major three-year Development Plan (1973–1975) and the indications are that it is succeeding in achieving its goals. Essentially, other than in those years of *major* external disruptions, the economy of Transjordan advanced rapidly after 1967. Of course, years of severe drought had an adverse effect, as was the case before 1967. Would a greater amount of foreign economic aid have accelerated the rate of growth? All the evidence, both before and since 1967, shows that funds available for investment were significantly in excess of actual utilization. The constraint was clearly the problem of technical and managerial personnel, in part a result of the large numbers of Jordanians working in the Arab oil states. The authors of the 1973–1975 Development Plan suggest that the Government "take all the necessary steps to convince Jordanians working abroad to come back and work in Jordan."[30]

I would suppose that the clearest example of my thesis is the economy of Iraq. It is a country very well endowed with natural resources—in addition to crude oil. Revenues from crude oil output were rising almost steadily since the early 1950s and, by and large, capital resources were no constraint with respect to economic development. Without going into detail, the evidence shows that in agriculture and industry there has been a slow growth, or stagnancy, since the later 1950s. Despite the growing oil revenues, national income per capita increased by less than 2% annually between 1958 and 1970. The recent large increases in oil prices will certainly raise Iraq's per capita income significantly. But whether this will bring about major improvements in its agricultural, industrial, and other sectors, is doubtful.[31]

Economists who have studied developing economies have come to recognize that, in most cases, it is the human factor, and not capital resources, which is mainly responsible for the rapid growth rate of some economies, and the stagnancy of so many others. The examples cited in this paper clearly illustrate this thesis. While the expansion of Arab financial resources, and a greater willingness to provide economic aid to the poorer Arab countries, may be helpful, in the final analysis the growth and development of these economies will depend on far more fundamental changes and shifts in economic polcies. This would involve their focusing far more strongly on economic development, a greater concentration on the development of human resources, and their effective utilization for peaceful economic development.

NOTES

1. *Middle East Economic Digest*, London, 19 April, 1974, pp. 439–42, 457.

2. International Monetary Fund *International Financial Statistics*, October 1974, p. 126;The figures derive from the Central Bank of Egypt, *Report of the Board of Directors for the Year 1971–72*, p. 29; The report stated, e.g., that in fiscal 1971/1972, Arab grants to Egypt amounted to E£ 122.3 million—$ 281 million.

3. International Monetary Fund, *International Financial Statistics*, December 1974, pp. 310–11.

4. Galal Amin, *Food Supply and Economic Development–With Special Reference to Egypt*, (London, Frank Cass and Co., 1966) p. 125.

5. Economist Intelligence Unit, *Quarterly Economic Review*, June 1965, p.7.

6. See, e.g., Donald Mead, *Growth and Structural Change in the Egyptian Economy*, (Irwin, 1967) p. 209; and for more recent years, see, Economist Intelligence Unit, *Quarterly Economic Review*, No. 3, 1974, p.11.

7. US Department of Agriculture, *Indices of Agricultural Production in Africa and the Near East*, June 1974, p. 18, and earlier issues; population growth rates were derived from International Monetary Fund, *International Financial Statistics*, October 1974, p. 126, and *1972 Supplement*, pp. 198–99.

8. Federation of Egyptian Industries, *Yearbook 1972*, Statistical Section, p. 8; *Yearbook 1968*, p.4.

9. M. Clawson, H. H. Landsberg; L. T. Alexander, *The Agricultural Potential of the Middle East*, (American Elsevier, N.Y. 1971) pp. 3–6; 131–32.

10. Central Bank of Egypt, *Annual Report for 1965–66*, pp. 21–23.

11. During those periods industrial production was increasing by an average of over 6% annually, see Mead *op. cit.*, pp. 286–88.

12. National Bank of Egypt, *Economic Bulletin*, Vol. XXI, no. 3, Statistical Section 7/1. b. Industrial production includes manufacturing, mining, crude oil production and refining, electricity, gas, and water.

13. B. Hasen, "Planning and Economic Growth in the UAR, 1960–65," in P.J. Vatikiotis (ed.), *Egypt Since the Revolution*, (Allen and Unwin, London, 1968) p.26.

14. Fuad El Taher, "Entrepreneurship in the United Arab Republic": The Eve of the Economic Plan 1960–65", *Economic and Business Review*, 1969, p. 29.

15. For a more detailed analysis of the Five Year Plan and the period until the latter part of the 1960s, the reader is referred to E. Kanovsky, *The Economic Impact of the Six Day War: Israel; the Occupied Territories; Egypt; Jordan*, (Praeger, N.Y. 1970) Part III.

16. *Middle East Economic Digest*, 17 August, 1973, p. 944.

17. *Middle East Economic Digest*, 6 September, 1974, pp. 1019–1020.

18. *Middle East Economic Digest*, 30 August, 1974, pp. 997–98; 6 September, 1974, pp. 1019–20.

19. *Economist*, 2 November, 1974, p. 37.

20. Ziad Keilany "Socialism and Economic Change in Syria," *Middle Eastern Studies*, Vol.9, no.1, 1973, p. 61. Other estimates would indicate a growth rate of about 8% annually. See Syrian Arab Republic, *Statistical Abstract 1973*, pp. 762–63, and earlier issues. The latter present estimates of net domestic product at factor cost, in 1963 prices, going back to 1953.

21. Official national accounts are available only since 1950, but a mission of the World Bank which visited Syria in 1954 stated that "one of the most noteworthy features of the Syrian economy has been its rapid growth over the last two decades ... Agriculture and industry have both featured prominently in this development." See the International Bank for Reconstruction and Development, *The Economic Development of Syria*, (The Johns Hopkins Press, Baltimore, 1955) pp. 18–23. S. A. Makdisi estimated that the average growth rate of national income between 1946–1948 and 1955–1957 was about 8%. See S.A. Madisi, "Syria: Rate of Economic Growth and Fixed Capital Formation 1936–1968," *Middle East Journal*, (Washington, Spring 1971) Vol.25, No.2, p.163.

22. These estimates are based on the latest official revisions of the national income accounts. See Syrian Arab Republic, *Statistical Abstract 1973*, p. 758–59. Earlier official publications are often at complete variance with the latest publications. For example, the *Statistical Abstract 1968*, p. 430 presents an index of per capita national income which indicates that in 1964 it was 28.5% *lower* than in 1956. The revised estimates would indicate an *increase* of 6.9%. There are many other major contradictions in the various series presented.

23. *Middle East Economic Digest*, 5 April, 1974, p. 403.

24. This writer is working on a study of the economy of Syria as part of the research project of the Horowitz Institute of Tel Aviv University, "The Economic Implications of Peace in the Middle East." This study is scheduled for publication in 1977.

25. *The Economic Development of Syria*, 1955, pp. 18–23; Challah, *Economic Development and Planning in Syria, 1950–1962*, (Unpublished Ph.D. Dissertation, University of Oklahoma, 1965) pp.60–62.

26. US Department of Agriculture, *Indices of Agricultural Production in Africa and the Near East*, June 1974, p. 60, and earlier issues. Because of the wide annual fluctuations in Syrian agriculture, three-year periods are preferable as the terminal points.

27. United Nations, *Studies on Selected Development Problems in Various Countries in the Middle East*, 1971, p. 36; Syrian Arab Republic, *Statistical Abstract of Syria 1973*, p. 154.

28. *Middle East Economic Digest*, 2 August 1974, p. 88.

29. E. Kanovsky, *The Economic Development of Jordan*, (University Publishing Projects, Tel Aviv, 1976).

30. The Hashemite Kingdom of Jordan, *Three Year Development Plan 1973–1975*, p. 330.

31. For details and sources see E. Kanovsky, *The Economic Development of Iraq*, (The Horowitz Institute, Tel Aviv University, May 1974).

The Egyptian Economy
Between the two wars

Eliezer Sheffer

Egypt is a poor country with a per capita annual income of E£ 100, equivalent to approximately $ 200–250 (depending on whether official or effective rates exchange are used). It also has a rapidly growing population pressing on its limited natural resources and is facing formidable economic problems, which in recent years have been further aggravated by the continuing conflict with Israel. The growth record of the economy since the mid-1960s has been a poor one—less than four percent per annum. This rate was considerably lower than in most other developing nations and left only a narrow margin for raising average income levels. Out of this relatively small annual increment in total resources, a progressively growing share has been allocated to military expenditures, thus severely limiting the amount of resources available for development and improvement of the living standards of the population.

The efforts to advance rapidly and simultaneously on various fronts, which characterized Egyptian economic policy in the late 1950s and early 1960s, were successful only for a limited period. Despite the substantial amounts of foreign aid obtained in the early 1960s, it was soon realized that total resources did not suffice to meet simultaneously the requirements of a rapid military build up and an increase in the productive capacity of the economy and well-being of the population.

The shortage of foreign exchange became the dominant constraint on economic expansion. The first serious balance of payments crisis occurred in 1965, when Egypt was unable to repay its foreign debts and to finance its rapidly mounting import bill. This compelled the Government to introduce an austerity policy, aimed at reducing consumption and limiting development expenditures, for the purpose of saving foreign currency. The Six Day War of 1967 halted the resumption of economic recovery for several years. The consequences of the war were devastating to Egypt's economy, both directly and indirectly: the closure of the Suez Canal, the loss of the Sinai oilfields, the physical damage to the canal area and the decline in tourism intensified the economic recession. Total gross national product contracted by 2.5 percent in 1967–1968. Despite an annual grant totaling some $ 250 million from Arab oil-producing states following the Khartoum agreement of August 1967, Egypt was forced to further reduce its imports and development outlays, in order to balance its external accounts.

It now seems that the effects of the mounting military expenditures were even more detrimental to Egypt's economy than the direct damage. Egypt had never acknowledged the 1967 defeat, and immediately embarked on a military build-up and preparation for another war. This required an increasing share of total economic resources. Direct military spending, excluding the cost of weapons supplied by the USSR under special agreements (whose terms were never revealed), have risen from 9.5 percent of the GNP in the mid-1960s to 15 percent in 1970–1971, and to 20 percent of the GNP in the years 1973 and 1974. This was largely at the expense of investment which, as a consequence, declined from 18 percent of the GNP to only 12 percent. The cumulative amount of direct military expenditures exceeded E£ 5 billion throughout the period between the two wars. This amount is more than twice as high as that allocated for development in the same years. The decision to divert resources from civilian to military uses had far-reaching adverse effects on the Egyptian economy. Egypt's weak economy was cracking under such a heavy military effort; it is not surprising that the period between the two wars was one of very slow economic expansion and near-stagnation in per capita consumption levels.

Egypt's capacity to acquire substantial resources over and above its Domestic Product was severely restricted between the two wars, as net capital imports were of negligible size. Its default in repaying foreign obligations in 1965 and 1966 damaged its credit worthiness, thus adversely affecting its ability to mobilize substantial commercial capital inflows. Western official aid, particularly that of the United States, was sharply curtailed at the same time as a result of political developments. Both these factors thus limited the size of the exernal trade deficit, which therefore could not significantly exceed the amount of the Khartoum grant.

After a certain improvement in the trade account due to the restrictive impact of economic stagnation on the volume of imports, expansionary policies were introduced in the second half of 1968. Some recovery from the devastating setback of the June War took place in the late 1960s but without lasting effects. After two years of relatively rapid economic growth, the scarcity of foreign exchange forced a slowdown in industrial activity in 1970–1971 as import requirements rose sharply. The realities of a continuing conflict with Israel, for a poor economy like Egypt's, soon reappeared. The current account deficit reached a dimension which could no longer be sustained and under prevailing circumstances this resulted in a reduction of the rate of economic growth.

The poor economic record of Egypt between the two wars must be looked at in the context of the 1967 war and the heavy military burden which followed. The accelerated pace of preparations for the next war left no other choice but to postpone development projects, and along with this the hopes of the people for an improved standard of living, to a more distant future. This was the kind of trade-off facing Egypt between the two wars.

The path chosen by the Egyptian Government was obvious and so were its economic implications. This may perhaps be best illustrated by the way in which the incremental resources were allocated throughout the period between the two wars. During the decade preceding the Six Day War development expenditures absorbed 20 percent of additional resources; only 11 percent were allocated for military uses. Between the two wars, however, over 40 percent of the increment to the GNP was allocated for military purposes and nothing at all for development. The value of gross fixed investment in every single year between 1967 and 1974 was below the 1965–1966 level of about E£ 380 million which implies a sharp decline in the volume of investment outlays in constant prices.

Consequently, Egypt's industrial capital stock and public utilities infrastructure were run down, with all the adverse implications this trend implied for long-run growth potential. The immediate effects were growing unemployment and underemployment rates, despite the increased manpower demands for the armed forces, and under-utilization of existing capacity due to inadequate supplies of imported raw materials and intermediate goods. The balance of payments situation further deteriorated in mid-1972, when prices of imported wheat and other basic commodities started to rise sharply. Delays in the repayment of foreign debt occurred in the first half of 1973, and Egypt experienced a second serious crisis in less than a decade in its balance of payments. The importation of essential inputs had to be further restricted, resulting in utilization of only 70 percent of total industrial capacity.

THE EFFECT OF THE OCTOBER WAR

The October War broke out in the midst of a period when the economy was at near stagnation, with extreme shortage of foreign exchange and mounting external debt pressures. The composition of the outstanding debt of some $ 3 billion was unfavorable. One-third of the total obligations were in the form of short-term credits. Another 40 percent had to be repayed within two years. Total payments of interest and principal on the medium and long-term debt alone, scheduled for 1974, amounted to over $ 400 million—equivalent to almost 40 percent of commodity export earnings in 1973. This was in addition to the outstanding arrears, the need to settle at least a part of the military debt to the USSR and the necessity of assuring the extension of the short-term credit facilities. This was the background to which Sadat referred in a recent statement that: "Egypt was on the verge of collapse in the autumn of 1973, without a single piaster of hard currency to pay its debts and uncertainty about the availability of a loaf of bread in 1974."[1] Such an expression may be regarded as an overstatement. Nevertheless, when combined with other information now available, it apparently indicates the gloomy situation of the Egyptian economy in 1973.

The October War has dramatically changed the whole economic outlook. The consequences of this war were entirely different from those of the Six Day War. The physical damage incurred was very small, the defeat on the battlefield was not total and the crossing of the canal entailed important political and strategic gains. The new external relationships that have evolved between Egypt and the United States, and with other Western nations, as well as with the Arab oil-producing states, improved Egypt's prospects for future economic development.

The Arab oil-producing states started in October 1973 to accumulate enormous amounts of wealth. The extent of their generosity toward Egypt may be decisive in its attempt to achieve sustained economic growth. So far, the Arab oil-producing states have financed a great part of the direct cost of the October War, by paying to Soviet Russia an estimated $ 1 billion for deliveries of weapons to Egypt. Economic grants of $ 500 million over and above the annual Khartoum grant of $ 250 million were extended immediately after the war to support

Egypt's shaky balance of payments. In reference to these special grants, Sadat had been quoted as saying: "The country had been saved by $ 500 million worth of aid from our Arab brothers which would not have been forthcoming if the Suez Canal crossing had not been made."[2]
Thanks to Arab grants, Egypt was able to finance an enlarged foreign trade deficit of some $ 660 million in 1973 and settle various debt arrears. At the Arab Summit Conference in Rabat at the end of October 1974, it is believed that an estimated annual sum of $ 1.3 billion for military aid, for a period of four years, was pledged for Egypt.

In addition to Arab aid, Egypt will probably obtain an enlarged inflow of economic aid from Western powers and international institutions. The new circumstances and aspirations are reflected in the interim development plan for 1975 and the Five Year Development Plan for the period 1976–1980. For the first time in many years these plans entail a steep rise in the volume of development expenditure and raise new hopes for the economic future of Egypt.

Will the October War prove to be a turning point in the economic history of Egypt? Is it likely that the dream of generations to witness the abolition of the extreme poverty of the people will be realized? The answer to these questions largely depends on political developments in the Middle East. Egypt's economic situation still looked very dismal toward the end of 1974. Immense economic resources were needed to cope successfully with its formidable economic problems. The achievement of a lasting recovery and sustained economic growth in Egypt depends largely on a political settlement of the conflict with Israel. This would make possible the transfer of resources from military to development purposes and would enable Egypt to mobilize all its national energy to cope with economic and social difficulties. It appears that for the first time in Egypt's long history there is a real chance of economic takeoff, in light of the unprecedented amount of foreign aid that has been made available. However, continued military conflict in the Middle East might spoil the new opportunities.

NOTES

1. *Financial Times*, 30 November, 1974.

2. *Ibid*.

The Growth and Power
of the Middle East
Oil-Producing countries

Benjamin Shwadran

The changes which have taken place in the relations between the oil-producing countries in the Middle East and the concessionaire companies since 1967 have been far-reaching and revolutionary in character; we are now beginning to experience their consequences though their full implications are as yet unpredictable.

Ever since the development of the oil industry in the Middle East early in the 20th century, the producing countries have struggled to obtain a greater share of the benefits of the oil resources of their territories and better conditions for the operation of the industry. From some 16% share of profits or 4–6 shillings per ton of oil produced, or some combination of both, the producers achieved by mid-century a 50% profit share from production. But the companies remained masters of the situation. They regulated the levels of production; they set prices; they decided where the oil was to be refined; they controlled the transportation facilities of the oil; and they determined where and to whom it should be sold. Although there was a Western inter-company and inter-governmental struggle for concessions in the Middle East, and this in itself is a fascinating story, all the major oil companies (and until the 1950s there were no others) operated as a cartel, not only in commercial practices but also in their dealings with the producing countries. They formed a strong stone wall which the producers could not break; even the bold step of Iran in 1951 in nationalizing its oil industry was foiled by the companies, and in the guise of an international consortium, the oil continued to be exploited on the same terms. Even the united collective efforts of the Organization of Petroleum Exporting Countries, OPEC, failed and for nine years OPEC strove to restore the price cut of 1960 without success. The period may properly be described as the era of the dominance of the companies.

During the period 1967–1973, decisive changes and forces have brought about the transformation of the relations between the producers and the oil companies. Some were internal developments stemming from inter-Arab relations while others were external determinants.

Right after the outbreak of the 1967 Six Day Arab–Israeli War the representatives of the Arab oil-producing and transporting countries met on 4–5 June and decided to stop the flow of oil to world markets and to prevent Arab oil from reaching, directly or indirectly, any country which supported or was obligated to support Israel. On 6 June, Syria announced that she had closed all the pipelines from Iraq and Saudi Arabia which crossed her territory. On the same day Lebanon announced that she had banned the loading of Iraq and Saudi Arabian oil tankers at the terminal in her territory. On the following day Saudi Arabia banned the loading of tankers whose destination were countries which supported Israel, and prohibited the export of oil.

This development of instituting an oil boycott against the consuming countries because of political considerations was a radical innovation in the history of the modern Arab movement. For up to then, the major Arab producers steadfastly and persistently refused to permit their oil, which they considered their own economic resource, to become a political weapon of the Arab movement. Yet the outbreak of the war in June 1967 had emotionally swept the Arab world and in the electrified atmosphere the major producers gave up their persistent stand and adopted the above mentioned measures. But the negative economic consequences of those measures were soon apparent and the producers rushed to revoke them. Less than a week after Saudi Arabia had prohibited the export of oil, the government permitted Aramco to renew its normal operations, Kuwait resumed her oil exports on 14 June, Iraq on 15 and Libya on 5 July.

For it became clear to all producers, after calmer tempers prevailed, that they suffered more from the boycott than the Western countries against whom it was aimed. However, to obtain the formal approval of the cancellation of the boycott by the Arab Summit Conference meeting at Khartoum in August–September 1967, the three major producers, Saudi Arabia, Kuwait and Libya, had to pay a very high price: they had to obligate themselves to pay annually $ 135 million for the war losses of Egypt and Jordan.

An Arab countermove soon emerged and brought into being a new organization in the Middle East. The hasty oil boycott pointed out to the three conservative major oil producers (Libya was then a conservative monarchy) the danger that threatened their very existence when their oil was used for political ends. *Al Ahram* of 8 September, 1967, explained that if the boycott had continued the Arab oil producers would have lost their world oil markets forever, and that Saudi Arabia and Libya would have suffered from unemployment. Representatives of the three producers, therefore, met in Beirut in January 1968 and established the Organization of Arab Petroleum Exporting Countries (OAPEC) whose basic purpose was the protection of the economic character of their oil. Membership in the new organization was severely restricted and practically eliminated all other Arab League states from membership. The three major producers aimed at securing themselves against being swept again by highly emotional fever which would embroil their oil in the Arab political struggle. They were determined in setting up OAPEC to guarantee the uninterrupted flow of oil to world markets and safeguard the Western investments in developing the oil resources of the Middle East. (Under the pressure of events in the Arab world the primary purpose of OAPEC was eroded, and during subsequent years membership was expanded to include practically all Arab oil-producing countries. However, not until the outbreak of the October War of 1973 did it actually operate as a political body.)

On the other hand the oil boycott of 1967 had very little impact on the European oil supply system for it lasted a very short time, and the Western European countries had learned their lesson from the first closure of the Suez Canal in 1956 and weathered the crisis easily and sucessfully, and without the assistance of the United States.

The steadily increased world demand for oil which began after the Six Day War was perhaps of great consequence to the development of the Middle East oil story, while production in the region—because of sabotage and other factors—decreased. At the same time the relations between the United States and Western Europe as regards oil supplies became tense. If we add the fact that both oil production and reserves in the United States began to decline in the 1970s, we realize the forces which brought about the changes in the relations.

The first major turn in the relations between the producers and the companies was perhaps (after the *coup d'état* on 1 September, 1969) Libya's successful achievement in defiantly raising the posted prices practically unilaterally, and in obtaining other very favorable terms at the end of 1970. There could be no doubt that American fear that the

Western European countries might meet Libya's terms at the expense of the Anglo-Saxon companies prompted the State Department to persuade the companies to accede to Libya's demands. This Libyan accomplishment was the beginning of the process which reversed the relations between the producers and the companies, and which is speedily reaching the stage of total elimination of the concessionaire companies in the area of production. The producing countries have become the masters of the situation; at a very rapid pace, they have obtained one concession after another from the companies, and now regulate and determine all aspects of the industry. Unfortunately for all concerned—producers, consumers, companies and governments—the transformation was not gradual to allow for accommodations by stages; it occurred by sudden leaps and bounds, which did not allow the producers, the companies or the consumers sufficient time to make sane and reasonable adjustments. Hence the acuteness of the present crisis.

Beginning with the Tehran Agreement of February 1971, the producers have succeeded in raising the posted prices; they have increased their share of the profits, restricted the companies to ever-smaller areas for exploiting their concessions, and eliminated all sorts of discounts the companies had previously enjoyed. Royalties had been reckoned as expenses: prices were adjusted with devaluations of the dollar and the pound sterling. The producers at first obtained a 25% participation in the companies. Payment for the participation was decided on the basis of the companies' book value, even though the book value was somewhat modified.

With the outbreak of the 1973 October War the process continued at breakneck speed. The producing countries unilaterally fixed prices and raised them almost 400% in less than three months. The Arab producers set up an embargo and cut production. While Iraq nationalized the Iraq Petroleum Company (excluding the British and French shares in the Basrah Petroleum Company, a subsidiary of the Iraq Petroleum Company), Iran practically eliminated the consortium, and took over the entire oil industry, only allowing the consortium access for a limited period of time to quantities of oil at full market price, less a commission percentage; the other Persian Gulf producers later obtained 60% participation in the companies, again for book value, which gave them undisputed control over production. We are told by the spokesman of Saudi Arabia that the era of 100% ownership of the companies by the producing countries is about to be ushered in. We will shortly know whether he is a good prophet or not. The process will begin with Saudi Arabia, to be followed by the other Persian Gulf producers; indeed, two days after Saudi Arabia made its announcement, Abu Dhabi followed suit.

What brought about these revolutionary changes? They were caused neither by the Six Day nor the October War, nor entirely by the international or Middle Eastern political situation. The thesis submitted is that they were the result of economic factors which in turn gave the producing countries their political importance.

In addition to their technical knowledge and know-how, their gigantic financial resources necessary to maintain and constantly expand the oil industry and the required world markets to dispose of the huge quantities of oil produced, the concessionaire companies had two basic advantages over the producing countries. World demand for oil was smaller than the supply; the relentless pressure of the producing countries for increased production in order to obtain additional income necessary to meet the current budgets and development programs saturated world markets, and the companies could manipulate and curtail production. The second advantage of the companies was the United States oil resources as an alternative to Middle East oil. The oil reserves and the level of production in the United States, controlled mostly by the very same American companies which were the concessionaires in the Middle East, were always a powerful whip in the hands of the companies against the Middle East producing countries. This power was demonstrated, of course, in 1956, during the first Suez crisis.

With 1967 the entire pattern began to change. The world demand for oil began to rise. The expanded economic growth of the developed countries, and the efforts for economic growth of the underdeveloped and developing countries were all based on oil, oil products and by-products. This increased the importance of, and dependence on, the producing countries. At the same time, both the oil reserves and production in the United States were steadily declining, while the demand in the United States for oil and oil products was constantly and rapidly expanding. The United States was fast becoming an importer of Middle East oil instead of, as it used to be, an exporter. The era of the producers had arrived. The process began with OPECs new-found power to impose a constant rise in posted prices, and in the speedy growth and expansion of the national oil companies in all branches of the industry. The producing countries made demands for greater refining facilities in their territories both for home consumption and for exports; they organized tanker fleets—small to be sure, but steadily expanding—to transport their oil. The march of the producers was proceeding apace and the world was inevitably approaching the energy crisis.

The October War of 1973 simply shifted the crisis to the center of world's political stage, and the world was sidetracked, unfortunately, from seeking a real solution. The panic which had overtaken the consumers was traumatic and they were confused, hysterical and demoralized in their immediate reactions to the crisis and by its potentially disastrous consequences. In addition to, and as a consequence of, the much higher prices of oil, the balance of payments problems of the consumer countries (which had been severe even before) now became acute. The outlook became gloomier with every price increase. The producers' oil revenues were no longer reckoned in millions, nor even in hundreds of millions, but in tens and even hundreds of billions of dollars. The industrialized nations would accumulate gigantic payment deficits, and the developing nations could not possibly survive for lack of means to purchase the oil, its products and by-products.

Because of the level of economic development, most of the producers could not possibly invest the bulk of their oil income in economic projects in their own lands—through purchases of capital goods and services in the consumer countries—nor would they invest them in long-term projects in those countries. Huge surpluses were accumulating in the hands of the major producing countries, which were a potential means of dominating and intimidating, if not manipulating, the financial and monetary structure of the Western world. The magnitude of the surpluses was at least frightening, if not terrifying. Various studies by financial and monetary institutions of high repute have predicted producer surpluses of $ 500 billion in 1985, provided prices remain stable until then. One study predicted a surplus of $ 1200 billion in 1989. A study initiated by the European Economic Community concluded that, even with the most optimistic outlook of high investments by the producing countries in Europe, and drastic reduction in the levels of consumption of the market members, the deficit in the balance of payments from the import of oil for five market countries would reach more than 90 billion dollars in 1978. The prospects would become even more ominous should the price of oil continue to rise.

The recycling of the petrodollar, should it succeed, might be a temporary stopgap to ease the pressure of the deficit. But it implies the acceptance of the high oil prices by both Europe and the United States. Before dealing with the problem of recycling, however, the basic issue, namely that of prices and supplies, should be tackled. The consequences of the energy crisis are a double threat, endangering the normal flow of oil to the consuming countries, and exposing their financial and monetary structures to willful manipulation by the producing countries. Is the situation as dismal as emerges from this picture? Are the consuming countries at the absolute mercy of the producers? Have developments since October 1973 been completely negative and hopeless? It would seem that, in spite of the bombastic boasts and threats by Arab spokesmen, a careful analysis of the pattern of events since the energy crisis would reveal a very cautious, hesitant retreat of the major Arab producers.

Let us begin with the embargo, unleashed especially against the United States for its direct support of Israel. It started with the most extreme ultimatum—the embargo would be lifted only after Israel had withdrawn from all occupied areas and the rights of the Palestinian Arabs had been guaranteed. In order to force the issue, the cut in supplies was to be increased each month by 5% until the terms were met. Less than two weeks later it was reported that the terms had been reduced to a timetable for Israeli withdrawal guaranteed by the United States; the monthly cutback of 5% was stopped and 10% of the cut was restored.

Ultimately, less than five months from its initiation, the embargo was lifted, even against the United States, and without any of the conditions having been met. All cutbacks were restored and production levels were in fact increased. As to the price of Middle East oil (the so-called posted price), it remained stationary from December 1973. All attempts by various interests and for a variety of reasons to increase the price were stubbornly, persistently and systematically stopped by OPEC every three months when its members met. True, the oil companies were steadily and consistently stripped of their interests and share in the profit, but prices remained stable. There were even pressures among the producers, weak pressures to be sure, to reduce the price level. Both OPEC and OAPEC have displayed an almost pathological fear of the formation of a consumers' organization to protect its members against the pressures and demands of the producer organizations. If indeed, as the producers' spokesmen often assert, they hold all the winning cards and the consuming countries are at their mercy, then the exaggerated fear and hysterical threats against the consumers' attempts at union are quite incomprehensible. These three indicators, among others, reveal the economic character of the struggle and the potential and real weakness of the position of the producers.

Despite OPEC's facade of unity of purpose and action, its member states have conflicting interests and objectives. In the end, they all—in differing degrees and for various purposes—depend on the consuming countries to take their oil and supply the revenue for the oil. Though they may disavow it piously or indignantly, they all dread the development and application of alternative sources of energy. Above all, they are afraid of a really strong and united consumers' union which by purely economic means could break their power. These factors have influenced the development and character of the embargo, which in the final analysis (except for the price increases) was totally ineffective. In spite of the extreme demands of the radical members of OAPEC, the embargo was lifted. In spite of the threats of the radicals to reduce production, Middle East oil production in 1973 was 16.9% higher than that of 1972, while the total world increase in output was only 9.2%. Iraq showed an increase of 35%, Saudi Arabia 28% and Abu Dhabi 26%, and with it the fourfold increase in billions of dollars. Of the major producers with huge revenue surpluses, only Kuwait actually reduced production (by about 8.2%), but the practice of restricting production in Kuwait long antedates the 1973 crisis.

It would seem that all the Middle Eastern producers, with the exception of Kuwait, are determined not only to maintain but also to increase production. It is as a result of economic considerations that prices were not increased, and Saudi Arabia was, apparently, sincerely desirous to reduce oil prices. Stabilization and certainly any reduction of prices would achieve two ends: it would make it possible for the consuming countries to buy more oil which the Middle Eastern countries are still interested in producing, and would—and this is perhaps more important—slow down or completely stop the development of alternatives. The fear of a consumers' union is well-founded, for such a union would indeed be capable of undoing some of the achievements and advantages of the producers. The inevitable conclusion, therefore, is that the only solution to the energy crisis, and its very dangerous financial and economic consequences, is a strong consumers' organization that would come to grips with OPEC, and out of which would emerge a solution which would make it possible for both to continue to exist and operate on the basis of mutual interdependence, rather than by the domination of one by the other.

The consuming countries, should they all unite, have at their command many powerful weapons. They can reduce consumption to a degree that would cause very serious damage to the production levels of the producing countries, even if prices are maintained artifically; they can speed-up the development and application of the various alternatives to oil; they can intensify production from newly discovered oil and gas-fields; and finally they can mobilize all their economic resources to force the producers through purely economic means (without boycotts, military invasions or confrontation), in principle not unlike the measures employed by the producers, to reduce prices and maintain supplies. What is sauce for the goose is sauce for the gander.

The consumers are moving in the direction of uniting and exercizing their power in the newly formed International Energy Agency. It is naturally a slow process, for the European nations—even though most of them, except France, are members of the IEA—are in it with only one foot, and are still torn between ultimate dependence on the United States in case, as they see it, IEA becomes a strong and determined counterfront to OPEC and antagonizes the Middle Eastern countries, and dependence on those very Arab countries, in the hope that by playing along with the Arabs they may arrive at some sort of understanding with them. For it is generally felt that the United States can afford to assume a strong position because its own energy resources would more than meet all its needs in times of necessity, while Europe and Japan must ultimately draw their oil from the Middle East.

However, such irresolution can only aggravate the situation. It would be at the expense of the United States, and even further decimate the Western nations, while solving nothing. A strong united front of the consumers is the only means of solving the crushing problem facing the Western World. Should IEA succeed, if and when it picks up momentum, then all the consumers will realize that it is their only alternative; then the murky international political situation might perhaps clear and the outlook become brighter.

The
Inter-Arab
Setting

Inter-Arab Relations

Daniel Dishon

The first part of this paper deals descriptively and in approximate chronological order with the shifting pattern of alliances and rivalries in inter-Arab relations between the June 1967 Six Day War and the 1973 October War. The second part relates to questions regarding the institutionalized forms of inter-Arab cooperation, the degree of solidarity achieved, and the role of Egypt as the focal state in the Arab world.

SHIFTING PATTERNS OF INTER-ARAB RELATIONS

"Progressives" versus "Reactionaries"

The period between the two wars represents a meaningful span of time in terms of inter-Arab relations. The Six Day War was clearly a turning point in the configuration of camps and combinations in the Arab world. On the eve of the war, the main principle of alignment and division was between those Arab states and regimes which styled themselves "progressive" and those which the "progressives" labeled "reactionaries."

The division into these two opposing camps produced the deepest split and constituted the most clearly defined cleavage the Arab world had known since the establishment of the Arab League in 1945. In the years 1965, 1966 and 1967 (until the war), the "two-camp" pattern came to be recognized and accepted as basic to the Arab scene, and the two terms: "progressive" and "reactionary" were common parlance.

The "battle order" issued by the then Supreme Commander of the Egyptian Armed Forces, Field Marshal (*mushir*) 'Abd al-Hakim Amer, on 14 May, 1967[1] illustrates how deeply rooted were these concepts. In its two short pages, the term *ad-duwal al-mutaharrira* ("the states liberating themselves"—a synonym for "progressive" states) appears 11 times, recurring in all the document's key phrases. It is obvious the author assumed that his readers (and listeners) knew exactly to which Arab countries the term was applicable and to which it was not. This assumption was perhaps not altogether justified, but the very fact that it was made and that a text as important as the "battle order" was drafted accordingly, is significant in itself. Moreover, the entire text is couched in terms implying that war against Israel was the concern of the "progressives" only. It went without saying that the "reactionaries" were not expected to take part in it. Furthermore, the wording gave a strong hint that the forthcoming war was likely to put an end to the "reactionary" regimes.

Only one month after Amer's order was issued, however, a totally new constellation of forces had come into being—partly as a result of the Arab states having closed ranks on the eve of the war, and partly as a result of its outcome. Against the background of the war, and with the emergence of a similar approach on the part of King Hussein and President Abdel Nasser toward the handling of the post-war situation, the Cairo–Amman axis was formed—an alliance between "socialist, revolutionary Egypt" and monarchical Jordan. The pattern of "progressives" versus "reactionaries" had been broken.

Another factor which contributed to the break up of this pattern was Egypt's growing dependence on the good graces of such arch-conservatives as King Faisal of Saudi Arabia, Shaykh as-Sabah of Kuwait and King Idris of Libya for their financial support.

At the other end of the old model, relations between Egypt and Syria, which together had formed the core of the former "progressive" camp, now rapidly deteriorated. The Egyptian–Syrian rift emerged in part because of Egypt's interpretation of the events leading to the Six Day War. In retrospect, the Egyptians came to feel that Syria had dragged Egypt into the war through false allegations of Israeli troop concentrations along the Israeli–Syrian border. When war actually came about, Syria had remained virtually inactive along its front. Later, the rift widened because of the ideological intransigence of Syria: almost alone in the Arab world Syria remained faithful to the earlier concepts and the old division into two camps. It was only in 1971, following Hafiz al-Asad's takeover late in 1970, that Syria began to revise its inter-Arab policy.

The "two-camp pattern" was thus disrupted within a very short time. This is not to say, however, that the division vanished completely. Awareness of the common characteristics which the "progressives" attributed to themselves (assumption of power through a military *coup*, an "anti-imperialist" foreign policy, Arab or Islamic socialism) did not entirely disappear. It became a kind of undercurrent, surfacing only rarely during the six years under review. Its residual existence made possible the occasional revival and exploitation of the appeal it had once held. All in all, however, during the six interwar years the answer to the essential issue governing inter-Arab relations, the question of who sides with whom and who opposes whom, was no longer dependent on the ideological factor, nor on the affinity of similar regimes.

Territories versus Principles

Instead, the issue which now determined the position of each Arab state in the web of inter-Arab relations was what the Arabs termed the "elimination of the traces of aggression." The basic division was between those who gave first priority to the regaining of their territories lost in the 1967 war, relegating to secondary importance their adherence to the principles which had guided the struggle against Israel, as against those whose first priority was "ideological purity" and faithfulness to the principles to which they had been committed for about twenty years, even though in the realm of practical politics such an approach made it more difficult to regain what they had lost. It was in the nature of things that those states which had lost territories belonged to the first group, while those which had not, belonged to the second. Syria constituted the exception: though part of its land was under Israeli occupation, it dissociated itself from Egypt and Jordan, and remained loyal both to the slogans of "the path of armed struggle" and to the ties of the "progressive" camp. This was the root cause of Syria's isolation within the Arab world, which lasted until Asad's rise to power in November 1970.

The new configuration evolved at the end of 1967, after the passing of Security Council Resolution 242 and the appointment of Gunnar Jarring, and found its earliest expression in the division between those who accepted the resolution (Egypt, Jordan, Lebanon) and those who rejected it (all the others). The rejection of the resolution on the part of the latter group, except for Syria, was purely declamatory, since none of their territories had been conquered and they had nothing to gain in any case from accepting it. Jordan and Egypt, for their part, did not make significant progress through their contacts with Jarring, and Egypt's main efforts were soon directed to the conduct of the War of Attrition. As a result, it was possible, until the Suez Canal ceasefire of August

1970, to blur the contrast between supporters and opponents of Resolution 242. The key phrase for Arab solidarity became: the "spirit of Khartoum"; i.e., the consensus—wide but not total—which was reached at the first Arab summit conference after the Six Day War, held in Khartoum in August and September of 1967.

A New Configuration

During the years 1968–1969 and up to the ceasefire which ended the War of Attrition in August 1970, the following basic configuration thus emerged:

- A Jordanian–Egyptian axis. The two states closely coordinated their stands at the UN, and their attitudes toward Jarring's mission and toward the Great Power talks on the Middle East.
- A loose grouping of the majority of Arab states which favored vague expressions like "the spirit of Khartoum," while neither supporting nor opposing the line taken by Egypt and Jordan.
- Two states which dissociated themselves from the rest: Syria at the radical, revolutionary, "progressive" extreme, and Saudi Arabia at the conservative extreme. Their attitudes found expression, *inter alia*, in their consistent refusal to take part in a new Arab summit meeting repeatedly called for by Jordan and Egypt. Indeed, it took two years to overcome Saudi Arabia's resistance before a new summit meeting was convened (in December 1969, in Rabat).

The reasons for Saudi Arabia's voluntary isolation were more complex than those of Syria. A combination of factors was at work. Some were rooted in Saudi "realpolitik," especially as regards the Arabian Peninsula: the war in Yemen flared up again a few months after the 1967 War, and the Saudis were therefore unwilling to cooperate with Egypt.[2] Another factor concerned money: at Khartoum, Saudi Arabia had agreed to pay the agreed upon "ransom" (i.e., an annual subsidy to be paid to Egypt and Jordan until "the elimination of the traces of aggression"), but it was plain that the other Arab states considered its contribution insufficient. The Saudis anticipated that at every inter-Arab meeting, and especially at a summit conference, new financial demands would be made on them and therefore sought to avoid such meetings.

Furthermore, Saudi Arabia had no desire to participate in any inter-Arab forum so long as the agenda included the Jarring mission, the Four Power talks, the Two Power talks, or any other attempt to attain a political settlement with Israel. King Faisal seemed to be waiting for the moment when he could say to the other Arab leaders: "All your various ways have failed; we have kept our own council and no one can accuse us of readiness to compromise over a settlement with Israel. Now that you have seen the error of your ways, start listening to me."

Low Tide of Pan-Arabism

The years 1968 and 1969 thus marked a low point in Pan-Arab activities. They were years which witnessed a relative rise in the strength of *wataniyya* (the patriotism of the individual state) as opposed to *qawmiyya* (Pan-Arab nationalism). The credibility of Egypt declined in the eyes of the Arab world, and its ability to exercise Arab leadership diminished. The general picture of the Arab world was one of a group of states lacking leadership, orientation and a common purpose.

Two "non-events" are striking evidence of this situation. Firstly, the Rabat summit conference failed in its objectives and Abdel Nasser himself explicitly acknowledged its outcome as a total failure.[3] Not one of the participating states was prepared to commit itself clearly to any concrete plan of future all-Arab action against Israel, though this was the central issue of the conference. Characteristically, four states boycotted the closing session: Iraq and Syria, because, to their minds, none of the anti-Israeli resolutions adopted were sufficiently warlike and radical; and Yemen and South Yemen, because their quarrel with Saudi Arabia, for all its marginality to the issues under discussion, was more important to them than the success of the summit.

The second "non-event" was the failure of Egypt to overcome the quarrels and mistrust between Jordan, Iraq and Syria so as to enable the so-called Eastern Command to become operational. (The Command was intended to coordinate the operations of the Syrian, Jordanian and Iraqi armies, and of the Fidayeen along the Syrian–Israeli and Jordanian–Israeli ceasefire lines with the purpose of waging a war of attrition there similar to the one then in progress along the Suez Canal.) On paper, the Command had been set up; in fact it did not operate.

In the light of subsequent events, it is worth noting that a war of attrition—i.e., a war limited in nature and static by definition—does not arouse the enthusiasm of the Arab world as did the wars of 1948, 1967 and 1973. Long before Egypt itself did so, the other Arab states came to regard static warfare as futile. The Egyptian attempt to draw the armies of Jordan, Syria and Iraq into a war of attrition on their respective fronts failed. The experience of having stood alone along the Canal was to become an important component of the Egyptian collective memory, strengthening Egyptian "separatism" as against Pan-Arab sentiment.

The Impact of the 1970 Ceasefire

Egypt's standing in inter-Arab affairs reached its low point in August 1970, when Abdel Nasser agreed to end hostilities along the Suez Canal. The latent split which had been implicit in the pattern of Arab relations since the end of 1967 was now clearly exposed. Egypt's acceptance of the ceasefire and the "Rogers initiative," and its agreement to renew Jarring's mission, now brought into sharp relief the contrast between those who had accepted Resolution 242 and those who had rejected it. Only Jordan stood by Egypt; most other Arab states, as well as the Palestinian organizations, withheld their support—some silently, others vociferously. They had not backed Egypt in the War of Attrition, but now condemned Cairo for terminating it (as Egyptian commentators bitterly observed on numerous occasions).[4] King Hussein's declaration addressed to Abdel Nasser—"Whatever you accept, I shall accept as well"[5] remained the only substantial encouragement Egypt received from any quarter in the entire Arab world.

Within one month, this nadir in Egypt's fortunes led to a reversal of the alliances in the Arab world which was both absurd and tragic. Abdel Nasser found himself compelled to aid his opponents in order to protect them from his only supporter: i.e., to rescue the Fidayeen in Jordan from Hussein. Only a few weeks earlier the Fidayeen movements had spoken out so vehemently against Egypt's new policy that Nasser had had to close the two broadcasting stations which he had placed at their disposal in Cairo. Yet such was the strength of inter-Arab pressures prompted by anti-Israeli and pro-Fidayeen sentiments, so pressing seemed the need to restore Egypt to a stronger position in the Arab world, that Nasser preferred to reverse his course. It is possible that his initial hesitations were deliberate, and that he delayed taking political action against Hussein until military developments in Jordan had clearly put the Fidayeen at a disadvantage. But in the final analysis he acted in September 1970 ("Black September") to rescue those who, in August (on the day following the Suez Canal ceasefire), had labeled him a "coward," and to stay the hand of the one Arab ruler who had sided with him.

Abdel Nasser's Death

The intervention in Jordan turned out to be Abdel Nasser's last political act. His death, on 28 September, initiated a new period in which centrifugal forces were to become stronger and more recognizable and to reassert themselves even in Egypt (cf. p. 195). In 1971 and the first half of 1972, regional foci crystallized; much multilateral Arab activity centered around them, but they did not become all-Arab concerns. One such focus was the Persian Gulf; there King Faisal of Saudi Arabia began his ascent to the rank of a central and active figure in inter-Arab affairs. Another focus—connected with the first—was the southern part of the Arabian Peninsula (the problems of Yemen and South Yemen). Yet another focus was North Africa, where a tendency emerged for the three North African states to draw more closely together.

However, the death of Abdel Nasser did not have an exclusively destructive effect on inter-Arab relations: Arab governments ceased fearing Egyptian subversion, and for that very reason eventually found it easier to let Sadat's Egypt take the lead again. Egyptian subversive activities (unlike the fear they generated) had actually ceased after the 1967 War, mainly as a result of Egypt's dependence on subsidies from the conservative regimes. It is noteworthy, in this context, that the Libyan and Sudanese *coups*—both in 1969—came about for local reasons and were not a result of Egyptian subversion or instigation. But fear and suspicion of the man who, during the 1950s and early 1960s, had attempted to overthrow virtually every regime in the Arab world, remained alive as long as Abdel Nasser did. When his charismatic and overpowering figure disappeared from the scene, and his mass appeal no longer had to be feared, there was initially less inclination to accord Egypt first place; but later on, when Sadat began to reassert his country's position, cooperation with him was accompanied by far less anxiety.

During the first year of Sadat's presidency, the emergence of the Federation of Arab Republics was at the center of inter-Arab developments. This is the subject of a separate paper in this book (see pp. 171-85), and will therefore not be dealt with here.

Toward the 1973 Wartime Coalition

At the end of 1971, the credibility of Egypt, and of Sadat personally, were almost nil largely because that year—which Sadat had proclaimed to be the "year of decision"—had ended so indecisively. During 1972, however, through a process many details of which are yet unknown, the credibility of Egypt was gradually rebuilt. New links were forged with those Arab states which were afterwards Egypt's chief allies in the October War.

It would appear that the military coalition was formed in concentric circles. The innermost circle comprised Egypt, Syria and Saudi Arabia. Only the Syrian leadership seems to have shared the secrets of operational planning. Saudi Arabia was apparently aware of the broad outline of the war plans and gave Egypt unstinting support. It was Saudi Arabia's financial backing which enabled Egypt to finance its military preparations. An intermediate circle comprised states which took on themselves certain specified obligations and partly fulfilled them even before the outbreak of war (for example, by sending to Egypt aircraft of Western manufacture). This group included—besides Saudi Arabia—Kuwait, Iraq, Sudan and Algeria. The remaining states formed the outer circle: their obligations and promises were vaguer and, in fact, their help was enlisted only during the first days of the war.

Again there were two states which stood apart: Libya which, even before the outbreak of the war, objected to it as "the wrong kind of war," and then cooperated with Egypt only with great reluctance while the war lasted; and Jordan, which did not believe the Arab armies had much of a chance, and eventually participated only at one remove (by sending a contingent to Syria but keeping the Jordanian–Israeli front quiet).

For Syria, the outbreak of the 1973 war marked the completion of its transition from the isolation of 1967 to the position of chief ally of Egypt. Simultaneously, Jordan traveled along the same road in the opposite direction.

What, then, were the general characteristics of the new coalition, constructed from the middle of 1972 onward and during the first ten months of 1973? For one thing, it provided additional confirmation that the previous pattern of "progressives" and "reactionaries" was no longer relevant. Within the previous two-camp pattern nothing could have been more incompatible than Egypt being closely linked to Syria and Saudi Arabia at one and the same time; yet, in 1973, the combination worked. It succeeded because the decisive criterion for Arab alignments had ceased to be the ideological classification of regimes; in its place the issues of the Arab–Israeli conflict had become the crucial guiding principle. Its application enabled Syria and Saudi Arabia to belong to the same camp.[6] Another characteristic was the reemergence of Egyptian centrality in the Arab world.

THE EMERGENCE OF NEW TRENDS

Inter-Arab Institutions Ignored

A salient characteristic of the entire period between the two wars, but one particularly in evidence during 1972 and 1973, was the abandonment by the Arab states of attempts to make inter-Arab cooperation dependent on the attainment of "institutionalized" forms. Almost all the measures taken and the contacts made in order to set up the October War coalition occurred outside the framework of existing inter-Arab institutions.

The Arab League played no part (except, perhaps, certain tasks undertaken by the Arab foreign ministers' meeting in Kuwait in November 1972, and by the League's Defense Council at its meeting in Cairo in January 1973). The institutions of the Federation of Arab Republics were not involved, despite the fact that the Federation's constitution empowers its Presidential Council to decide "on matters of peace and war."[7] The entire structure of alliance was erected through contacts which were mainly bilateral, or in small, informal groupings removed from any institutional setting. Even the one inter-Arab framework which had remained most universally accepted as an institution—the summit conference—did not act as an instrument for the preparation of the war, but was only convened after the war had ended.

This was more than just a change of method. The abandonment (for the time being) of the search for "institutionalized," constitutional forms of Arab unity signified de facto recognition of a trend which dates back to an earlier period: the break-up of the United Arab Republic in 1961. The after-effects of that traumatic experience have been evident ever since, in the recurrent use of the euphemistic term "the lessons of the past" whenever Arab unity and solidarity were under discussion. After 1961, the belief in the imminent establishment of a comprehensive Arab state "from the Atlantic Ocean to the Persian Gulf" could no longer be sustained. Gradually, the idea of comprehensive unity ceased to be a program of action for practical politics and became a vision of a distant, almost messianic future. In terms of immediate political action the sovereignty of separate Arab states came to be recognized as an existing fact. While lip service continued to be paid to the concepts of all-embracing unity, Arab governments could now afford to act as sovereign bodies without constant fear of criticism and without constantly having to measure up to the idea and the ideals of unity. The individual state as a sovereign entity had shown itself to be stronger than the many constitutional and statutory schemes, as well as the actual and projected federal and confederative plans which had been marshaled against it over the preceding 30 years. Each country had kept its army as the instrument of sovereign national policy, rather than subjecting it to the demands of the Collective Security Pact (1950) or the United Arab Command (1964). (The failure of an inter-Arab observer staff—which operated in Jordan in 1970 and 1971 to watch over the implementation of the Cairo Agreement between the Jordanian Government and the Fidayeen—belongs in the same context.)

A comparison between the structure (and even the very name) of the United Arab Republic, as it evolved between 1958 and 1961, and that of the Federation of Arab Republics, illustrates how much the idea of unity as an institutionalized process had lost in strength and persuasiveness in the decade between the breakup of the UAR and the establishment of the FAR in 1971: the institutions of the UAR were meant to govern; those of the FAR were at best intended to achieve coordination between a group of sovereign states.

The prevalence of these more recent tendencies and the pragmatic adjustment to their existence on the part of most Arab governments constitute the background to Qadhafi's outbursts against them.[8] He remained committed to the earlier concepts. Perhaps this is related to the fact that he (alone among present Arab leaders) had not yet become a public figure when the "lessons of the past" were learned. When he watched the entire Arab world moving toward acceptance of the new trends, Qadhafi came out, in 1972, with the suggestion of "merger unity" (*indimaj*) with Egypt—the final *cri de coeur* of a world outlook which already belonged to the past. It was the almost universally skeptical reception of Qadhafi's project which helped Sadat to revoke the promises made to Qadhafi a year earlier—in a moment of weakness—to avoid other pressures.

Solidarity Strengthened

Did greater acceptance of national sovereignty and the abandonment of rigid forms of cooperation yield a larger measure of solidarity for the

Arabs in 1973 as compared to 1967? The answer is undoubtedly affirmative, though it needs qualification.

Reference should be made to three areas: the oil embargo, financial aid and military aid. The oil embargo of 1973–1974 was perceived by the Arabs as an act of solidarity, which indeed it was. But paralleling the inter-Arab motive, purely economic incentives were at work: in economic terms, the time was right to obtain a rise in oil prices which would have seemed fantastic a year earlier. Yet, the concerted timing on the part of the oil-producing states, and their linking of the oil embargo to the aims of the October War, made the "oil weapon" an instrument of solidarity. As such, it left a powerful impression on the Arabs, who seized on it as a significant new element in the overall situation (especially in comparison with 1967, when the same attempt, made under different world economic conditions, failed altogether).

The financial aid rendered to the two "frontline states," before, during and after the October War, was undoubtedly much greater than in 1967 or in the inter-war years. It is, however, possible that the sum total of financial assistance, if calculated as a percentage of "free" income of the donors, decreased rather than increased.

Military cooperation in 1973 embraced more countries than in 1967. Some Arab states which had not taken part at all in the Six Day War (Morocco, Libya), or which had come too late to join the fighting (Algeria), actively participated in the 1973 October War. Not only were the expeditionary forces larger and from a greater number of states, but several of them also constituted a relatively greater proportion of the total combat strength of the states which sent them to the front. This was especially true of the Iraqi contingent in Syria which, in 1973, comprised a much higher percentage of Iraq's entire fighting force than did the contingent despatched to Jordan in 1967. Algeria and Kuwait also apparently sent a greater proportion of their total combat strengths to the fronts than had been the case in 1967.

Egypt–the Key Country

To conclude, a few words on Egypt as the "key country" in the Arab world—an expression which Muhammad Hasanayn Heikal used,[9] and which seems to describe the position of Egypt in the inter-war years most accurately. It was not a position of hegemony or of leadership, since in the period under review Egypt had neither the strength nor the means to force on the Arab governments a line unpopular with them.

Yet, the centrality of Egypt existed in a real sense. It was seen to operate both positively and negatively. In the former case, when Egypt's credibility was high and it believed itself capable of acting—it immediately became the very focus of Arab activity. In the latter case, when—due to weakness, domestic problems or marked inferiority in the conflict with Israel—Egypt was rendered incapable of taking the lead in inter-Arab affairs, no one else was able to take its place.

During the period here reviewed, three attempts were made by leaders of other Arab states to set the tone in inter-Arab affairs. The first attempt was by Houari Boumedienne, who immediately after the 1967 Six Day War tried to appear as the spokesman of all the Arabs. Within weeks, at the Khartoum summit, he found himself on the outer fringe of Arab affairs. The attitude towards Algeria on the part of the delegates to the summit, and the impression this made on Boumedienne, marked the beginning of Algeria's withdrawal from the "Arab East," and its subsequent concentration on North African and domestic issues. Next, Iraq made one of its customary attempts, noted at every stage of inter-Arab developments, to establish itself as the recognized champion of the Arab cause. This came to a head in August 1970, when Iraq attempted to take the lead in forming an Arab coalition against Egypt, against the "Rogers initiative," against the Suez Canal ceasefire, and against what it termed the "abandonment of the cause of the Fidayeen." Thirdly, Qadhafi attempted, after the death of Abdel Nasser, to don the deceased leader's mantle.

The three attempts had one thing in common: all of them failed.

At no time during these years was Egypt strong enough to make the Arab world at large adopt policies for which a fairly wide consensus did not exist in any case. At all times, Egypt remained strong enough to prevent any prospective rival from replacing it at the center of the stage. Looking at the Arab scene as a whole, this is one of the most significant conclusions to be drawn from the course of events between 1967 and 1973.

NOTES

1. *Amr qital raqm 1 ila dubbat wajunud al-quwat al-musassaha*, 14 May, 1975; reprints of the order, as distributed to Egyptian army units at the time, available in the Shiloah Center archives.

2. For the significance of the war in Yemen in inter-Arab relations, see *Middle East Record 1967*, pp. 107-09, 122-29, 140, 594-612; *MER 1968*, pp. 187-92, 835-45.

3. *Radio Cairo*, 24 December, 1969; *al-Ahram*, 5 January, 1970.

4. For example, *al-Ahram*, 4 August, 1970.

5. *Radio Amman*, 26 July 1970.

6. In addition to considerations stemming from Saudi Arabia's stand in the Arab–Israeli conflict, this change in Saudi attitudes was influenced by the cessation of hostilities in Yemen (where the war had virtually ended in 1970), by the expulsion of the Soviet advisers from Egypt in 1972 and the subsequent weakening of Soviet–Egyptian ties, and by Faisal's conviction that developments in the Persian Gulf area had taken a turn which now allowed him freedom of action elsewhere.

7. *Al-Ahram*, 18 April, 31 August, 1971.

8. For example, his statement that the FAR would lead to unity "a hundred years from now"; *Kull Shay'*, 19 August, 1972.

9. "*Balad al-miftah*," *al-Ahram*, 24 March, 1972; in a similar sense—"*quwat at-tamasuk*" ("rallying power"), *al-Ahram*, 14 April, 1972.

The Federation
of Arab Republics

Varda Ben-Zvi

While the major trends described in the preceding paper were unfolding, an attempt was made at creating a formal framework of Arab unification, which contrasted oddly with the prevalent approach and the reluctance to form supra-national bodies. The Federation of Arab Republics, the antecedents of which date back to 1969, was a somewhat atavistic attempt to apply ideological precepts which had been prevalent in earlier periods of Arab nationalism in its "Unionist"—i.e., pan-Arab—mould, and to translate them into a program for action. It mirrored approaches prevalent in the past but no longer fashionable at the time the scheme was conceived. It assumed a faith in the attainability of new and larger, formally constituted Arab political units which did, in fact, no longer exist. Yet it resulted, in 1971, in the establishment of an institutionalized federal organization binding together several Arab states and—technically speaking—still in existence at the time of writing. The fact that it ran counter to the dominant trend of the time—a reliance on solidarity based on *ad hoc* arrangements—largely accounts for the fact that, almost immediately, it became totally ineffectual.

CHRONOLOGY OF EVENTS

The following chronological outline lists the main stages which led to the establishment of the Federation of Arab Republics.

In May and September 1969, respectively, military *coups* brought new regimes to power in Sudan and Libya. The new leaders, Ja'far an-Numeiri and Mu'ammar al-Qadhafi, both described the change of government in their respective countries as a revolution which purportedly followed the footsteps of Jamal Abdel Nasser's Egyptian revolution and declared their desire to forge close relations with Egypt.

Numeiri would have been satisfied with the strengthening of bilateral ties between Egypt and Sudan, but at the prodding of Qadhafi, the three leaders—Abdel Nasser, Numeiri and Qadhafi—met in December 1969 in Tripoli. On 27 December, 1969, a joint communiqué was published which, after a few weeks, became known in the Egyptian media as the "Tripoli Charter."[1] Cooperation between Egypt, Sudan and Libya was based on this Charter until November 1970.

On 8 November, 1970, at the conclusion of the first series of talks held after Nasser's death, the leaders of the "Tripoli Charter States," Anwar Sadat, Numeiri and Qadhafi, proclaimed their decision to draw a plan for the establishment of a federation (*ittihad*). In mid-November 1970, Hafiz al-Asad took control of the Syrian regime following a long period of internal strife. A brief visit by Asad to Cairo resulted in Syria's joining the scheme for the projected federation on 27 November.

In mid-April 1971, Numeiri withdrew from four-party discussions then being held in Benghazi. On 17 April, the leaders of Egypt, Libya and Syria announced the establishment of the Federation of Arab Republics and published its Basic Provisions. The federal Constitution was then published in August 1971[2] and went into effect after popular approval was given by referendum in each of the three member-states on 1 September, 1971. On 2 September, Egypt changed its official name, "The United Arab Republic"—the name given in 1958 to the united Egyptian–Syrian state which it had retained despite Syria's secession in 1961—to "The Arab Republic of Egypt."

In the last months of 1971 and the first months of 1972, the bodies of the Federation were set up in accordance with the Constitution. Sudan continued to regard herself as a member of the group of "Tripoli Charter States" but maintained that, by establishing the Federation, the other members had ignored the existence of the Charter. Egypt, Libya and Syria, for their part, viewed the Federation as a development evolving out of the Tripoli Charter and until 1972 spoke of the future participation of Sudan as a matter of course, to be realized as soon as Sudanese domestic conditions would permit.

Although the Libyan–Egyptian attempt at complete unification (to be referred to below) was made outside the framework of the Federation, it is important to note here that, in August 1972, Egypt and Libya announced their decision to bring about full unification between them within one year. In July 1973, however, Sadat indicated that the time was not yet ripe for the merger project.

TERMINOLOGY AND INSTITUTIONS

The Tripoli Charter was originally a joint communiqué (*bayan mushtarak*). In conformity with the political parlance of the day, the communiqué emphasized "the revolutionary alliance" and the common goals of "the revolutions of Sudan, Libya and Egypt." In order to pursue these common goals, the communiqué stated, the three leaders had decided to meet once every four months in order to survey the progress made toward their realization and to establish joint committees in various fields for the purpose of implementing cooperation between their states.

A few weeks after the issue of the communiqué, communications media in Egypt began to refer to it as an "agreement" (*ittifaq*) and shortly thereafter as a "charter" (*mithaq*). The intention behind the new term was, no doubt, to give a more prestigious title to a document which was originally a routine statement. The change in name did not, however, impose any new obligations on the leaders who originally signed the communiqué.[3]

The governments thus quickly adopted the new name used by the media—if, indeed, they did not coin it themselves. Since then, Egypt, Libya and Sudan were referred to by official spokesmen and by the media as the "Tripoli Charter States."

In November 1970, when the leaders of Egypt, Libya and Sudan announced their decision to "draw up a plan to be included in a detailed agreement between them which would outline the steps and stages leading to the establishment of a union (*ittihad*)" between their states, the exact meaning of the framework to which they were referring was not clarified.[4]

Soon after the November 1970 declaration was issued, Dr. Jamal al-'Utayfi published an article in *al-Ahram*, in which he listed various possible connotations of *ittihad*. He noted first, as the November declaration itself had done, that the projected establishment of a united tripartite leadership and its auxiliary committees, would pave the road toward the creation of the *ittihad*. The *ittihad* itself was no more than a stage on the path to *wahda*, i.e., full unity between the peoples of the Arab nation. As a preliminary stage, it could take several forms: a federal state within which each state would forgo its (international) identity (*shakhsiyya*) while retaining wide autonomy in the management of internal affairs; a confederal state within whose framework each state would maintain its (international) identity while the member states maintain a common body to deal with international relations; or (an even looser) form of "association by mutual agreement" (*ittihad at-tawafuq*) similar to the framework of the Arab League, the European

Council or the British Commonwealth, where several states agree on the realization of common goals and to this end maintain permanent bodies of which their representatives are members. In al-'Utayfi's opinion, the November 1970 declaration referred to such an "association by mutual agreement," but one in which the bonds between the member states were stronger than those between members of the Arab League.[5] Al-'Utayfi's article did not elicit any official reaction, let alone official approval, but a close study of the Basic Provisions of the Federation and of its Constitution attests to his acumen.

In the present paper, the term "Federation of Arab Republics" will be employed only because it is the accepted translation in Western languages for *ittihad al-jumhuriyyat al-'arabiyya*, and not because we are dealing with a federation in the accepted sense of the word.[6] (It is noteworthy that the *official* translation of *ittihad* in Egypt is "confederation" while in Libya it is "federation."")

Upon entering the Federation the member states did not relinquish sovereignty to the slightest degree. Shortly before the referendum, held to approve the Constitution of the Federation, Egyptian President Anwar Sadat explained in an address to the nation:

> We reached this formula while Abdel Nasser was still alive; we said that any union (*wahda*) would begin with a federation (*ittihad*) of the united Arab republics, in the sense that each republic with all its bodies...would be an independent personality...and each republic would be a strong unit (*wahda*) in itself... From all these strong, independent units the federation...or a strong state (*dawla qawiyya*) will be built, because (if) each unit within the federation is a strong state...then the federation itself or the federated state itself will certainly be a strong state."[8]

The first Article in the Constitution of the Federation speaks of the establishment of a federal state (*dawla ittihadiyya*) called the "Federation of Arab Republics." Both the Basic Provisions and the Constitution set forth in great detail the establishment of common bodies, as required in the accepted sense of a federation: a Presidential Council headed by a chairman, a Council of Ministers, a Federal National Assembly (parliament), a Federal Constitutional Court, and Specialized Federal Councils. The duties and authority of these bodies are clearly defined. But the wording and the content of the various clauses of the Constitution make it clear that actual authority rests only with the Presidential Council comprising the presidents of the member states: it is the Presidential Council that appoints the members of the Council of Ministers, determines the subjects it is to deal with and defines the authority of each minister; establishes the Specialized Federal Councils; calls the Federal National Assembly into session, and is empowered to decide on its dissolution; determines the composition of the Constitutional Court and appoints its president; and prepares the proposed budget of the Federation. All the other bodies of the Federation are in fact advisory bodies only.

According to Article 8a of the Basic Provisions and Articles 14a, 18, 31, and 70 of the Federal Constitution, every decision made by the Presidential Council must be a unanimous one. Thus the fact that the chairman of the Presidential Council is considered the president of the Federation is virtually meaningless: he cannot make any decisions without the consent of the other members of the Presidential Council.

Article 14 of the Constitution deals with the scope of federal authority. In the fields of economy, education, culture and legislation, the essential authority of the Federation is limited to the drawing up of a common policy and coordinating the member states' activities. In foreign affairs, the Federation is empowered to establish the general principles of foreign policy and to decide on "questions of peace and war."[9] In defense matters it is charged with the organization and supervision of the defense of the Federation as a whole—not the defense of each member state. Political power, the actual conduct of foreign policy, diplomatic representation, the organization of domestic political activity, control of the army, taxation and foreign trade—all these remain within the jurisdiction of the member states, and none of the federal bodies, not even the Presidential Council has direct authority in any matter regarding the individual citizens of the member states.

Apart from giving formal expression to the desire for union, the Constitution was apparently intended to ensure the maintenance of the political status quo in each state and in the relations between them as it existed immediately prior to their association. According to Article 64 of the Constitution, federal authorities are permitted to intervene to restore security and order—even in the event that a formal request to do so could not reach them—in any one of the federated states, should it be threatened as a result of internal or external disturbances. Against the background of the then geographic, demographic, political and military realities, it would appear that this article reflected primarily Egypt's willingness at that time to protect Qadhafi's regime.

MOTIVATION FOR SEEKING TRIPARTITE LINK

The interest of Libya and Sudan in their association with Egypt under the Tripoli Charter was obvious in light of the situation obtaining in their own states and in the Middle East as a region at the time. The new leaders, for whom the first years in power were marred by several plots and attempted counter-*coups*, were much in need of the moral—and substantive—support they received from Egypt. Following the rise to power of Qadhafi and Numeiri, Abdel Nasser paid two formal visits to Libya (25–30 December, 1969 and 20–26 June, 1970) and two to Sudan (1–2 January and 24–29 May, 1970), in marked contrast to his habit in preceding years of not leaving Cairo to visit other Arab capitals. On every occasion, he lavished praise on the regimes of Libya and Sudan and the personal qualities of the men who led them. His demonstrative cooperation with them in the framework of the "Charter States" represented a political achievement for the new leaders, who could hardly point to any rapid achievements within their own countries. Through their alliance, as manifested by the Charter, the Sudanese and Libyan rulers were able to put their countries on the map of inter-Arab relations.

Bilateral relations between Egypt and Libya and between Egypt and Sudan were tightened by the dispatch of hundreds of Egyptian advisers: military and internal security personnel, administrators, financial experts, transportation and engineering specialists, agricultural and industrial development experts, doctors, nurses and medical technicians, educationalists, etc.[10] The formal existence of the tripartite Charter, however, helped to minimize complaints of Egyptain "domination" which would otherwise have caused greater alarm to Libya and Sudan.

Nor was Libyan and Sudanese support of Nasser insignificant for Egypt at this time. Firmly—and at times vociferously—Qadhafi and Numeiri supported all of Nasser's steps during and after the War of Attrition (when most other Arab countries did not). They rejected Syrian and Iraqi attempts to woo them as leaders of "young revolutions" and stressed the primacy of the Egyptian revolution. Libya "defected" from the Maghreb by showing preference for the ties she had established with Egypt. Despite their distance from the borders of

Israel, Sudan and Libya participated in the conferences of "the confrontation states" which Nasser convened. They supported Egypt's line at the various all-Arab and Islamic meetings of 1969 and 1970. Qadhafi's call for the "Pan-Arabization of the Battle" (qawmiyyat al-ma'raka) was presented as a parallel to Nasser's appeal: "Everything for the sake of the battle." Libya and Sudan did not come out against Nasser when he accepted the Rogers initiative, thus bringing about the end of the War of Attrition through the August 1970 ceasefire. Following Iraq's condemnation of Egypt after the ceasefire acceptance, Libya and Sudan supported Iraq's expulsion from a commanding role on the eastern front. When civil war erupted in Jordan in September 1970, Numeiri and Qadhafi essentially performed Nasser's work for him by condemning King Hussein: because of Nasser's ambivalent relations with the Fidayeen organizations, it served his purpose to have others protest their decimation.

Moreover, while himself attacking the USSR and its role in the Middle East, Qadhafi did not censure Egypt for her ties with the Soviet Union. In addition, her relations with Libya assured Egypt of a bond with a state independent of the Soviet Union for arms supplies, and capable of acquiring arms from the West, principally France, without the limitations of the embargo imposed by France on the states who had participated in the Six Day War of 1967. Furthermore, as an oil-rich state, Libya was expected to serve as an important source of financial assistance for Egypt.[11]

Egyptian media repeatedly spoke of the untapped potential to be realized by closer ties between the Tripoli Charter States; the consolidation of some fifty million Arabs—the populations of the three states—into one front; the concentration of an enormous economic potential; the possibility of decisively influencing Arab oil policy; joint strategic control of both the southeastern Mediterranean and the Red Sea; and the huge strategic hinterland that Sudan and Libya could provide for Egypt. (During the War of Attrition, for instance, Egypt transferred her military colleges to Libya and Sudan, as well as aircraft units not actually participating in the fighting, to keep them well out of the range of Israel's air force.)

At the same time, Egypt had its reservations—certainly during Nasser's lifetime. When Qadhafi first demanded, in May 1970, to turn the vaguely-phrased Tripoli Charter into a binding and formal union, Nasser refused. His attitude was based to a large degree on the bitter lessons learned from the unsuccessful Egyptian–Syrian union of 1958–1961. Moreover, grappling with the outcome of the Six Day War, he apparently realized that a meaningful formal union would entail dividing the federated Arab states from the rest at a time when its declared policy was comprehensive all-Arab cooperation. If Nasser had not died at the end of September 1970, cooperation between Egypt, Libya and Sudan might possibly have remained a matter of the Tripoli Charter only.

SADAT'S ACCESSION; DECISION TO FEDERATE

Nasser's death was followed by a period of disorientation in Arab affairs, characterized by the echoes of the inter-Arab war of words for and against the August 1970 ceasefire, the profound impression left by the Jordanian civil war, and the need for a decision on the future of the ceasefire along the Suez Canal. Qadhafi, who had behaved toward Nasser with the reverence befitting a student towards his mentor, could now afford to bring pressure to bear on the new president of Egypt as well as on the leader of Sudan, and could urge them forward in the establishment of formal union between their states. Under the circumstances, Sadat agreed—perhaps quite willingly.

At the conclusion of the traditional period of forty days' mourning after Nasser's death, the leaders of the Tripoli Charter States announced their decision to establish a federation. Although it was presented by the leaders as the logical continuation of the Tripoli Charter and as the fulfillment of Nasser's plan, the decision was a sharp deviation from his stubborn reservations against a clear-cut formula for union. If measured by Qadhafi's zeal for immediate unification, however, the declaration of November 1970 was moderate enough and more in keeping with Sadat's views as well as being the only formulation possible in light of Numeiri's stand. In the latter's opinion (which was greatly influenced by domestic considerations), a federal union would be premature until such time as the following basic conditions had been met: a stable, consolidated regime in effective control and a minimal degre of economic independence in each state; and greatly strengthened economic and cultural relations between the member states. Steady effort in this direction, Numeiri claimed, would encourage a popular desire for union, so that it would come about naturally without having to be imposed. Because of this position, the November declaration did not name a date for the proclamation of the federation, and for the time being the group of the Tripoli Charter States remained very much as they had been.

Libya's and Egypt's dependence on Sudan as a member of the tripartite group decreased with Syria's joining the Tripoli Charter late in 1970 and becoming a candidate for the future federation. In April 1971, Sudan withdrew from the group, and Sadat, Qadhafi and Asad published the Federation's Basic Provisions.

For Qadhafi, the Provisions obviously represented at least the partial fulfillment of his doctrinaire demand for immediate, formal, union. He probably thought that a legal document would be more effective in securing an Egyptian commitment to defend his regime and that membership in the federation would assist him in promoting his views in the Arab world at large. On the other hand, he was forced to accept "Ba'thist" Syria into the federation, despite his own vehement denunciations of that party, and despite his calls for the elimination of all parties in the member states and for setting up mass organizations on the model of Egypt's Arab Socialist Union.

Sadat—in an address to the nation on 30 August, 1971—spoke of the Federation as being "essential for the battle." He added, however, that "the Federation of Arab Republics which we are founding...is not only for the sake of the battle and the confrontation states... No...this is an answer to the state of disintegration which the Arab nation is today experiencing."[12] But there is no doubt that Sadat—who at that time had not yet eliminated his opponents at home and had not yet worked out his general attitude on the Middle East crisis—had succumbed to Libya's pressure. Perhaps he hoped (unjustifiably, as it turned out) that his agreement to the establishment of the Federation would halt the incessant Libyan pressure for the proclamation of a complete Egyptian–Libyan merger. With regard to Syria, Sadat hoped for the creation of strong bonds which, at that juncture, were desired by both sides. A close Syrian–Egyptian bond was difficult to establish on the bilateral plane because of the unhappy residue still left by the break-up of the United Arab Republic. According to Arab views current at the time,[13] Sadat agreed to join the Federation at a time when Egypt's standing in the inter-Arab arena had fallen low; by joining it Egypt would improve her stature.

Asad, for his part, was apparently agreeable to any measure that would return Syria to the center of inter-Arab relations by establishing her as Sadat's chief ally, thereby finally "living down" the after-effects of having caused the break-up of the union with Egypt. In addition, he was eager to further increase the isolation of Iraq's rival Ba'th regime from Egypt. When the opportunity presented itself, he grasped it. Syria's interest in closer military cooperation with Egypt also played a part in Asad's decision.

The formal steps which became incumbent upon the member states following the declaration of April 1971 were carried out at a rapid pace. After the federal Constitution was approved by plebiscite in September, the Presidential Council held its first session in Cairo in October 1971. Sadat was elected Chairman of the Presidential Council of the Federation, and Cairo was chosen as its capital. In December 1971 the seven members of the Council of Ministers were appointed,[14] and in January 1972 they swore allegiance in Sadat's presence. It was decided that, instead of maintaining diplomatic representation, each member state would have a resident minister and an office in the capital of the other member states. The Federation's flag was hoisted in all three capital cities on 1 January, 1972. The Federal National Assembly held its first session in Cairo in March. In April, councils for information, foreign affairs, planning and economy, transport and transit services, culture and education, and scientific research were established, each subsequently appointing sub-committees to discuss and make suggestions in specific areas.[15] In June 1972, the establishment of a Federal Constitutional Court was announced. Between October 1971 and February 1973, the Presidential Council held six sessions. (No further meetings were reported.)

THE FAILURE OF THE FEDERATION; QADHAFI'S MERGER PLAN

But the federation as a living organism, even in the limited sense of an "association by mutual agreement," has never functioned.

At the conclusion of every session of the Presidential Council, unofficial sources reported serious differences of opinion among the three leaders. Sadat and Asad refused to comply with Qadhafi's demands for a "return to Islam" which would entail the banning of alcoholic beverages, discrimination against non-Muslims, and support for Muslims in various parts of the world (possibly bringing the Federation into conflict with powers having Muslim populations, such as the Soviet Union, India and China). Definite agreement was expressed only on matters for which it was easy to find consensus, for example: declaring support for the Fidayeen organizations, criticizing King Hussein's position, or censuring the United States for supporting Israel.

In 1972, Qadhafi began to censure Syria for her growing reliance upon the USSR, and to oppose Egypt's agreement to the renewal of UN Representative Jarring's diplomatic mission to the Middle East. Eventually, Qadhafi began to censure Sadat for not waging war against Israel.

In 1971 and 1972 Qadhafi approached Algeria and Tunisia, two states outside the Federation, with proposals for union; they were rejected.

The most convincing proof, however, of the failure of the federal framework as a meaningful structure was Qadhafi's insistent demand for immediate merger–union (*wahda indimajiyya*) with Egypt. He first made the demand in February 1972, a mere six months after the Federation was founded. Leaving Sadat with little time to ponder his next moves, Qadhafi, in July 1972, made public his discussions with Sadat on the matter and demanded immediate implementation of the promises Sadat had purportedly made. Qadhafi argued that real union required abandoning the independent identities of the states involved and their merger into one single state; since the Federation had not even formed an army of its own, he said, it could certainly never lead to true unification.

For as long as he was able to postpone implementation of any practical measure, Sadat appeared to acquiesce to Libyan pressure. On 2 August, 1972, Sadat and Qadhafi published a joint statement declaring their intention to establish "complete union" (*wahda kamila*) between their respective states by 1 September, 1973. The decision, they stated, was made "with all respect for the Constitution of the Federation and for the jurisdiction of its authorities."[16] Various steps towards this unification were discussed in meetings held by the two presidents during 1973, and in seven joint committees. Qadhafi, however, felt progress to be too slow, and during an extended stay in Cairo (22 June to 9 July, 1973) he attempted—unsuccessfully—to explain his position to collocutors of every rank in the Egyptian establishment. Then, between 18 and 21 July, some 50,000 Libyans began a march into Egypt with the intention of forcing Sadat to sign the instrument of union.[17] An Egyptian roadblock on the way to Alexandria halted their progress. Sadat received a delegation from among the marchers, and issued a statement declaring his commitment to the original declaration, specifying 1 September, 1973, as the date for official unification.

But, as events turned out, Qadhafi failed; it was precisely his zeal and extremism which now permitted Sadat to openly oppose immediate unification without risk of being blamed for "anti-unionist" policies.

Union never came about. Sadat's address on 23 July, 1973 (Egyptian Revolution Day) marked the end of successful Libyan attempts at pressure. In that address, Sadat referred to the Federation, which had almost been forgotten in the commotion surrounding the Libyan–Egyptian union scheme. He said:

> One of the fundaments upon which Israel bases her strategy is the discord and disunity of the Arab nation... In the midst of the ashes of defeat, and in the midst of the pain and dissolution, three states, Egypt, Syria and Libya, have arisen and established—for the first time—a Federation (*ittihad*)...that forms one state, the Federation of (Arab) Republics, with a Council of Ministers and a National Assembly. And I say, whether these bodies function regularly or less than regularly, the very existence...of the desire of three states to create one state and thereby deal a heavy blow to the strategy of Israel (means) that...defeat and disintegration have not made us forget our goals and our faith in our unity. I say that even if this were the only significance (of the Federation), it is sufficient to ennoble the existence of the Federation and to impart radiance and glory to this illustrious action. It is being carried out; it is going forward slowly—but surely. And that is what is important.[18]

At that time, Sadat did not mention Syrian and Egyptian preparations for war against Israel—preparations that were already at their height—but he did stress the degree of inter-Arab understanding that had been achieved through bilateral contacts, particularly Egyptian–Syrian relations, which he called "fully coordinated" and "mutually trusting."

While the Federation became increasingly less significant and while Arab media concentrated on the merger of Egypt and Libya, Egypt and Syria had steadily drawn closer to each other and had grown increasingly distant from Libya. Syria and Egypt did not include Libya in their planning for the 1973 war. Indeed, on the second day of the war Qadhafi publicly criticized their methods. It is obvious that for several months prior to the war, and also while it lasted, Egypt maintained close ties with Arab states outside the Federation (especially Saudi Arabia)—much more so than with Libya, a member of the Federation and a candidate for unification with her. During and after the Arab Summit Conference in Algeria which followed the war, Libya's isolation, and the fact that she had been relegated to the fringe of inter-Arab affairs, became even more obvious.

CONCLUSION

The decision in 1971 of the presidents of Egypt, Syria and Libya to establish the Federation had served their short-range political ambitions. When the circumstances changed, short-range goals altered along with them and there was no longer any need to lend content to a structure which had never been intended to go beyond cooperation between independent and sovereign states.

In a message which Sadat sent to Qadhafi and the Libyan Revolutionary Council in May 1974, he argued his opposition to complete union under the then circumstances. What he said could equally well be applied to the federal concept:

> The method of declaring unification without prior studies and without basic agreement is a dangerous method. I say frankly that I do not believe in a policy of raising banners. A slogan that does not express a verified reality proves all too quickly a disappointment for the masses and provokes negative reaction. It also leads the rest of the world to believe that we are lacking in seriousness—the seriousness with which we must handle our affairs. It is no secret that after so many proclamations of unions made in different places on different occasions, the world has come to expect, with each such proclamation...the termination (of the scheme) as well.[19]

NOTES

1. *Al-Ahram*, 28 December, 1969; English text in BBC's *Summary of World Broadcasts*, 30 December, 1969, quoting *R. Cairo and R. Bayda'*, 27 December, 1969.

2. For their full texts, see "The Declaration of the Establishment of the Federation of Arab Republics and Basic Provisions of the Federation," *al-Ahram*, 18, 30 April, 1971; "The Constitution of the Federation of Arab Republics," *an-Nahar*, 21 August, 1971, (For an English translation of the Constitution see *MEJ*, vol. 25, 1971, pp. 523-29.)

3. No process of formal ratification of the "Charter" was initiated in any of the three states.

4. *Al-Akhbar*, 9 November, 1970. The term *ittihad* had gradually come to mean a framework less binding than one of full unity (*wahda*) between two or more Arab states. Already in the late fifties, prior to the declaration of the Egyptian–Syrian union of 1958, the possibility of a "Federated Union" (*wahda ittihadiyya*) between the two states was spoken of. In February 1958, the short-lived union between the Hashemites of Iraq and Jordan was established and called the Arab Federation (*al-ittihad al-'arabi*). In abortive talks held between April and June 1963 the leaders of Egypt, Syria and Iraq proposed new plans for a *wahda ittihadiyya* between their states. In all these cases, *ittihad* was translated into Western languages (by the member states themselves, as well as by outside observers) as "federation" or, at times, "confederation."

5. Jamal al-'Utayfi, "As'ila hawl i'lan al-ittihad al-thulathi," *al-Ahram*, 19 November, 1970.

6. For the accepted connotations of the terms "federation" and "confederation," see, e.g., Harry Back, Horst Cirullies and Gunter Marquard, *POLEC: Dictionary of Politics and Economics* (Berlin, 1967); Joseph Dunner (ed.), *Dictionary of Political Science* (London, 1965).

7. Peter K. Bechtold, "New Attempts at Arab Cooperation: The Federation of Arab Republics, 1971–?," *MEJ*, vol. 27 (1973), p. 167.

8. *Al-Ahram*, 31 August, 1971.

9. The Presidential Council, however, had no say in the preparations, on the part of Egypt and Syria, for the war in 1973.

10. Sudan's hopes for substantial financial assistance from Libya did not materialize. On the other hand, Egypt and Libya both aided Numeiri's return to power after an abortive counter-*coup* in July 1971, although Sudan had by then withdrawn from the Federation.

11. In retrospect, it seems that with the exception of the fixed payments Libya made to Egypt in keeping with the decisions made at the 1967 Arab Summit Conference in Khartoum, Egyptian hopes for substantial financial assistance from Libya remained unfulfilled.

12. *Al-Ahram*, 31 August, 1971.

13. For example: Fu'ad Matar, *Ayna asbaha 'Abd an-Nasir fi jumhuriyyat as-Sadat* (Beirut, 1972), p. 8.

14. The Council was expanded when five additional ministers were appointed in December 1972.

15. The suggestions proposed by these sub-committees are almost identical to the hundreds of suggestions that various bodies within the Arab League had

been making for years. For example, the Council on Information and Education proposed the establishment of special committees for the revival of Arab heritage, for the education of the working classes, for coining Arabic terms to replace foreign expressions, and for considering the establishment of a federal university.

16. *Al-Ahram*, 3 August, 1972.

17. The Libyans claimed it was a spontaneous march; the Egyptians—that it was government-sponsored.

18. *Al-Ahram*, 24 July, 1973.

19. *Al-Ahram*, 26 May, 1974.

Formation
of the
Egyptian-
Syrian
Axis

Nasser and Sadat, 1967–1973: Two Approaches to a National Crisis

Shimon Shamir

In Egyptian contemporary history, the six years from the war of June 1967 to the war of October 1973 are divided into two equal parts: the first three years constitute the last phase and the lowest ebb of the period of Jamal Abdel Nasser, and the succeeding three years constitute the initial and formative stage of that of Anwar as-Sadat. This division in no way disrupts the intrinsic unity of the period. In the life of Egypt, the six years constitute a single chapter which is marked in its entirety by an agonizing crisis stemming from the trauma of the 1967 defeat.

Seen in perspective, the defeat could be regarded as the culmination of a series of failures on the part of the Nasserite regime; yet, for most Egyptians it came as an unexpected blow. It shook the foundations of their society and initiated a period in which everything in Egypt—to use the words of Muhammad Hasanayn Heikal—was "disintegrating, crumbling and falling apart."[1] With all its shortcomings, the Nasserite Revolution had been regarded in Egypt as a source of hope for a future of prosperity and dignity. The shattering of the power and prestige of Nasserism cast a heavy shadow as to the validity of its vision, and adversely affected the Egyptian self-image. Egyptians began to question their ability to progress in the conditions of the modern world and achieve genuine national regeneration. A phrase coined in those days, and which reflected the subjective perception of the import of that crisis, referred to it as a "civilization challenge" to the Egyptian existence.[2]

To stand up to this challenge, the Egyptian leadership had to undertake a long line of difficult tasks. These may be grouped into three sections, corresponding to the three facets of the crisis. Firstly, to "erase the traces of the 1967 aggression," that is, to restore the territories whose loss had diminished the stature of Egypt. Secondly, to reinforce the political system which was wavering after the authority of the ruling elite had been shaken, the relevancy of its program had faded away, the cohesive forces of the community had grown weaker and pressures on the state's administration and economy had increased. And thirdly, to rehabilitate Egypt's international standing, both in the inter-Arab sphere in which Egypt's influence had considerably decreased, and in the global sphere where Egypt's dependence on the USSR had reached dangerous proportions.

Nasser and Sadat each dealt with these problems in their own fashion. The differences in their policies can, of course, be attributed to the rapidly changing circumstances—but only in part. Their respective policies often reflected distinctly different approaches to the problems at hand. In spite of the fact that Nasser and Sadat belonged to the same generation, had similar social background, grew up in the same political environment, shared the same ideological tenets and were for two decades close associates, it is possible to point out a number of differences in personality and outlook which set them apart.

Nasser's leadership has often been characterized as "a leadership of response."[3] His policies were usually formed as reactions to the challenges he encountered on his way. Nasser's responses were often bold and imaginative but at the same time also impulsive, emotional and reflecting the frantic militancy of the Cairo demonstrations of his youth. When he had seized power he saw before him "a role in search of a hero," and he stepped in to fill the void and lead a historic process of transformation in Egypt and the whole region. He became the *za'im* of a millenarian pan-Arab movement and measured himself and his actions by this scale.

Sadat, on the other hand, preserves in his personality many of the traits of rural Egypt. He has the realism and the shrewdness of the Egyptian fellah and takes pride in these qualities.[4] "One of the differences between me and Nasser," he wrote in his memoirs, "was that Nasser belonged to those people who live constantly at their nerves' edge."[5] Sadat is much more composed, he is discreet and calculated. Nasser's successor is a down-to-earth pragmatist who shuns the rhetorics of messianic movements; and he remembers well that it was thanks to his ability to maintain a low profile that he survived throughout the 18 years of serving under Nasser, in times when more assertive persons were purged and disappeared, one by one, from the political scene.[6]

To give a full account of developments in Egypt under Nasser and Sadat, in the 1967-1973 period, would exceed the scope of this paper. What would be attempted here is rather to present a characterization—by necessity only in a generalized and schematic form—of the distinct approaches of these two leaders to the three facets, mentioned above, of the crisis afflicting their society.

STRATEGY IN THE CONFLICT WITH ISRAEL

As a result of the defeat in the Six Day War, Egypt lost the Sinai Peninsula, with its economic resources and strategic key points, as well as her control of the Suez Canal, and was forced, subsequently, to evacuate the three Canal cities.

The implications of this defeat were very sharply focused on the personality of Nasser. It was Nasser who had miscalculated in 1967 and embroiled the other "confrontation states" in a premature war, and thus it was Nasser who was to blame for the Arab defeat. Since the major decisions on the moves towards escalation in May 1967 were his and his alone, nobody felt a need to shoulder with him the responsibility for the defeat in June. This fact was to influence Nasser's basic position on the issue of confrontation with Israel during the three years which followed.

Thus, the phrase which was coined immediately after the war's end—"erasing the traces of aggression"—was not merely rhetorical: it was the essence of Nasser's approach to the problem. He aspired to obliterate his failure by turning back the pages until the situation would once again approximate, as closely as possible, that prior to the Six Day War.

Accordingly, his primary objective was to prevent any crystallization of the Israeli military victory into a new relationship between the Arab world and Israel which would constitute an historic achievement of Zionism. Nasser, who had led the Arab armies to defeat, had no desire to lead the Arab states into a regional settlement which would contradict the maximalist Arab aspirations, conveniently expressed in the phrase "restoration of the legitimate rights of the Palestinians." One of the first features of his policy to emerge after the war was the formulation of a set of principles which would preclude any such development. Thus, at the Khartoum summit meeting, the four "Noes" were formulated as a binding Arab consensus: no peace with Israel, no negotiations, no recognition and no compromising on the rights of the

Palestinians. In dozens of speeches and statements, Nasser posited the equation that any direct peace talks with Israel were tantamount to surrender. His efforts to forestall any movement towards direct negotiations were rhetorically presented as a struggle for the very "survival" of Egypt and of the entire Arab world.

The operative goal was the restoration of the territories lost in the war. True to his basic motives and concepts, Nasser placed his emphasis on the return of every inch of Arab soil, for any territorial compromise would have amounted to at least a partial recognition of the finality of his own defeat.

The ideal model was the 1957 Israeli evacuation of Sinai which, at the time, required no substantial concessions on the part of Egypt. However, Nasser understood that the magnitude of the 1967 defeat made it impossible for him to expect full evacuation of the territories without any reciprocity on his part. Although he had never made an unequivocal public statement on the recompense he was willing to offer, it apparently included such elements as partial demilitarization; international guarantees; some form of Israeli usage of the Suez Canal; exclusion of the Gaza Strip problem from the Egyptian–Israeli bilateral controversy; and a non-belligerency agreement.[7]

The practical significance of his proposal may be summed up as a return to the 1957–1967 period of relative calm, with the addition of arrangements which would reduce, but not eliminate, the chances of the outbreak of another war. The outer limit of the concessions was delineated by Nasser so as to prevent any transfer of concrete assets to Israel as her gains of the Six Day War (expressed in the principle "no concession of a single inch of Arab soil") while leaving open the option for embarking, at some point in the future, on the second stage, i.e., the solution of the "1948 problem" (expressed in the principle, "no bargaining over the rights of the Palestinians").

This position could be seen as some improvement on the traditional Arab attitude of unreserved animosity, and it may have held some possibility of further improvement in the future, but it definitely was not a peace offer. In spite of some vague references to the desirability of peace—made mostly in the period immediately after the war and before the Egyptian forces were adequately rehabilitated—Nasser did not withdraw his categorical rejection of the Jewish State. When pressed on the issue of genuine peace, he would argue—citing statements of Israeli leaders—that in the choice between territories and peace Israel had opted in favor of territories, and therefore the only possible solution was an imposed settlement in the spirit of his proposal. For this matter, the Israeli proposal of 19 June, 1967, to evacuate the whole of Sinai in return for true peace, could not be regarded by Nasser as satisfying his demands, for it did not refer to *all* the Arab territories,[8] and Nasser saw himself responsible for the Golan Heights, the West Bank, the Gaza Strip and Jerusalem—no less than the Sinai Peninsula. The Israeli proposal, however, was soon retracted and replaced by the dictum of "no return to the 1967 border."

Nasser was thus saved by the Israelis from the need to put his position to further tests and was allowed to maneuver in the political arena with such ambiguous expressions as "a peaceful settlement" on "a just peace," and to get away with it. It was probably the ambiguity of the latter expression in the text of Security Council Resolution 242—in addition to the French version of the withdrawal stipulation—which made its acceptance a relatively simple matter for Nasser.[9] However, if Nasser's basic attitudes and motivations are taken into consideration, his following statement can be taken as a faithful expression of his position: "To give up an inch of occupied Arab land is impossible and not in my hands; to accept negotiations with Israel is impossible and I will not consent to it; to sign a peace treaty with Israel is impossible and not in my capacity; to recognize Israel is impossible and not in my capacity."[10]

Nasser's strategy for attaining his goal was a combination of what was termed "the military solution" and "the political solution."[11] In broad terms, and disregarding short-lived fluctuations, it may be described as a strategy intended to produce escalating pressures upon Israel so as to impose on her the evacuation of the territories within the framework of a settlement which would not go beyond the above-mentioned outer limits. This strategy was described in Egypt, schematically, as consisting of five elements:[12]

a. Building up an Arab military capacity in order to pose a growing threat to Israel. To this end, in the first stage, the forces of Egypt itself had to be rehabilitated. Next, military plans had to be prepared for "the mobilization of Arab resources." This planning (e.g., the Muhammad Fawzi plan) was intended, among other things, to confront Israel with two formidable commands—one in the south and one in the east, both coordinated and directed by Egypt.

b. Drawing the USSR into increased involvement in the Israel–Arab conflict, to the point of active participation in the arena of operations. (On relations with the superpowers, see pp. 3–49.)

c. Neutralizing American support for Israel. It was calculated that though it was hard to expect actual American support for the Arabs, pressure could be applied on the US to adopt an "even-handed" policy which would suffice to deprive Israel of the capacity to withstand the combined Arab–Soviet pressure.

d. Activating the blocs of states friendly towards the Arabs—in the Afro–Asian world, and to a certain extent in Europe as well—to exert pressure on Israel. The various bodies of the UN were expected to substantiate this pressure by "giving teeth" to their resolutions.

e. Conducting a constant war of attrition on all the fronts which bordered on Israel. The Fidayeen organizations were assigned the role of carrying the War of Attrition into Israel's territory and its population centers.

These five points are, of course, not on the same level of importance, and from March 1969 the fifth point, attrition, became distinctly the main instrument of Egyptian strategy. Nasser had incorporated it into a four-stage concept of progress described as: holding the ground, deterring, eliminating the aggression and achieving final victory.[13]

Shortly before Nasser's death, the results of this strategy could be summed up as a grave disappointment: a) the Egyptian army had indeed been rehabilitated, but the Arab states rejected the ambitious plans for mobilizing Arab forces under Nasser's command; b) the USSR had become actively involved in the fighting, but this very involvement, because of its attendant risks, steadily led to a Soviet interest in de-escalation; c) the US, particularly with its Rogers Plan, had indeed grown closer to the Egyptian position, but had not retracted her demand that the Arabs pay for the evacuation of territories by a peace agreement; d) the various international blocs had complied by lavishing expressions of support for the Arabs, but it also became clear that no factor, other than the two superpowers, had any effective influence on the Middle Eastern arena; and finally e) the War of Attrition was painful enough for Israel but it hurt the Arabs even more. In July 1970, Nasser was compelled to accept a ceasefire thus, in fact, throwing into question the effectiveness of his basic strategy.

Sadat's numerous statements on the Arab–Israeli conflict have made it clear that, so far as basic attitudes were concerned, he did not differ much from Nasser. Sadat's hostility to Israel was evidently fed by a stronger undercurrent of Islamic and anti-Jewish bias,[14] while in Nasser's attitude the notion of Israel as an "Imperialist outpost" evidently loomed larger; however, both regarded the establishment of the State of Israel as an act of injustice, a historic challenge to the Arab world and a constraint on Egyptian strategic and political interests.

Yet, on the level of practical politics, Sadat's rise to power opened an avenue for a reconsideration of the Egyptian position in this stage of the confrontation with Israel. It created an opportunity for a more pragmatic and innovative approach. As concerns personal motives, Sadat was free of Nasser's psychological burden of responsibility for "the disaster"; and with regard to national strategy, he had again a free hand—for Nasser's strategy, as seen above, had reached an impasse just on the eve of Sadat's accession to power. And, indeed, it seems in retrospect that Sadat did possess the necessary adaptability and boldness to utilize this greater latitude for crystallizing a somewhat different approach to the problem. The essence of Sadat's approach, as will be seen below, was the extension of the scopes of both the diplomatic and military options for Egypt.

Evidently, the political manuevering which was typical of Sadat's first months in office reflected a search for a new course and a resolution to explore, through the US, the potentialities of the diplomatic option. After sending out "feelers," in January 1971, he publicly took two steps which showed a higher degree of flexibility than that revealed by Nasser. On 4 February, in a speech to the National Assembly, he suggested an interim agreement for the extension of the ceasefire to a limited period which would allow for the clearing of the Canal and its re-opening to shipping, provided Israel made a partial withdrawal from the eastern bank of the Suez Canal, within the framework of a timetable for the implementation of the Security Council resolution (i.e., total withdrawal). On the 15th of that same month, in reply to Jarring's note, Sadat proposed signing a peace agreement with Israel, to include mutual recognition of "sovereignty, territorial integrity and political independence," in exchange for complete withdrawal from the territories occupied in June 1967; the Palestinian issue was mentioned in the reply indirectly by way of the demand for the "just settlement of the refugee problem, in accordance with the resolutions of the UN."

The precise significance of Sadat's proposals is debatable, but they were probably more than a propaganda ploy and less than a radical transformation of the position towards Israel. A year and a half later, Sadat explained to his generals—in the 24 October, 1972 meeting of the Supreme Council of the Armed Forces[15]—that the "Initiative" (*al-mubadara*, as his February statements came to be known in the Egyptian political jargon) was motivated by two considerations. First, he wanted to gain time. The second Egyptian extension of the ceasefire was going to expire by the end of the month and he knew that in case hostilities were resumed he could not expect any Soviet assistance, for the Soviets were preparing for the Communist Party Congress, scheduled for the end of March, and had made it clear that the last thing they wanted at that time were complications in the Middle East. Furthermore, for the same reason, Sadat said, they delayed the delivery of missile batteries assigned for the defense of Upper Egypt (the Aswan High Dam) and that was a crucial factor in considering the resumption of war. Second, it was necessary to find a way to cross the Canal with minimum losses. Sadat explained that the proposed interim agreement was designed to allow his forces to cross the Canal and thus give Egypt, six months later, when the agreement would expire, a more substantial military option in case Israel refused to evacuate the Sinai Peninsula.

Other explanations given by Sadat were that the reopening of the Suez Canal was a "winning card" with Western Europe and the world in general and that the proposals would project a positive image of Egypt's policy and expose Israel's "intransigence." In his memoirs, Sadat has the following to say on the *mubadara*: "Israel suffered a grave shock because it had based its policy on the argument that no Arab leader existed who would be ready to sign a peace agreement with her. Thus, for the first time the Arabs managed to embarrass Israel in her relations with her allies 2the US3."[16] Sadat expediently left open the question of whether his proposals had been made initially in good faith or were meant to embarrass the Israelis.

All these *post factum* explanations do not necessarily reflect the whole truth and there are many indications to the effect that Sadat wished seriously to explore the potentialities of American mediation for achieving progress towards the realization of the Egyptian goals. In any case, Sadat's diplomatic offensive soon lost its momentum. Sadat found Israel's reply to Jarring totally unacceptable and the Israeli readiness to negotiate an interim, or "special" agreement (originally an Israeli idea) as having been motivated by the intention of eventually freezing the interim agreement situation indefinitely or simply stalling for time without seeking any change in the present situation. The US, said Sadat, simply accepted the Israeli thesis that Egypt did not possess substantial bargaining power and thus it would be better to await further Egyptian concessions.[17]

Whatever the case, three central resolutions appear to have crystallized during Sadat's first months in office: a) endorsing Nasser's two basic tenets, i.e., the restoration of *all* the territories lost in 1967 and the safeguarding of the rights of the Palestinians—while leaving the definition of these rights open to a wide range of interpretations, from the establishment of a Palestinian state *alongside* Israel, to its establishment *instead* of Israel; b) continuing the development of the Egyptian capacity for a substantial military option, preferably without returning to a war of attrition; c) upgrading the diplomatic expressions of readiness for peace with Israel on the basis of an overall settlement, in accordance with the Arab interpretation of Resolution 242.

The nature of the peace settlement suggested by Sadat was unclear, and most certainly did not coincide with the Israeli concept of genuine peace. As seen above, Sadat shared with Nasser the view that the Jewish State was an incursion on the Arab world, and like him he compared the ultimate fate of Zionism to that of the Crusaders and the Mongols.[18] The nature of the desired peace settlement, according to Sadat, was not a historic reconciliation with Israel, but the termination of hostilities to be imposed on Israel rather than negotiated in a bilateral fashion. Like Nasser, he wished to leave open the option of dealing with "the 1948 problem" after "the 1967 problem" was satisfactorily solved. The difference lay in the fact that, Sadat—sincerely, insincerely or undecidedly—projected the notion that stage two, "the final solution," was beyond the responsibility and capability of his generation.

An Egytian analyst described "Sadat's Doctrine" in the following terms: "[The doctrine of] President Sadat has been established on a clear fundamental concept, namely that the Arab–Israeli struggle is a struggle which would last for generations and—as a long experience has shown—it is beyond the capacity of any single generation to shoulder the tasks of generations. Hence, it is necessary to determine for each generation the specific tasks and objectives it should achieve in the framework of this struggle ... In the specific circumstances of the present realities, the tasks of the new Arab generation, according to Sadat's concept, are confined to the elimination of the consequences of the

1967 aggression, [i.e.,] to liberate the occupied Arab lands and gain recognition for the right of the Palestinian people to establish a national state in Gaza and the West Bank. The other tasks are beyond the arena of responsibility of the October War generation and the coming generation will have to bear their burden."[19]

The most decisive resolution adopted by Sadat (which may turn out to have been the major decision of his whole career) was to resort to the "military option," namely to activate the armed forces in a massive form and within the framework of a well-defined overall strategy.

In order to properly evaluate this decision, it should be borne in mind that for reaching that decision Sadat had to overcome not only what he termed "the barrier of fear" in face of Israeli military superiority, but also the skepticism of his own people. At that time, as many indications have shown, significant groups within the Egyptian elite, political as well as intellectual, did not believe Egypt *had* a military option, and increasingly tended to assume that the only way out of the crisis, on the basis of Egyptian interest, was to seek a compromise of sorts which would allow Egypt to divert its resources to development.[20]

Subsequently Sadat explained that he had actually been compelled to undertake the risks involved in this decision. He said that the following developments, of the 1971–1973 period, had forced his hands:

a. The intolerable state of Egyptian morale, domestic situation and public climate stemming from the seemingly endless no peace–no war situation, which threatened an "internal explosion";

b. The alarming deterioration in Egypt's position and prestige in the Arab world;

c. The "lack of response," to his initiative in February 1971, the purpose of which had been to "examine the peace intentions of the US and of Israel";

d. The tendency on the part of the two superpowers to integrate a Middle Eastern *status quo* into their global detente;

e. The rapid solidification of the Israeli occupation of Arab territories through Israel's "creation of facts" in these territories.[21]

There is no way of knowing to what extent these developments only intensified and supplied pretexts for a decision which had already been made when Sadat took office, or whether the decision took shape gradually from the developments which followed his assumption of power. The military option, in principle, had never been discarded and as seen above the "political solution" and the "military solution" were never seen as mutually exclusive. During a part of 1971, Sadat concentrated on his contacts with the US diplomats seeking their consent to his concept of an interim agreement. However, toward the end of 1971 ("the year of decision"), having abandoned these efforts, he shifted the stress to the military option, but without discarding the diplomatic option altogether. He evidently considered various types of military action but his overtures to the Soviets did not yield the results which he deemed then necessary for substantiating a military initiative. In April 1972, he told Brezhnev that "things could be moved only by means of a military operation, namely a great Arab offensive" which would compel Israel to accept the ruling of an international conference, just as the North Vietnamese offensive of January 1972, "compelled the US to return to the Paris talks" and accept the evacuation settlement.[22] Most probably, the basic elements of the strategy which was implemented in October 1973 had been formulated, one at a time, after mid-1972.

After the October War, it has been sometimes suggested that this military offensive had in fact been designed by Nasser. Heikal, in particular, propagated this version, referring to such military plans of the Nasser period as Liberation One, Two and Three, and Defense Plan 200.[23] This has not been admitted by Sadat, and Gen. Gamasi even denied it vehemently, explaining that those plans had been nothing but training or defensive plans.[24] It is, indeed, entirely plausible that although Nasser had considered a number of military options, the strategy of the October War was conceived by Sadat and his aides.

Instead of the Nasserite strategy of a protracted and escalating process of multi-frontal pressures, Sadat developed a concept of a two-stage concentrated effort. Sadat's strategy called for, firstly, a large-scale military offensive which would have a limited objective but would be sufficient to break the stalemate and affect the balance of power; and, subsequently, a comprehensive diplomatic offensive which would give expression to the newly acquired Arab leverage and achieve the Arab targets. The adoption of this strategy involved several major decisions on the part of Sadat:

a. The resumption of hostilities should take the form of an all-out war, investing the total military capacity in a concentrated offensive operation;

b. The offensive should be co-ordinated, from the outset, with only one other Arab army, the Syrian;

c.   The oil weapon should be utilized to give weight to the offensive;
d.   Having secured the maximum military aid obtainable from the USSR, the diplomatic offensive would be based on a sharp turn towards the US;
e.   The focus of diplomatic activity would be a peace conference at which Arab representatives would negotiate with Israel's representatives under UN auspices.

The difference between this approach to the problem and that of Nasser is obvious. Rather than gradually mobilizing Arab military capacity, Soviet involvement and international political support in order to prevail over Israel at an unspecified moment in the future, Sadat chose to begin with an almost unilateral action, utilizing those resources which were at his disposal at the time. He expected Arab, Soviet and international forces to rally to his side as a consequence of his decision to take action and not as a prerequisite for that action.

True, not all the constituents of this strategy were original and some became feasible only as the result of new circumstances which had not existed in Nasser's time. Certainly the employment of the oil weapon was a new factor which became operational only at some time in early 1973, with the change in attitude of the oil-producing countries in response to the situation in the world energy markets. But the strategy as a whole definitely bears the stamp of Sadat's approach.

The key-factor in Sadat's strategy was the new concept of a limited war, purposefully set into a political grand design. Even the pro-Nasser Heikal had to admit that "it was a long time before Egypt became ready to accept the idea of a limited attack aimed primarily at opening up political possibilities"[25]—thus implying that the breakthrough in strategic thinking was achieved in Sadat's time.

The characteristics of Sadat's approach were reflected in the resolution to exhaust the potentialities of each move to the limit: during the military phase, committing the full military capacity of Egypt and undertaking all the risks involved in order to ensure maximum chances of success; and, during the diplomatic phase, ignoring some of the *taboos* of the Arab world and executing a rapid shift in political orientation to the fullest extent necessary to achieve his goals.

Before his strategy could be made applicable, Sadat had to make another decision, perhaps the most difficult of all. When considering a military operation the greatest fear was that the Israeli Air Force would resume its deep-penetration strikes into Egypt which, since the War of

Attrition, had become a nightmare to all Egyptians. It was for this reason that the leaders of Egypt brought their full powers of persuasion and pressure to bear on the Russians in order to obtain land-to-land missiles and new interceptor aircraft which, they believed, were necessary to deter Israel from striking into the depths of Egypt. In mid-1972 Sadat realized that the USSR did not intend to supply him with these weapons for the precise reason which had impelled him to ask for them: they would release the main brake on the resumption of warfare. Sadat decided to expel the Russians and prepare for an offensive with the weapons he possessed.

According to Sadat's subsequent account of the developments prior to the October War, once the Soviets were expelled he had a free hand to work out and implement his concept. He promptly instructed the Minister of War, Ahmad Sadiq, to prepare the army, relying only on those means which were at his disposal, so that the "military option" would become operational by 15 November, 1972, after the US elections. However, it seems that among the Egyptian commanders, including Sadiq, disbelief in Egypt's ability to go to war without the arms that had been requested from the USSR was widespread. In October, it appeared to Sadat that Sadiq was dawdling because of his skepticism. He was replaced by Ahmad Isma'il, and at that stage the flow of arms from the Soviet Union was resumed (see above, p. 42). Additional time was given to the military commanders to complete basic preparations by January 1973 and indeed, in that month the basic concepts of the military offensive were crystallized and an Egyptian–Syrian joint command was set up.

In April 1973, Sadat and Asad met at Burj al-'Arab where the crucial decision to go jointly to war was taken. Contingency planning considered May 1973 as an optional date for the offensive but, according to Sadat, this was discarded because of Israel's state of alert, the Nixon–Brezhnev summit meeting, and promises of more weapons from the Soviets. In all likelihood, the decisive consideration was the fact that the Egyptian army had not sufficiently completed its preparations, neither had military coordination with Syria and political coordination with Saudi Arabia been fully worked out. All this was achieved in the subsequent months, mainly in the August bilateral meetings.[26]

In the event, when Sadat's strategy was implemented in October 1973, it achieved most of its goals, despite the overwhelming Israeli victory in the second stage of the war. In the aftermath of the war, Sadat could pride himself on the fact that: "For the first time since the establishment of Israel, we (the Arabs) have succeeded in learning the lessons, taking the proper considerations into account, delineating a program of action and seizing the reigns of the initiative, politically as well as militarily."[27]

THE INTERNAL REGIME

Indications of stagnation and decline had already been visible in the Egyptian Revolutionary regime even before the Six Day War, but it was the shock of defeat which brought matters to a head. In the wake of the war, Nasserism, as a system of ideas and comprehensive program, lost much of its validity and the authority of the Nasserite regime was eroded. With the decline of national consensus, the cohesion of the political community noticeably diminished. For the first time in many years, clashes occurred between Muslims and Copts. Workers went on strike in several industrial plants and student demonstrations reached alarming proportions in scope and level of violence. Protests were made by intellectuals—among them the most prominent figures in the cultural life of Egypt—against the excesses of the revolutionary regime. Petitions were presented even by functionaries of professional associations, despite the fact that they were part and parcel of the regime. The protest movement focused on the demand for *taghyir* (change) and even though there was no agreement as to the nature of the desired change, the actual enunciation of the demand challenged the legitimacy of the political system.

The discontent at the "no war—no peace" situation nourished the crisis. The ever expanding military expenditure, which, according to Egyptian sources, totalled $ 10 billion, brought development to a standstill. The rate of economic growth was slowed down to below 4%: the increase was totally absorbed by the high birth rate and growing public consumption (mainly for the army), and the Egyptians were told to tighten their belts. Sadat himself admitted subsequently that on the eve of the October War Egypt did not possess the financial means to ensure daily food supplies. Public services, especially in Cairo, were so neglected as to cause grave difficulties to the public. Draftees who had been serving since the war in Yemen had not been discharged and new recruits, who now included university graduates as well, were given no date for the termination of their service.

In times of national emergency a society is, of course, capable of bearing burdens heavier than these, but in this case the strains were accompanied by a credibility gap. With faith in the approaching campaign so low, many Egyptians were skeptical about the justification of the sacrifices demanded of them and feared that they were to no avail.

The differences between Nasser and Sadat in personal and political assets found expression in different domestic policies. Four areas where these differences were manifested will be described below: leadership, ideology, political institutions and the socio-economic system.

In the post-1967 crisis, Nasser's renowned charisma, based on his "heroic performance and messianic message,"[28] was no longer there to serve him. Two of the major components of his public image had been weakened by the defeat: the halo of power and success which had so much attracted the masses, and his image as a "son of Egypt" which had made him a focus of identification for them.

For the Egyptians, the man who appeared on television, on 9 June, and in gloomy tones accepted responsibility for the defeat, could no longer be identified with the star that had risen in their sky some twelve years earlier and whose frequent triumphs had been the source of their pride. During his last three years, Nasser was a leader with little credibility and limited pwer; he was beaten and ailing.

Similarly, Nasser's personality lost its appeal as a symbol for identification to the Egyptian public. The defeat and its aftermath brought out those of his qualities which did not tally with what is commonly regarded as the Egyptian character or temperament: his tendency towards hasty decisions and adventurous policies, and the ruthlessness in which he suppressed his political adversaries. Many Egyptians now referred to him in private as *al-wahsh*—the wild beast.

To all appearances, Sadat's personal qualifications were hardly more promising. His public image was dull and he had commonly been regarded as Nasser's "yes-man" devoid of any talents in his own right. His assumption of power was popularly greeted by the saying, *Mat al-wahsh, hadir al-jahsh*—"The wild beast is dead, and the jackass is here." Many regarded Sadat's accession to power as the last straw in Egypt's humiliations. Sadat's various proclamations, in his first year in office, of "deadlines" for the resumption of the war against Israel to which he inevitably failed to adhere, only increased the scorn with which he was viewed by the Egyptian public and particularly the intellectuals. He appeared as the perfect anti-hero, lacking any aura of success.

Yet, gradually, Sadat revealed some aspects of his character which rendered him more agreeable to the Egyptians, especially to the lower classes, and facilitated popular identification with him. Rather than setting himself up as the revered leader of an historic liberation movement, Sadat appeared as a traditional headman, managing the affairs of his community in a paternal fashion. In his public appearances he reflected the Islamic outlook, the values of the Egyptian village and the folk wisdom of the popular classes. Sadat himself described the constituents of his identity in the following terms: *rootedness* in the age-old traditions of Egypt, *solidity* which comes from the tie with the land, and *faith* in Islam.[29] Sadat also impressed the Egyptians with two resolute decisions which he took, in May 1971 and July 1972, the one in domestic and the other in foreign matters. As the result of all these, his public image seemed to be somewhat improved, while still remaining at a relatively low level.

Another problem which Nasser had to face was the decline of his ideology, the doctrine of Nasserism. It is, of course, an open question whether a political community at all needs a formal ideology; however, in Arab society—anguished as it has been in modern times by the disintegration of the traditional system of belief and the crises of identity and disorientation—the need for every body politic to have an ideology has become an accepted norm of political life. Nasser himself had regarded the ability to crystallize an "authentic" ideology as a criterion for the vitality of his regime and the validity of his leadership.

His problem was that the doctrine expressed in the 1962 National Charter had never actually taken root in Egypt. After 1967 it became even clearer that the Charter, with its pseudo-Marxist Third World jargon, was not in tune with the rhythm of Egyptian life and did not relate sufficiently to the values and problems of Egyptian society. Principles such as "dissolving the differences between the classes," and "the alliance of the working forces of the people" remained abstractions with no hold in reality, and they were inseparably associated with the failures of the Nasserite socio-political system.

Nasser recognized the legitimacy of the demand for change and for programmatic re-orientation. In order to meet this demand he presented, in 1968, the "Program of 30 March." However, the Program contained nothing that was new, nor did it include any reference to the basic issues of the time, except for a call to mobilize the national resources for the campaign and activate the institutions of the Arab Socialist Union (see below).

Formally, Sadat never relinquished Nasserism. He maintained that his regime remained loyal to the Nasserite movement, and that he himself was treading Nasser's path. The Nasserite charters, constitutions and programs remained in force, and the principal institutions of the previous regime were preserved.

In actual fact, Sadat laid open the possibility for a comprehensive revision of Nasserism. Without attributing the responsibility directly to Nasser, Sadat spelled out the numerous failures of the preceding regime. The media were allowed to go even one step further, and they accordingly made bitter and hostile attacks on Nasserism.The following extract from *al-Musawwar* is characteristic:

> The past had two aspects: that of the facade, and that of reality. The facade was splendid: it included the abolition of capitalism, of feudalism, of exploitation and of factionalism, along with the struggle against Imperialism, the strengthening of the military, a fair deal for peasants and workers, the realization of social justice, industrialization of the country and unification of the Arab nation from the Ocean to the Gulf.
>
> This splendid facade dazzled us at first, as it dazzled the entire Arab nation... The Arabs believed in this aspect of the past, a belief which had almost become an ideology. The master of this past became a demigod: to honour him, statues were erected and sacrifices were made; institutions and organizations were created hailing his name and fostering his ideology.
>
> This was the facade. As to the reality, matters were utterly different... The practical implementation was made here (in Egypt); we the Egyptians alone were those who had to carry its burden. And it bore no resemblance whatsoever to the facade.[30]

The "de-Nasserization" process created a certain void in the life of Egypt. Into this void Sadat cast several slogans and catch-phrases—such as "Science and Faith" and "the Building of the Modern State"—which reflected the characteristics of Sadat's outlook but never attained the level of a well-ordered program. Sadat, as a pragmatist, was not likely to formulate a doctrine of "Sadatism." The basic documents adopted during this period, such as the Permanent Constitution of 1971 and the ASU Guide to Political Action of 1972, reflected some nuances of Sadat's policies but offered no ideology.

This development was welcomed by Egyptian intellectuals who had resented the imposition of Nasserism upon all spheres of life, and by the Egyptian public in general who had become weary of Nasserite indoctrination. However, for Sadat, there was also a political price to pay: de-Nasserization cast a certain shadow over the legitimacy of his hold on Nasser's inheritance and enabled the ambitious Qadhafi to stake a claim for succession as the Nasserite movement's true leader. Up to the very outbreak of the October War, the Egyptian regime was on the defensive against the ideological fervor of Qadhafi who preached an Arab–Islamic revival in a style reminiscent of Nasser in his early days.

The real nature of the political institutions of Nasser's regime had been questioned even before 1967 but, as seen above, it was only after the defeat that they were openly challenged. The purges which followed the defeat exposed the inner mechanism of the power structure of the regime. The revelations about acts of negligence committed by the military leadership, the 'Amer affair, the public trials of the heads of intelligence, the open frictions with 'Ali Sabri, the clashes over the secret *apparatus* within the ASU—all these laid before the Egyptian public a picture of a brutal struggle for power within the regime's top echelons. The persons involved in the struggle, who were designated in a derogatory manner as "the centers of power," were inextricably bound up with Nasser's political system and the institutions of his regime.

Seen against the background of these revelations, Nasser's recurrent promises to institute a "rule of law" in the country were given little credence. With the decline of his charismatic authority the need to institutionalize his rule became more acute. Nasser managed to defend his position by conducting a series of political purges and by strengthening the instruments of surveillance and coercion, but he had to pay a price. He became the prisoner of his own system, controlling the "centers of power" only by playing the one against the other. He lost the ability to carry out a genuine legitimization process,[31] and thus the "Program of 30 March" turned out to be no more than an exercise in manipulating externalities which did not affect the essence.

Sadat's accession to power set him on a collision course with the "centers of power," if he was not to become their puppet. The clash occurred during the first half of May 1971, when his sudden and decisive move placed all the powerful personages of the top Nasserite echelons behind bars; he then found himself in full control of the ruling apparatus of the state. This opened a rare opportunity to reorganize the political institutions and restore their authority.

Sadat, indeed, declared that he intended to carry out a radical reform in the entire internal political structure, making it subject to the law, institutionalizing and regulating its functions, and subordinating it to the rights and interests of the individual citizen. He proclaimed the establishment of the "State of Institutions" to replace the "State of Secret Recordings." May 15 was designated as a holiday commemorating the birth of the "Reform Movement." Sadat outlined a program for the development of the executive, judicial and representative authorities so as to make Egypt a modern democratic state. He promised to put an end to the harassment of citizens, arrests without trial, confiscations of property and the suppression of the freedom of speech.

The "Reform Movement" yielded very little. As a matter of fact, it became obvious that Sadat had no intention of restricting his own powers in any significant way, nor to make any substantial changes in the political system. Throughout that period, it remained a centralized one-party regime, with all decision-making powers invested in the presidency and political control exercised through an internal security system. Indeed, it seems that the Egyptian public, accustomed to promises of reform which never materialized, did not treat Sadat's proclamations with undue seriousness in the first place.

Yet Sadat, more temperate and paternalistic by nature, did moderate the style of government to a fair extent. In many cases political exiles were repatriated, persons under arrest were released, the restrictions on the press slightly lifted, sequestration of property abolished, and the status of blacklisted intellectuals rehabilitated. These changes were perceivably welcomed by the Egyptian public which was weary of almost two decades of Nasserite authoritarianism.

In the economy, liberalization distinguished Sadat from Nasser in a more substantial way. Initially, Nasser's state-controlled economic system had registered considerable accomplishments, but by the mid-sixties, economic growth had sharply declined. Nasser's "transformation to Socialism" had similarly yielded at the beginning some improvements for the workers and peasants, but after the mid-sixties no more progress had been made in this direction and the post-1967 crisis had considerably aggravated the conditions of the lower classes.

Sadat, with his more conservative outlook and greater pragmatism, opted for a new direction of development following mainly Western patterns. He gradually removed doctrinaire socialist elements from the system and Marxist interpretations of the National Charter were repudiated. The public sector was no longer represented as a realization of the ideal of nationally owned means of production, but rather as a type of economic organization which was sufficiently flexible to suit the changing requirements of development.

Liberalization policies were more substantial in the socio-economic system than in the political system for obvious reasons. While in politics Sadat had no true interest in replacing the autocratic regime which he had inherited, in the field of socio-economics a real need existed for a re-alignment in order to attract capital investments from the Arab oil-producing and Western industrialized states. 'Abd al-'Aziz al-Hijazi, at that time Deputy Prime Minsiter, explained that just as the economy had to undergo the phase of "Egyptianization" in the 1950s and the phase of "Arab Socialism" in the 1960s, so it was now moving into a period of "Economic Openness" which necessitated a considerable degree of liberalization in the economy.[32]

In practical terms, various restrictions on banking and foreign trade were lifted. The private sector was granted full legitimacy and considerable encouragement, and at some point even the possibility of selling part of the public sector's assets to private owners was discussed. It is difficult to tell to what extent this policy has affected in practice the distribution of wealth in Egypt, but it has definitely exposed Sadat's administration to the accusation that it was carelessly allowing the social gap to increase.

INTERNATIONAL POSITION

For the Nasserite regime, the role Egypt played in the international arena was more than a matter of foreign policy—it was a historic mission, the *raison d'être* of the Revolution, and it was here that Nasserism had scored its greatest successes in the fifties. However, on the eve of the Six Day War, the international position of the Nasserite regime was already on the decline and Egypt had lost a good deal of her leverage, both in inter-Arab and global politics.

Egypt's leverage on the inter-Arab level had stemmed originally from Nasser's influence over the masses in the Arab world, an influence which could be manipulated in order to pressure the ruling elites of the Arab states (in the name of *'Uruba*). In the mid-sixties—following the disintegration of the union with Syria in 1961, the failure of the 1963 Tripartite Federation and the entanglement in the Yemen war—this leverage had diminished and the conservative states' resistance to the bloc of "progressive" states under Nasser's leadership became more vigorous.

On the global level, Nasser's leverage ensued from his ability to play the two superpowers one against the other, with the full backing of the Afro–Asian bloc (in the name of "Positive Neutralism"). But here again, with the relaxation of the cold war and the decline of the Afro–Asian bloc, Nasser's blackmailing tactics lost a good deal of their effectiveness. In the mid-1960s the United States, weary of Nasser's game, even refrained from renewing its food supplies to Egypt.

The 1967 defeat accelerated this process and Egypt lost her offensive posture. She became dependent on the economic and military cooperation of the Arab states and, even more so, on Soviet military and political aid. The international prestige of the Nasserite regime reached a low ebb and references were being made in the world press to "the sick man on the banks of the Nile."

This development in Egypt's relations with the Arab world was particularly humiliating for Nasser. He became dependent on the aid of precisely those Arab states which for the preceding two years he had been denouncing. Nasser, the leader of the "liberated" bloc, was forced to seek assistance from the "reactionary" regimes headed by Saudi Arabia. At the Khartoum Conference the latter promised him aid amounting to an annual subsidy of £ 95 million, which was meant to compensate him for the financial losses resulting from the Six Day War (mainly the closure of the Suez Canal), but not much more than that.

Nasser was compelled to bury his hatchet and terminate the ideological warfare within the Arab world, but it was too late to change his political image. Consequently, the regimes of the Arab world, almost all of which had been under attack by Nasser at one time or another, were not too anxious to make substantial sacrifices in order to aid Egypt in her distress. This was very clearly manifested at the 1969 Rabat summit conference when the Arab states rejected Nasser's program for the "mobilization of resources," making him leave the conference frustrated and enraged. Had it not been for the pro-Nasserite *coups* in Libya and Sudan, which allowed him to form a subsitute mini-bloc and thus somewhat repair his position, his great pan-Arab venture might have appeared at the end of his career to be in shambles.

Sadat, on the other hand, was not entirely tied down to the residues of the Nasserite period and the road was open for him to put relations with the Arab states on a new footing. Sadat was evidently aware of this fact. On one occasion he analyzed, in retrospect, the traditional obstacles to Arab cooperation in these terms: firstly, he said, there was the ideological conflict between different types of regimes; secondly, the rivalry and jealousy between the Arab rulers; and thirdly, the imposition of superpower competition on inter-Arab relations.[33] All these, he felt, should be eliminated in order to achieve effective Arab collaboration.

True to his concept, Sadat abandoned the pretensions and aspirations for Egyptian hegemony over other Arab states. He changed the country's official name from the "United Arab Republic" to the "Arab Republic of Egypt." Egyptianism became a strongly stressed theme in his statements, to the relief of the other Arab regimes and the joy of many Egyptians who had never approved Nasser's imposition of Arabism on their society. In the same vein, Sadat set down the principle that inter-Arab relations should be based on pragmatic considerations of mutual interest, and not on rhetorical slogans and visions of grandeur.

This position was resented by Sadat's neighbor to the west, Col. Mu'ammar al-Qadhafi, who remained faithful to the spirit of messianic Nasserism. Throughout most of this period, Sadat was under heavy pressure from Qadhafi to implement the union between the two countries, according to Egypt's commitments under the terms of the federation pact. For Sadat, whose domestic position was none too firm, this pressure (culminating in Qadhafi's "grand march" on Cairo in July 1973) was highly disturbing. Yet, in Sadat's estimate, cooperation with Saudi Arabia was more important than union with Libya. While the latter would have deflected him off course, away from his major objectives, the former could aid him in reaching them. His *rapprochement* with King Faisal was met with criticism, and exposed him to the accusation that he preferred Arab wealth (*tharwa*) to Arab revolution (*thawra*). But, it was these practical politics which led to the creation of the Cairo–Riyad axis as the basis for the military-diplomatic offensive of October 1973.

Egypt's growing dependence on the Soviet Union, as the result of Nasser's actions and policies, was probably the greatest setback for Nasserism, which—it should be remembered—had started originally as a liberation movement. In less than a decade and a half, the Soviet posture developed from seemingly disinterested assistance to a real threat to Egyptian sovereignty.

Two main stages may be distinguished in this process. The first began immediately after the 1967 defeat when Nasser became totally dependent on the Soviets for the rehabilitation of his army. The second came with the escalation of the War of Attrition and the intensification of the Israeli Air Force's deep penetration strikes in late 1969 which, in turn, led Nasser to seek Soviet protection for Egyptian air space. In both cases, Soviet aid was indispensible and without it Egypt's strategic and political position would have been critically paralyzed.

In the first case, the rehabilitation of the army was carried out by the Soviets on an unprecedented scale. Up to the end of 1968, the Soviets siphoned into Egypt weapons valued at $ 2.5 billion without pressing for any financial return. In the second case, SA-3 missiles as well as other arms were rushed into Egypt, and regular Soviet anti-aircraft units and MiG-21 pilots assumed responsibility for protecting vital zones in Egypt.

Nasser was not unaware of the implications of dependency on the USSR, but since the campaign against Israel was of the highest priority he was prepared to reconcile himself to it. As seen above, according to his basic strategic concepts, the Soviets were expected to play an active part in uprooting the Israelis from the occupied territories. Yet, it seems that Nasser's tendency to lean on the Soviet Union was not adopted entirely out of necessity but he was predisposed to take this line. It should be remembered that his formative years as a political leader were those of the rise of Afro–Asian "positive Neutralism" as an anti-imperialist movement sympathetic to the Soviet Union. Some of his greatest achievements had been associated with the USSR, such as the triumph over the Baghdad Pact, the building of the Aswan High Dam, the industrialization of Egypt, and the modernization of the army.

The United States, on the other hand, represented for Nasser a hostile power with which he had clashed bitterly at several points along his political course. As the writings of his close associate Heikal have shown, his distrust of the Americans and antagonism towards them were deeply implanted in his outlook. Both Heikal and Sadat have described Nasdser as "a leader of the Cold War period."[34]

Nasser stated clearly that "Egypt would not remain neutral between friends and enemies." The United States (with whom diplomatic relations had been severed after the Six Day War) was associated with Israel and could in no way be expected to offer the types of aid provided by the USSR. Despite the Rogers Plan and other US attempts to accommodate Egyptian demands, the United States remained for Nasser a constraint which had to be neutralized and not a potential partner. He did try to maintain with the United States what Sadat described as "a thin line of communication"[35] (which became of considerable importance on the eve of the August 1970 ceasefire) but his hopes lay mainly with the Soviet Union.

In Nasser's view, therefore, it was expedient to receive Soviet guidance on political as well as military matters, to provide the USSR with bases in Egypt, and to welcome the presence of nearly 20,000 Soviet military personnel on Egyptian soil. According to revelations made after his death, he was ready to give the command of the air force to Soviet generals and was eager to sign a treaty of alliance with the USSR.[36]

But there was a limit to this readiness and Nasser tried to draw the line in domestic affairs. The greater his dependence on the Soviets grew, the harsher was his attitude to leftist and pro-Soviet elements in Egypt. However, even this last line began to be breached towards the end of the period. His weak stance towards the Russians compelled him, in April 1970, to recall the pro-Soviet 'Ali Sabri, and appoint him—shortly after he had been deposed—liaison officer with the Soviets. (It was subsequently argued that it was this humiliation which precipitated his physical deterioration and ultimate heart failure.)[37]

Sadat had a number of reasons to reconsider that policy. At the time of his accession to power, following the trauma of the restoration of 'Ali Sabri, a sense of disillusionment with the Soviets had set in to the Egyptian leadership (and most notably in military circles). According to Sadat, when Nasser returned from his last visit to the USSR—the prolonged visit of June-July 1970—he was depressed by the inflexibility of the Russians and the harsh terms they had set for supplying the arms he requested; he told Sadat that the Russians were "a hopeless case."[38]

Sadat saw Soviet hands behind the "centers of power" who tried to undermine his position. It was only with great difficulty that he managed to coordinate with the Soviets the removal of 'Ali Sabri, and he had to pay a recompense for it in the form of the May 1971 Treaty of Friendship and Cooperation which he deeply resented.[39]

The Soviets were quite high-handed with Sadat. They did not esteem him very highly and considered him a transitional ruler only. His urgent requests for military assistance, in his trip to Moscow in March 1971, were turned down and Sadat tended to blame the Soviets for having been left without any capability of action at the close of his "year of decision."

Conversely, he had good reasons to upgrade his relations with the United States. In the Egyptian political spectrum he was closer to the Right and he had great admiration for Western technology and management methods. The economic exigences prescribed a re-orientation towards the industrialized western world and the pro-US oil-rich conservative Arab regimes. To rehabilitate Egypt's international and inter-Arab position, it was definitely necessary to demonstrate a capacity to maneuver between the super-powers and at that stage it meant movement towards the United States.

Above all, Sadat firmly believed that the key for restoring the lost territories was in the hands of the United States which was the only power to possess the necessary leverage over Israel. He did not expect to bring the United States to take this course of action through Egyptian pressure, but rather through collaboration based on areas of overlapping interests. This was the basis for his intensive contacts with the US diplomats on the question of an interim agreement, during the first half of 1971. It was in the course of these negotiations that he publicly issued a call to President Nixon "to put the screw on Israel."[40]

Realizing, at the end of that phase, that the United States was not ready to apply a one-sided pressure on Israel, Sadat was reinforced in his conviction that a military action had to come first. This made him turn to the Soviets once again. The military option was contingent—according to the Egyptian assessment—on the supply of strategic weapons, particularly ground-to-ground missiles and MiG-23 aircraft. Sadat's requests to the Soviets to supply him with these arms grew increasingly desperate. Between October 1971 and April 1972 he rushed off to Moscow three times to beg the Russians for their supply, but to no avail.

Apparently, in mid-1972, Sadat crystallized a new evaluation of the problem. He realized that Nasser's formula, namely reconciliation to Soviet patronage in order to receive, by way of return, active Soviet aid towards the restoration of the territories, was not operative. On the contrary, the stronger the Soviet hegemony in Egypt grew, the less ready they became to invest efforts and undertake risks in order to aid Egypt to achieve that purpose. Despite the considerable degree of convergence of political positions, the practical implication of their policy was the solidification of the stalemate in the Israeli–Arab arena.

Sadat also viewed Soviet–American detente, which was taking shape at that time, with great anxiety. Agreement between the two superpowers he feared would induce the Soviets to abandon their insistence on the restoration of Arab territories. It could only work for reinforcing the *status-quo* and creating conditions which would be very difficult for Egypt to upset.

Sadat, therefore, reasoned that if the Russians were reluctant to aid Egypt in going to war, their presence in Egypt could only be a hindrance. It was better to maintain a military option with the weapons presently in Egypt's possession than to forego it completely. In addition, Soviet presence was not consistent with the two-phase strategy formulated by Sadat: it restricted him from pressing the button for launching the military phase, and would certainly have hampered the shift towards the United States during the diplomatic phase. In July 1972, with the culmination of the frictions between Sadat and the Kremlin, Sadat took the crucial decision and the Soviets were told to leave.

Having ousted the Soviets, Sadat was in no haste to turn towards the United States. He apparently discarded the option of turning at that point to the Americans because, as long as the military operation was the imminent step, Sadat could not forego Soviet military assistance altogether. Therefore, even after July 1972, Sadat continued his efforts to maintain a certain degree of cooperation with the USSR, in order to draw the maximum military aid obtainable from that source. In October 1972, a certain improvement in relations was achieved, and in February 1973, an even more significant thaw took place.

In May 1973, Fu'ad Matar, a Lebanese journalist who had excellent connections in Cairo, reported in a conversation with Qadhafi: "I found out that there had been a change in the Soviet position, and that they had become convinced that if Sadat was resolved to fight they must help him and satisfy his demands, for the following considerations:

should he win, they would share the fruits of his victory; should he fail, he alone would have to pay the price of defeat." In an article written from Cairo at that time, Matar reported additional weapons and electronic equipment having been promised by Soviet Ambassador Vinogradov to Sadat at a meeting in mid-May.[41]

The foundations of Soviet–Egyptian cooperation during the October War were thus laid during 1973. There are many indications that full understanding was not in fact attained between the parties, and the Soviets were not certain about the definite date of the attack till a very late stage. Although Sadat complained that the arms he had received were not all that he had expected and been promised, they definitely included what the Soviets had not been supplying to him before they were ousted from Egypt, including some of the long-desired missiles. Thus, by forcing their hands, Sadat had succeeded in obtaining the armaments required for the military offensive, as well as the Soviet "umbrella" which insured him against total collapse in face of the inevitable Israeli counter-strike.

The promptness with which Sadat turned to the United States at the end of the War reflected clearly the fact that the shift had been premeditated and Sadat had never abandoned his belief that the ultimate vehicle for achieving his present target was diplomacy in collaboration with the United States.

• • •

Three years after Sadat succeeded Nasser, the relationship between their public images had become reversed. While at the outset of Sadat's administration it was commonly asked how a person as mediocre as Sadat could step into the shoes of a leader of such historic stature as Nasser, it has now become customary in Egypt to point out Sadat's merits by contrasting them to the weaknesses of Nasser.

Indeed, during the few years of his rule, Sadat has displayed skills so unexpected that there are observers today who believe that Sadat had intentionally maintained a low profile during Nasser's period, in order to prevent his liquidation in one of Nasser's political purges.[42] Since he became Egypt's president, Sadat has convincingly demonstrated political sophistication and shrewdness, capacity to make difficult decisions, a good sense of timing, and flexibility in the choice of methods coupled with an adherence to ultimate targets.

Nevertheless, Sadat's capacities should not be overstated. Reviewing Sadat's moves over a period of three years, in the light of his accomplishment in the October War, one is tempted to regard them all as corresponding systematically to a preconceived blueprint. This, certainly, was not the case. Many of Sadat's steps were taken, groping in the dark, as mere improvisations, and possibly on the basis of some wrong assumptions as well. With all his achievements, Sadat still confronts a somber reality in which all the crucial problems of Egypt remain as yet unsolved, and it is not at all certain that he possesses the concepts and programs which could lead to their solution.

NOTES

1. Muhammad Hasanayn Heikal in an interview with Ahmad Isma'il, *al-Anwar*, 18 November, 1973.

2. Accordingly, the symposium on the October War, held at Cairo University on 27–31 October, 1975, devoted a whole section to the "civilizational aspects" of the war.

3. See Heikal's series of articles on the Nasserite period in *al-Anwar*, 12, 14, 16, 18 July, 1975.

4. See 'Abd al-Sattar Tawila's book on the "Six Hours War" serialized in *Ruz al-Yusuf*, 7 October, 1974.

5. Serialized in *al-Ahram*, 28 September, 1975.

6. See Salim al-Lawzi's view on this subject in *al-Hawadith*, 8 February, 1974.

7. See *Middle East Record (MER)*, Vol. III (1967), p. 266.

8. The 19 June, 1967, resolution reads: "Israel offers to sign a peace treaty with Egypt on the basis of the international borders and Israel's security needs. According to the international border, the Gaza Strip is within the territory of the State of Israel. The peace treaty will have to guarantee the freedom of navigation in the Straits of Tiran and in the Gulf of Aqaba (*mifratz shlomo*), freedom of navigation in the Suez Canal, air rights over the Straits of Tiran and the Gulf of Aqaba, and the demilitarization of the Sinai Peninsula. Until a peace treaty is concluded, Israel will continue holding the territories she now holds." The Minister of Foreign Affairs was authorized to discuss details of this resolution in his talks with the representatives of the US administration. This he did shortly afterwards. (Text of resolution in Shiloah Center Archives.)

9. The following passage from Heikal is particularly revealing: "Nasser was always sceptical about Resolution 242. At one of his regular meetings with senior army commanders, which took place on 25 November, only three days after the passing of the Resolution, he said to them: 'Let me tell you a few facts. Everything you hear us say about the UN Resolution is not meant for you, and has nothing to do with you. If you look at what the Israelis are doing in the occupied territories it is perfectly obvious that they are never going to evacuate

these areas unless they are made to do so. Please remember what I have said before—what has been taken by force can only be recovered by force. This is not rhetoric: I mean it...If I were Levi Eshkol or Moshe Dayan I would do the same thing as they are doing; they want to expand and now they think they have the chance to expand. I don't see that even if they wanted to they could withdraw, because they have fed their people with too many hopes and promises. What they are saying now will inevitably harden into official policy and they will become bound by it. So you don't need to pay any attention to anything I may say in public about a peaceful solution.'" Mohamed Heikal, *The Road to Ramadan*, (London 1975) p. 54.

10. Heikal, "Abdel Nasser's Talks in Moscow," *al-Ahram*, 12 July, 1968.

11. Subsequently, the combination itself was referred to in Egypt as "the military solution."

12. See the analysis of this problem in Heikal's articles, e.g., *al-Ahram*, 3 July, 1970; 3 March, 1972; *al-Anwar*, 24 May, 1973.

13. Speech on 10 April, 1968, *al-Ahram*, 11 April, 1968.

14. See, for example, his speech at the al-Husayn Mosque, in which he described the Jews, using the Quranic expression, as a people "condemned to degradation and deprivation," *al-Ahram*, 26 April, 1972.

15. The record of that meeting is presented in Musa Sabri, *watha'iq harb uktubar*, Cairo 1974; and appears to be, mainly, authentic. See pp. 39–41, 62.

16. Serialized in *al-Ahram*. The quotation is from the 24 October, 1975 issue. It should be noted that just as the term "peace" (*salam*) does not denote in Arabic full reconciliation, so for Sadat, the meaning of "peace agreement" falls short of the Western purport of this term. "Peace agreement" is not a peace treaty, he explained, for even the 1949 armistice can be termed a "peace agreement"; Musa Sabri, *loc. cit.*

17. The gap separating the positions of the two parties was summed up by Brig. Y. Raviv—who was at the time the military secretary of Minister of Defense Moshe Dayan—in an article in *Ma'arachot*, the IDF monthly. According to Raviv the following Israeli demands were not met by Sadat: An Egyptian commitment not to resume warfare (Sadat offered a ceasefire limited in time); a self-contained agreement (Sadat wanted to make it conditional upon proceeding to the implementation of full withdrawal according to a predetermined time-table); prohibiting the crossing of the Suez Canal by substantial Egyptian forces (Sadat wanted Egyptian military formations on the Canal's east bank); withdrawal from the Canal zone only (Sadat said in an interview to *Newsweek* that he wanted the Israelis to withdraw beyond the al-'Arish-Ras-Muhammad line); opening the Canal for Israeli ships (Sadat spoke of cargoes only); and certain other demands concerning the status of the evacuated area, the stationing of UN troops and the determination of inspection arrangements. According to Raviv, the first two issues were the crucial stumbling blocs.

Y. Raviv, "Nisyonot muqdamim le-hesder benayim ben yisrael le-mitzrayim (ba-shanim 1971–1972),"*Ma'arachot*, April–May 1975, pp. 2–17. See also Musa Sabri, *loc.cit.*

18. See Sadat's Speeches 14 May, *al-Ahram*, 15 May, 1971; 10 June, *al-Ahram*, 11 June, 1971; also his "October Paper," *al-Ahram*, 1 May, 1974.

19. Lutfi al-Khuli, "Sadat's Political Doctrine," *al-Ahram*, 11 June, 1975.

20. See the author's "Some Arab Attitudes toward the Conflict with Israel between 1967 and 1973," in G. Sheffer (ed.), *Dynamics of a Conflict*, (Atlantic Highlands 1975) pp. 185–199.

21. Sadat's speech on 1 May, 1973, in Mahalla al-Kubra, *R. Cairo*, 1 May—*BBC*, 3 May, 1973.

22. Interview to *Ruz al-Yusuf*, 13 January, 1975; to *al-Hawadith*, March, 1975.

23. *Road to Ramadan*, pp. 155f.

24. Interview to *al-Akhbar*, 29 May, 1975.

25. *Road to Ramadan*, p. 168.

26. Sadat in an interview to Musa Sabri, *Akhbar al-Yawm*, 3 August, 1974; to *Ruz al-Yusuf*, 12 September, 1974, 13 January, 1975; to *al-Usbu' al-'Arabi*, 9 October, 1974; Heikal, *Road to Ramadan*, pp. 10–14, 180–82.

27. "The October Paper," *al-Ahram*, 1 May, 1974.

28. R. H. Dekmejian, *Egypt under Nasir*, (Albany 1971) p. 5.

31. See Robert Springborg, "Patterns of Associations in the Egyptian Political Elite," in G. Lenczowski (ed.), *Political Elites in the Middle East*, (Washington 1975) pp. 83–108.

32. *Al-Musawwar*, 24 August, 1973; *al-Ahram*, 14 August, 1973.

33. Sadat in an interview to Salim al-Lawzi, *al-Hawadith*, 26 April, 1974.

34. Heikal in an interview to *BBC*, 20 June, 1975, Sadat's speech on Radio Cairo, 14 April, 1975, *al-Ahram*, 15 April, 1975.

35. Sadat's memoirs *al-Ahram*, 24 October, 1975.

36. Sadat's interview to *as-Siyasa* (Kuwait), 9 September, 1975; speech at the People's Assembly, 14 March, 1976; *al-Ahram*, 15 March, 1976, interview to al-Lawzi, *al-Hawadith*, March 1975.

37. An interesting account of this affair appears in *al-Jadid*, 7 May, 1971.

38. Sadat's interview to al-Lawzi, *al-Hawadith*, 26 April, 1974.

39. Sadat's interview to *as-Siyasa* (Kuwait), 9 September, 1975.

40. Sadat's speech, 20 May, 1971, *R. Cairo*, 20 May; *BBC*, 20 May, 1971.

41. Fu'ad Matar in *al-Nahar*, 16, 17, 19 May, 1973.

42. Al-Lawzi in *al-Hawadith*, 8 February, 1974.

29. Sadat's speech to the ASU Central Committee and the People's Assembly, 28 September, 1972, *R. Cairo*, 28 September—*BBC*, 30 September, 1972.

30. Salih Jawdat, in *al-Musawwar*, 15 March, 1974.

Continuity and Change in the Ba'th Regime in Syria

Itamar Rabinovich

The question of continuity and change is an issue of general interest in the study of the Ba'th regime in Syria. Though the formal continuity of the regime and the party has been preserved since 1963, both underwent profound changes which were to culminate in the intra-Ba'th *coups* of 23 February, 1966 and 14 November, 1970. Within this framework the years 1967 to 1973 are of particular interest because of the seizure of power in the middle of the period by Hafiz al-Asad. Asad's policies were shaped to a considerable extent by his efforts to solve the problems he inherited from the regime he had dislodged on 14 November, 1970, but his efforts and success have been constrained by the legacy which he inherited as a major figure of that very regime.

Asad's most notable success has been in coping with the problems of institutionalizing and stabilizing relations within the Ba'th ruling group. During its first years in power the Ba'th eliminated all real opposition in Syria and became the sole effective power in the country. In the absence of significant extra-Ba'th opposition, relations within the Ba'th elite became the crucial issue of Syrian politics and the failure to regulate these relations had plagued the Ba'th regime between 1963 and 1970.[1]

The intra-Ba'th struggle was particularly fierce during the first phase of the regime, between March 1963 and February 1966. The *coup* of 23 February, 1966 reduced the number of factions and issues involved in this struggle but also produced new conditions which perpetuated it.

For one thing the *coup* was staged by a heterogeneous coalition within which differences were sometimes more apparent than common ground. Typical was the rivalry between the predominantly 'Alawi faction of Salah Jadid and the predominantly Druze faction of Salim Hatum which undermined the stability of the regime throughout 1966.

Of more lasting importance was the conflict which developed between Salah Jadid and Hafiz Asad. In addition to the personal and ideological differences between these two 'Alawi officers their rivalry concerned one of the major issues of Syrian–Ba'th politics: the relationship between the Ba'th Party and the dominant faction in the Syrian Army. During the years 1963 to 1966 the former became an instrument of the latter, providing it with a legitimizing ideology, a cadre of activists and loyal bureaucrats and a framework for institutionalized political activity. But even after the emasculation and final ouster of the historic Ba'th leadership, the party did not become a fully malleable tool in the hands of the military.

The circumstances of the *coup* of 23 February gave this pattern of relations a peculiar twist. Salah Jadid, the central figure of the new regime, found himself retired from the army in February 1966 and sought to exercise his power from the position of Assistant Secretary General of the Syrian Ba'th. Jadid realized the critical importance of controlling the army and was not satisfied with his informal status among the Syrian officer corps as the leader of their strongest faction. He tried to develop the military section of the Ba'th Party into an organ that would also give him formal authority over all party members in the army. This led in time to friction between the army and the party; Hafiz al-Asad, Commander of the Air Force and Acting Minister of Defense, emerged as the champion of the military establishment's interests in opposition to the party.

Asad himself articulated the army's position in a lengthy report which he presented to the Regional Congress of the Syrian Ba'th in March 1969. He charged among other things that "within the army, particularly after the defeat of 5 June, 1967, the party leadership played a destructive role, the like of which had not been played by the most reactionary and anti-popular governments in Syria. It kept trying to incite CoS Suwaydani by maintaining personal contacts and directing the affairs of the army and the factions in it without the knowledge of the Minister of Defense and outside the command's meetings...these matters did not end with the Chief of Staff but went so far as the maintenance of contacts outside the regular chain of command with the army's rank and file."[2]

In the confrontation which took place during this party congress in March 1969 Asad demonstrated the military superiority of his faction, but refrained from taking over the government. He was apparently unwilling to take full power into his hands before he was assured of control of the party. Such control was necessary for a smooth transition of power and for maintaining at least a semblance of continuity of Ba'th Party rule. When Asad finally did seize full power in Syria on 14 November, 1970, he did not act of his own choosing in as much as he responded to a challenge posed by his rivals.

This course of events offers a partial explanation for the relative cohesion of Asad's regime which is in such marked contrast to the Ba'th experience in the periods 1963 to 1966 and 1966 to 1970. It was highly significant that Asad did not come to power as the senior partner in a victorious coalition but as the sole unquestioned leader of a broad military and civilian faction. This enabled him to relinquish the principle of collective leadership, a previously cherished tenet of Ba'th political doctrine, and gradually to build up a presidential regime bolstered by a personality cult.

The more pronounced military bias of the Asad regime served to simplify the relationship between its military and civilian sectors. The primacy of the military in Asad's system had been established almost two years before his takeover, and the civilian party militants and functionaries who joined him probably had no illusion with regard to their relative position in the hierarchy of power. The cooperativeness of the civilian party hierarchy has had a paradoxical effect on the image of the Asad regime. In contrast to previous periods the military was not called on to intervene openly in the proceedings of the party, nor did it feel the need to be heavily represented in party forums. Thus the apparent predominance of the civilians has served to cloak the military character of the regime. When the Syrian Ba'th Party held its Fifth Ordinary Regional Congress in May 1971, some six months after Asad's rise to power, his control of a reformed party organization and the harmony between that organization and the regime's military core were apparent.[3]

It is a corollary of the stability of Asad's regime that little is known about its most vital aspect, the inner structure and workings of the Ba'th military. Information about these issues in earlier periods of Ba'th rule has been derived primarily from altercations and revelations which came in the wake of intra-party squabbling. The scant information which has percolated through, however, suggests that in its essence the Asad regime is a continuation of the original Ba'th political system in that it is based on a hard core of army officers attached to their factional leader by primordial ties—personal, family and sectarian. The change has been in the coherence of this hard core after November 1970, and its ability to manipulate the other components of the Ba'th political system in a smooth and efficient manner.[4]

While less crucial than the organization of the power structure within his regime, the most salient feature of Asad's domestic policy in the years 1970 to 1973 was his attempt to reduce the antagonism between the regime and the urban middle classes and to acquire legitimacy for the regime.

One of the distinctive features of the Ba'th regime in Syria as it developed in the years 1963 to 1966 was the dichotomy between the new ruling elite and the urban population. The regime's public base narrowed still further after the ouster of a considerable number of party leaders and members in February 1966. The February *coup* also underlined some of the characteristics which had alienated a significant part of the middle classes in the country's major cities in the three previous years: the regime's sectarian composition, secular approach and radical image. The practical consequences of the antagonism between the Ba'th and the urban population were aggravated by the political remoteness and ineffectuality of those social groups which could have been a source of public support for the regime.

While this did not pose an immediate political danger to the regime it did signify a fundamental weakness that could have become critical in times of crisis. The regime's awareness of the hostility, or at least alienation, of important segments of the urban population explains, at least in part, the somber mood which reigned in Syria between 1966 and 1970. The country was practically closed to foreign visitors and Syrians themselves rarely traveled abroad. There were shortages of consumer goods and the government dealt heavy-handedly with its political opponents.[5]

Asad, who has shown himself to be a more pragmatic and less doctrinaire politician than his partner-rivals of the late 1960s, has addressed himself to this problem since November 1970 in a different manner. He has sought to reconcile the urban middle classes by restructuring the regime and redressing some of their concrete grievances. Asad's determination to bring about such a reorientation of Syrian domestic politics was reflected in the first policy statement issued by the new regime on 16 November. He further elaborated on the subject in the first major speech he delivered, after the "corrective movement" of 14 November, 1970. Asad called for the creation of "a comfortable domestic atmosphere" and for the generation of confidence "among all classes and the progressive and patriotic elements" in order to strengthen the home front. He promised a permanent constitution and a legislative assembly and emphasized in a clear departure from the political terminology of the previous years the importance of "the citizen's liberty and honor."[6]

The implementation of this new policy of "openness" began during the last weeks of 1970 and continued during the years 1971 to 1973.

One series of measures set the regime on firmer constitutional ground. A legislative People's Assembly was appointed in February 1971 and, on 12 March of the same year, Asad was elected president for seven years. Provincial elections were held in 1972 and in 1973 a permanent constitution was promulgated and a new legislative assembly elected.

The Ba'th since 1963 had attached non-Ba'th representatives to the Syrian cabinets chiefly in order to demonstrate that the regime rested on a broad rather than a strictly partisan basis. Later on, the slogan "leading party" was adopted so as to depict the role of the Ba'th as the leader of a coalition of revolutionary movements. Asad developed this line further in 1972 by setting up the "National Progressive Front" in which the Ba'th participated, along with the Communists, the Nasserists and Akram Hourani's faction. By vesting the National Progressive Front with status and authority, although not with actual power, Asad sought to mollify those who objected to the notion of exclusive Ba'th domination without actually loosening the party's hold.

Another series of measures was designed to create a better public atmosphere in Syria. Asad, who had explicitly declared his intention to act to placate disaffected elements, followed his statements with gestures directed at such discontented groups as the Sunni community, the religious hierarchy and commercial circles. Thus, several political prisoners were released and a number of political exiles were allowed to return; a number of emergency decrees were cancelled; travel to Lebanon was allowed without travel permits; the policy of "socialist transformation" was reasserted, but a measure of economic liberalism was promised. The importation of consumer goods was facilitated and efforts were made to attract Arab and Syrian money from abroad.[7]

The impact of this policy was reinforced by the success of Syria's new line in inter-Arab relations described below. In previous years the regime's radical and doctrinaire line and Egypt's rejection of its legitimacy had isolated it in the Arab world. The improvement of Syria's standing and the active role it began to play in inter-Arab politics consequently removed a major source of complaint against the Ba'th regime.

But the policy of mollifying the Ba'th regime's opponents contained an inherent flaw. Perceptive observers were bound to notice that the essence of the regime was unchanged and that its new domestic policy consisted essentially of a series of gestures that were calculated to mask its true nature. Furthermore, the liberal policies of the Asad regime supplied the currents of opposition with opportunities to voice their sentiments. Thus in the provincial elections of 1972, which were held in a relatively free atmosphere,, several of the government's candidates were defeated by traditionalist candidates. The regime was then forced to intervene in order to prevent a serious political embarrassment.

Still more embarrassing were the demonstrations and other manifestations of opposition in Syria's central cities in February 1973 in protest against the proposed draft of the new permanent constitution, the reduced status of Islam, the formalized status of the Ba'th party and, in a more implicit way, the dominant position of the 'Alawis in the Ba'th regime. In view of the scope and intensity of the opposition, the Ba'th amended the constitution and restored the former position of Islam.[8]

The manifestations of opposition in 1972 and 1973 thus illuminated the peculiar position of the Ba'th regime in Syria after ten years in power. On the one hand the regime was, and felt, secure enough to experiment with constitutional reform and it handled the opposition with dexterity and confidence. At the same time the emergence and impact of the opposition bore witness to the regime's tenuous hold over significant segments of the Syrian population.

Syria's policy in the Arab–Israeli conflict has traditionally been closely linked to its Arab policy and to the shifts in its domestic politics. The *coup* which brought Asad to power was triggered by the altercations which followed Syria's abortive intervention in the Jordanian civil war and, as early as his first few weeks in office, Asad presented his own different approach to the problem faced by Syria as a result of the Six Day War.

The immediate outcome of the Six Day War constituted a twofold challenge for the Syrian Ba'th regime. Since the regime had based its claim to legitimacy in part on its claim to possess a doctrine that would lead the Arabs to victory over Israel, it now was faced with the need not only to explain that the doctrine still held true, but also to explain away its own military defeat. Secondly, the regime continually had to prove to

Syrian public opinion that it was doing its utmost to regain the Golan Heights and that, in any case, it was doing no less than the other Arab regimes which had lost territory as a result of the Six Day War.

Following a few weeks of confusion in the summer of 1967, the Ba'th regime formulated a policy that was designed to solve these problems. The Ba'th stated that military action remained the only way open to the Arabs in the Arab–Israeli conflict and that the liberation of the Golan Heights would be achieved as part of an over-all military solution. Attempts to regain territory lost in 1967 through diplomatic bargaining were futile. Theoretically, this line was diametrically opposed to Egypt's policy, which sought the return of Sinai through a political settlement provided the conditions of such a settlement conformed to Egyptian requirements. In practice there was no such diametrical opposition since the Ba'thists did not fully oppose Egypt's experimentation with a political option. The Syrian regime expressed its fundamental reservations with regard to this policy, voiced its doubts, and would not endorse Security Council Resolution 242, but it refrained from explicit denunciation of Egyptian policy.

For one thing the Syrians were not convinced that the Egyptian approach was doomed to fail. They felt that if Egypt reached an agreement over the Sinai, Cairo could not ignore the Golan Heights, i.e., there might be some prospects for Syria in Egypt's policy. Soviet and Egyptian pressures on Syria not to obstruct Egyptian policy reinforced these Syrian considerations.

The weakness of this policy was the regime's susceptibility to criticism for preaching war while not in fact investing effort and taking real risks to recover the Golan Heights. The answer to this problem was already sketched out in 1967: the bestowal of maximum support for the Palestinian organizations and especially for operations carried out from Jordanian and Lebanese territory. The Syrian regime knew how to tread carefully the fine line between explicit backing of this activity and fostering the impression that credit for it was due to Syria.

For the most part, Syria executed this policy successfully and suffered minimal damage compared to Egypt, Jordan, and even Lebanon during the years 1967 to 1970. Despite even a reduction of military activity on the Golan front, little public criticism of the Syrian regime was heard. During 1970 a slight change was noticeable in Syrian policy—the army was built up, the regime's confidence increased, and the government conducted a more active and aggressive border policy. But the contradiction latent in the policy of encouraging Palestinian organizations while maintaining minimal involvement finally became apparent in September 1970 when civil war broke out in Jordan.

The Ba'th regime was forced to make a very difficult choice. The situation was further confounded by domestic political developments, as Jadid's faction tried to exploit the situation in order to embarrass and weaken Asad and his military supporters. As mentioned above, these attempts finally forced Asad's hand and he seized full power in Syria in mid-November 1970.

Asad's more pragmatic approach to these issues had already been evinced before the events of the summer and fall of 1970 by his advocacy of close military and political cooperation with other Arab regimes in disregard of ideological differences or even animosities. This approach was confirmed after his rise to power by Syria's participation first in the Tripoli Charter with Egypt, Libya and Sudan and then in the tripartite federation with Egypt and Libya. Nasser's death in September 1970 reduced the threat of a Nasserite resurgence in Syria and facilitated Syrian cooperation with Egypt by eliminating residual mistrust.

The new bias of Syria's Arab policy was clearly reflected in Asad's speech of 5 December, 1970. Asad placed the chief stress on the formation of a broad united Arab front that would mobilize the totality of Arab resources and lead to an all-Arab participation in the forthcoming struggle.[9] Three weeks earlier his rivals had been advocating a policy which called for cooperation with progressive regimes only, and had denounced the Iraqi regime and Syria's participation in Arab Summit conferences.[10]

A further step in the same new direction was taken during the Ba'th Party Congress in May 1971. The "political report" presented to the Congress recommended that the party relinquish its total rejection of Security Council Resolution 242, which had led Syria into a diplomatic impasse and, while adhering to its fundamental principles, adopt a more flexible policy. The analysis which accompanied this recommendation contained a number of observations which elucidated Syria's outlook. It pointed to the clear distinction to be drawn after 1967 between the Palestine problem and the issues of the territories lost in the Six Day War. The Arab position with regard to the former was defined as the insistence on the rights of the Palestinians "without a precise definition of these rights." Syria and Egypt alone of all the Arab countries were seriously confronting Israel. The Palestinian organizations were on the retreat and hardly effective. Altogether Israel was becoming stronger and new methods for confronting it ought to be found.[11]

It took almost a year until the change in Syria's policy was made public. The occasion was Asad's speech on Revolution Day, 8 March, 1972. The Syrian President explained that the circumstances in which Syria found itself required simultaneous military and political action. Such combined action would implement the two fundamental goals: 1) liberation of the territories lost in 1967; and 2) restoration of the rights of the Palestinian people. Asad then went on to say that when the interpretation of Security Resolution 242 reflected these fundamental aims, it would receive Syrian support. His statement amounted to a qualified acceptance of the resolution.[12]

These developments in Syria's Arab policy and in the regime's approach to the Arab–Israeli conflict were crucial for the emergence of the Syrian–Egyptian axis on the eve of the October War. An agreement to go to war together could hardly have been conceived in the state of Syrian–Egyptian relations before the end of 1970. The degree of mutual confidence and proximity of outlook that had been reached after that time made such an agreement possible. All the same, however, the similarity of outlook and restoration of confidence were relative and had their limits. Syria was a rather passive partner in the process that led to the war. The process was initiated and led by Egypt and was designed according to the Egyptian conception as subsequently presented by President Sadat on 16 October, 1974. Despite the changes which had taken place in its position since 1970, Syria did not fully share this conception, and this remained an inherent source of tension in the Egyptian–Syrian alliance. The fact that Syria found itself playing a junior role in the partnership further exacerbated this tension. Its outcome can already be seen in the conduct of the October War and the political developments which have resulted from it.

NOTES

1. On the political history of Syria and the Ba'th during the period, see T. Petran, *Syria* (London 1972); I. Rabinovich, *Syria under the Ba'th, 1963*–1966 (Jerusalem and N.Y. 1973); N. van Dam, "The Struggle for Power in Syria and the Ba'th Party (1958–1966)," *Orient* (Hamburg, March 1973), p.14; M. H. Kerr, "Hafiz Asad and the Changing Patterns of Syrian Politics," *International Journal*, XXVIII (Autumn 1973), pp. 689–706; and M. Maoz, *Modern Syria* (Heb.), (Tel Aviv, 1974).

2. Excerpts from the report were quoted in *al-Anwar* (Beirut), 15 November.

3. *Reports and Resolutions of Fifth Regional Congress* (Damascus, 1971).

4. A number of developments in 1974 and 1975 could indicate that a change had taken place in this respect. In the wake of the October War changes were introduced in the upper echelons of the Syrian Army and defense establishment. In a *Newsweek* interview in June 1974, Asad admitted vaguely to intra-party opposition to his policies (see the official version as distributed by the Syrian News Agency on 3 June, 1974). The Ba'th Party Congress of April 1975 did not proceed smoothly and at least one prominent army officer, the Commander of the Air Force failed to be reelected to the Syrian Regional Command.

5. For details, see O. Tabor, "Syria," in D. Dishon (ed.), *Middle East Record, 1969–1970* (Jerusalem, 1977).

6. *Radio Damascus*, 5 December, 1970.

7. See Petran, pp. 248–58.

8. *Al-Hayat*, 20, 23, 25, 26 February, 1973; *an-Nahar*, 1 March, 1973.

9. *Radio Damascus*, 5 December, 1970.

10. See the partial text of the resolutions and recommendations of the Tenth National Congress of the Ba'th in *al-Nahar*, 14 November, 1970.

11. *Reports and Resolutions of the Fifth Regional Congress*, pp. 55–57.

12. *Radio Damascus*, 8 March, 1972.

Jordan
and the
Palestine
Issue

The Jordanian Entity in Changing Circumstances, 1967–1973

Uriel Dann

The major contention of this survey is that the socio-political characteristics of Jordan in 1973 were essentially the same as those of Jordan in 1967 prior to the Six Day War. One may state even more sweepingly that with respect to these characteristics, Jordan has remained essentially unchanged throughout its existence as a state, from its establishment shortly after World War I as Transjordan to this very day. The reason is not, of course, that Jordan's existence has been untroubled, but that the forces which formed and maintained the "Jordanian entity" have succeeded to date in finding answers to all the challenges which have arisen—challenges which have indeed been most demanding.

It is impossible to discuss the question of the "Jordanian entity" without first defining its nature, its supporters and their strategy, and its opponents.

The official designation of the state—The Hashemite Kingdom of Jordan—conforms strictly to reality: Jordan is a monarchy vested in the Hashemite dynasty, with the ruler as cornerstone of the political structure both in fact and in law. This regime is characterized by a conservatism which regards with suspicion all radical movements, regardless of their origin or their character. It upholds that Arab nationalism which owes its functional origins to "The Great Arab Rebellion" of the *Sharif* Husayn b. 'Ali, Amir of Mecca,[1] during World War I, and which maintains that the Hashemites have to this very day an historic and—as descendants of the Prophet—even an Islamic claim to national leadership. Ideally, it is the Hashemites' mission to work towards Arab unity within the Arabian Peninsula and the Fertile Crescent. (For a variety of reasons which cannot be pursued here, but which have always been perfectly convincing to the Hashemites themselves, they have never regarded Egypt as authentically Arab. The Maghreb, though closer than Egypt to Arabdom by Hashemite standards, is excluded by the barrier of the Nile civilization.) The entity has traditionally been linked in alliance to the West—Britain formerly, the United States now—from which it receives vital economic and diplomatic aid, and whose lead it follows in global politics. It requires a strong standing army, loyal to the King's person.

Those who support this conception of the Jordanian entity are, first of all, the King and the members of his extended family, the *"Sharifs"*; a circle best described as "the King's friends"— consisting of a score of individuals who hold key positions as personal advisors and top executives, regardless of their origin; the Bedouin (most of whom are no longer nomads but maintain their social uniqueness), who constitute the shock troops of the army; the villagers and small townspeople on the East Bank, especially in the south. Those who support the entity from outside, for different reasons and at different levels of commitment, are the United States, Britain, the Arab monarchies and most non-Arab Muslim states.

Those who oppose the entity are the Palestinian Fidayeen organizations and, at the risk of over-simplification, the Palestinians in general, as well as an undefined stratum of intellectuals conspicuous for two generations on the East Bank. Externally, the entity is opposed by all Arab circles committed to socio-political radicalism.

The focal points for these elements, whether friendly or hostile, are the King or the Palestinian organizations. Until now those who support the entity have shown an incomparably greater degree of consistency, resilience and readiness for sacrifice that those who oppose it.

The consequences of the Six Day War for Jordan were reflected in a number of different ways:

1. The war did not directly affect the East Bank—the territorial, historical and political power-base of the "Jordanian entity" as defined above;

2. Jordan lost the Palestinian West Bank, and with the West Bank that half of its population which was culturally and professionally "advanced";

3. Jordan emerged from its isolation within the Arab world, at least temporarily, because of the distinguished part its army played in the fighting, and because its losses gave it a common bond with Egypt and Syria;

4. The disastrous defeat of the Arab armies served further to legitimize the Palestinian organizations; it also accorded them a

momentum which confronted the established Jordanian entity with a challenge the likes of which, as regards both character and intensity, it had never faced;

5. The war did not undermine the Hashemite ruler's faith in himself as the kingpin of the Jordanian entity, the policy-maker and the allocator of resources. This point is the key to the history of Jordan during the period under review in this survey—as well as during the periods before 1967, and since the 1973 October War.

In the light of the foregoing, the basic considerations which governed King Hussein's thinking between the two wars can be described as follows:

1. Whatever happened, a situation had to be maintained in which the King could make decisions with regard to the East Bank on matters which he considered vital to the "Jordanian entity." On the other hand, it was necessary to act with caution and flexibility before concluding that all-out confrontations were inevitable.

2. The implications of the loss of the West Bank went far beyond the mere shrinkage of Jordan's material resources. For the physical absence of the Hashemites on the West Bank cleared the way for a Palestinian presence there—even if at one remove, given the Israeli occupation—thus providing a focus of loyalty for the Palestinians of the East Bank. This, in turn, would of necessity strike at the very heart of the Jordanian entity. Furthermore, Hussein regarded acceptance of this loss as tantamount to abandoning the heritage he had received from his forebears, and to renouncing a mission he was not entitled to give up. Thus, his return to the West Bank was for him an unwavering objective, second in importance only to that of maintaining his position on the East Bank.

3. Because of the overriding importance of the above-mentioned points, Jordan's emergence from its intra-Arab isolation was viewed as a desirable but incidental outcome of the war. The goodwill of the Arab world in general, and coexistence with the radical Arab regimes in particular, were definitely subordinate to the above-mentioned primary considerations.

4. Although the Palestinian organizations were enemies, an open collision with them had to be avoided as far as possible. This restraint is to be explained by Hussein's character as well as by his overall tactics since coming to power: he has always been aware of

the unbridgeable chasm between his own basic objectives—as regards both the East Bank and the West Bank—and those of the Palestinian organizations.

5.   The State of Israel was not a primary consideration *per se* during this period or any other since 1957. Israel was never in the forefront of those working to undermine the King's power and overthrow the political entity with which he identified himself. It was, nevertheless, a rival which in June 1967 had proven once again, and more convincingly than in the past, its power to injure him when circumstances generated a confrontation. It came into possession of that property—the West Bank—which he so coveted. As a result of his evaluation of the situation between 1967 and 1973, Hussein took an opportunistic and pragmatic attitude toward Israel. In practice this meant no "heating up" of the conflict, maintaining contacts of sorts and avoiding significant concessions—all on the assumption that Israel would not initiate a violation of the *status quo* to his detriment.

Given these considerations, Hussein was faced with two main problems during the period between the two wars. Firstly, how could he repel the Palestinian menace to the "Jordanian entity"? Secondly, how could he re-align the West Bank with that entity?

The history of Hussein's relations with the Palestinian organizations between the two wars falls into two periods, with the fighting of September 1970 forming a dividing line. The first period is characterized by the growth of the organized Palestinian presence in Jordan from virtually nothing to a peak at which the organizations threatened to overthrow the "Jordanian entity." The second period is that of Hussein's counterattack by which he crushed the organizations in Jordan.

The growth and development of the organizations in Jordan is a process which can be traced back to the 1950s. It is a process whereby an amorphous mass of "refugees" dependent on charity became a separate entity which aspired to nationhood and self-determination. The concentration of Palestinians within the East Bank—where they have come since 1967 to constitute nearly half the population[2]—made a confrontation between the two entities inevitable, sooner or later. The acceleration of this process of nationbuilding after the Six Day War is bound up with the post-war atmosphere image of the "confrontation states" and their leaders—above all Abdel Nasser—as the collective guardians of the Palestinians, responsible for their future.

Israel easily foiled the attempts made by the Palestinian organizations during the months immediately after the war to establish themselves in the West Bank. As a result, the focus of their activities shifted to the East Bank. From the beginning of this shift, and until the crisis of September 1970, the position of the organizations on the East Bank improved spectacularly. Apart from the overall situation in the Arab world and the self-generating quality of success, the important reason was Hussein's demonstrated unwillingness to confront the organizations overtly. The explanation for Hussein's attitude—surprising at first sight—is rooted in his personality and, in particular, in his tendency to postpone as long as possible decisions which require extreme action. This strain contradicts his generally accepted image and runs counter to the stubbornness which is also an integral part of his character. Hussein does not decide easily or rapidly. However, when he reached the conclusion in September 1970 that there could be no coexistence between him and the organizations in Jordan, he ceased to hesitate.

While it is not necessary to chronicle in detail the relations between Hussein and the Palestinian organizations prior to the crisis of September 1970, it is useful to outline the main stages.

The Karama action of the Israeli army in 1968 provided a dramatic beginning. On 21 March, Israeli forces, including armor and aircraft, raided the Fath concentrations at Karama, east of the lower Jordan, in the most intensive action of its kind since the 1967 war. There is little reason to doubt that the raid was carried out more or less as planned. Moreover, effective opposition came from the Jordanian army rather than from the Palestinians.[3] Yet, for a variety of reasons—among them the unexpectedly heavy casualties on the Israeli side—"Karama" turned into a political victory of the first order for the Palestinian organizations. It immediately became throughout the Arab world a saga of Palestinian heroism which contributed more than anything else at the time to changing the image of the Palestinian from that of a "refugee" to one of a fighter for his honour and country on a par with, or even superior to, the established Arab armies. Even Hussein jumped on the bandwagon by proclaiming his army the comrade-in-arms of the Fidayeen. In so doing, however, he became psychologically and tactically dependent on the initiatives of the Palestinian organizations. During the two and a half years after Karama, relations were characterized by Hussein's courting of these organizations. He publicly justified their existence, identified himself with their aims, competed with them over declarations of enmity toward Israel, and even accepted their infiltration into the very seats of power, where they emptied Government agencies of their authority and compelled the King to dismiss their enemies, some of whom were his most loyal friends. All this in return for the organizations' "recognition" of Jordan's sovereignty, carefully defined and hedged about in "agreements" which were unworkable, and usually inoperative from the moment they were signed. There were a host of minor "understandings" and "undertakings"; the more pretentious agreements, however, were those of November 1968 and June 1970.[4]

A number of half-hearted and isolated attempts by Hussein to out-maneuver or paralyze the organizationss did not turn the tide. They merely served to accentuate the King's basic enmity and, by their utter and quickly conceded failure, further lowered his prestige. The outcome was inevitable. By the spring of 1970, at the latest, the Palestinians had set up a virtual state within the state which, if it did not carry out all the civil functions, at any rate neutralized the King's authority over much of the country, including Amman. The collective ego of the organizations and the individual egos of their members were inflated to grotesque proportions. Hussein and his family were no longer safe from molestation, and were denied entry into areas which the organizations considered vital to their security.

The standing of the polity which Hussein headed deteriorated, along with his own, among his supporters and the silent majority which registered the general trend. Those who believed in the Jordanian entity and benefited from its existence, including the heads of the army, began to doubt Hussein's will or ability to fight back. There were those who threatened to take the initiative out of the King's hands and engage the organizations without his consent. Others prepared positions of retreat for themselves. Political activists, who had in the past opposed the regime and lain low during the ten years of Hussein's unquestioned supremacy before 1967, organized themselves as the "National Gathering" (*tajammu' watani*), the declared object of which was to bring the sides closer in the interest of "national unity," but which in fact served to weaken still more the regime's stand against the organizations. In June 1970 seven of its members were included in the Cabinet in a singular—but futile—gesture of appeasement.

This phase closed with the attempt on Hussein's life on 1 September, 1970, by members of Na'if Hawatima's "Popular Democratic Front for the Liberation of Palestine," which gave priority to the struggle against

Hussein over that against Israel.[5] With the hijacking of international passenger planes by George Habash's "Popular Front for the Liberation of Palestine" a week later, their landing in Jordan, and this organization's refusal to release them or their passengers while on Jordanian territory, it was made dramatically clear not only to the world, but to Hussein himself, that the Hashemite Kingdom was on the verge of collapse. Finally convinced that he could wait no longer, Hussein decided to smash the organizations in Jordan and sweep their remnants out of the kingdom. He hesitated to the last, but once he had made up his mind he did not budge. Details of method were another matter, and in this respect consistency did not bother him.

On 16 September, 1970, Hussein declared military government throughout the country and the administration passed into the hands of army officers under his direct command. Early next morning the army started to attack Fidayeen strongholds in the capital.[6] It should be stressed that during the ten months before the final destruction of the organizations in Jordan, in July 1971, the army was up against stubborn resistance. To begin with, the reconquest of Amman was no easy task. It took at least five days of bitter fighting for the army to gain strategic control, although pockets of resistance were not eliminated until long after. During the same week, Salt and Zarqa'—the key cities flanking Amman on the west-east axis—were retaken. The northern towns remained in the hands of the organizations for a few weeks longer, but by the end of the year the Fidayeen were at last dislodged from there as well and restricted to tenuous encampments in the hills around Jarash and 'Ajlun, where they hung on until they were finally driven out of Jordan the following July.

During this time, Hussein was faced with a united front of disapproval from the Arab states, expressed most actively by Syria and Iraq. Within days of the outbreak of fighting in Amman, Syria staged a military invasion of at least tank-brigade strength, with artillery (but no air support), thinly camouflaged as a Palestinian liberation action. The Syrian operation was liquidated after a week of fighting under pressure from the Great Powers, threats of Israeli intervention, and failure in the field. Iraq maintained a strong force of about three divisions which took up positions around the strategic junction of Mafraq. However, Hussein's decision to ignore their presence—despite some anxiety—was justified by events; the Iraqis remained inactive throughout, and in January 1971 finally departed for home in a huff. Kuwait suspended its financial aid and Libya severed relations. The "moderates," chiefly represented by Egypt, Tunisia and the Sudan, carried out at least a pretence of sustained diplomatic pressure in favor of the organizations.

The formal results were again a number of undertakings—this time with the Arab states as sponsors and quasi-guarantors—of which the "Cairo Agreement" of 27 September, the "the Amman Agreement" of 13 October, and the "Second Amman Agreement" of 14 December, 1970, are the best known. These, and other, agreements purported to set down the terms of coexistence as between two equal contracting parties. But equality had become a fiction since September 1970. Every new round of fighting, negotiations, agreement and resumption of fighting saw Hussein emerge better off than before. Of all those engaged in the struggle he was the only one who saw his strategic object clearly, and pursued it relentlessly; this object was to restore his sovereignty over Jordan or, in other words, to restore the "Jordanian entity."

The reasons for his success stand out clearly in retrospect. For once Hussein reappeared as the embodiment of the Jordanian entity, the army—not merely the officers—was with him. The Transjordanian population in general hated the Palestinian organizations whose members, so far as the Transjordanians were concerned, were boastful and domineering foreigners. Further, the "National Gathering" collapsed in the face of the King's anger and determination just as manifestations of organized civilian opposition had collapsed on earlier occasions, both in his and in his grandfather's time. As for the Palestinian organizations themselves, they were neither united nor psychologically equipped to hold out in an actively hostile Arab environment, and they certainly were not prepared to confront the army in a head-on clash. Finally, they broke and ran. Another important factor was that the Arab governments, while giving the organizations diplomatic and financial help, and taking their side in the war of propaganda, stopped short of all-out support. In this regard it should be noted that neither Egypt not Iraq broke off relations with Hussein until he published his plan for a federation with the West Bank early in 1972, thus bringing a new dimension of expansionism into his struggle with the organizations. Not even the most radical of the Arab states were at any time prepared for a military showdown with Hussein on behalf of the organizations, apart from the abortive attempt by Syria mentioned above (which cannot be viewed as a blatant exception, considering the hesitancy with which it was undertaken and the limited resources committed).

organizations from Jordan and the 1973 October War do not show any change in the basic trend thus far established.

The traditional Jordanian entity had successfully dealt with the most dangerous challenge it had ever faced, and those who had represented that entity would not consider endangering it again. Two distinct "styles" of dealing with the Palestinians became apparent during this period—that of Hussein, and that of Wasfi at-Tall. Tall, member of a prominent family long established in and about the town of Irbid, was appointed prime minister for the fifth time (according to the official count) on 28 October, 1970. A fortnight earlier the King, having returned the military governorships to civilian officials, could claim that military rule had, for all intents and purposes, been terminated.[7] However, both the opinions and personality of the new prime minister ensured that this distinction would make no difference—as spokesmen for the Palestinian organizations had indeed claimed from the first.[8] From the moment of Tall's appointment to his assassination 13 months later, this active, courageous, and tactless man was the very nemesis of the Palestinian organizations, as well as the Palestinians as such. While he certainly controlled and directed the removal of the organizations from Jordan—or what had remained of them by the time he took office—he did no more than carry out the policy to which Hussein had already committed himself.

Where Tall differed from the King was in his attitude toward the West Bank and its place in relation to the Jordanian entity. Hussein's deep commitment to regaining this territory has been described. Tall, on the other hand, seems to have believed that the loss of the West Bank represented a gain to Jordan. This was consistent with his view of the Palestinians resident on the East Bank as an alien element unassimilable by the Transjordanian nation then emerging there. His last term in office is replete with administrative meaasures, often accompanied by offensive expressions, which tended to loosen the connection between Jordan and all things Palestinian. He could not, however, disavow the fundamental communion between the two banks which his royal master postulated, though it seems that such a course would have been his personal preference.

The bullets of "Black September" put an end to the man and his style in Cairo, on 28 November, 1971.[9]

From Tall's murder until after the October War, the dominant style was that of Hussein, regardless of whether the premier was Ahmad al-Lawzi or Zayd ar-Rifaʻi, his abler successor. Hussein's style was that of the mailed fist in a velvet glove. Beneath the smooth phrases, vague promises and vacillations, lay his own resolve to maintain Jordan under the control of its traditional rulers who drew their strength and support from Transjordanian society—villagers, townspeople and Bedouin. To maintain this end, the organizations must not be allowed to return.

Whereas Hussein changed his policy toward the Palestinian organizations halfway through the period under survey here, his policy concerning the West Bank remained the same throughout. The explanation for this constancy is clear; Hussein's basic stand on both issues—the Palestinian organizations clear; Hussein's basic stand on both issues—the Palestinian organizations and the West Bank—was derived from a consistent concept of his own place in the scheme of things. His policy, on the other hand, was of necessity largely determined by outside factors. In the East Bank, the growing strength of the organizations after 1967 compelled Hussein to reexamine his policy, and ultimately to reverse it. In the West Bank, the decisive factor was the Israeli occupation, and neither the fact of occupation, nor its characteristics so far as Hussein was concerned, changed during the six years. It follows that there was no need for Hussein to change either his designs for the future or his policies in the present. As to the former, at an early staage after the 1967 war, certainly no later than the beginning of 1969, Hussein's concept, to which he still adheres, crystallized: the West Bank was wrested from Jordan; therefore any settlement—that is, any Israeli pullback—would have to be based on its return to Jordan as the party concerned. Then, with Jordan in possession, the "Palestinian people" on the West Bank[10] could exercise its right to self-determination by means of a referendum. There were three options to choose from: fusion with Jordan as one state, as before the 1967 war; total separation; or, autonomy within a federation headed by the Hashemite king. Hussein's choice, as he made clear time and again between the two wars—and time and again since—was for a federation which he regarded as the consummation of a communion of destinies decreed by history between the peoples of both banks. He came nearest to spelling out this view in detail on 15 March, 1972, when he published his plan to turn the "Hashemite Kingdom of Jordan" into a "Federated (*muttahida*) Arab Kingdom" on both banks of the Jordan.[11] The operative clauses of the proposed federation foresaw the King as the head of state with his federal capital in Amman, one army under the supreme command of the King, and federal judiciary, legislative and executive authorities, the last "to guarantee the kingdom's security, stability and prosperity." Each region would have in its respective capital—Amman and Jerusalem—its own judiciary, legislative and executive authority. It is worth noting that, in contrast to many earlier and later pronouncements, Hussein did not on this occasion mention a referendum to be held prior to establishing the federation. Presumably "a long series of...consultations which we [Hussein] have had with people's representatives" mentioned in the statement, all "unanimously" in favor of the plan, served instead as an appropriate expression of the people's will.

Hussein's obvious inference—that West Bank compliance could be assumed—merits a brief examination. The "long series of consultations" with West Bank residents acclaiming the federation is plausible enough. Ever since the loss of the West Bank, Hussein had cultivated its goodwill with all the means at his disposal, but with ambiguous results. One reason is that the criteria of his acceptance on the West Bank are obscure, the evidence is contradictory and in any case there must have been fluctuations in the extent of support. But it is characteristic of the nature of the many-stranded relationship between Jordan and the West Bank, which goes back to early mandatory days, that Hussein could at all times produce a respectable showing of followers for such an ostensibly reasonable program as a federation between the West and the East Banks, particularly when the premise was an end to the Israeli occupation. As to Hussein's unmistakable confidence in a referendum, it would be rash to impute to him cynicism alone, or irrational faith in the attractions of his rule. It is true that previous elections in Jordan might appear wanting as measured against Western standards. More important, however, is the age-old practice—as old as Islam, and older—of accepting the guidance of the government in matters political, so long as the government—"the State", *dawla*—reasonably fulfills its part as guardian of peace and order, is not overly oppressive, and respects the privacy of the subject. The Jordanian state is capable of fulfilling such conditions. This Hussein intuitively understands, hence much of his optimism. There is undoubtedly a fringe of nonconformists of all descriptions, but they are not "the people."

In the history of the period, Hussein's proposed federation marked a new departure in his relations with the Arab governments. Apparently, they shared his appraisal concerning the feasibility of the project—once Israel had withdrawn, to be sure—and they reacted with nervous hostility.The pattern of 1947–1948—when the Hashemite ruler of Transjordan appeared as the deeply distrusted savior of the West Bank from Zionism—was repeating itself. But it soon became clear that the of its success, were unfounded. The annexation of 1948–1949 had come about because the Palestinians rushed into Abdallah's arms in fear of an impending Israeli conquest, and because Israel then regarded this annexation as the best of the practicable possibilities. In 1972 neither of these conditions obtained, and Hussein's plan remained a declaration of intent.

That the plan remained merely a declaration of intent is a result of Hussein's failure to reach agreement with Israel between the two wars. Although the relevant material is still inaccessible as a whole, from the existing bits of information one can piece together a reasonably convincing picture. It would seem that Hussein held secret talks with Israel in a rational atmosphere—this too in the tradition of his house. He was prepared to concede certain minor "border adjustments" which, one may guess, involved the Latrun bulge and the Qalqiliya area; he was prepared to give up the Jewish Quarter in the Old City of Jerusalem; and to establish some kind of combined municipal administration in Jerusalem. But he was not prepared to budge beyond that.

Seen in this light, the significance of the changes in the relations between Hussein and the various Arab governments during the period under survey is not great. They were of necessity the outcome of the two fundamental aspects of his own policy: confrontation with the Palestinian organizations and his aspiration to regain the West Bank, as well as changing considerations of the other Arab leaders, which were not always directly connected with Hussein's problems. This makes it possible to account for the marked improvement in Jordan's Arab position during the months before the October War. Without Hussein's altering his own attitude, Iraq, Egypt and Syria lifted their diplomatic and psychological boycott. Iraq did so because of the growing tension in its relations with Iran and Syria, Egypt because of President Sadat's increasing "Egyptism," and Egypt and Syria together in readiness for the projected war against Israel. Hussein was not party to the planning of the war, nor did he have prior knowledge of the impending attack, but for these very reasons it was necessary to keep him favorably disposed.

The beginning of the period under review—the Six Day War—was a fateful event in the history of Jordan. The significance of the October War is less clear. So far, it is reasonable to say that for Jordan it constituted a vast reshuffling of the deck, involving the reopening of options which were closed during the previous years. Nonetheless, there has been no change in the nature of the "Jordanian entity," nor in the basic approach of those who rule it.

NOTES

1. Great-grandfather of the present King Hussein; he lies buried in Jerusalem at the Haram ash-Sharif, next to the Dome of the Rock.

2. Estimates vary. Certain authorities claim they are a majority, but most believe they are rather less than one half. An exact determination is impossible in the absence of objective criteria.

3. For a concise description of all aspects of this affair, see D. Dishon (ed.), *Middle East Record (MER) 1968*, (Jerusalem 1973), pp. 365-73, 386, 404-05, 588.

4. The last formal agreement was signed on 15 September, 1970, a few hours before Hussein set in motion the machinery for the destruction of the organizations. It is inconceivable that the King signed it in good faith, but its 13 points demonstrate the rank the organizations had by then obtained, as partners and rivals of the supposedly sovereign state.

5. It is interesting to note that Hawatima alone among the leaders of the prominent Palestinian organizations was born in the East Bank.

6. It seems that in the South—from Kerak to Ma'an—the organizations were eliminated during the last days *before* 16 September, by concerted action of the local townspeople, the Bedouin and the army. However, their hold on this area had never been strong.

7. King Hussein at his press conference of 14 October, 1970 (*R. Amman*, 14 October).

8. A Palestinian spokesman (*R. Damascus*, 16 October). Both sources as quoted in D. Dishon (ed.), *MER 1969–1970* (Jerusalem, 1977).

9. For a view that during this period Tall forced his general conception as regards the Palestinian question on a reluctant Hussein, see A. Susser, "The Transjordanian Elite, Wasfi at-Tall and the War against the Terrorists," *Occasional Papers*, Shiloah Center, Tel Aviv University, 1974 (Heb.). I do not sup-

port this view, though Mr. Susser and I are divided chiefly as regards the extent, and not the nature, of Tall's influence.

10. Palestinians in the East Bank, according to Hussein, have their corporate being inextricably interwoven with that of the "Jordanian people"; they may exercise their individual right to opt out and, by implication, lose thereby their rights of full citizenship.

11. For a full tranlation of the King's statement regarding this plan, as broadcast by *R. Amman*, on March, 1972, see BBC, *Summary of World Broadcasts*, (The Middle East and North Africa), 17 March, 1972, pp. A/6–A/11. The statement is of great interest as a full and reasoned exposition of Hussein's "Palestinian ideology"—as he wished the world to accept it, but also without a doubt as he essentially believed himself. As far as we can know, his belief as expressed then is still intact.

The Institutionalization
of Palestinian Nationalism
1967–1973

Gabriel Ben Dor

Research on the recent political history of the Palestinians has been a field of notoriously slippery ground. Yet, further research on this subject in general, and on the institutionalization of Palestinian nationalism in particular is definitely called for. It is of great potential interest not only to scholars studying the Arab–Israeli conflict or recent Middle Eastern political history, but in theoretical terms also to students of what political sociology calls "comparative institution building," as well as to those scholars concerned within the discipline of international relations with what might be called, for lack of a better term, "diplomacy without sovereignty."[2]

This study is not concerned directly with these two theoretically important issues. Rather, it is an attempt to assess the role of the Palestinians in Middle Eastern politics in general, and the Arab–Israeli conflict in particular, between 1967 and 1973. In so doing an effort will be made to avoid the trap which Reinhardt Bendix calls the "fallacy of retrospective determinism,"[3] that is, to rewrite the history of the Palestinians in the period between 1967 and 1973 with wisdom of hindsight regarding what happened in October 1974 in Rabat, even though at given points events and developments subsequent to the October War are alluded to in order to develop a more illuminating comparative perspective on the inter-war period, which constitutes the focus of the analysis. Finally, this paper will attempt to demystify the subject. No other Middle Eastern issue is as fuzzy and beclouded by ever-present myths and fallacies as that of the Palestinians or Palestinian nationalism. In the minds of most Israelis, no other issue is identified so closely with Israel's fears of being destroyed by the Arabs and replaced by a Palestinian Arab state. In the minds of concerned Arabs, no other issue is identified to such an extent with what they perceive to be the great historical injustice done to them by Zionism. For such reasons, as well as those relating to the difficulties of data gathering, objective sources are scarce to come by. Scholarly studies do not abound, though at least one recent study on the subject represents a notable and outstanding exception to this unhappy state of the field.[4] Therefore, it may safely be stated that there is a pressing need to treat the Palestinian issue in a scholarly manner, though this treatment will be on the whole necessarily on a high level of generalization and will describe and analyze the Palestinian issue within the framework of the Fidayeen organizations or the PLO without reference to particular Palestinian organizations, although the differences between them are great and significant. These differences, however, ought to be kept in mind. The available literature does describe the differences between the various organizations, mostly along ideological, factional, and to some extent, personal and sociological lines.[5]

Within the limitations of space, this paper attempts to achieve four objectives. First, to periodize the years between 1967 and 1973. Secondly, to present the perceived goals of the PLO between 1967 and 1973. Thirdly, to assesss which of these goals were achieved and which were not, or, in other words, to make up a catalogue of accomplishments as well as failures; to describe what might be termed "the state of the PLO" at the outbreak of the 1973 October War,[6] and finally, in the concluding remarks, to draw some lessons from the analysis of the period with regard to the subsequent development and fortunes of the PLO.

A PERIODIZATION OF THE INTERWAR PERIOD

In order to avoid an overly complicated approach and prolonged discussion, it might be sufficient to speak generally of two periods: from 1967 till 1970 and from 1970 to 1973. The first period is characterized by what might be termed guerrilla warfare along classical, or quasi-classical lines,[7] more or less within Israeli-administered territories, in an attempt to bring about an uprising of the Arab population. The period from 1970 to 1973 is characterized by terrorism pure and simple and no longer by guerrilla tactics.[8] A more sophisticated periodization, however, would seem to give three stages.

The first, which can be called "the take-off period" of the PLO, would run from 1967 to some time in 1969. At this stage its activities were characterized by three motifs. One feature was an attempt to bring about a "popular war" against Israel—a "popular war" in inverted commas, because it is a technical term in a different context. A second characteristic of these years was a build-up of military strength. This gained momentum especially after the Battle of Karama in March 1968. Some people have claimed that this was a turning point, which, indeed, seems to be true to a large extent: up to then, the organizations had had difficulty in recruiting manpower. From this point on, they sometimes had more recruits than they could absorb.[9] The third process that took place between 1967 and 1969 was the takeover of the PLO by al-Fath and its allies in February 1969[10]—a move that put at the disposal of the Fidayeen a very potent political instrument, as well as an organizational and symbolic rallying point.

The second period could be "the attempt to consolidate gains." It began in 1969 and ended in 1971, and was a very dismal phase for the Palestinian organizations. In this period too, two major developments took place, the first of which was the growing involvement in inter-Arab politics and an attempt to radicalize both Palestinians and Arabs in other countries.[11] The second development was of such importance that its significance scarcely needs any further elaboration: the civil war in Jordan and the breakdown of Palestinian power there, which meant, of course, the end of the dream of an "Arab Hanoi" or a Fidayeen State and of a significant autonomous territorial base, adjacent to Israel's longest border.[12]

The third stage, 1971-1973, was marked by "the politics of institutional survival." This stage witnessed above all, in terms of military methods, terrorism abroad, that is, outside the Middle East. That period was also characterized by a great deal of "politicking" within and between the organizations; as well as some attempt to adapt to restrictions and limitations that stemmed from the political environment, from having to fight and to survive as a political organization without a territorial base or the hope of gaining one in the near future. The profile of the organizations on this period was, on the whole, much lower. One shrewd observer of Middle East politics, P. J. Vatikiotis, wrote a book at that time in which he inserted a chapter at the last minute called "The Decline of the Guerrillas."[13] It seems that he went too far and overstated the case. By the end of 1973, the organizations had managed to survive, although they were not more active than in the years 1972 and 1973.

It would appear from analyzing the three stages that transition from stage to stage had not been thought out beforehand, and did not fit any preconceived notions as to how the movement should conduct itself.

Rather, these stages were a response to tactical exigencies which the inter-Arab and international environment had created.[14]

One may argue that the Palestinian militants were fortunate in that the emergence of their movement coincided with a period in Arab history in which implementation of the dream of Arab unity—at least in the messianic, grand, pan-Arab nationalistic terms—while not by any means abandoned, was postponed to the indefinite future. It was reduced to the kind of thing one pays lip-service to, or one is tied in with, in terms of semantics and symbols, or perhaps one is really committed to, but one does not hope to achieve immediately.[15]

To that extent, all the movements antithetical to messianic pan-Arabism, such as state nationalism,[16] had gained some legitimacy in the mid-1960s. In this sense, the Palestinians certainly would have had much greater difficulty in legitimizing themselves in the 1950s, when things were different in the Arab world. The issue of Palestinian versus pan-Arab nationalism became important and discernible in Palestinian political thought in the wake of the Six Day War, often with the reversed formula "the liberation of Palestine will help create Arab unity" rather than the other way around, as was customary before 1967. The decline of messianic pan-Arab nationalism as an idea also coincided with the decline of conventional Arab military might against Israel in 1967—which helped create a climate for the Palestinian efforts to generate guerrilla warfare in the late 1960s.

THE MAIN GOALS OF THE PLO

Just what were the Fidayeen organizations trying to accomplish in this period? From the available sources[17] ten main goals are discernible, which the organizations were trying to accomplish at various times—sometimes emphasizing one, sometimes another in response to changing circumstances. The first goal (not necessarily in order of preference or priority) was, of course, the most obvious one: not to let the Palestinian issue die in a period which witnessed the momentary Arab paralysis in the aftermath of the Six Day War, a number of attempts to reach political settlements of various types, and a prolonged period of calm between the Egyptian–Israeli cease-fire of August 1970 and the October War in 1973. The second goal was to damage and demoralize Israel as far as possible, militarily, politically, economically and psychologically. The third goal was to involve the Arab countries in a more intensified version of the Arab–Israeli conflict, a tactic for which the guerrillas' role in instigating the outbreak of the Six Day War furnished a precedent.[18]

The fourth goal was to raise the level of Palestinian consciousness and to build, or as the Palestinian thinkers sympathizing with the Fidayeen frequently perceived it, "re-build a more cohesive Palestinian political community."[19] The fifth goal was to involve in the Arab–Israeli conflict, or to be more specific, in the Palestinian–Israeli conflict, remote third parties from overseas; the sixth was to attempt to radicalize at times the Palestinians and at times other Arabs;[20] and the seventh, to bring about a guerrilla style uprising of the population in the territories occupied by Israel in the Six Day War in 1967.

The final three goals appear to be the most important, not necessarily in the view of the Fidayeen but rather in the added perspective of our retrospective analysis. The eighth goal was to acquire a "veto power" over the implementation of the Arab commitment to restore "the legitimate rights of the Palestinians"—and in this context it should be noted that the Palestinian slogan of "self-determination"[21] was directed not just against Israel, but also against Arab regimes. This is a crucially important point. The ninth goal was to build a new Palestinian national center through a new, relatively modernized, elite with a central institutional framework capable of extracting and absorbing resources from the inter-Arab and international environments. This goal is reflected in the very title and main theme of this study—the institutionalization[22] of Palestinian nationalism. Finally, it was necessary for Palestinian nationalism to establish its legitimacy. An attempt was made to legitimize the PLO and its affiliate organizations on three levels: among the Palestinians themselves, on the inter-Arab plane and in the international arena as a whole.

MAJOR FAILURES AND ACCOMPLISHMENTS

What were the major failures and accomplishments of the organizations in this period? There were six major failures. First, we may safely state that the Palestinians, all their efforts notwithstanding, were no real military factor of any significance against Israel or any Arab regime which wanted to wrest control away from them. Secondly, despite claims to the contrary made by some observers of the Palestinian Arab scene, very few Arabs other than some Palestinians were radicalized. Thirdly, notwithstanding their historical efforts, the Palestinian organizations showed no capability of establishing independence from the Arab regimes.[23] Fourthly, they could not gain an autonomous territorial base, notwithstanding their legalized foothold they have since late 1969 in the 'Arqub region in southeastern Lebanon (which is no more than a springboard for occasional raids into Israel, not an autonomous territorial base which has been absolutely essential for successful guerrilla warfare waged elsewhere in the world).[24] Fifthly, notwithstanding their institutional capabilities, the Palestinian organizations were unable to reach an ideological consensus regarding what is to be done and how to accomplish it.[25] Sixthly, despite Soviet help from 1968 on, a point made *inter alia* by Maoz[26] and Eran,[27] the Palestinians failed to gain unequivocal backing or support from any major world power or superpower.

The main accomplishments are five. The most important one by far has been the ability to build and, even more crucial, to maintain, an institutional framework of Palestinian politics which did not fall apart despite fratricidal tensions, conflicts, dissension and occasional splits.[28] The institutional framework survived and withstood the test of time. Anyone familiar with the history of Palestinian politics can appreciate the significance of this fact.[29]

Secondly, the Palestinians have apparently managed to create a new elite, relatively modern in its conception,[30] methods and the symbols it employs. If one wishes to pursue this point further one should examine the role in the Palestinian movements of youth and women, as well as the patterns of organizations, the uses of technology and the kind of symbolism in terms of communication. Now, when we say new, relatively modern elites, we wish to put them on an equal footing with some of the radical Arab states, no more and no less—in terms of generational belonging and in terms of conception, language used and ideological source of conviction. It seems that in this respect there is a great deal of similarity.[31]

In a sense, without having a state, the Palestinians affiliated with the PLO did undergo the kind of revolution which the radical Arab states underwent in the 1950s and the 1960s.[32] A relatively new national political center which reflects some very important traditional cleavages of the Palestinian political community (such as the people from the mountains versus the people of the coastal plain, Christians versus Muslims, urban versus rural, etc.) has been created in the PLO.[33] As far as the traditional elites on both the West and East Banks of the Jordan are concerned, they have remained relatively stable.[34] However, the point is that this PLO-dominated center did, more or less successfully, pre-empt the possibility of the emergence of other centers or of others who might try to take over the PLO center.[35]

The Palestinians as such, in accepted sociological terms, have been a relatively modernized society in comparison with the surrounding Arab societies. They were fairly highly urbanized, having fairly high rates of literacy, etc. Therefore, it is misleading to analyze the great societal changes in Palestinian society without comparing them with the surrounding Arab countries. Societal changes in the Palestinian communities were unique mainly in one sense—as a society, it is a "multi-state" society.[36] Palestinian society can be regarded as a unit, but it is embedded in different political systems. For that reason, unlike in most other societies in which the peripheries of society build up the center, here we have a direct effort to build a political center and then tie the rest of the society to it. This is a unique process of political sociology: rather than politics starting from society, we have here the political center trying to rebuild the society. The Palestinian organizations tried to do this fairly consciously. They accomplished this through terror and assassinations coupled with an ability to extract Arab support, as well as by their ability to create a feeling that the PLO's leadership was the first Palestinian one in decades which was capable of at least some accomplishments. There was also a feeling that this was a leadership unequivocally committed to its cause. It was dynamic and dedicated. Again it seems that there is a striking similarity in the kinds of feelings aroused by the self-styled revolutionary leadership of the so-called radical Arab states and by the PLO leadership. It seems indeed that the general analogy of the PLO leadership with that of the radical Arab states is on the whole very useful.

The fourth accomplishment of the Palestinians has been their ability to set up a nucleus for future political action in anticipation of the advent of more favorable circumstances. Again, this seems true, notwithstanding the decline of their guerrilla-type actions in 1971–72. There was at that time a nucleus for future political action either in the Middle East or overseas.

Finally, the Palestinians created patterns of political competition similar—and this is the third time this point is made—to that of other Arab "revolutionary" regimes, and by this time their level of institutionalization was such that they did have resources worth fighting for and competing for by this period. Even though other Arab regimes did want to penetrate the Palestinian movements and did create movements of their own for their own political purposes (e.g., the Syrians—as-Sa'iqa; or the Iraqis—ALF) these organizations established and operated by the radical Arab states were absorbed within the framework of the PLO, even though they had been created originally to some extent to compete with it. Thereby, the Arab states operating these organizations, tacitly as well as explicitly, contributed to the legitimacy of the PLO, thus recognizing and demonstrating its value and stability, as did the radical PFLP and PDFLP.[37]

Have the failures outweighed the accomplishments? If the major accomplishment is the building of a durable institution as a nucleus for potential future political action, then the question still remains what is to be done with the power stemming from the aforementioned potential. One cannot yet say, definitely, whether the failures outweigh the accomplishments.

THE PLO AT THE OUTBREAK OF THE OCTOBER WAR

What kind of picture of the PLO emerges at the outbreak of the October War? It seems that five points are particularly noteworthy. The first is—if we look at the 1967–1973 period in its totality—that the PLO could neither contribute significantly to the Arab war effort nor seriously disrupt relative calm between the Arabs and Israel, when all other parties were interested in maintaining it for the moment. It proved ineffective during the fighting and it proved ineffective in provoking fighting when others were not interested in doing so.[38] Secondly, as it turned out later (a fact which was already noticeable in the inter-war period but in a very incipient form), the PLO itself did not completely grasp this during the 1967–1973 period[39] and its leaders were to comprehend it only after the October War.

Thirdly, when one takes a good look at the realignment and reorganization of the Arab information and propaganda efforts in the inter-war period,[40] one sees a curious and conspicuous co-existence of the "Palestine issue" with the issue of the "occupied territories." The twin slogan of "liberating the territories" and "restoring the legitimate rights of the Palestinians" was then born. These two became so intimately intertwined that they might justly be regarded as interdependent.[41] They were two sides of the same coin, two inseparable components of the same slogan, which was the mainstay of the Arab propaganda effort. This, it seems, worked greatly in the interest of the Palestinians. Inasmuch as the immediate tactical goal and even the long-range (that is, five or six years to a decade) goal of the Arab regimes after 1967 became the recovery of the territories lost in 1967, it was coupled with the slogan of restoring the rights of the Palestinians.[42] Thus, in the long run one could not be done without the other. An Arab leader could not arrest the momentum to regain the territories without having to satisfy at least some significant portions of the leadership and public opinion in the politically conscious strata in the Arab world that something had been done to satisfy the legitimate aspirations of the Palestinians. Otherwise, a war against Israel would have turned into a completely selfish effort over a few square miles; radical Arab leaders who were not involved directly in the effort to "liberate" the territories grasped this point and used it very adroitly in propaganda maneuvering. Qadhafi's condemnation of Egyptian and other efforts to concentrate on the issue of the territories,[43] even during the very days of active fighting in October 1973, is one example in point.

Fourthly, through this interdependence of the issues of territories and "restoration of the legitimate rights of the Palestinians," at this point the stage was set for the emergence of a sort of semi-veto power in the hands of the PLO against any semi-permanent settlement between Israel and the Arabs. This semi-veto power was wielded through the use, or—if one wishes—the activation of the formula of the "restoration of the legitimate rights of the Palestinians." The process culminated in October 1974, at the Rabat Arab Summit Conference, where the PLO became the institutional custodian, so to speak, of the Palestinian rights; that is, they now almost had the last word in determining whether or not the legitimate rights of the Palestinians were being satified, thereby untying the hands of those Arab regimes involved in negotiating a settlement, perceived to be in their own national interest, vis-à-vis Israel. This was true notwithstanding the inability of the Palestinians to do anything about the August 1970 Egyptian–Israeli cease-fire which they had violently opposed, and following which their relations with Egypt in particular, but also with others, had deteriorated markedly.[44]

The fifth point is that the PLO constituted a target for political action by a number of factors external to the immediate Middle Eastern regional political sub-system. In simpler terms, the PLO set itself up as a political ally of powers either inside the region or outside the region, above all the Soviet Union, which were potentially or actually interested in disrupting a possible settlement not to their liking.[45] In other words, if a settlement were to be reached between Israel and a number of other Arab countries which was distasteful to a radical Arab state not directly involved, or to an outside major power such as the Soviet Union,[46] one of them or any combination of them could utilize the alliance with the PLO to attempt to disrupt that settlement while using and acting within the legitimate language and framework of inter-Arab politics. This is an important point which remains true, it would seem, at the time of writing. It has not been fully realized because so far its potential has not been fully exploited.

CONCLUSION: THE LONG-TERM LESSONS

What are the long-range conclusions from this analysis of the Palestinian organizations between the two wars?

It appears that the most important lesson to be learned is that the fortunes of the PLO, notwithstanding a great many statements to the contrary, basically still depend on the patterns of the Arab–Israeli conflict, its intensity and the importance of the continuing Arab commitment to the Palestine issue. Although the PLO has attempted to shape the pattern of the Arab–Israeli conflict, even its political power is predominantly moulded by this very pattern.

The PLO is an excellent moral facade[47] for various Arab states for purposes of propaganda. This has given rise to an incorrect assessment of its real political power. To some extent, probably to a very limited extent only, the PLO can and does influence the patterns of the Arab–Israeli conflict, but much more than that, it is influenced by the conflict. The PLO cannot seriously threaten, and certainly cannot coerce, any Arab regime into doing what it does not wish to do, even though the PLO does have a great deal of nuisance value to a given Arab regime, and even though it has managed to assassinate one major Arab leader (Jordanian Prime Minister Wasfi at-Tall, in Cairo, in November 1971—who was killed by Black September members).[48] Despite the assassination attempts, the structure of Arab politics today is such that all regimes (which are—except for Lebanon—basically authoritarian in character) have ample coercive power to put down easily any attempt by the PLO to utilize terrorist or guerrilla methods[49] to force an Arab regime into doing what it really does not wish to do. Therefore, were the extent of the Arab commitment to the Palestine cause, or the intensity of the Arab–Israeli conflict, to decline, the PLO's room to maneuver would be greatly limited. The importance of this point cannot be over-emphasized.

As usual in the Arab Middle East, Lebanon represents to some extent, and in some ways only, a spurious exception to most of the statements made in this paper in regard to the PLO's political impact on the other Arab states. To put it very bluntly, Lebanon is being coerced to do what it does not wish to do not by the PLO but rather by two factors that have been coercing Lebanon throughout its existence: other Arab states and the reluctance to upset its anomalous internal balance.[50] These two fully account for the treatment of the PLO by the Lebanese Government, which is different from the kind of treatment it is getting from any other regime of the "confrontation states" along Israel's boundaries. It is certain that if Lebanon had not been caught in this dilemma on the inter-Arab scene as well as domestically, the PLO would have been in a very different position in Lebanon. If one looks at the development of the crisis in 1969, which led to the Cairo Agreement,[51] it seems that without the two Lebanese constraints mentioned above, the PLO would not have accomplished what it did accomplish there. Thus, Lebanon is seemingly an exception to the thesis that the PLO cannot coerce Arab states into doing what they do not want to do. In Lebanon, however the PLO has played the role of a filter through which previously existing political sources of tension became active.

As for the radicalizing impact of the PLO within Lebanon, at least to some extent the Lebanese exception is more real. Again, the unique situation there accounts for that. This, however, must be qualified by what may sound as somewhat deterministic, but is nevertheless true. There have been many sources of radicalization and periodic outbursts within certain strata of Lebanese society (certain Muslim areas, some urban centers such as the city of Tripoli). What has taken place there is a substitution: that is, the sources of radicalization used to come from the other Arab countries while now the Palestinian mediating element has become the filter through which external Arab inputs percolate into Lebanon. This element is, in Lebanon, the most radical institutional manifestation of the kind of Arab nationalism that the Lebanese leadership has traditionally feared. Indeed, the radicalizing influence and the troublesome massive presence of the Palestinians in Lebanon have played a major role in the bloody civil war of 1975–1976.

As long as the Arab states do maintain a strong commitment to the

Palestine issue and to the fight for "the restoration of the Palestinians' rights," there is a semi-veto power in regard to when these rights are restored, what kinds of rights, at which points could one say that Palestinian rights have been restored to the point where one could proceed with political settlements disregarding the Palestine issue. It seems that the Rabat Arab Summit Conference did confer (the process had started even before Rabat) some such semi-veto power on the PLO. This, however, is based on the assumption that the fundamental pattern of the Arab–Israeli conflict, including the very highly emotionally charged commitment of the Arab states to the Palestine issue, continues. Were the Arabs to renounce that responsibility, there would be nothing the PLO could do about it, and this is the overridingly important point.

In this context, an intriguing question arises: why was there no euphoria among the Palestinians after Rabat commensurate with the rather emotional reactions the Rabat decision caused in Israel? At least three reasons can be elaborated through speculation, for no hard data are available as yet. Firstly, the Palestinian leadership was disappointed on at least two scores. They seemed to know full well that the Rabat Conference and, thereafter, Arafat's reception at the UN were accomplished primarily through the use of the Arab oil weapon, and through the emergence of a relatively united Arab world (in tactical terms), and that this had nothing whatsoever to do with their own achievements, strategy or ideology. They were not doing anything better in October 1974 than in October 1973, or October 1971, or at any other time. The Rabat Conference and the UN General Assembly in the fall of 1974 demonstrated more than ever the impotence of the Palestinians in accomplishing anything major, except through the institutionalized sovereign channels of the Arab states. No Palestinian with any intellectual approach to politics can disregard this very basic fact; the achievements at Rabat and the UN did not result from anything Palestinians did for themselves, but were given to them through Arab power, and if Arab power chose not to give them such accomplishments, then they could not have achieved them. Secondly, the Palestinian leadership may have felt that they were at, or already beyond, the peak of their international power, accompanied by a virtual international "festival" when they were at this summit, supported by Arab power which was also more or less at its height; and even at this peak they were still not capable of coercing Israel into giving them any territory or even negotiating with them. Therefore, the future may have looked much bleaker than before. Thirdly, and this is really only speculation, there seems to have been a general sense of confusion among the Palestinian leadership surrounding the question: "Where do we go from here?" After they had gained international legitimization, had received standing ovations in the UN and elsewhere, the next step was not at all clear and it seems that there was a great deal of confusion, which ought not to be underestimated.

The second lesson from the 1967–1973 period is that the PLO and the Palestinian organizations after the Six Day War needed two major elements in order to transform themselves into a real power to be reckoned with in the Middle East: institutionalization and control over some significant chunk of autonomous territory. One of these two was achieved to a large extent; the Palestinians did manage to institutionalize their political structure, and this has been a major political accomplishment indeed. However, in so far as the control of autonomous territory was concerned, they completely failed. Until this is achieved one way or another—and it is difficult to see how it can be achieved—dependence on the Arab regimes for some of the very basic needs of the Fidayeen, such as arms supplies, cannot be avoided. This last is very basic indeed: although arms supplies have been delivered to some extent from the Soviet Union, but mainly through the Soviet clients in Eastern Europe, and these can be obtained even notwithstanding the hostility of the Arab regimes, there is simply no way physically to get them into the hands of the Palestinians without the cooperation of the Arab countries.

The USSR's assessment of the PLO depends on the USSR's assessment of the role of the PLO in the inter-Arab system: as long as the USSR assesses that it does have a role, it is going to maintain some sort of relationship with it in order to pre-empt the possibility of the PLO falling into the hands of someone else with whom the USSR may be on bad terms. The USSR may be unhappy about a possible settlement say between Egypt, Jordan and Israel; if and when the Soviet Union wants to disrupt that possibility, it appears that the PLO is an excellent instrument for the purpose. There is some evidence that some people in the PLO have been thinking along such lines ever since the convening of the Geneva Conference in December 1973, and some PLO leaders believe that this is one of their strongest cards. Regardless of how true this is from the Soviet point of view, it did come up among the Palestinians, rightly or wrongly, and one cannot be sure that they are altogether wrong. In late 1974 it became known that there is a major disagreement between the PLO and the USSR on the very basic question of the right of Israel to exist. There is also Soviet unhappiness regarding many other things the PLO has been doing, and, as Sovietologists and others[53] have pointed out, the USSR paradoxically was a latecomer to recognizing the PLO as the sole legitimate representative of the Palestinian people, and there are many differences of opinion between the USSR and the PLO. It should be borne in mind, therefore, that the Soviet support for the PLO is very far from unequivocal,[54] though, of course, it is an important source of support to reckon with.

It is clear that to the extent that the Fidayeen are unable to gain control of autonomous territory, their leaders are also in physical danger in case they disrupt the patterns of the conflict as the Arab states would like to see those patterns. One should remember George Habash's close to eight months' imprisonment in Syria in 1968.[55] Although today it would be far more difficult—for obvious reasons—for any Arab regime to imprison a major Palestinian leader, were the patterns of the Arab–Israeli conflict to change, and were the Fidayeen to oppose them to the detriment of what the Arab countries would consider their interests, it seems clear that the lack of an autonomous territory would reduce the political capabilities of the Palestinian organizations to a bare minimum.[56]

Thirdly, connected to the second lesson, no matter how one speculates, one cannot really be clear as to what the various components of the PLO—and the PLO is very far from being a homogeneous organization[57]—would do if they were given a chance to acquire a territorial base; it appears that some components of the PLO realize full well the very importance of such a possible move. So far, the PLO, as has been mentioned, has not fallen apart as an institution, despite some expectations to the contrary.[58] However, no great test has had to be passed as yet, and no such revolutionary inducements have been offered to the PLO as to rival the possibility of an autonomous territorial base. The ongoing argument in the PLO is well known on the question of what to do if parts of the territories held by Israel were to be evacuated. There has been some very lukewarm compromise over setting up a "national rule" (*sulta wataniyya*), etc., but the issue is far from having been determined or settled. In fact, it appears that the PLO is very badly split on this issue and rightly so, because it is on this that the survival of an independent political capability of the Palestinians in the future may very well depend. One cannot be sure what they would do if this were to be offered as an inducement, which has not been the case so far, notwithstanding a great many speculations to the contrary.

The whole issue of the PLO ideology is somewhat confused; one sees a very interesting kind of process, whereby, because of difficulties in formulating an ideology, there is no PLO ideology except on the lowest common denominator of agreement to liberate Palestine along the lines of the establishment of a secular democratic state, etc.[59] The ideological formulation takes place within the separate organizations and even there, as a number of scholars have pointed out, the relatively sophisticated elaboration is done in the left-wing organizations, the PFLP and the PDFLP, where the ideologizing, however, is completely unrealistic. The more realistic ideologizing, if one might call it that, of the Fath is very unsophisticated and very crude[60] and the product is barely worthy of the name ideology.

This is true with regard to strategy as well. The basic point is that what the Palestinians accomplished between the two wars was to build up an institutional capability, so to speak, to "strategize."[61] We do not see very profound strategic thinking nor the execution of the little dose of strategy that was in fact crystallized; nor do we see, as has been pointed out, that the accomplishments which we do perceive came to being as a result of strategic thinking. As already indicated, often the opposite occurred—the kind of strategic thinking that existed[62] led to failures and unintended activities led to accomplishments.

Finally, it is difficult to determine to what extent the PLO's domination[63] of the Palestinians—and in the year following the October War it seemed clear that there was such a domination—could be challenged. All kinds of powerful political factors in the region have been interested in challenging the domination. The present domination is obvious. It is not certain to what extent other institutions, other political organizations or simply other elites, could successfully challenge the PLO, which, as has been said, between the wars did manage to pre-empt the Palestinian political center. This question is very much open and, needless to say, does have some political significance in terms of the ongoing diplomatic momentum, because the PLO issue might become very salient; as has been pointed out, the stage of the Arab–Israeli conflict following the October War does involve diplomatic momentum for something more than an immediate interim settlement,[64] and when that happens the PLO's power rises disproportionately to its military capabilities.

In this context it may be appropriate to end by calling attention to paradoxes inherent in the role of the Palestinians in 1967–1973. A great many people interested in Middle Eastern politics tend to attribute, both to the Soviets and the Arabs a very diabolical, Machiavellian type of mind, grand designs and plans of such nature. Our research on the Palestinians certainly indicated nothing of this sort. If anything, it seems the paradox is—and this is often true in political life—that the accomplishments, the most important achievements of the Palestinians, were really unintended consequences of what they tried to do. They failed in almost everything they tried to do consciously; they failed to take over any territory for an "Arab Hanoi" or a Fidayeen state; they failed to be a real nuisance to Israel militarily; they failed over and over again and yet, to a large extent as an unintended consequence of what they were trying to do, they managed to institutionalize, they managed to gain legitimacy, they managed to gain something which might be called a semi-veto power at least over the implementation of the Arab commitment to the rights of the Palestinians.[65] They thought they would be a factor in the Middle East in disrupting periods of relative calm, but in this they also failed. Thus, the final paradox is that the Palestinians, the most violent of any Arab factor in the conflict, the ones who opposed diplomacy and the diplomatic approach towards a solution of the conflict, who rejected most violently the idea of negotiating with Israel,[66] are the ones who benefit most from the series of negotiations and this, it seems, is the greatest paradox we can point out; the factor which most opposes diplomacy gains most from diplomacy, the factor which wants to fight most, can fight least. Perhaps this can be a lesson to all analysts of political affairs in this troubled and complicated part of the world.

NOTES

1. For a review of the theoretical issues related to institution building, see Gabriel Ben Dor, "Institutionalization and Political Development: A conceptual and Theoretical Analysis," *Comparative Studies in Sociology and History*, 17/3, July 1975, pp. 309-329.

2. This term has been adopted from the idea of "Authority without Sovereignty" as expressed by Dan Horowitz and Moshe Lissak in an article with that title, in M. Lissak and E. Guttman (eds.), *Political Institutions and Processes in Israel*, (Jerusalem, 1971). Horowitz and Lissak used their term with reference to the Jewish Community under the British Mandate. In some respects, there are

similarities between Zionism and Palestinian nationalism. Interestingly, this theme is fairly frequent in the writings of several important Palestinian intellectuals.

3. Reinhard Bendix, *Nation-Building and Citizenship*, (New York, 1964), p. 13.

4. William B. Quandt, Fuad and Jabber Ann Mosely Leach, *The Politics of Palestinian Nationalism*, (Berkley and Los Angeles, 1973).

5. On the structure of the PLO, see e.g., Daniel Heraidstveit, "A Profile of the Palestinian Guerrillas," *Cooperation and Conflict*, XVII (1972) 13-36, and A. Yaniv, *PLO–A Profile*, (Jerusalem, 1974).

6. A number of stimulating efforts along such lines were made before the October War. See, for instance, Quandt, et al., *op. cit.*; Mirko Aksatijevic, "Reflections on the Palestinian Resistance," *Journal of Palestine Studies*, II (1972), 111-119; Yehoshafat Harkabi, "Fedayeen Action and Arab Strategy," *Adelphi Papers*, No. 53 London, 1968; Hisham Sharabi, "Palestine Guerrillas: Their Credibility and Effectiveness," *Center for Strategic and International Studies, Georgetown University, Supplementary Papers* (Washington, 1970); idem, "Palestine Resistance: Crisis and Reassessment," *Middle East Newsletter*, January 1971; Michael Hudson, "The Palestinian Arab Resistance Movement, its Significance in the Middle East Crisis," *Middle East Journal*, 23 (1969), pp. 291-307; idem, "The Palestinian Resistance: Developments and Setbacks 1967–1971," *Journal of Palestine Studies* (1972), pp. 64-84.

7. Y. Harkabi, *op. cit.*; idem (ed.), *On the Guerrilla*, (Tel Aviv, 1971); J. Bowyer Bell, *The Myth of the Guerrilla*, (New York, 1971).

8. See, for instance, the interesting but impressionistic account of Gerard Chaliand, *La Resistance Palestinienne*, (Paris, 1970); Ehud Yaari, *Strike Terror: The Story of Fatah*, (New York, 1970); J. Laffin, *Fedayyen–The Arab–Israeli Dilemma*, (London, 1973).

9. Sharabi, *Palestine Guerrillas: Their Credibility and Effectiveness*.

10. Quandt, "Political and Military Dimensions of Contemporary Palestinian Nationalism," in Quandt *et al, op. cit.* pp. 67-71. At the Fifth Palestinian National Congress in Cairo in February 1969 al-Fath got 33 seats, as-Sa'iqa and the PFLP—12 each, while the Palestine Liberation Forces (PLF—its commando affiliate) got 15 seats. In response, the PLA, and PFLP refused to participate; al-Fath managed to dominate the PLO executive committee (of 11 members, 4 were Fath members and 3 were its sympathizers); from this point on Arafat, the Fath leader, became the PLO Chairman.

11. Doubts, however, were raised at times as to the capacity of the Palestinian movement to radicalize the Arab world. See, for instance, Ilyas Murqus,

Al-Muqawama al-Filastiniyya wa-al-Mawqif al-Rahin, (Beirut, 1971). The viewpoint held by the PFLP and the PDFLP is described in detail in Chaliand, *op. cit.* See also idem. "Le Double Combat du PDFLP, *Le Monde Diplomatique*, July 1970. I. Abu Lughed, insists on the vanguard role of the Palestinians in *Shu'un Filastiniyya* (No. 11, July 1972; on this see also Y. Harkabi, *The Problem of the Palestinians*, (Jerusalem, n.d.) pp. 15-16.

12. The problems of this stage were analyzed in detail by Hudson, *op. cit.* and Aksentijevic, *op. cit.*, as well as by Hisham Sharabi, "Liberation or Settlement: The Dialectics of Palestinian Struggle," *Journal of Palestine Studies*, II (1973), pp. 33-48.

13. P. J. Vatikiotis, *Conflict in the Middle East*, (London, 1971).

14. To some extent, this is an example of what political scientists (for instance, Charles E. Lindblom) would call "The Science of 'Muddling Through'." *Public Administration Review*, XIV (1959), pp. 79-88.

15. The previous stage had led to what Malcolm Kerr called *The Arab Cold War*, (3rd Edition, New York, 1971). The transformation to the post-messianic stage of Arab nationalism is analyzed in Ben Dor, "Unity and Disunity in the Arab World," *Seqira Hodshit*, September, 1973, pp. 3-13.

16. See H. R. Sharabi, *Nationalism and Revolution in the Arab World*, (Princeton, 1966), ch. VII; and introduction to Sylvia G. Gaim (ed.), *Arab Nationalism: An Anthology*, (Berkley and Los Angeles, 1962). See also Adel Daher, *Current Trends in Arab Intellectual Thought*, (RAND Corporation, 1969).

17. The major sources for the study of contemporary Palestinian politics have been: the Beirut periodicals and newspapers: *Shu'un Filastiniyya*, *Filastin al-Thawra*, *al-Hadaf* (PFLP oriented), *al-Muharrir*, *al-Wafa*, *al-Hurriyya* (PDFLP oriented); the Amman publication: *Al-Fath*; the articles, surveys and chronologies published in the *Journal of Palestine Studies*, (published since 1972, in Beirut, jointly by the Institute of Palestine Studies and Kuwait University); and radio broadcasts (such as the *Voice of Fath*—Cairo; and the *Voice of Palestine*—Damascus).

18. Y. Harkabi, *Fedayeen Action and Arab Strategy*.

19. In the view of the PLO, Palestinian society had to be rebuilt along with the Palestinian polity. The PLO's ambitions have always included a strong element of social, as well as political, consciousness.

20. See, in addition to the previously quoted sources, *Ma'rakat al-Muqawama al-Filastiniyya, fi Waqiha al-Rahin*, (PDFLP), (Beirut, 1969); and *Al-Tariq al-Qawmi li-Tahrir Filastin* (ALF), (Beirut, 1970).

21. See, for instance, the final communiqué of the Palestinian Popular

Congress of April 1972, in the *Journal of Palestine Studies*, I, (Summer, 1972), pp. 177-180; and Leila S. Kadi, *Basic Political Documents of the Armed Palestinian Resistance Movement*, (PLO Research Center, Beirut, December 1969).

22. The concept of "institutionalization" is used here in the sense developed by Samuel P. Huntington in his by now classic "Political Development and Political Decay," *World Politics*, XVII (1965), pp. 386-430 and *Political Order in Changing Societies*, (New Haven, 1968).

23. This has been a crucially important point for the Palestinian movements ever since their inception. See Fuad Jabber, "The Regimes and the Palestinian Revolution 1967–71," *Journal of Palestine Studies*, II/2 (Winter, 1973) pp. 79-101 reprinted in Quandt, *et al.*, *op. cit.*, pp. 86-199.

24. See also Harkabi, *On the Guerrilla, passim*.

25. See Quandt, *Politics of Palestinian Nationalism*, pp. 94-112.

26. Moshe Maoz, "Soviet and Chinese Relations with the Palestinian Guerrilla Organizations," *Jerusalem Papers on Peace Problems*, 4, March, 1972.

27. Oded Eran, "The Soviet Union and the Palestine Guerrilla Organizations," *The Shiloah Center Occasional Papers*, (Tel Aviv, 1971).

28. Arafat took great pride in this. See interview with him broadcast by *Sawt al-Thawra al-Falastiniyya*, Radio Cairo, August 1972, and reprinted in the *Journal of Palestine Studies*, II (1973), p. 174.

29. See for instance, Yehoshua Porath, *The Emergence of the Palestinian Arab Nationalist Movement, 1918–1929*, (London, 1974); Ann Mosely Leach, "The Palestine Arab Nationalist Movement under the Mandate," in Quandt *et al.*, *op. cit.*; J. C. Hurwitz, *The Stuggle for Palestine*, (New York, 1950); Naji Alush, *Al-Muqawama al-Arabiyya fi-Filastin, 1914–1918*, (Beirut, 1967).

30. Hudson, in his "The Palestine Resistance..." pp. 291-307, develops a sophisticated comparative typology of political movements in the contemporary Arab world and reaches a similar conclusion.

31. Numerous studies exist on the character of these radical Arab elites. For a few representative views, see Amos Perlmutter, "The Arab Military Elite," *World Politics*, XXII, January 1970, pp. 269-300; Manfred Halpern, "Middle Eastern Armies and the New Middle Class," in John J.Johnson (ed.), *The Role of the Military in Underdeveloped Countries*, (Princeton, 1962), pp. 277-316; H. Sharabi, *Nationalism and Revolution in the Arab World*; Monroe Berger, *The Arab World Today*, (New York, 1964), ch. 10; and Eliezer Beeri, *Army Officers in Arab Politics and Society*, (New York, 1969).

32. To a certain extent, the decline of Ahmad Shuqayri from the leadership of the PLO signifies the decline of the entire traditional elite. For some characteristic views of the elite, see Shuqayri's memoirs: *Araba'un 'Aman fi'l Hayat*

al 'Arabiyya wa al-Dawliyya, (Beirut, 1972), and his *'Ala Tariq al-Hazima wa'l Muluk wa'l Ru'asa'*, (Beirut, 1972).

33. This point is made, for instance, forcefully and emphatically in Vatikiotis, *Conflict in the Middle East*, ch. IX.

34. A number of surveys and studies carried out by Israeli scholars on the West Bank (hitherto unpublished) clearly indicate a high degree of stability of the traditional political elites there.

35. The concept of "Center" is used here in the sense developed by Edward Shils in his "Center and Periphery" in the *Logic of Personal Knowledge, Essays Presented to M. Polanyi*, (London, 1961), pp. 117-130. See also Daniel Lerner, "Some Comments on Center-Periphery Relations," in Richard L. Merrit and Stein Rokkan (eds.), *Comparing Nations*, (New Haven, 1966), and ch. 1. "Centers and Periphery in Society and Social Science," in J. Peter Nettl, *Political Mobilization*, (New York, 1967).

36. The multi-state character of the Palestinians is clearly demonstrated in the tables of their geographic distribution. The Palestinian estimate for 1970 is based on Nablil Shaath, "High Level Palestinian Manpower," *Journal of Palestine Studies*, I (1972), p. 81, as slightly amended in Ibrahim Abu Lughod, "Educating a Community in Exile: The Palestinian Experience," *Journal of Palestine Studies*, II (1973), p. 97. The Israeli estimate is based on the official figures of the Israeli Foreign Ministry (1974).

	Palestinian Estimate (1970)	Israeli Estimate (1974)
Jordan		
East Bank	900,000	600,000
West Bank	670,000	650,000
Gaza	364,000	400,000
Israel	340,000	530,000
Lebanon	240,000	150,000
Syria	180,000	130,000
Kuwait	140,000	150,000
Egypt	33,000	
Iraq	14,000	Other Arab
Persian Gulf	15,000	Countries 130,000
Libya	5,000	
Saudi Arabia	20,000	
US	1,000	
Latin America	5,000	Western
West Germany	15,000	Countries 150,000

37. Note the following declaration by PFLP leader George Habash: "...it is our duty to support the Palestine Liberation Organization, by attempting to raise its political, organizational and, in particular, military standards, by attempting to fight from within the framework of the Liberation Organization, so that it may rise to the level which will enable it to undertake such a task." *Al-Hadaf*, 24 March, 1973.

38. An analysis of the diplomacy and speeches of the 1967 and 1973 Wars, as well as of the War of Attrition, reveals that references to the Palestinians were minor and almost incidental. The 1973 War certainly demonstrated that the role of the Palestinians in the total Arab war effort was insignificant.

39. An analysis of the writings and speeches of Palestinian leaders clearly indicates this. See for instance the survey of the PLO's ideology and objective in Quandt, *The Politics of Palestinian Nationalism*, pp. 94-113.

40. Cf. Yehoshafat Harkabi (ed.), *Leqah Ha-Aravim mi-Tevusatam*, (Tel Aviv, 1969); A. L. Tibawi, "Towards Understanding and Overcoming the Catastrophe," *Middle East Forum*, XLIV (1968), pp. 35-43.

41. This was well demonstrated, for instance, in Sadat's main speech during the October War (on 16 October, 1973), in which, however, the Palestine issue as such was not central.

42. Nevertheless, the UN Security Council Resolution 242 of 22 November 1967, which, during the inter-war period was the basis for a number of major diplomatic efforts involving Israel, Egypt and Jordan speaks only of "...a just settlement of the refugee (not the Palestinian) problem." Meron Medzini, ed., *Israel's Foreign Relations–Basic Documents, 1948–1972*, (Jerusalem, 1972), p. 475).

43. See for instance, *al-Balagh*, 8 October, 1972, as quoted in the *Journal of Palestine Studies*, II (1973), p. 163.

44. See Jabber, "The Arab Regimes and the Palestinian Revolution," pp. 89-90; Sharabi, "Palestine Resistance: Crisis and Reassessment."

45. *Filastin al-Thawra*, 16 August, 1 September 1972; *Al-Nahar, al-Hadaf*, 2 September 1972.

46. Cf. Maoz, *op. cit.*; Eran, *op. cit.*; L. Romanecki, "The Arab Terrorists in the Middle East and the Soviet Union," (Jerusalem, Hebrew University, Soviet and East European Research Center, 1973).

47. Numerous attempts have been made to utilize the Palestine issue within the moral as well as judicial framework of international relations. See, for instance, W. T. Mallison Jr., and S. V. Mallison, "The Juridicial Characteristics of the Palestinian Resistance: an Appraisal in International Law," *Journal of Palestine Studies*, II (1973), pp. 64-78.

48. On Black September, see Laffin and the Maoist interpretation Gilbert Mury, *Septembre Noir*, (Paris, 1973).

49. There has been a great deal of thinking in the Arab world as well as among the Palestinians themselves about the potential and the limits of guerrilla warfare, especially in the context of the struggle against Israel, but also in more general terms. See, for instance, Akram Dayri and Major Haytaam al-Ayyubi, *Nahw Istratijiyya 'Arabiyya Jadida*, (Beirut, 1969); Abu Hamman, *Al-Muqawama Askariyyan* (Beirut, 1971); and Shawqi Khayrallah, *Al-Tariq Ila al Quds* (Beirut, 1973).

50. Lebanon is aptly characterized by Hudson as the "Precarious Republic" in a book by that title, (New York, 1968). He explains perceptively the strains, stresses and constraints of Lebanese politics.

51. Hudson, "Fedayeen are Forcing Lebanon's Hand," *Mid East*, (Washington, DC.) February, 1970, pp. 7-14.

52. In a survey reported in Halim Barakat, "Social Factors Influencing Attitudes of University Students in Lebanon Towards the Palestinian Resistance Movement," *Journal of Palestine Studies*, I (1971), it was found that, among students in Lebanon, "sectarianism is the most highly significant determining factor of attitudes towards the Fidayeen."

53. Eran, *op.cit*; Maoz, *op.cit*.

54. Eran, *op. cit.*

55. Jabber, p. 86. This was coupled by a number of other restrictions on the PFLP in Syria, reported in *al-Hurriyya*, 16 September, 1968. Numerous similar examples can be quoted in regard to Egypt, needless to say Jordan, and even Iraq.

56. This fear is pervasive in the writings of Palestinian intellectuals. Indeed the events of 1970 in Jordan and to a lesser extent in Egypt seem to justify such fear amply. Quandt, *op. cit.*, p. 96 quotes a Fath representative: "The Arab countries have their specific problems, their own interests which condition their thinking and determine their action." (Quotation taken originally from Gilbert Denoyan, *El-Fatah Parle: Les Palestiniens Contre Israel*, (Paris, 1970).

57. Cf. Heraidstveit, "A Profile of the Palestine Guerrillas," pp. 13-36.

58. Arafat himself mentioned this as to the greatest accomplishment of the PLO in the difficult years of 1971 and 1972, in an interview in *Filastin al-Thawra*, January 1973.

59. See, for instance, the "Aims of the Political Program of the Palestinian Revolution Adapted by the 11th Palestine National Congress, Cairo, 12 January 1973," in the *Journal of Palestine Studies*, II (1973), pp. 169-73.

60. Cf. Quandt, *op. cit.*, pp. 94-111.

61. See Arafat's views in *Filastin ath-Thawra*, 1 January, 1973.

62. Beyond what Lindblom called "the science of muddling through," the strategy that was actually prusued was that referred to as "incrementalism" in David Braybroke and Charles E. Lindblom, *Strategy of Decision*, (New York, 1963).

63. As pointed out before, this was, in general, pre-emptive domination, that is denial of domination to others. The actual hold of the PLO on the Palestinians had to be tenuous as long as the vast majority of the Palestinians lived under tight Israeli and Jordanian control. In these areas, the PLO could—and did—build up considerable sentiment in its favor, but had difficulty translating it into political or military power.

64. Nadav Safran, "The War and the Future of the Middle East Conflict," *Foreign Affairs*, 52 (1974), pp. 215-236.

65. The resolution of the 11th Palestinian National Congress (*op. cit.*, p. 190) expresses the idea clearly in part I, article 15: "In its official Arab relations the Liberation Organization concentrates on protecting the interests of Palestinian citizens in the Arab homeland and expressing the political will of the Palestinian people, and the Palestinian revolution, within the framework of the Palestine Liberation Organization, will continue to be the highest command of the Palestinian People; *it alone speaks on their behalf on all problems related to their destiny, and it alone* through its organizations for struggle *is responsible for everything related to the Palestinian's people's right to self-determination.*" (italics added.)

66. *Ibid.*, particularly Part I, article 2, and Part II, article 2.

Political Factors
and trends in the
Israeli-Administered Territories

Elie Rekhess and Asher Susser

THE POLITICAL CHARACTERISTICS OF THE WEST BANK

During the period of Jordanian rule, the West Bank had been administratively integrated as part of the highly centralized Hashemite Kingdom. However, in the political sphere, the integration of the Palestinians was marginal and power was concentrated in the hands of the King and his supporters from the Trans-Jordanian elite, backed by the Jordanian internal security services and the army in which the East Bankers also filled the key positions and manned the major part of the front-line units. All national political institutions were concentrated on the East Bank and West Bankers did not serve in posts which would allow them to be directly involved in the major decision-making process.[1]

The main opposition to the regime which rejected the traditional "image of Jordan"[2] and all it stood for, was concentrated mainly in the West Bank and led by political parties such as the Arab Nationalist Movement (ANM), the Ba'th and the Jordanian Communist Party (JCP). Yet these had not been allowed to operate freely since all political parties had been banned since 1957.

Those who held positions of leadership in the West Bank were mainly from the traditionally notable and wealthy families whose influence was limited to their respective communities. Their source of authority, based on their social standing and wealth, was of a strictly local nature.

Interregional diversity (as between the semi-industrialized, more modernized and more radical town of Nablus and the mainly agricultural and conservative town of Hebron), personal rivalries and the regional administrative divisions of the West Bank under Jordanian rule, all served as additional factors preserving the East Bank's predominance over the West Bank and preventing the emergence of an independent West Bank political leadership.

Following the Israeli occupation in June 1967, the political circles aligned with the Hashemite establishment continued to seek guidance mainly from Jordan, the more radical groups tended to identify more with the PLO and the "progressive" Arab states—particularly Egypt—while the stand of the Communists was formulated to a large extent in accordance with Soviet policy.

The three major political forces directly concerned with the control of the West Bank—Israel, Jordan and the PLO—formulated their policies toward the West Bank during the initial period of Israeli administration.

Israel saw Jordan as the future partner for a settlement over the West Bank and did not favor the establishment of a Palestinian entity or the emergence of a local representative leadership. Contact with the population was to be maintained on a local basis by means of the various municipalities and chambers of commerce. Seeking to control the West Bank with a minimal security effort, the Israeli authorities strove to promote a process of normalization in which the local population would be able to continue to live their daily lives much as before the occupation. These considerations dictated a firm line against those seeking to disrupt this process whether in Fidayeen organizations or in political organizations designed to promote civil unrest and protest against the occupation.[3]

Another central aspect of the process of normalization was Israel's policy of open bridges which allowed for the maintenance of continued contact between the population and Jordan and the Arab world in general, which corresponded with Israel's policy of continuing to regard the population's political future as tied to Jordan.

Jordan continued to regard the West Bank as an integral part of the Hashemite Kingdom, and like Israel opposed the formation of any separate Palestinian entity or West Bank representative leadership. The open bridges policy and the maintenance of economic ties between the two banks, enabled Jordan to preserve its influence over the population and at times to impose economic or other sanctions against those who deviated from Jordanian policy.

The Palestinian organizations stressed the necessity of an armed struggle for the liberation of the occupied territories and of all Palestine. In order to achieve this aim the organizations sought to carry out extensive Fidayeen operations within the occupied territories in an effort to disrupt the process of normalization of Israeli rule and to limit cooperation between the population and the Israeli authorities. Claiming to be the sole representative of the Palestinian people, the PLO similarly rejected any form of separate West Bank political initiative.

THE FORMS OF POLITICAL ACTIVITY UNDER ISRAELI RULE

The absence of an autonomous West Bank leadership and the allegiance of the various political circles to their external patrons led the majority of West Bankers to abstain from independent political initiatives in regard to the future of the area immediately after the Six Day War. Nevertheless, a small group of leaders, from among those previously associated with the Hashemite establishment as well as the anti-Hashemite political groupings, promoted the concept of the Palestine entity. This initiative was mainly associated with figures such as Hebron Mayor Muhammad 'Ali al-Ja'bari, 'Aziz Shihada, a lawyer from Ram'allah, and Dr. Hamdi Taji al-Faruqi, a former leading member of the Jordanian Ba'th party, also of Ram'allah.[4]

On 11 June, 1967, Israeli officers were approached by two Palestinian politicians who suggested a meeting of about 50 Palestinian leaders to be convened in Ram'allah. Their aim was to constitute an assembly which would then request the government of Israel to recognize them as representatives of the Palestinians and negotiate with them the establishment of a separate Palestinian entity on the lines of the UN Partition Plan of 1947.[5]

The solution sought by those aligned with the Palestinian entity was not clearly defined. While they insisted on the right of the Palestinians to self-determination, the supporters of the entity idea generally sought to preserve the association with Jordan by means of an eventual federation between Jordan and the postulated Palestinian state. However, from the writings of Muhammad Abu Shilbaya, one of the main Palestine entity supporters, the long-term aim seemed to be Palestinian domination of both banks. Though they were not alone in demanding changes in the relationship with Jordan, they differed from other groups in their advocacy of local initiative to secure this aim while still under Israeli occupation and by agreement with the Israeli authorities, before an overall settlement with Arab states.[6]

Israel did not respond to this initiative, Jordan strongly criticized it, and Fidayeen opposition was manifest in the firing of a bazooka shell at Faruqi's home in December 1967.[7]

A second trend advocated reunion with Jordan, cooperation with the Arab countries and the rejection of any separate contacts between the

West Bank leadership and Israel. This trend was supported by a heterogeneous and incongruous coalition of pro-Hashemites and circles associated with the radical political parties. The latter strove to establish a National Front which would unite representatives of the various political groups and parties in a coordinated effort to resist the occupation.[8]

By July 1967, 25 West Bank leaders, mainly from East Jerusalem, had already constituted themselves as the Supreme Muslim Council—headed by Shaykh 'Abd al-Hamid as-Sa'ih, and including both members of the Hashemite establishment such as Anwar Nusayba, former Defense Minister and Ambassador to London, Anwar al-Khatib, former Jordanian Governor of the Jerusalem district, and anti-Hashemite figures such as 'Abd al-Muhsin Abu Mayzar and Ibrahim Bakr, associated with the Ba'th party.[9] These initial steps toward political organization failed however to produce the intended National Front.

Firm Israeli countermeasures such as the deportation of as-Sa'ih, who also headed the High Committee for National Guidance (in September 1967), and Ibrahim Bakr (in December 1967), served as a deterrent against such local political activity. Furthermore, differences between local leaders associated with the Hashemite establishment and those associated with the radical political parties, on the future relationship with Jordan and the question of the Palestine entity, also prevented the formulation of a joint political program. Pro-Hashemite leaders withdrew from this form of political activity while those associated with the radical political parties, the Ba'th, the ANM and the JCP, were also divided amongst themselves on the question of the form and objectives of resistance to the occupation. While the Ba'th and the ANM supported an armed struggle for "the liberation of Palestine," the Communists supported "at the present stage" a political struggle for the "elimination of the traces of aggression."[10]

Though the National Front did not materialize, circles associated with this initiative drew up a draft "National Covenant for the Present Phase of the Arabs of the West Bank" (*al-mithaq al-watani al-marhali li-'arab ad-daffa al-gharbiyya*) published in the Lebanese press in October 1967.

The Covenant stressed the general Arab character of the struggle against Israel and rejected the notion of a Palestinian entity to be established in agreement with Israel. As for the future relationship with Jordan, the Covenant supported the unity of the two banks but called for changes such as the establishment of a national government which would abandon Jordan's pro-Western orientation, establish a democratic regime and organize the army on the basis of national service.[11] The substance of the Covenant in effect called for the Palestinization of Jordan, since the implementation of such demands would lead to the transfer of power to the Palestinian majority, both in the administration and the armed forces—the mainstay of the Hashemite regime—while simultaneously detaching Jordan from its traditional Western allies. These demands, as well as the fact that it was submitted for publication by the PLO bureau in Lebanon, suggest that those who had drafted it belonged to circles associated with the anti-Hashemite opposition parties which had made such demands prior to 1967.

Radical circles continued their efforts to organize clandestine bodies to direct resistance against the occupation and it was apparently toward the end of 1968 when the Committee for National Solidarity (*lajnat at-tadamun al-qawmi*) was formed in Nablus by members of the JCP and the ANM. This was to be followed by the formation of similar committees in other West Bank towns, which were to coordinate their activities with the National Gathering (*at-tajammu' al-watani*) opposition in Jordan.[12] Apart from organizing protests against the occupation, the Committee had also sought to undermine the position of the generally pro-Hashemite traditional leadership, which had also adopted a relatively moderate stand toward the Israeli authorities, and generally opposed the disruption of the process of normalization under occupation.

However, this renewed attempt at political organization by the radical groups was similarly frustrated by Israeli deportation of leaders involved and by the limited degree of cooperation between the various radical parties. While the Communists continued to restrict their activity to political action,[13] elements associated with the ANM, from which the PFLP had emerged, became increasingly involved in Fidayeen activity, thus leaving the organization of protest mainly in the hands of the Communists, who continued to organize independently and formed various front groups such as the Popular Resistance Front in the West Bank (*jabhat al-muqawama ash-sha'biyya fi ad-daffa al-gharbiyya*). The PFLP on the other hand, at least until the beginning of 1969, also engaged independently in the organization of unrest through underground groups such as the West Bank Students' Union which had operated under its auspices.[14]

Israeli security measures severely hampered the efforts of the radical groups to organize, thus serving to advance the process of normalization, as well as indirectly maintaining the stability of the traditional leadership.

The frustration of the radicals by Israel only illustrates one facet of West Bank inability to organize politically. As shown below, attempts by other elements to launch political initiatives were similarly stopped short by a combination of external factors. These, though guided by conflicting interests, jointly prevented their success.

An alternative plan to that proposed by Palestine entity supporters in June 1967 was proposed by Musa al-'Alami. 'Alami's plan suggested the replacement of the Israeli occupation with neutral control for five years to enable the holding of a referendum to allow for Palestinian self-determination and to decide on the future relationship with Jordan.[15] This proposal was rejected by the Palestine National Assembly (PNA) of July 1968, which declared anyone who lent support to "an entity and international protection to be an enemy of the Arab Palestinian people and the Arab nation."[16]

Nevertheless, two local leaders, Hamdi Kan'an of Nablus and Muhammad 'Ali Ja'bari of Hebron persisted in efforts to attain some form of representative status for the West Bank leadership. It seemed that these leaders were motivated by the desire to limit Israeli presence and at the same time to attain a new political status for the West Bank before a Jordanian return to the area. Their efforts bear witness both to their intentions and to the constraints which hampered them.

As mayor of Nablus, the most prominent political center in the West Bank, Kan'an had attained since the occupation the status of a leading West Bank political figure and he appeared to be striving to turn his post of mayor into a position of political leadership extending beyond the local level.

At the end of 1968 Kan'an called for municipal elections, and this was attacked by the Jordanian media as an attempt to form a West Bank representative body, toward the establishment of a Palestinian entity. It did in fact seem that Kan'an at this early stage of the occupation was already striving to ensure some form of autonomy for the West Bank in the framework of a future federation with Jordan, as he himself openly demanded after the civil war in September 1970.[17]

In an attempt to improve his relations with Jordan, Kan'an openly supported the civil unrest called for by King Hussein at the beginning of February 1969. This was followed by a deterioration of his relations with the Military Government, which led Kan'an to make efforts to restore order in Nablus. He met with little success and unrest continued, mainly under the influence of radical groups. With Kan'an under pressure from all sides, the local leadership was not prepared to lend him support in his efforts to restore order. Now isolated and unable to control the town, Kan'an resigned in March 1969.[18]

Ja'bari, due to his authoritative leadership in the Hebron area, was from the outset more independent in his political behavior than other leaders in the West Bank. In the initial period after the Six Day War, he was the most outspoken in his rejection of Jordan's claims to the loyalty of the population of the area, and also adopted a more moderate stand toward the occupation, illustrated by his success in preventing manifestations of protest in the Hebron area and his frequent criticism of Fidayeen activity in the West Bank. Furthermore, he openly questioned the representative character of the Palestine National Assembly, in which, he maintained, West Bankers had no say. These views of Ja'bari were the background to his continued support for local political initiative which he sought to realize by repeated calls for a conference of West Bank leaders.[19]

But Ja'bari too encountered difficulties in pursuing an independent line. He believed that the intensive Fidayeen activity in the Hebron area in late 1969 was directed in part against him personally because of his moderate attitude toward the Israeli authorities. It seems indeed that this activity was partly intended to undermine Ja'bari's control over the Hebron area as a result of his support for local political initiative and consequently, in mid-November 1969, Ja'bari declared that he was "quitting politics," indicating that he would no longer discuss political issues including the idea of the Palestine entity. The affairs of the occupied territories, he maintained, were part of "an Arab case adopted by the Arab States."[20]

However, Ja'bari renewed his independent activity at the beginning of 1970. Yet his intention of using meetings of notables of the Hebron area in March 1970 as a stepping stone to the establishment of wider regional forums not only met with Fidayeen warnings, but was also prevented by the Israeli Government.[21]

In the face of continued outside opposition to local initiatives, those who tended to favor the idea remained a minority.

THE IMPACT OF THE CIVIL WAR IN JORDAN

The civil war of September 1970 in Jordan no doubt had a profound impact on the West Bank, and the demand for a new relationship with Jordan now attained a greater sense of urgency.

While some leading figures in the West bank called for the severance of all connection with the regime in Jordan, and formed political groups calling for the establishment of a Palestine entity, it seemed that most local leaders acted according to a realistic appraisal of the political situation, and avoided steps which would lead to detachment from the regime in power on the East Bank, and from the Arab world in general. Despite the widespread hostility expressed against the Hashemite regime in the wake of the civil war, it became clear that the political factors which had militated against local political initiative until then still prevailed.

Though a traumatic experience for West Bankers, the civil war did not alter the basic positions of Israel, Jordan, Egypt and the Palestinian organizations which rejected local political initiative. Most West bank leaders therefore remained reluctant to assume any representative status. Local leaders did at first show signs of intending to take some form of independent initiative but no real immediate change took place in the West Bank political scene.

On 26 September, 1970, after a meeting attended by Anwar al-Khatib and Anwar Nusayba of Jerusalem, Mayor Hajj Ma'zuz al-Masri, Hikmat al-Masri, Qadri Tuqan and Hamdi kan'an of Nablus and Mayor Ja'bari of Hebron, it was already clear that most of these leaders had no intention of severing their relations with the regime in Jordan, and they refused Kan'an's proposal to issue jointly an anti-Hussein statement.[22]

In mid-October four Nablus leaders, Qadri Tuqan, Hikmat al-Masri, Ma'zuz al-Masri and Rashid Nimr, traveled to Cairo via Beirut in what Tuqan described as a private visit to express condolences to the Egyptian leadership following the death of President Nasser.[23] However, the object of the mission seemed to be to consult the PLO, Jordan and Egypt on the policy West Bank leaders were to adopt in the light of the civil war. In Beirut, talks were apparently held with PLO representatives, and in Cairo with the Jordanian ambassador, President Sadat and members of the oppositional National Gathering from Jordan.

It appeared that the talks held in Cairo clarified to West Bankers that local political initiative under Israeli occupation was unacceptable in the view of the outside Arab parties concerned. On his return, Tuqan told the press that the West Bankers did not agree to any change concerning the formation of a Palestinian state or local autonomy, until after an Israeli withdrawal after which "we will turn to Hussein...[since] we know how to deal with him logically."[24]

Yasir Arafat later re-emphasized the Fidayeen stand in particularly strong terms. He disclosed that he had been approached in Amman by certain West Bank personalities who had sought his permission to hold a conference in the occupied territories which would declare the separation of the West Bank from Jordan. He, however, made it quite clear that he saw such a step as an effort to establish "a distorted Palestine state" and threatened exponents of such an idea with execution.[25]

The generally restrained reaction of West Bank leaders to the civil war in Jordan was staunchly criticized by Hamdi Kan'an, and groups from the young intelligentsia who attempted to organize politically. The most widely publicized of these groups was the Palestinian National Gathering (at-tajammu' al-watani al-filastini) formed in October 1970, and headed by Yusuf Nasir.[26] The group associated with the editorial staff of al-Quds[27] reportedly sought to form a new leadership and to establish a Palestinian entity in the occupied territories. The group was also associated with a proposal similar to that previously made by Musa 'Alami to ask the UN to conduct a referendum in the occupied territories to allow the local population to determine its future.

From the outset, the group seems to have had very little room for maneuver and its members were at first even afraid to identify themselves or openly publish their views. Israel did not favor their political organization and their activity was also criticized by Fidayeen radio stations which referred to the group as "tools in the hands of Israel and Imperialism"; Jordanian media took a similar stand.[28]

Hamdi Kan'an, on the other hand, now openly demanded the formulation of a new relationship with Jordan and rejected Hussein's stand of self-determination for the West Bank only after liberation. At the beginning of December Kan'an published a statement in al-Quds calling on Hussein to amend the constitution so as to provide for Palestinian self-rule in the framework of a federal union between the two banks.[29]

Though Kan'an and the new groups such as the Palestine National

Gathering did represent a certain trend of opinion favoring independent political initiative, the available political alternatives made their chances of success extremely remote. Israel, perhaps even more than before, regarded Jordan as partner for a settlement and did not favor local political organization. Furthermore, any local representative body would have to face the impossible situation of adopting a political program that would not arouse the Fidayeen and the Arab world against them nor lead to their deportation by the Israeli authorities.

The fact that most West Bank leaders continued to allow the determination of their political future to rest with external political factors, and refrained from taking any drastic steps which could signify their detachment from Jordan, should not, however, be interpreted to mean that they were prepared to return to the pre-1967 mode of Jordanian rule. Even before the civil war it appears to have been generally accepted that changes ought to be made in the future relationship with Jordan, and the events of September only served to give greater justification to this trend. There now seemed to be a more widespread support for the idea of a referendum under UN control of the occupied territories before any return of Jordanian rule, both among the local leaders such as Ja'bari and others and the young intelligentsia.[30]

Though most local leaders were not prepared to act independently, Nablus leaders were prominent in seeking involvement in political developments concerning the West Bank. This was illustrated by the participation of Qadri Tuqan, Hikmat al-Masri and Rashid Nimr in talks held in Beirut during February 1971 on the question of the establishment of a Palestinian state. These talks followed unofficial American contacts with PLO leaders to sound out their views on the establishment of either a separate Palestinian state in the West Bank and the Gaza Strip or a Jordanian—Palestinian federation or a Palestinian government in exile.[31]

The Nablus leaders, however, did not depart from the stand of Jordan, the PLO and Egypt, which continued to refect the notion of a Palestinian state in the West Bank and the Gaza Strip and reaffirmed their support for the unity of the two banks and the efforts of Egypt and Jordan to achieve a peaceful solution to the conflict.[32] Yet in April, following further clashes in Jordan, which again aroused protest in the West Bank, Nablus leaders such as Hikmat al-Masri, Rashid Nimr, Walid ash-Shak'a and Hamdi Kan'an as well as other leaders in the northern West Bank, coupled their denunciation of events in Jordan with statements stressing the right of the Palestinians to self-determination.[33]

Jordan's growing sense of power, particularly under the premiership of Wasfi at-Tall, led to firm and immediate Jordanian countermeasures. Jordan prepared a black list restricting the entry of certain West Bankers, including the signatories of the Nablus petition, and other figures known to be anti-Hashemites or Palestine entity supporters such as Muhammad Abu Shilbaya. Instructions were also issued for the arrest of certain West Bank personalities, and Hikmat al-Masri was in fact arrested in April during a visit to Amman.[34]

In May these restrictions were lifted and it appeared that while taking a firm stand against deviation from Jordanian policy, the Government adopted a softer line when West Bankers refrained from outspoken criticism of the regime. This tendency was also illustrated by Tall instructing government ministries to assist and give better service to West Bankers visiting Jordan.[35]

The reaction in the West Bank to the final expulsion of the Fidayeen organizations from Jordan in 1971 was more moderate than it had been in September 1970. It seemed that West Bank leaders realized now even more than in September that protest on their part would result in futile confrontation with the regime, which was now all-powerful. The Jordanian Government on its part also made special efforts to explain to local leaders the background to the measures taken against the Fidayeen organizations. Anwar Nusayba, although describing the events as "deeply shocking and not inevitable," said that "the Jordanian action must be seen in the context of limited action, aimed at eliminating a security threat within Jordan."[36] It seems that West Bankers distinguished between the military struggle between the regime and the Fidayeen organization and what had appeared in September as an indiscriminate "massacre of the Palestinians" as had been presented by Fidayeen media at the time.

Though Jordan was now clearly in a powerful position to assert its influence on affairs in the West Bank, attempts were made mainly by Ja'bari to continue independent political activity. At the end of July, he approached the Israeli Military Government and requested permission for a conference of West Bank leaders to discuss the idea of self-determination of the West Bank and the Gaza Strip as a step toward the establishment of an independent Palestine state. Another reason he gave for his request was the need to discuss the Lebanese threat to boycott West Bank agricultural and industrial products, as Lebanon had claimed that Israeli products were also being exported in these consignments. A call for such a convention, limited, however, to the economic question, came from the Mayor of Bayt Sahur, Nikula Abu 'Ita. Though Ja'bari reportedly assumed that the elimination of the Fidayeen in Jordan would make the Military Government more receptive to his idea, the authorities rejected his request and only approved that of Abu 'Ita.[37]

No political action was taken and the resolutions centered on the economic question and the sending of a delegation to the Arab League.[38]

THE PREDOMINANCE OF ISRAEL AND JORDAN

The two years preceding the October War were characterized by a political stalemate on the question of a Middle East settlement, a continuation of the process of normalization of Israeli rule, and Jordanian superiority over the Palestinian organizations in their competition for influence in the West Bank area.

The attitudes of West Bank leaders toward local political initiatives remained unchanged and they continued to concentrate on local affairs and day-to-day problems. The lack of political initiative in the international arena allowed the question of West Bank involvement in a political settlement to be avoided.

Israel and Jordan were now, more than before, the two dominant factors influencing West Bank affairs. But the Fidayeen organizations, though defeated both in the West and East Banks, did not resign themselves to Israeli and Jordanian predominance and attempted to strengthen their ties with the West Bank.

The developing process of normalization reached a new height with the Military Government's decision to hold municipal elections. This decision also came in response to calls for elections by Hamdi Kan'an as well as young professionals and intellectuals who sought to replace the traditional leadership.[39]

After the publication of the order to hold elections, both Jordan and Fidayeen organizations expressed their staunch opposition.[40] In the West Bank itself, pro-Hashemites and radical nationalists also opposed the elections in line with the stand adopted by Jordan and the Fidayeen organizations that elections under the occupation would mean indirect recognition of Israeli rule. Incumbent mayors in addition to accepting this view saw no reason to endanger their position.[41]

Following Jordan's call to boycott the elections and Fidayeen threats against both candidates and the electorate, the Military Government took action to induce the population to carry out the Israeli order for elections.

The Military Government made it clear to leaders in Nablus, which was the main center of opposition to the elections, that if elections were not held an Israeli officer would be appointed to run the municipality. A week before the scheduled date of elections in Nablus, Hikmat al-Masri was arrested for allegedly attempting to obstruct elections but was released shortly afterwards. It was also pointed out to merchants that a boycott of the elections would lead to administrative restrictions on exports to the East Bank.[42]

Israel's resolution apparently made Jordan realize that the elections would be held and that continued opposition on its part could lead to the non-participation of its supporters, thus possibly paving the way to the election of candidates less favorable toward it. In view of this, Jordan softened its opposition[43] and after the election officially recognized the newly elected mayors and councils. In order to maintain its position of influence over the West Bank, which it preserved to a large extent through existing local institutions, Jordan had no choice but to accept the fact of elections held under Israeli rule.[44]

The elections took place on 28 March in the northern West Bank and Jericho, and on 2 May in the rest of the area. The results did not represent any substantial change in the control of veteran and traditional leaders in the town councils.[45] In Nablus and Hebron, both mayors were reelected and there were only minor changes in the Nablus town council.[46]

The fact that the electorate was limited by Jordanian law to males over 21 who owned property on which they paid municipal taxes of at least JD 1 per year restricted the possibility of independent candidates winning widespread popular support. The vast majority of this limited electorate was more inclined not to cooperate with those who sought to replace the traditional leadership.

On 15 March, in the midst of Israeli preparations for the elections, Hussein announced his federation plan. At a time when Israel's firm control of the West Bank was being demonstrated, for example by the implementation of its decision to hold elections, Jordan sought to strengthen the loyalty of the population to the Hashemite regime. At the same time, Hussein also aimed to provide a solution of his own to the problem of Palestinian self-determination in order to reduce the potential influence of the Fidayeen organizations in the West Bank.

The plan provided the West Bankers with the promise of autonomous rule after the liberation, and was intended to give at least partial satisfaction to the various circles in the West Bank which had demanded changes in the nature of the West Bank's relationship with Jordan, particularly in the light of the civil war.

As for the local reaction, some Palestine entity supporters and radical nationalists rejected the plan, but apart from leaflets distributed by Communists in the West Bank and a demonstration by Nablus schoolgirls there were no widespread manifestations of opposition.[47]

Hussein's promise of a new relationship between the two banks to be implemented after liberation satisfied most of those previously associated with the Hashemite establishment. However, as it became clear that the prospects of the plan's implementation in the near future were remote, leaders such as Ja'bari, who had not rejected the plan, continued to advocate the need to take some form of political action *before* liberation. Immediately after the announcement of Hussein's plan, he called for a meeting of West Bank mayors to discuss the plan.[48] No such meeting materialized, yet Ja'bari persisted in his efforts to guarantee a new status for the West Bank. In May 1972, he urged that the newly elected mayors of the major towns be given the power of the former district governors whose functions had ceased in 1967.[49]

Despite the fact that Hussein's federation plan was not an ideal solution for all West Bankers, it was generally accepted that any alternative to the Israeli occupation should be welcomed, particularly since no other seemed realistic at the time.

An article in *al-Quds* illustrated this trend, maintaining that as Hussein's plan was an alternative to the occupation which all West Bankers rejected, "we should not concern ourselves with the means by which the elimination of the occupation is achieved."[50]

Jordan, during this latter period, continued to demonstrate its ability to influence West Bank affairs in the economic and administrative spheres by imposing and later lifting customs duty on West Bank products and by imposing various administrative restrictions on the freedom of movement between the two banks. The appointment of Tahir al-Masri to the new post of Minister of State for the Affairs of the Occupied Territories in the Zayd ar-Rifa'i cabinet, formed in May 1973, also signified the regime's desire to demonstrate its consistent interest in and attachment to West Bank affairs.[51]

The PLO, however, did not remain idle in the face of growing Hashemite influence. Basing its activity on support from radical nationalist circles in the West Bank, the PLO made efforts to counteract the hold of both the Israeli and Hashemite factors.

At the beginning of April 1972 a Popular Palestinian Convention and the tenth session of the PNA were held in Cairo. About 100 West Bankers were invited to participate in the Popular Convention. It was reported that some were willing to participate; however, the Military Government clarified that anyone taking part in the conference would not be allowed to return to the West Bank. Jordan on her part stressed that since the conference was being convened to discuss the destruction of the Hashemite Kingdom, such participation would be regarded as treason. As a result of these stands of Israel and Jordan, none of the West Bankers invited took part.[52]

The convention and the assembly reaffirming the sole representative character of the PLO totally rejected Hussein's federation plan linking it with the municipal elections as an Israeli–Jordanian plot against the Palestinian revolution. As an alternative to Hussein's plan, they called for the unity of the East and West Banks and the Jordanian and Palestinian peoples in a joint struggle against the Hashemite regime and Israel. A new form of unity of the two banks was to be attained by the overthrow of the Hashemite regime and the establishment of a national democratic regime which would provide the base for the liberation of all Palestine. The convention maintained that though Israel and Jordan had prevented the participation of West Bankers it represented the national aspirations of the entire Palestinian people.[53]

Toward the end of 1972, the PLO Executive Committee called for the formation of "a committee of national unity in the West Bank and the Gaza Strip in order to resist Hussein's designs which aim at the liquidation of the [Palestinian] cause."[54] The eleventh session of the PNA, held in Cairo in January 1973, called for the strengthening of the ties of national unity and the struggle of the Palestinians in the occupied territories, in Israel and outside Palestine. Following these resolutions the

PLO increased its efforts to establish a national front in the West Bank which would operate in coordination and cooperation with the Palestinian organizations, would plan "a military and popular struggle" and strive to "put an end to the Israeli aggression."[55]

In accordance with this policy of the PLO, the Palestine National Front (*al-jabha al-wataniyya al-filastiniyya*) was established in the West Bank in August 1973. It seems that Communists in the West Bank were the driving force behind the organization of the front though it included West Bankers previously associated with the Ba'th, the ANM and some independent figures.

'Arabi 'Awwad, a prominent West Bank Communist leader[56] and one of the Front's central figures (deported from the West Bank in December 1973),[57] repeatedly stressed that "that Palestinian National Front is an integral part of the PLO."[58]

In May 1974, at a meeting of representatives of the main organizations of the PLO, 'Abd al-Muhsin Abu Mayzar (deported from the West Bank in December 1973) represented the Palestinian National Front, which was formally recognized at this meeting as the PLO representative in the occupied territories.[59]

The Palestinian National Front began to show signs of activity shortly after the 1973 October War. Firm Israeli countermeasures, such as the deportation or arrest of prominent members of the Front, seem to have hampered its efforts to entrench the organization. Nevertheless this had not prevented a steadily increasing influence of the radical national forces aligned with the PLO in the West Bank.

SUMMARY AND CONCLUSIONS

1. A major characteristic of West Bank politics has been the influence of external events, particularly in the international arena and the sphere of Jordanian–Fidayeen relations, on the attitudes adopted and the form of political action taken by the local population. Accordingly, the period between 1967 and 1973 can be divided into two main phases:

In the first phase, from June 1967 until mid-1971, the international arena was characterized by a series of diplomatic efforts for a settlement of the Middle East crisis. In the sphere of Jordanian–Palestinian relations this phase was governed by a continuous struggle for power between the Hashemite regime and the Fidayeen organizations, which culminated in the elimination of Fidayeen presence on the East Bank.

Intensive diplomatic activity on the one hand, and the Fidayeen–regime struggle in Jordan on the other, motivated West Bankers to attempt to define their future relationship with Jordan and encouraged some to strive to achieve a form of autonomy before the conclusion of the struggle in Jordan, or the attainment of a settlement to which they were not party. Yet the unclear future of the East Bank at the time made it all the more difficult for the population to define clearly its stand toward both Jordan and the Palestinian organizations, and leaders often vacillated between pro-Hashemite and pro-Fidayeen views. The civil war in Jordan in September 1970, though leaving a long-lasting feeling of disenchantment toward the regime in Jordan, did not lead to any drastic steps against the regime, which from then on enjoyed complete control in the East Bank.

The second phase, from mid-1971 until the October War in 1973, was characterized by political stalemate in the international arena and the steadily growing power of the Hashemite regime in contrast to the profound weakness of the Palestinian organizations.

In these circumstances the question of local involvement in a future political settlement lacked a sense of urgency, and most in the West Bank preferred to maintain a favorable relationship with the regime in Jordan. The Palestine entity debate was relegated to the sidelines and relations with the Hashemite regime steadily improved at the expense of the popularity of the PLO.

2. The three main political forces directly concerned with the political future of the area—Israel, Jordan and the PLO—though due to a variety of conflicting interests, all jointly prevented local political initiative. The stand of these three political forces, as well as the general stand of the Arab states on the question of the settlement of the conflict, dictated the form of local political activity and the views adopted by the local population

Israel's influence was facilitated by the very fact of its direct control of the area; Jordan continued to maintain contact with the area and influence over the population through the open bridges and its control of the East Bank; the PLO, which claimed the sole legitimate right to represent the Palestinians as the only recognized Palestinian political body, had a measure of authority to define the permitted political activity of the population. Fidayeen organizations had the ability to use violence or the threat of violence as a means of controlling local politics.

The continued control of West Bank affairs by external forces, the loyalties of the population to divergent outside Arab factors, interregional diversities and personal rivalries all served to prevent the emergence of one recognized all-West Bank leadership. As a result, West Bankers were unable to attain a consensus of opinion on the crucial question of the political future of the West Bank and its relationship with Jordan.

3. The local leadership, though generally accepting a stand against local political initiative, was however not prepared to remain totally passive in determining the future of the West Bank. They had sought a measure of involvement in coordination with the main external political forces, Jordan, the PLO and Egypt, in initiatives for a peaceful settlement that had been made during this period. During the latter period of political stalemate, abstaining from any initiative of their own, local leaders continued to concentrate their activities on local day-to-day problems in the spheres of education, economic development, etc.

The local leadership throughout most of the period was not party to efforts by the more radical circles to disrupt the process of normalization. Their economic interests, which had played an important role in their reluctance to oppose the Jordanian regime, seem to have similarly determined their relatively moderate stand toward the Israeli authorities. However, they continued to express their genuine opposition to the occupation by submitting protest memoranda against various Israeli measures, or by making anti-Israeli statements in the press.

This form of protest was not prohibited by the Israeli authorities. By restricting themselves to such manifestations of opposition, local leaders refrained from an outright confrontation with the Military Government while at the same time demonstrating their loyalty to the Arab cause.

4. Generally, attitudes in the West Bank on the political future of the area could be classified as follows:[60]

a) The idea of the unity of the two banks was supported by the vast majority from both major political groupings, those previously aligned with the Hashemite establishment and those previously associated with the radical anti-Hashemite political parties. They were also united in their rejection of local political initiative involving agreement with the Israeli authorities. However, these two groups differed fundamentally on the question of future relations with Jordan.

While the anti-Hashemites sought the Palestinization and republicanization of Jordan, the pro-Hashemite circles tended to accept Hussein's line of more moderate reform after liberation.

b)   Though generally favoring the unity of the two banks, a minority group, which included elements from both the above-mentioned groups, sought to ensure by agreement with Israel some form of autonomous status for the West Bank before liberation.

c)   A third trend supported the official line of the Palestinian organizations, which rejected a solution based on Security Council Resolution 242 and called for the establishment of a Palestinian state in the entire area of former Palestine. This view was not openly advocated on the West Bank though it gained support among sections of the student population and radical intellectuals.

With Israel in control of the West Bank, Jordan and the Palestinian organizations competed to maintain influence in the area. Moreover, Israel's policy of normalization, which allowed for the preservation of the connection with Jordan, gave the Hashemite regime an advantage over the Palestinian organizations in maintaining a political foothold in the area, particularly after the elimination of the Fidayeen presence on the East Bank. Efforts made by the Palestinian organizations to disrupt this process were frustrated by Israeli security measures. Elements in the population aligned with the Fidayeen organizations, and anti-Hashemite in their political outlook, were unable to organize. This in turn had the effect of preserving the internal political *status quo* with the traditional and generally pro-Hashemite leadership remaining in power, following the neutralizing of their potential rivals by Israel.

5)   The local population was united in its desire for a rapid termination of the Israeli occupation, but relied on external forces to bring about such an Israeli withdrawal. The fact that Jordan, during the period up to the October War, seemed to be the only possible partner for a settlement with Israel over the area led to a growing realization on the part of West Bankers that their political fate would continue in the future to be connected with the Hashemite regime, and their political stands were to a large extent governed by this consideration.

The strengthening of the PLO since the October War and particularly since the Rabat summit resolutions, and the growing international recognition of the PLO as the sole representative of the Palestinians, have altered Jordan's status in regard to the West Bank. The impact of these resolutions on the internal West Bank political situation—the standing of the local leadership vis-à-vis its potential opposition in the more radical circles and the general political orientation of the population—depends to a decisive degree on events in the inter-Arab and international arenas and on the feasibility of actually implementing the Rabat resolutions.

NOTES

1. U. Dann, "Regime and Opposition in Jordan Since 1949," in M. Milson (ed.), *Society and Political Structure in the Arab World*, Humanities Press, 1974, pp. 145-81.

2. For a detailed outline, see U. Dann, "The 'Jordanian Entity' in Changing Circumstances 1967–1973," in the present volume.

3. J. Kimche, *Palestine or Israel*, (London, 1973) pp. 259-60; *Middle East Record (MER), 1968*, (Jerusalem, 1973) pp. 243, 245, 254, 295.

4. While Mayor Ja'bari had previously been a long-standing supporter of Hashemite rule in the West Bank, Shihada and Faruqi had been associated with the opposition. The former seemed to be motivated more by his ambition for recognition as an all-West Bank leader while the latter having opposed Hashemite rule in the past sought to take advantage of the new situation to implement Palestinian self-determination.

5. *MER 1967*, p. 282; Dan Bavly, *An Experiment in Co-existence*, (London, January 1971). Those who favored the establishment of a Palestinian entity usually referred to the 1947 partition resolution; however, it was generally understood that such an entity, to be approved by Israel, could not extend beyond the 4 June, 1967 borders.

6. *MER 1967*, p. 283; *New Middle East (NME)*, March, October 1969, March 1970; *New Outlook*, November-December, 1969; *Quds*, 10 March, 24 July, 1969, 26 May, 28 August, 1970.

7. Kimche, *op cit.*; *MER 1967*, p. 283.

8. D. Farhi, "Society and Politics in Judea and Samaria," *Ma'arakhot* (Heb.), June 1971.

9. *MER 1967*, p. 293.

10. *MER 1967*, pp. 293, 294; *Anwar* (Weekly Supplement), 2 February, 1969, *Shu'un Filastiniyya*, April, 1974.

11. *Hayat*, 6 October, 1967; *MER 1967*, p. 283; Farhi, *op. cit.*

12. The National Gathering, formed in Jordan in 1968, was headed by the veteran Jordanian opposition leader Sulayman Nabulsi and included members previously associated with the banned political parties in Jordan.

13. A gradual change was, however, taking place in the JCP as indicated in the party's growing support for an armed struggle and participation with other Communist parties in the establishment of *quwwat al-ansar* in 1970. Nevertheless, the West Bank communists continued to concentrate on political activity.

14. *Jerusalem Post (JP)*, *Quds*, 7 January, 1969; *Lamerhav*, 9 January, 1969; *Ma'ariv*, 2 March, 7, 9 July, 1969; *Ha'aretz*, 7 March, 1969, 5 August, 1970.

15. *MER 1968*, pp. 449, 450.

16. *MER 1968*, p. 431.

17. *MER 1968*, p. 450; *Difa'*, 26 December, 1968, 4 January, 1969; *Quds*, 2 January, 1969.

18. *Ha'aretz*, 6 February, 12 March, 1969; *Ma'ariv*, 6, 9, 14 March, 1969; *JP*, 16 March, 1969.

19. *MER 1967*, p. 282; *MER 1968*, p. 449; *Anba'*, 2 May, 1969.

20. *Davar*, 5 November, 1969; *JP*, 19 November, 1969.

21. *Ma'ariv*, 9, 10, 23, 24 March, 1970; *Ha'aretz*, 10, 24 March, 17, 24, 26 April, 8 September, 1970; *R. Cairo, Voice of Fath*, 24, 26 March 1970—*BBC*, 26, 31 March, 1970; *JP*, 3, 17 April, 1970.

22. *Quds*, *Anba'*, *JP*, 27 September 1970; *Ma'ariv*, 28 September, 1970; *Davar*, 19 October, 1970; *NME*, November, 1970.

23. *Davar*, *JP*, 11 October, 1970.

24. *Israel Broadcasting Authority (IBA)*, 21 October 1970—*BBC*, 23 October 1970; *Quds*, 22 October, 1970; *Ma'ariv*, *JP*, 23 October, 1970; *Yediot Aharonot*, 30 October, 1970.

25. *Musawwar*, 13 November, 1970.

26. An East Jerusalem Christian who studied in the United States. In a *New Outlook* interview, April 1971, he maintained that the group was established after the Rabat Summit of December 1969. However, it seems that the civil war prompted them to attempt more concrete steps toward political initiative. Shortly before Rabat there had been reports of Palestine entity supporters who intended to send a memorandum to the Summit calling for recognition of Israel, establishment of a Palestinian state in the West Bank and Gaza Strip and a pledge from the Summit that these territories would not be returned to Jordan and Egypt. It is not clear whether the memorandum was in fact sent, but those behind it were apparently later involved with the Palestine National Gathering.

27. The editorial staff of *al-Quds*, particularly Muhammad Abu Shilbaya, had continuously called for a local political initiative and had supported the Palestine entity idea.

28. *JP*, 9 October, 1970; *Ha'aretz*, 21 October, 1970; *Davar*, 13, 30 October, 1970; *Quds*, 22 October, 23 November, 1970; *R. Baghdad, Voice of the Central Committee*, 16 October, 1970—*DR*, 20 October, 1970; *'Amman al-Masa'*, 26 October, 1970; *Yediot Aharonot*, 19 October, 1970; *Ma'ariv*, 26 November, 1970; *New York Times*, 6 December, 1970.

29. *Yediot Aharonot*, 19 October, 1970; *JP*, 26 October, 1970; *Davar*, 30 October, 1970; *Quds*, 7 December, 1970.

30. *Hayat*, 22, 23 December, 1970.

31. *Ma'ariv*, 7 January, 1971; 12 February, 1971; *Hayat*, 1, 3 February, 1971; *al-Usbu' al-Arabi*, 15 February, 1971.

32. *R. Amman*, 16 February, 1971; *Quds, Anba', Ha'aretz, JP*, 18 February, 1971; *Quds*, 21 February, 1971; *Quds, Hayat*, 25 February, 1971; *Ha'aretz*, 4 May, 1971; Y. Harkabi (ed.), *The Arabs and Israel* (Heb.), no. 3-4, Tel Aviv, 1975, pp. 164-65. Though having shown identification with the Palestinians in the civil war, West Bankers had not generally followed the Fidayeen political line, and had in the main accepted the Rogers' initiative rejected by the PLO.

33. *Quds*, 4, 6, 7, 8, 11, 15 April, 1971; *Ha'aretz*, 4 April, 1971; *Anba'*, 6 April, 1971.

34. *Ha'aretz, JP*, 18 April, 1971; *Ma'ariv*, 18, 22 April, 1971; *Anba'*, 23, 30 April, 2 May, 1971; *Quds*, 26, 29 April, 4 May, 1971.

35. *Anba'*, 17, 24, 30 May, 1971; *Quds*, 21 May, 1971; *Ma'ariv*, 21 May, 1971.

36. *Ha'aretz*, 20, 23 July, 1971; *Ma'ariv*, 19, 20 July, 1971; *Anba'*, 21 July, 1971; *JP*, 22 July, 1971.

37. *Ma'ariv*, 22 July, 1971; *New York Times*, 23 July, 1971; *Davar*, 26 July, 1971; *Ha'aretz*, 4, 6 August, 1971.

38. *Ma'ariv*, 19 August, 1971.

39. *Anba'*, 11 February, 9 March, 1972; *Quds*, 9 March, 1972; *Ma'ariv*, 17 March, 1972; *Ha'aretz*, 15 September, 1972.

40. *Ha'aretz*, 28 November, 1971; *R. Amman*, 27 November, 1971—*IMO*, 27 November, 1971; *JP*, 12 December, 1971; *Ma'ariv*, 12 January, 23 March, 1972; *Times*, 10 February, 1972; *Hayat*, 16, 27 February, 25 March, 1972; *R. Cairo, Voice of Fath*, 27 March, 1972—*BBC*, 29 March, 1972.

41. *JP*, 28, 29 November, 12, 21 December, 1971.

42. *Ha'aretz*, *JP*, 22, 24 March, 1972; *Ahram*, 25 March, 1972.

43. *Anba'*, 15 March, 1972.

44. *IBA*, 19 April, 1972—*BBC*, 21 April, 1972; *JP*, 18 May, 1972; *Anba'*, 18 August, 1972. Ram'allah's newly elected mayor was not recognized by the Jordanians as they continued to regard Nadim Zaru, deported in 1969, as acting Mayor.

45. Shaul Mishal, "Anatomy of Municipal Elections," *Hamizrah HeHadash*, Vol. XXIV (1974), No. 1-2.

46. *Ha'aretz*, *Ma'ariv*, *Davar*, 29 March, 1972; *Ha'aretz*, 31 March, 1972; *Davar*, 3, 4 May, 1972; *Times*, 4 May, 1972.

47. *Ma'ariv*, 16 March, 1972; *Anba'*, 19, 20, 23 March, 1972.

48. *Anba'*, 16 March, 1972; *IBA*, 18 March, 1972—*BBC*, 21 March, 1972.

49. *JP*, 18 May, 1972.

50. *Ma'ariv*, *Ha'aretz*, 16 March, 1972; *R. Amman*, 19 March—*IMTP*, 19 March, 1972; *Quds*, 20 March, 1972; *Anba'*, 9 June, 1972.

51. *Ha'aretz*, 13 February, 3, 29 June, 1973; *JP*, 3, 10, 25, 29 May, 1973; *R. Amman*, 26 May, 1973—*BBC*, 29 May, 1973.

52. *Ma'ariv*, *Davar*, 2 April, 1972; *Al-Hamishmar*, 3 April, 1972.

53. *Harkabi*, pp. 175-203.

54. *Quds*, 7 September, 1972.

55. *Middle East News Agency*, 10 January, 1973—*Daf Yomi*, January 1973; *Ha'aretz*, 18 January, 1973; *Shu'un Filastiniyya*, April, 1974.

56. The central role of the Communists in the establishment of a political body directly affiliated with the PLO serves as a further illustration of the trend in the JCP toward closer cooperation with the Fidayeen organizations. It should be noted that Fu'ad Nassar, First Secretary of the JCP, was admitted as a member of the PNA in January 1973.

57. *GPO/D*, 10 December, 1973.

58. *Shu'un Filastiniyya*, April, 1974; *Filastin ath-Thawra*, 2, 9 January, 6 February, 12 June, 1974; *Nahar*, 30 May, 1974; *R. Cairo, Voice of Palestine*, 31 May, 1974—*QY*, 2 June, 1974.

59. Harkabi, p. 216.

60. *Quds*, 20 February, 15 May, 1969; *JP*, 25 July, 1969, 28 August, 1970; *NME*, September, 1970. D. Farhi, *op. cit.*.

The Arab
Environment

Continuity and Change in Saudi Arabia, Yemen and South Yemen, 1967–1973

Haim Shaked and Tamar Yegness

In so far as internal processes and foreign policies (local, regional and international) are concerned, the Kingdom of Saudi Arabia, the Yemeni Arab Republic[1] and the People's Democratic Republic of Yemen[2] constitute three sovereign entities which should be considered as three separate centers within the geopolitical context of the Arabian Peninsula and the Middle East. Not only are their social and economic make-up, regimes, political ideologies, self-image and interests, as well as their capabilities and policies, unidentical—they are also governed by divergent outlooks on goals and roles.

Yet, the geographical proximity of these three countries, internal changes within each of them, their sensitivities concerning various political, economic and security matters, as well as the lack of equilibrium in their relative military and economic strength, created during the last decade an inter-relationship between Saudi Arabia, Yemen and South Yemen, or combinations of two out of these three. In each of the three cities of Riyad, San'a and Aden, there was a growing awareness of the relevancy of events in the two other neighboring countries, and of the importance of decisions made in the adjacent capitals and the trends reflected by these events and decisions. Furthermore, if the fundamental processes in these three countries during the period under review are analyzed, it would be discovered, not without some feeling of surprise, that—in spite of the salient differences in the orders of magnitude, basic social, political and economic characteristics, and the degree of acuteness of various internal issues—the three states had more in common than first meets the eye.

Formally, the regimes of each of these three countries are quite different from each other. While Saudi Arabia is a monarchy, Yemen—which had been split for several years into two rival states—came to be during the period under review a unified republic. South Yemen, for her part, emerged during the same period as a "people's democratic" republic. Still, the three regimes faced a similar problem—that of constant tension between revolutionary currents and conservative, traditional forces. This tension between tradition and revolution or, to some extent, between gradual evolutionary change and sudden revolutionary upheaval, became pronounced in recent years by a series of political takeovers in Yemen and South Yemen. Saudi Arabia, in contrast with her two neighbors, did not undergo a *coup d'état* or change of regime. However, any in-depth analysis of the internal situation in Saudi Arabia reveals that one of its basic political problems was the threat of revolution. Indeed, one of the major problems with which Saudi rulers were faced was that of the maintenance of a delicate and complex balance between the preservation of tradition and threats posed to its continued existence through forces stimulated by a consistent governmental attempt to implement a policy of gradual modernization.

Another dimension of the analysis of the political texture of each of these countries is that of the source of power and authority of the ruling institution. In each of the three states, the question of political loyalty has become acute in recent years and remains unresolved. In Yemen and in South Yemen, as well as in Saudi Arabia, the politically (and, to a large extent, the militarily) significant parts of society are its more traditional elements—and their basic loyalty still goes either to the extended family or to the tribal, i.e., traditional social framework. Not only are the societies of all three fragmented, but their segments are also in conflict with each other and all share a strong tradition of decentralism and preference to local, limited, and particularistic interests. Indeed, one of the central internal issues—common to all three states—has been that of a regime attempting to establish or to enhance a centralized governmental system, while a tradition of centuries is being shattered through the processes of modernization and the creation of tools, by the government, for its implementation.

The wars of 1967 and 1973, significant as they are in the development of the Arab–Israeli conflict, do not provide a convenient point of reference for the analysis of the dynamics of continuity and change in the internal process and external policies of Saudi Arabia, Yemen and South Yemen. Furthermore, it is doubtful whether these two dates are of decisive importance in the political history of these countries. Any attempt to restrict the analysis of continuity and change in Saudi Arabia,

Yemen and South Yemen to the period 1967 to 1973 is therefore both arbitrary and misleading.

For all three, it is the period of the late 1950s and early 1960s which marks the emergence of political change which has affected their politics and moulded their overall image. In Yemen, the social and political forces which surfaced with the outbreak of the revolution in 1962 had been fermenting since the late 1950s within and outside the country—e.g., "the Free Yemenites." In South Yemen, too, the internal struggle emerged toward the late 1950s and early 1960s—with Britain's attempts to create federations (1959—the Federation of Arab Emirates of the South which, in 1962, changed its name to the Federation of South Arabia), and with the crystallization of the "Front for the Liberation of the Occupied Southern Yemen" (FLOSY), and the "National Liberation Front" (NLF)[3] and their acute rivalry.

The year 1967 was, however, significant for the two Yemens. Toward the end of that year, South Yemen became independent after a period of some 130 years of alien rule. Thus, South Yemen turned from a post (or outpost) of the British imperial system into a political entity which hoped and was expected to stand on its own feet. The foreign power which had tried for a long time to freeze, or even to reverse, the socio-political processes at the tip of the Arabian Peninsula and its southern coast was no longer in control and the laying down of the "rules of the game" was transferred from the hands of British governments and representatives to local political forces. A relative political freeze of generations, imposed by an outside power, thawed, and freedom of action, maneuver and conflict came to rest in the hands of the indigenous political factions and leaders.

Yemen was in a somewhat similar situation in 1967. The major revolutionary change had occurred there earlier, toward the end of 1962, when Imam al-Badr's short-lived rule was overturned by a sudden military *coup d'état*. The revolution, the prolonged civil war which ensued and the massive external intervention (by Egypt and Saudi Arabia) which characterized that war, introduced a strong turbulence into the traditional Yemen of the Imams Yahya and Ahmad. By 1967, Yemen was in a very different social, political, economic and military condition than it had been five years before. At the end of that year, the last units of the Egyptian expeditionary force were evacuated (to a large degree, as result of the Six Day War). The formal and practical disengagement of Egypt from a direct involvement in the Yemeni scene provided more freedom of action to local forces within Yemen and to her immediate neighbors—Saudi Arabia and South Yemen. In consequence, in 1967 Yemen entered a new phase, some aspects of which were identical with the South Yemeni situation.

In this sense, Saudi Arabia was a different case. From its inception, the present Saudi Kingdom has been free of foreign domination. Rather than 1967, it was the year 1964—during which King Faisal took over complete power from King Sa'ud—which was an important landmark in the contemporary history of Saudi society, its internal politics and external policies.

In Yemen, the "watershed" of the phase which began in 1962 was the year 1970, in which the Yemeni Arab Republic came to control the whole of Yemen after an agreement reached between the Republicans and the remnants of the Imam's forces under the auspices of Saudi Arabia and with Egyptian consent. The years 1967 to 1970 were characterized by the completion of the long and painful process of an exit from the political stage by the "royalists," namely, the Hamid ad-Din (or Mutawakkilite) family. On the other hand, the original founders of the Republic had not managed to secure complete political power. After the termination of the civil war in the first part of 1970, it became obvious that alternative forces—such as tribal elements and the so-called "third power"— had become the politically significant powers in Yemeni politics. Thus, the powers which were intermediates between the staunch supporters of the Imamate and the original Republicans of 1962, assumed a position of ever-growing importance in Yemen's political life. During the period of 1970 to 1974, the expectations of the supporters of the Imamate faded almost completely. On the other hand, the expectations of the original founders of the Republic were far from being fulfilled. A long and bloody civil war, which raged intermittently from 1962 to 1970, ended with a formal change of the regime in Yemen but without victory for either of the two main protagonists.

Two important political processes occurred in Yemen during the period under review. The first process began before 1967, but became more pronounced after that year, and particularly after 1970: the change in the relative political weight of the tribal forces and their confederate alliances in Yemeni politics. The Yemeni tribes, and in particular the Zaydis from the mountain region, had been for centuries the core of the political and social institutions in Yemen. Their loyalty, or a shift in that loyalty, was for many generations a decisive factor in the stability of any government in Yemen. During the civil war, these tribal forces shifted their support between the Imam's and the Republican camps. However, with the evacuation of the Egyptian army in 1967 and the termination of the civil war in 1970 it became evident that the most important single tribal power, under the leadership of the head of the Hashid tribal confederation, 'Abdallah al-Ahmar, became the determining force in Yemeni politics. In other words, a few years after the take-over of Imam al-Badr's palace in San'a by the Republicans—the (Zaydi) tribal elements re-emerged as the decisive political element on the political scene—this time within a republican system and under a new leadership, that of a tribal chieftain rather than the Imam.

The second process—connected with the first, and presented here as a hypothesis which requires additional checking and documentation—was the "re-Zaydification" of political power in Yemen. An important impetus for the 1962 revolution had been the attempt by personalities who regarded themselves as representatives of the deprived and exploited Shafi'i population of Yemen to acquire a political role which, they thought, they deserved. Indeed, for a certain period of time, during the earlier phases of the civil war, it seemed that the Shafi'i segment of Yemeni society was about to establish an identity between itself and political power and government. More recent developments in Yemen proved that the Shafi'is had not succeeded in accomplishing a complete takeover of power from the Zaydis. While the fact that 'Abdallah as-Sallal, the first leader of the Republican revolution, was himself a Zaydi had no direct bearing on the delicate Zaydi-Shafi'i balance, his successors in political power reflected the traditional preponderance of the Zaydis over the Shafi'is. The positions held by the Zaydis toward the end of the period under review added to the internal tensions—religious/ideological, social and political—which have characterized Yemen during the last two decades. If the hypothetical observation about the "re-Zaydification" of Yemeni politics is correct, one should expect more upheavals in Yemen.[4]

In South Yemen, the watershed of the period under survey was in the second half of 1969. In June of that year, President Qahtan ash-Sha'bi was deposed by the leaders of the more radical faction of the NF—'Abd al-Fattah Isma'il al-Jawfi, Salim 'Ali Rubay', and Muhammad 'Ali Haytham (replaced in August 1971 by 'Ali Nasir Muhammad Husni as Prime Minister, Defense Minister and member of the Presidential

Council). As far as one can ascertain from the fragmentary and meagre sources of information available on South Yemen, political affairs during the period under review were characterized by a dual process: firstly, a consistent attempt was made to secure a total NF control of the government, the administration and all other institutions in the country; secondly (and simultaneously), intense conflicts and rivalries raged among different factions within the NF, which were trying to take over the party from within the NF, and thus impose on South Yemen that particular character which the faction vying for power thought it best for South Yemen to assume. The main milestones in this double process since South Yemen's independence in 1967 were: the Fourth Congress of the NF (held in Zinjibar in March 1968); the deposition of Qahtan ash-Sha'bi (June 1969); and the Fifth Congress of the NF (March 1972)—the resolutions of which reflected the solidification of the extreme leftist-radical wing of the ruling NF party.

Political change in South Yemen during the period under review focused on five elements. Firstly, an acute power struggle within the NF, which was heavily shrouded in ideological terminology. In South Yemen this rivalry took place among various radical, leftist factions and not—as in other parts of the Arab world—between "right" and "left," or "conservative" and "progressive" viewpoints. It should be emphasized that in spite of the ideological phraseology of the political rivalry—as reported in various sources—there was a strong personal element which fed, and perhaps aggravated this struggle. A second focus of political activity was the attempts by the NF to use the military forces as one avenue through which to bring about complete control over the country. At the same time, various party factions tried to use the same institution as a tool for a takeover of the NF party. The history of the establishment of the various military units in South Yemen by the British authorities is an interesting issue in itself which has yet to be researched, reconstructed and recorded. It is sufficient to mention here that the British had set up various military units, not necessarily because South Yemen was facing a meaningful external threat but rather in order to create an internal balance within and between various centrifugal forces in South Yemen. Since 1967 the state (or more precisely the NF party) had tried—with some measure of success—to take over, through reorganization and purges, not only all the indigenous military and armed forces which the British had left behind after their evacuation of Aden, but also those military units which were set up after independence. The setting up, in mid-1970, of "popular militia" units and of "revolutionary commands" which were under the authority of the party was part and parcel of this process. Consequentially, even if, potentially, the regular army could have emerged as an independent political center of power—in reality this did not occur between 1967 and 1973.

A third focus of political activity was closely connected with the considerable amount of tension between Aden and its hinterland, and in particular between Aden and Hadramaut. The background of, and reasons for, this rivalry as well as its development, form an interesting and complicated chapter in South Yemen's recent history. Suffice it to mention here that Aden, as the center of political power, tried to break up the large area of Hadramaut into three parts (by dividing it at the end of 1967 between the Fourth, Fifth and Sixth Governorates) and thereby facilitate the imposition of central authority over the various ideological, military and tribal factions which have been reluctant to accept this authority. This tension between Aden and Hadramaut as well as constant restlessness within the latter have stayed on the agenda of South Yemen's leadership.

A fourth focus of political activity resulted from the ambivalent attitude of the government to the tribes, which can be summed up as follows: an attempt to break the tribal structure as a framework for loyalty while simultaneously attempting to absorb the tribes and to integrate them within a more comprehensive social, economic and political system.

Finally, one should not overlook an important characteristic of the 1967–1973 period—that of external subversion. In South Yemen, external subversion assumed various forms (sabotage and violence by local tribes; hostile propaganda by political exiles) and originated from different sources (mainly from Saudi Arabia—but to some extent also from Yemen). During the period under review, subversion had its ups and downs, but never ceased to be an important element on the South Yemen scene. Without attaching too important a role to this element as a factor determining South Yemen's internal affairs, one should bear in mind that under a certain external and internal constellation, this problem may surface again and become acute.

Unlike Yemen and South Yemen, where deep political upheavals occurred during the years 1967 to 1973, in Saudi Arabia the year 1974 marked a decade of King Faisal's rule. In contrast with the two neighboring countries, where the political power rested at the top, in the hands of complex groupings—the centrality of King Faisal in Saudi Arabia's political life became a major characteristic of the Saudi scene.

In spite of the plethora of reports about the way of life of members of Saudi Arabia's royal family, there is very little authoritative knowledge of the real machinations of power in that country. Ostensibly, the same court, under similar conditions—but with a personage other than King Faisal at its top—would be run in a somewhat different manner. King Faisal's domestic rule could be summarized as follows: through a very complicated system of agents, alliances, balances, intimidation, bonuses, etc., he accomplished the impossible. In spite of circumstances which should have, theoretically, generated upheavals—he maintained a stable government. Furthermore, he succeeded in allowing gradual development while simultaneously preventing any serious internal political shake-up. To this day, there are no parties, no real trade unions, and no channels for free expression of opinion within the country. Undoubtedly, the huge income from oil, the rise of s young, less traditional elite (graduates of foreign law and business administration schools, and not necessarily members of the royal family), the growing sophistication of new weapon systems acquired by the military establishment, as well as the modern training which their absorption and maintenance require—created in recent years strong tensions which threatened the very basis of the Saudi regime. However, an assessment of the overall situation in Saudi Arabia at the end of 1973—in comparison with the beginning of 1967—reveals that even if these tensions did surface (e.g., the conspiracies of 1969 and early 1970), they did not assume a momentum sufficient for toppling the regime. If it were right to assume that one of the problems which troubled Faisal as king and ruler was that of the perpetuation of the government, or *dawla* (with all the classical Islamic connotations of this word)—he managed to safeguard it. Probably only a radical change would allow all htose latent forces which are imprisoned in Saudi society to surface, and then we shall perhaps be able to analyze them and to find out when and how they started to develop.

In as much as the declared and actual foreign policy of Saudi Arabia during the last decade is concerned, there was also a remarkable consistency. Carefully and gradually, King Faisal worked toward the buttressing of his position as one of the main leaders of the Arab world. Apparently, he was guided in this regard by two basic principles. Firstly, where there was a danger of a meaningful, direct or indirect, threat to Saudi Arabia's supremacy in the Arabian Peninsula. King Faisal did not hesitate to steer his relations with other Arab states to the verge of open crisis (e.g., during the early stages of the Egyptian military intervention in th stages of the Egyptian military intervention in the Yemen civil war). Secondly, while acting in a way which should improve his bargaining position (including a shrewd utilization of oil income)—and in spite of his declared and practical involvement in Arab affairs and the Arab–Israeli conflict, he refrained from altering his pro-Western orientation, particularly his relations with the US. One aspect of King Faisal's activities in foreign affairs has been neglected in many studies. This aspect, as many others, is connected with the personality of King Faisal and with the strong awareness of an Islamic mission which had accompanied him for many years, and particularly since he ascended the throne. The importance of this awareness should not be exaggerated to the extent of saying that King Faisal's acts were determined solely by the awareness of a religious mission and not by tactical or other considerations. Still, it would appear that the conviction that he was "trustee" of Islamic affairs had been a strong, perhaps even dominant, guideline in King Faisal's actions, including his involvement in the October 1973 War, its preparation and aftermath.

During the six years under review, Saudi Arabia, Yemen and South Yemen underwent considerable economic change. From the point of view of economic and financial power, Saudi Arabia began to stand out not only in local and regional, but also in international terms. In this regard, Saudi Arabia happens to stand on one side of the fence and the two Yemens on the other. Yet, even in the economic sphere, the three share, in reverse, a common problem—that of resources. In Saudi Arabia, the main problem is an unrestrained and sudden overflow of financial (as against a dearth of human) resources, and the main dilemma is how to invest and distribute them properly. In the two Yemens, the main issue is an acute lack of resources, both economic and human, essential for any meaningful development and modernization. In all three, these problems were aggravated between 1967 and 1973. The independence of South Yemen brought in its wake both a severance from Britain and the localization of responsiblity for the fate of a large, backward area. The resultant distribution of the very limited economic resources of the city of Aden over the vast, but poor, rural and tribal hinterland; the growing needs which were a natural outcome of independence; the closure of the Suez Canal and, consequently, the shift of major sea routes and the subsequent disastrous effect on the port of

Aden as a major source of income—all these presented the leadership of South Yemen with an insurmountable problem, influenced their political ideology and orientation, and nourished extremist, revolutionary and radical leftist attitudes. As to Yemen, the termination of the civil war in 1970, and the consequential need for an accelerated pace of reconstruction and rehabilitation as well as satisfying the (sometimes conflicting) demands of Zaydi and Shafi'i segments of the population, constituted a major problem with which Yemen's leadership was constantly confronted. Their attempt to implement the slogans of progress and modernization, and thereby to satisfy the expectations which the propagation of these slogans generated, was confronted with the realities of the lack of essential infrastucture, means and know-how.

Paradoxically, Saudi Arabia, although on the "giving end," belongs to the same club of countries faced with a grave economic problem. The growth by leaps and bounds of Saudi Arabia's oil income during 1974 provided a solution to all the financial problems of the regime. Yet, it created a new problem—that of the tension created by the need to absorb the unexpected bounty which descended on the country, by the uneven distribution of the new wealth, and by the debates about the way in which the income should be properly invested. Thus, for different reasons, the economic situation in all three countries gave birth to massive socio-political tensions and difficulties.

The relationship between the Saudi, Yemeni and South Yemeni regimes during the period under review is a chapter which has not yet been fully researched. Because of its military and financial strength, and leadership, Saudi Arabia has overtowered the two other states, particularly after the Egyptian exodus from Yemen in 1967 and even more so after Gamal Abdel Nasser's sudden death in September 1970. Between 1970 and 1973, the *rapprochement* between Yemen and Saudi Arabia was swift and meaningful and, before long, brought about a growing dependence of the former on the latter. At the same time, Saudi Arabia made successful efforts to prevent, by various means and tactics, any attempt to unite Yemen and South Yemen, while instigating tribal elements in South Yemen to act against the NF government there.

The Khartoum conference of August 1967 brought about, among other things, attempts to stop the civil war in Yemen and the beginnings of a dialogue between Egypt and Saudi Arabia about the fate of the Yemeni Republic. It took, however, three years for a meaningful shift in Yemeni–Saudi relations to occur. The attempts made after 1967 by

Imam al-Badr's supporters to undermine the Republic did not convince the Saudis that placing their bets on Badr's forces would be the best way to safeguard Saudi Arabia's interests in the southern part of the Arabian Peninsula. Consequently, their military and financial support to the Imamate's supporters dwindled and the pathetic attempt of the latter to occupy and control at least the northernmost tip of Yemen was doomed. During the year of 1970, the resources of the Imam's supporters became exhausted to the extent that they could no longer prevent an agreement—actively supported by the Saudis—between the Republic, tribal forces headed by 'Abdallah al-Ahmar and "the third force." During that year the circle closed: the Republic, which had from its inception been dependent on Nasser's Egypt—at the time the arch-enemy of Saudi Arabia—gained Saudi recognition and, before long, became dependent on Saudi economic aid.

This dependence was not unconnected with the relations between Saudi Arabia and South Yemen which—during 1967-1973—were constantly hostile and even deteriorated in 1969 to border clashes (the Wadi'a incident). The rivalry between the two hinged primarily on ideological differences: the fortress of Islamic conservatism against the self-declared *avant-garde* of Marxist (and Maoist?) revolutionarism. During the whole period under review, Saudi Arabia saw in South Yemen an outpost of subversion against the conservative, traditional alignment in the Arabian Peninsula, hence Saudi Arabia's willingness to provide South Yemeni exiles with political refuge, to support and even initiate subversion within South Yemen and to assist South Yemen's enemies (such as the aid provided to the Sultan of Oman against the Dhofar rebels). Hence, too, Saudi Arabia's apprehensions of a possible union between Yemen and South Yemen—which might add to the power of the South Yemeni radicals.

The mixture of hostile and friendly relations between Yemen and South Yemen added a measure of complexity to this entangled relationship. A long tradition of a "hot" and partially undefined border, as well as ideological debates about the nature and mission of the "true" revolution and, therefore, the right to represent the real "Yemen," played a role in the oscillation of this relationship toward tension, which was symbolized by the dropping of the word "South" from the official name of the People's Republic of South Yemen and the addition of the term Democratic in the new name in November 1970. Incidents along the border between Yemen and South Yemen in March 1972, and

Yemen's occupation of the island of Qamaran in early October 1972, did not improve the deep suspicion between the two states. Typically, however, when the relations between the two reached a zenith of tension they publicly agreed, at the end of October 1972 in Tripoli (Libya), to work toward the implementation of a union between them. Typically again, nothing more than marginal and impractical committee discussions ever came out of this declaration.

The attitudes and policies of the three states concerning the Arab–Israeli conflict merit a separate analysis, and is beyond the scope of this paper. It is enough to mention here that, out of different motivations and outlooks, all three took a strong anti-Israeli stand, not only in the declarative and attitudinal spheres but also in action. Commensurate with her self-assumed role of leadership in radicalism and "true revolutionarism," South Yemen provided, during the period under review, moral and other support to the extremist Palestinian Fidayeen organizations led by Na'if Hawatma and Dr. George Habash. Apparently, in June 1971, South Yemen also provided a base for the units which attacked the "Coral Sea," and in October 1973 the port of Aden served as a base for the unofficial embargo imposed by Egypt on the Bab al-Mandab straits. Saudi Arabia, on her part, supported Egypt, Jordan, and the PLO (i.e., Fath), and became an unequivocal spokesman of the Arab world concerning a full Israeli withdrawal from the administered territories and the restoration of Palestinian rights. Undoubtedly, she played a major role in the crystallization of the Egyptian–Syrian axis which led to the war of 1973, and even sent military units to the "eastern front." One point which was prevalent in Saudi statements on the conflict during the years 1967–1973 was her total rejection, based on an Islamic-Arab reasoning, of Israel's occupation of east Jerusalem. Faisal's expressed wish to "pray in Jerusalem" was but one expression of this idea. Yemen, which did not lag behind her two neighbours in making or joining anti-Israeli statements, was not in a position to make any substantial contribution, political, military, or economic, to those Arab states or Palestinian organizations who claimed to lead the Arab world against Israel. The common attitude of these three states against Israel, however, was not a contributing factor to improved relations between them.

NOTES

1. Hereafter: Yemen. From late 1962 until 1970, Yemen was actually divided into the Yemeni Arab Repubic and the Mutawakkilite Imamate of Yemen.

2. Hereafter: South Yemen. In November 1970 South Yemen's official name (assumed after independence in 1967) was changed from the "People's Republic of South Yemen" to the "People's Democratic Republic of Yemen."

3. During the year of 1967, the NLF emerged as the stronger party and took over South Yemen. In December of that year the NLF changed its name to the "National Front." It has since remained the ruling party of South Yemen.

4. On June 13, 1974, a *coup d'état* occurred in Yemen in which the newly formed Revolutionary Command under Ibrahim al-Hamdi, an army officer, dissolved both the Republican Council and Consultative Council. The new regime strengthened its relations with Saudi Arabia.

Foundations of the Ba'th Regime in Iraq since 1968

Uriel Dann

A connection can be seen between the Six Day War and the accession to power of the second Ba'th regime in Iraq[1] in as much as the war further undermined the government of President 'Abd ar-Rahman 'Arif. It must be stressed, however, that that government was already shaken at the time, and its ruined prestige—the result of failures, scandals, lack of a political base and, finally, an atrophy of willpower—would probably have brought about its speedy downfall in any case. The Ba'th takeover, engineered by retired Maj. Gen. (*liwa'*) Ahmad Hasan al-Bakr, had been anticipated for months before it took place. Similarly, the 1973 October War cannot be said to constitute a break in the contemporary history of Iraq, though one point of significance will be mentioned below.

The second Ba'th regime has been the rule of a political party such as Iraq has never experienced in the past. It is instructive to observe how the rulers themselves have understood this party rule as applied to the condition of their country. The Assistant Secretary-General of the Iraqi Ba'th, Saddam Husayn at-Tikriti, concluded a press conference on 9 April, 1974, as follows:

> Respecting our relations with civilians and the military: I did not say there are civilians and soldiers in the Party. In the Party one does not speak of civilians and soldiers. We say, rather, "Comrade Major So-and-so belongs to the Party, and Comrade Division Commander So-and-so belongs to the Party." The instructions of the national leadership are obligatory even on a general. This is our Party rule, and this is the procedure, in fact and not in theory. From the president of the state to the lowliest among us, the Party has the power to influence the course of the policy which we have proclaimed to the men sitting in tanks, to those manning

309

machineguns along the eastern border [Iran!], and to those
who stand ready to fight for all that is necessary to Iraq and
to the Arab homeland. The armed forces are a non-partisan
body which accepts orders. This was agreed on in the
National Charter, and it is just. And I can state that there
exists no factor capable of threatening the Revolution."[2]

This bold and sweeping assertion conforms to the reality of Iraq as it
has been since 1971; it is without doubt the consummation of a desire
which possessed the present rulers on the day of the takeover in July
1968.

The juridical foundation of Ba'th rule is laid down in the quasi-
fundamental laws of the country: the Provisional Constitution of 16
July, 1970, and the National Action Charter of 15 November, 1971.[3]
The Provisional Constitution, Paragraph 39, states, *inter alia*, that
members of the Revolutionary Command Council (RCC), on assuming
their posts, are sworn faithfully to work toward "Unity, Freedom and
Socialism"—the sacrosanct slogan of the Ba'th founding fathers.
Although no explicit mention is made of the Party here, the preceding
paragraph authorizes the RCC to coopt additional members from among
the regional (i.e., Iraqi) Ba'th leadership. This is the only instance of the
term Ba'th in the entire document, but it establishes the domination of
the Party on the constitutional plane. Like its counterparts in the Arab
world since 1952, the RCC is sovereign or, in the words of the Iraqi
Provisional Constitution of 1970, it is "the Supreme Authority (*al-hay'a
al-'ulya*) in the State." As such it has absolute executive and legislative
powers. Not even the Constitution restricts its power, for it is empowered to amend the Constitution by its own decrees. The President of the
RCC—who according to the Provisional Constitution effectively controls its general activities and its decision-making processes in particular—is the former Major General, later Field Marshal (*mushir*), Ahmad
Hasan al-Bakr, who is also *ex-officio* President of the Republic, and as
such head of state and Commander-in-Chief. In addition, he is Chairman of the Council of Ministers—i.e., Prime Minister—and Minister of
Defense. Among his powers is the appointment and dismissal of ministers, which is not subject to any constitutional restriction. He is Secretary General of the Ba'th Party—or to use the proper designation, of the
"Ba'th Party Regional [Iraqi] Command." There can be few parallels
to such concentration of key posts; it reflects, however, the reality of
power of the second Ba'th regime. In view of the aforesaid, it is evident

that the Vice-President of the RCC should also be the Assistant-Secretary General of the Party, and as such occupy the second position in the state.

The National Action Charter of 1971 is a wordy document the import of which can be stated in brief as expounding the Party's claim to absolute rule, since the Provisional Constitution itself does not do so. It reiterates the main provisions of the latter and interlocks them with the Ba'th's program as it has been articulated at their "National" and "Regional" congresses, with their unflagging stress on "revolution" and "popular mobilization," on socialism, liberation and on Arab unity. The Charter emphasizes the central position of the Ba'th Party in the Iraqi state—indeed this seems to be its chief *raison d'être*. At the same time, it opens the door for cooperation with other "patriotic and progressive forces." It pays a great deal of attention to the role of the army in the "national struggle." The effective implications of these points will be examined later.

How then has this regime worked? With regard to the two main figures of the regime, Bakr and Saddam Husayn—whose functions the Constitution and the Charter have rationalized into the appointments of President and Vice-President of the sovereign body—it is the junior who has gradually come to play the prominent role. Saddam Husayn is a relative of Bakr's, who originally reached the top of the pyramid through Bakr's patronage.[4] He has been known for some years as the strongman of Iraq. It is easy to misunderstand this point. Saddam is much younger than his uncle (by several removes) Bakr, and has long assumed the main burden on rule. Bakr is ill, and is said to have been depressed by the death of his wife. But their teamwork seems to have been unimpaired on the whole. In quite recent crises Bakr still showed the drive and ruthlessness which have always been a hallmark of the regime; his undoubted prestige has always been an important, perhaps a vital, asset of Saddam.

Bakr and Saddam Husayn, then, are the heart of the ruling party. This party has proved to be a living entity with a will to rule that is fully consonant with the aspirations laid out in the two documents quoted above. It has built up its instruments of pwoer which will be outlined later on. Conversely, that concentration of power which is generally believed to be in Iraq a contestant for rule, namely "the Army," has so far been a fiction as far as a dichotomy "Party versus Army" is concerned. The Iraqi officer corps is a body of persons whose profession gives them control over the tools of power; it is traditionally associated with concepts of "progress," "honor" and "achievement" and tends to foster cliques which, as opportunities present themselves, are capable of toppling a government. But it is not, by virtue of its structure, history or experience, an establishment moulded to exercise sustained rule. The "military governments" in Iraq so far, when closely examined, were not actually military governments. Rather, they were regimes in which certain senior officers imposed their wills, directly or indirectly, in the absence of an institutionalized civilian government capable of policy decision and implementation.[5]

Thus, so long as the Ba'th retains the will to rule, so long as it succeeds in preserving its various organizational instruments, and so long as it manages to prevent the growth of a resolute opposition—the army will remain an aggregate of individuals. No doubt a sudden onslaught could destroy the regime by eliminating two or three of its key members. But at the socio-political level the regime has no rivals at present—which is not, of course, to say that it has no enemies.

How then has the Party, in practice, maintained the conditions which have prevented the growth of organized groupings capable of competing in a power struggle? Above all, how does the Party maintain control over the army as a framework of units commanded by men with the means of posing a physical threat? At this point the history of the regime must be considered.

The Iraqi Ba'th, from its inception a generation ago up to the present, has been essentially a civilian organization whose constant objective was to achieve and maintain power over the state. To accomplish this objective it has invariably needed help from the military, and army officers have often been prominent among its members. However, its nature as a non-military, or extra-military, association has never thereby been affected.[6]

The *coups* of 17 and 30 July, 1968,[7] together with the intervening fortnight are a demonstration of this contention. In the final months before their seizure of power the Ba'th leaders combined with certain officers in central command and staff positions who had otherwise no Ba'th past or sympathies, but who bore a grudge against the then rulers. Together they toppled the government of 'Abd ar-Rahman 'Arif and Yahya at-Tikriti, a relatively simple task. During the second half of July 1968, the Ba'th and its military allies presented to the outside world a coalition government in which the latter held the key posts of Prime

Minister and Minister of Defense. The developments of those two weeks show how in Iraq a closely knit group of civilians capable of pursuing a well-defined goal can overcome rivals among the army who lack political acumen and experience. A brief period of intense maneuvering—mostly behind the scenes—which included the suborning of officers from the opposite camp culminated in the dramatic but bloodless *coup* of 30 July which saw, in rapid succession, the deployment of an armored unit at the right place and time; the arrest of a few key opponents; a "First Proclamation"; and mass demonstrations praising the fulfilment of the revolution.[8] By the end of the day, Bakr's Ba'th Party was in sole control. The political history of Iraq from then until the October 1973 War—and beyond—falls into two phases. The first phase lasted between two and three years. It was characterized by the gradual elimination of a group of senior officers within the Ba'th whose standing assured them of prominence after the takeover, but whose hold over sections of the armed forces and connections within the officer corps gave them an independence distasteful and potentially dangerous to Bakr and his immediate collaborators. The main Ba'th officers involved were Generals Salih Mahdi 'Ammash and Hardan 'Abd al-Ghaffar at-Tikriti. They started their careers under the regime as deputies to Bakr, and Interior and Defense Ministers respectively, and finished it within three years—the former as an ambassador in comfortable and powerless exile, the latter as a victim of assassins' bullets in Kuwait. Their defeat was due to their inferiority in the game of politics when played against rivals of supreme talent and willpower, who worked through a superbly organized machine.

The second phase, which began around the spring of 1971, fulfilled the objective which Bakr and Saddam Husayn doubtless had in mind from the very beginning: the rule of the Party *sans phrase*, where they themselves, as sole leaders of the Party, succeeded in relegating division commanders and General Staff officers from being partners in government to the status of technicians carrying out orders under supervision—just as Saddam Husayn described the situation at the press conference quoted above.

Among the assets required to achieve and maintain control over a political society like that of Iraq, there is one that is absolutely essential—the uninhibited and relentless passion for power. The cardinal aim of Bakr and Saddam Husayn has been to exercise supreme power; all else seems secondary. To maintain such power in contemporary Iraq

one must shrink from nothing. The ways of the regime are best understood by observing what has occurred on the political scene over the last
seven years. The most impressive feature is the regime's routine use of
political murder. Under the guidance of Saddam Husayn this irreversible way of removing an adversary has become an established tool of
statecraft. Political murder is not, of course, uncommon in this or some
other parts of the world. The difference seems to be that in today's Iraq
it has come to look less like the product of cruelty, or panic, or the urge
for revenge, than a calculated means for the safeguarding of the regime,
to be applied deliberately, institutionally, unemotionally as it were, and
with due regard for appearances. When necessary, the last proviso is the
first to be jettisoned. More conventional measure have also abounded,
of course—economic and professional sanctions, intimidation, imprisonment, exile, hangings, bribery and, quite often, a combination of the
aforesaid.[9]

The second prerequisite, which goes well with the first, is the ability to
rule. Tacitus says of an unsuccessful emperor that when tested he
proved not to be *capax imperii*—he was no ruler. By contrast, Bakr and
Saddam Husayn have proven that they are nothing if not that.[10]

These qualities—the will and the ability to rule—are the essential
conditions for the successful application of the instruments of government. Foremost among these is a complex system of security arrangements, some more institutionalized, some less, some of the kind found
elsewhere, some quite peculiar to Iraq under the Ba'th. It may be said
that they have all had Saddam Husayn as mastermind and director. The
supreme security agency has been the General Office, accountable to
the Party's Regional Command, that is, to Saddam Husayn. The Genral
Office, directly or indirectly, has controlled a variety of subordinate
bodies. Some of these—the police, the Criminal Investigation Department, the censorship—are not Iraqi or Ba'th innovations. However, it is
worth noting that they have all been kept at a high efficiency (though
they may not have invariably been handled with high intelligence), and
their officials have often been professionals who had served in previous
regimes. Other organs seem to be peculiar to the present regime, such as
the assassination teams—semi-permanent and more than semi-
professional—which have fulfilled the assignments alluded to above. In
addition, "shop stewards" have apparently been attached to the HQ
of each army formation—from the battalion level upward—in order
to keep a watchful eye on things in general, and the commanding officer

in particular. These men have usually been subalterns or senior NCOs, and although they do not appear on establishments, they seem to be organized according to a fixed and quite complex Party hierarchy, and they report upward ultimately to the General Office. It is they who have been the main instrument for keeping the army under control, and it may be assumed that their nominal commanders hate and fear them accordingly. At the same time the Party—Saddam Husayn is credited with having initiated the scheme in person—has taken care to found a solid infrastructure of dedicated junior officers recruited from the Party militia and sluiced through special training courses. Their number is said to be several thousand, and they give substance to the work of the "shop stewards." Needless to say, the Party has not neglected the positive approach either: "morale officers" *are* on the establishment of each unit, the role of the army as bearer of the revolution has been constantly stressed and lauded, and conditions of service for all ranks are continuously upgraded. But this policy is not peculiar to Ba'th Iraq.

Naturally, all these qualities and elaborate constructions do not secure the regime from the risks of overthrow. The possibility remains that one day one commander will outwit his young commissar, put his Party subalterns out of action one way or another, and train his guns on the Palace of the Republic. But for such an operation to succeed, preparation, involving coordination, is necessary, and the regime has worked hard and well to ferret out all plotting in its initial stages. Even more important probably, its reputation for having succeeded in doing so has imbued potential plotters among the officer corps with a sense of futility and awe. However that may be, so far the system has worked. The regime may also come to its end through the chance murder of Bakr or Saddam Husayn which is easier to accomplish than a full-fledged plot, and would almost certainly have the same result, though with some delay. But the contemplation of chance murders is beyond the scope of this survey.

It is not the purpose of this survey to analyze the politics of the regime in any detail. However, several basic policy positions, and one dilemma, emerge, all of which go far to providing a key to events in Iraq since 1968.

The term "Ba'th" and the slogans associated with its history inevitably give a general impression of unrest—of radicalism and mission, activism and revolution, subversion and demagogy. Moreover, there is little in the antecedents or behavior of the Ba'th rulers to counter this

association. And again, the domestic as well as the regional opportunities undoubtedly afford full play to the mischief the Ba'th has come
to symbolize in the worst suspicions of its enemies. Yet these same
rulers have proven over and again that they are realists first and last.
They want to stay in power, and they know that in order to succeed they
must judge precisely the limits beyond which it is unsafe to go, and
which interests they can distrub only at their own peril. But they are
Ba'this, and a reputation for sioth or timidity might easily prove to be a
surer road to perdition for them than living up to their image of boldness. This is the dilemma, and it goes far to explain the contradictions
constantly apparent in the policies of the regime.

Domestically, Iraq has a diversified political tradition. Fundamentally this diversity is bound up with the communal scene—Sunni
Arabs, Arabic-speaking Shi'a, Sunni Kurds and various micro-
minorities—which still constitutes a mixture rather than a compound. It
is this communal profusion which mainly accounts for the centrifugal
tendencies noticeable in the socio-political history of Iraq, though it is
worth noting that the oil industry added a non-communal catalyst at a
relatively early date.[11] The dominant—and domineering—community
in Iraq continues to be the Sunni Arabs who make up hardly a quarter of
the population, despite the passing of two generations of statehood. The
Ba'th regime, Pan-Arab nationalist by definition, is the very epitome of
Sunni Arab preponderance in Iraq (even if individual Shi'is have occasionally reached the top of the Ba'th pyramid), and the present rulers
have shown by word and deed that they intend to preserve the character
of Iraq as bound up in that preponderance. On the other hand they are
patient and observant politicians—in sharp contrast to their predecessors of 1963. As a result, the politics of the regime since 1968 have been
a curious, but consistent and highly characteristic, combination of
unchanging strategic aims and flexible tactics. The determination to rule
is paramount, but Bakr and Saddam Husayn have shown from the start
a gift for timing, maneuver and ostensible compromise which is wholly
admirable in politicians, and in their case has occasionally approached
statesmanship.

Three instances may suffice to characterize the domestic scene under
the second Ba'th regime:

a) The regime has endeavored four years to create an image of itself
which disguises the Ba'th monopoly of power. Agreements have been
signed over the last years, and decrees issued, which provide for a legis-

lative and a "National Progressive Front" which included by 1974 political entities other than the Ba'th—the Communists, Kurds hostile to Mulla Mustafa Barzani, and various nationalist splinters. The Council of Ministers has a minority of members put up by those bodies and may thus be presented as a patriotic coalition or, to use the technical term, as representing the "National Progressive Front." However, none of the departments handed to non-Ba'this are politically sensitive (usually the non-Ba'this serve as ministers of a state, i.e., without departmental responsibility).[12] Moreover, membership in the infinitely more important RCC is reserved exclusively for Party members, despite requests by the non-Ba'th partners of the National Progressive Front for its broadening. But though power has been strictly kept within the Ba'th, some prestige and emoluments have been shared, and hence, presumably, tension and the risks of open violence have lessened.

b) An acid test of anti-Imperialism throughout the Third World is the readiness of regimes to come to grips with Western oil companies. The present Iraqi regime has been as raucous in its declarations as any, and its credibility in this respect has been doubted by its declared enemies alone—such as its fellow Ba'this of Damascus. But beyond the sound and fury oil flows freely, and in increasing quantities. "Nationalisation," though highly touted, has so far affected only two of the three foreign producers—the Iraqi Petroleum Company and the Mosul Petroleum Company; the satisfyingly inclusive appellation of the first camouflaging the fact that the Basra Petroleum Company has remained untouched.[13] Even Saudi Arabia has gone further.

c) The Kurdish problem is another example of the regime's dexterity. There can be no doubt at all that the regime was never ready to grant autonomy in any meaningful sense to the Kurds on Iraqi soil. No Iraqi regime since British mandatory times ever was, and the indivisibility of Iraq as part of the Arab territorial heritage has always been one of the Iraqi Ba'th's fundamental tenets. Whenever the conflict blazed into violence, the Ba'th rulers surpassed their predecessors in premeditated ferocity; Mulla Mustafa Barzani himself had been the subject of an assassination attempt in 1971 which failed narrowly, and sensationally. But Bakr and Saddam Husayn also surpassed their predecessors in their restraint; the "Four-Years Statement" of 11 March, 1970 was a muster of quite surprising concessions coldly calculated to buy time for consolidation. Significantly the Baghdad authorities avoided the term "agreement" which would have acknowledged the Kurds as contractual partners. This aim achieved, a unilateral and innocuous "Kurdish Autonomy Law" followed on 11 March, 1974, and—reluctantly at first—another bout of savage repression. When this campaign failed as before, largely because of Iranian aid to the Kurds, the regime resorted to a radically new departure: by signing the Algiers Agreement of 6 March, 1975, which legitimized the position that Iran had already in fact acquired in the Shatt al-'Arab river, Saddam Husayn purchased the Shah's promise to abandon the Kurds. The future of the "Kurdish problem"—that of reconciling an alien nation within Iraqi borders to (an Arab) Iraqi rule—is certainly not solved for Iraq. But the Ba'th regime has again proved its unfettered agility.

The foreign policy of the Iraqi regime has been actuated by the desire—dictated by reason as well as by sentiment—to remain true to Ba'th fundamentalism on the one hand, and to disarm suspicion and avoid unprofitable hostility on the other. Here the regime has been *a priori* in a more difficult position than at home, since abroad it lacks the means of coercion on which its domestic policy is so reliant. Consequently, the regime has adopted a defensive stance in most of its foreign confrontations. Its basic considerations have been twofold—to be accepted on equal terms by the comity of nations, primarily of course Arab nations, and to maintain its domestic position. Both have been responsible for the restraint the regime has shown—by and large—vis-à-vis the activism of Iran. This attitude culminated in the Algiers Agreement of 6 March, 1975—whereby undivided Iraqi sovereignty over the Shatt al-Arab, Iraq's only outlet to the Persian Gulf, was sacrificed for the chance of putting an end, at least temporarily, to the running sore of the Kurdish insurrection. Consideration for its image as a good neighbor accounts at least in part for the massive participation of Iraq in the October War on the Syrian front and for the prompt withdrawal of its forces after the ceasefire. It was a genuine instance of Arab cooperation just when the chances of causing the rival Ba'th regime serious harm—by abstaining from help or by overstaying their welcome—must have seemed attractive to the Iraqis. On the other hand, the political and ideological aspects of the Palestine problem have posed no difficulty to the regime. Iraq is a pillar of the "Rejection Front" which refuses to countenance a non-military solution of that problem. It is a stand which is in keeping both with Iraq's historical extremism on this matter and with Ba'th principles, while the remoteness of the fighting line has made unheroic circumspection unnecessary. Cooperation with the USSR, close as it is, was founded on a rationally considered community of interests in the area and has not, by that token, got out of hand. The Soviet–Iraqi "Treaty of Friendship and Cooperation" of 9 April, 1972, unlike its Egyptian counterpart, did not assign to the USSR a stronger position vis-à-vis its Arab partner than the latter was willing to countenance in the longer run. From the Iraqi point of view it may be said that the relationship has conformed to the guiding principles articulated at the head of this paragraph. (Here, as elsewhere, the contrast with the first Iraqi Ba'th regime of 1963 is striking. Then the regime roused the active malevolence of the USSR—a remarkable feat given the "objective anti-Imperialism" of the Baghdad rulers, as conceded by Moscow. It did so mainly through its persecution of the Iraqi Communists, but also by its diplomatic maladroitness in general.)

Occasionally, Ba'th fundamentalism—or Pan-Arab radicalism—has gained the upper hand, even if that meant wanton perturbation of foreign relations, and a reinflaming of ancient suspicions. That the Persian Gulf is "Arab" seems to have remained a first principle which no consideration of expediency has been able to blur. Concomitant with the Arab character of the Gulf is the leading role envisaged for Iraq in that region. This in turn inspired in the earlier 1970s overt claims to Kuwaiti off-shore islands, bickerings with Saudi Arabia, support for the Omani rebels and, above all, a confrontation with Iran which found vent in Iraqi subversive activities in Iranian Khuzistan ("Arabistan") and Baluchistan, and in an adamant refusal to recognize the Iranian occupation of strategic islands at the outlet of the Gulf. The Algiers Agreement with Iran, mentioned above, has blunted the animosity between these two countries, and undoubtedly improved the regime's reputation for neighborly moderation throughout the Gulf in general.

Iraqi relations with Syria are a special case. The Ba'th group which took power in Iraq in 1968 is related to the historic "National Command" of Michel 'Aflaq and Salah Bitar which was ejected from Syria by the Ba'th officers led by Jadid and Asad. Since then the Ba'th rulers in Baghdad and Damascus have been rival contestants for orthodoxy and pursue each other with the venom peculiar to such relationships. This, however, is not the whole story. It must not be forgotten that relations betwen Syria and Iraq have been unsettled through most of recorded history. The technological and economic developments of our own generation have complicated matters further. Two problems stand out, with no final solution in sight. Iraq depends on the Syrian littoral for the marketing of much of its oil; though the strategic pipelines to the Gulf will obviate this need, practical considerations weigh heavily against a radical switchover in the foreseeable future.[14] Even more fundamental is the question of the Euphrates waters, vital to Iraqi agriculture and as vital for the industrialization of Syria. Since the amount of water available is limited, it is Syrian against Iraqi needs—with Syria, up-river, exercizing the stranglehold. So far the Iraqi rulers have shown, by and large, more restraint than their Syrian counterparts—partially, no doubt, because geography has put Iraq in the weaker position, but also in keeping with the grand tactics of the Baghdad regime.

In reviewing the foreign relations of the Ba'th regime in Iraq after 1968 even the unsympathetic observer would probably admit that Bakr and Saddam Husayn have shown statesmanlike qualities of a considerable order—a capacity for patience and self-command, decision making and agonizing reappraisals. These qualities have complemented the combination of inexorable purpose and flexible procedure which has served these men on the domestic scene. On consideration, it is easy to account for the longevity the regime has shown, much greater already than any of its predecessors since the 1958 revolution.

The "foundations" of the second Ba'th regime hardly affect the social scene. There has been no lack of declarations; development projects and agrarian reform have proceeded, though at a rather leisurely pace. But it is not unfair to state that social problems have come a poor second after security and politics. There certainly was no breakthrough during the first five years of the regime.

NOTES

1. The first Ba'th regime in Iraq was that of 'Ali Salih al-Sa'di, February–November 1963.

2. *Iraq News Agency* report of 10 April, 1974.

3. For the 1970 Constitution, see *Jumhuriyya* (Baghdad) 17 July, 1970. For the National Action Charter, *ibid.*, 16 November, 1971. An English translation of the National Action Charter appeared in *Summary of World Broadcasts*, (BBC, London), Part IV, 19 November 1971, pp. A/1-A/19.

4. Both of them, like several other prominent personalities of the regime, hail from Tikrit, north of Baghdad—which reflects the tendency in the Arab world to this day of political power concentrating in certain regions or even towns. Another famous native of Tikrit is Saladin, the conqueror of Egypt and a Kurd

to boot. Perhaps for these reasons Bakr and Saddam Husayn are not known to have presumed on this tie with the hero of modern Arab historiography.

5. For an elaboration, see U. Dann, "The Iraqi Officer Corps as a Factor for Stability—an Unorthodox Approach," paper presented at the Symposium on the Military and State in Modern Asia, the Hebrew University of Jerusalem, July 1974. H. Z. Schiffrin (ed.), *Military and State in Modern Asia*, (Jerusalem, 1976) pp.259–68.

6. Syria provides the obvious contrast.

7. Both dates appear in what may be called the Ba'th calendar of blessed events.

8. For a good detailed description of these two weeks, see O. Bengio, "Iraq," in Dishon (ed.), *Middle East Record 1968 (MER)*, (Jerusalem 1973), pp. 520-21.

9. For details, see chapters "Iraq" in *MER 1968, 1969-70, 1971* (the last-mentioned volume in an advanced stage of preparation).

10. The Nazim Kazzar conspiracy of 30 June 1973, affords a good case-study of the rulers' reaction to a sudden crisis. Nazim Kazzar, then Director of Security, succeeded in taking the regime by surprise when he sprang a plot with the aim of establishing a new, "purified," Ba'th polity, involving the liquidation of the incumbents. Both Bakr (who returned that day from a state visit abroad) and Saddam Husayn, but especially the latter, reacted with speed, decisiveness and sang-froid. The rising was crushed within the day; its leaders were executed. (For an account of the affair, see D. Kehat, "Kazzar's Abortive Coup, June 1973" (Hebrew), *Occasional Papers*, Shiloah Center, Tel Aviv University, 1974.)

11. Or rather, a basically non-communal catalyst. In Kirkuk, the earliest center of exploitation, the oil workers are mainly Kurds, the tradesmen Turcomans, the officials Sunni Arabs. The perennial conflict between these "classes" has thus acquired some characteristics of communal strife.

12. In November 1974, of 29 ministers four were Kurds, four Communists and one a non-Ba'th Arab Nationalist.

13. Written in the summer of 1975. The Basra Petroleum Company was nationalized in December 1975.

14. The inauguration, early in 1977, of a pipeline from northern Iraq to the Anatolian coast has further emancipated Iraq from Syria in this field.

Continuity and Change
in the Political Regimes of
Sudan and Libya, 1967–1973

Haim Shaked and Esther (Souery) Webman

There are basic characteristics which are common to the political dynamics of the Sudan and Libya in recent years. Each of the two states is located on the fringes of two centers: the Sudan borders on the Arab Middle East and "black" Africa; Libya is situated between the *Mashriq* and the *Maghrib*. This obvious but significant factor has had implications on the process which has shaped the historic image of these countries and influenced events in recent times. Moreover, both countries border on Egypt which has for many years played a dominant role in influencing its neighbors. It is no coincidence that the Sudan and Libya have been involved in recent years in plans for tripartite or dual federations and other forms of institutionalized cooperation, with Egypt as the common denominator. Both the Sudan and Libya experienced military *coups d'état* in May and September 1969, respectively. It is doubtful whether there was any direct connection between these two *coups*, but the fact that the military in both countries did oust an "old regime" and set up a new one based on army officers at least created an external similarity, and perhaps also an internal dynamic typical of the type of regime that has been set up in the wake of military *coups* in the Middle East in recent times.

Some central problems are common to both the Sudan and Libya. With differences in style and emphasis both have exhibited over the last four or five years considerable tension between the declared revolutionary ideologies and the day-to-day realities, which have posed for the new regimes complex problems of modernization, economic development and national integration. For some generations both have suffered the strains of a duel between the governing political and socio-economic centers and the periphery. The clash between South and North in the Sudan is well known. Less known, but not of less importance, are the strains in the relationship between the Nile region and the peripheral east and west of the Sudan. In Libya, there is tension between the coastal area, which contains most urban settlements in the country and is more open to external influences, and the interior—which is primarily a desert inhabited in parts by semi-nomadic tribes. There has also been a traditional rivalry between Tripolitania and Cyrenaica. Moreover, in recent years both countries have faced a critical problem inherent in the attempts by their rulers to create an infrastructure suitable for a new national identity, appropriate to the self-image of the ruling institution. This in turn also involved the problem of developing a cadre endowed with the proper revolutionary ideologies, which would support the regime, and which would both serve as a unifying factor and as an agent for the acceleration of those processes in which the regime is interested. While there is, in this sphere, a basic similarity between the two countries as to abstract objectives, the ways chosen have differed. During part of the period under review here, an attempt was made in the Sudan to set up institutions and to develop an ideology along the lines established in other Arab countries where a military *coup d'état* has taken place, but with an emphasis on the peculiar Sudanese circumstances that necessitate specific solutions. A similar attempt was also made in Libya, but with a strong emphasis not on the specific Libyan character of the revolution, but rather on the more general, Arab and Islamic, "circles"—a conception which the Sudan could never adopt, *inter alia*, because of its Southern problem.

In this context it is noteworthy that both countries have devoted much deliberation to their links with Egypt. In the early years of the revolutionary regime in Libya, its leaders were active in attempts to develop, strengthen and even impose close contacts with Egypt, while Egypt has exhibited growing reservations. The Sudan, by contrast, was hesitant about its connection with its northern neighbor—even when Egypt was interested in developing its ties with the Sudan. Their deliberations over the wider Arab circle have been no less weighty. However, as was the case with regard to Libya's and the Sudan's relationship with Egypt, the starting point as well as the results of these deliberations differed. The Sudan, for the most part, tried to compromise and mediate between rival trends in the Arab world. In contrast, Libya has tried to impose its own views on Arab opinion. As for the Arab–Israeli conflict, neither the Sudan nor Libya are "confrontation states," but here too, there are deep differences between their respective attitudes to the conflict.

This comparison between the two states perhaps serves to illuminate a number of processes and phenomena of recent years—but it might also be misleading. As already said, the descent from the generalization to a scrutiny of details reveals important differences between the Sudan and Libya. Each of these two countries has a separate history, and a different social and economic structure and political tradition. If the political image and structure of the two states during the years 1967–1973 is, among other things, a derivative of their less recent histories, it would follow that there are significant differences between them. One of these—which certainly influenced events in the Sudan and Libya between 1967 and 1973—is the degree of crystallization of national identity. It can be said that Sudanese national identity is stronger by far than the Libyan, and that the self-image of their respective regimes have been very different both in the style of action and in "the national role" which their regimes assumed and cultivated. Moreover, the Sudan has been in the shadow of Egypt ever since its occupation by Muhammad 'Ali, and in the course of time, and due to the prevailing circumstances, a kind of "Sudanese complex" has developed in so far as her relations with Egypt are concerned. Libya, on the other hand, has a long history of independence from outside Arab domination, though there is some justification for the contention that the Cyrenaica region has for a long time been apprehensive of Egyptian penetration or even occupation. An analysis of the economic and financial situation of the two countries also reveals a fundamental difference. There is no need to expound on the Libyan affluence resulting from oil revenues since the early 1960s. The Sudan, on the other hand, has for a long time suffered from severe economic problems. Furthermore, up to 1969 the regimes of the Sudan and Libya were very different. In Libya, there was a continuity of monarchic rule, while the Sudan went through shattering political convulsions—from a parliamentary regime upon independence in 1956, through a period of military revolutionary rule under Ibrahim 'Abbud, then back to parliamentary rule until the *coup* of 1969. Since the 1969 *coups,* both political and ideological activity of the regimes in the two countries has been unidentical. Generally speaking, the Sudanese regime since 1969 has strongly underlined the handling of domestic problems, while the Libyan regime has concentrated mainly on external politics. The revolutionary regimes that have taken shape in both countries during the period under discussion have thus assumed different shapes. To a certain extent, these differences are molded by the different personalities of Numeiri and Qadhafi.

THE INTERNAL POLITICAL SITUATION IN THE SUDAN

The watershed in Sudanese internal politics and external affairs in recent years is, chronologically, in May 1969, when the Numeiri regime came to power through a *coup d'état*. The period which that *coup* ended began in October 1964, when the Sudan experienced an event which is rather rare in modern Arab history: the return of the army to barracks after five years of military rule following a civilian *coup* that reinstated a government similar to that which had existed before the Ibrahim 'Abbud *coup* of 1958. Thus, any methodical discussion of continuity and change in the Sudan in the last decade must relate to two periods: the one that began in 1964 and lasted till mid-1969, and the second that began in mid-1969 and has continued to the present day. The second period can also be sub-divided into two phases, the first of which lasted until July 1971. During this period, the main efforts of the revolutionary leadership headed by Numeiri were devoted mainly to the elimination of actual and potential opposition forces. Two clear stages can be discerned in this continuous effort. The first was characterized by an alliance between Numeiri's supporters and radical-leftist forces against the traditional-religious elements, the most dangerous of which were the Ansar—the supporters of the Mahdi's family and the Umma Party. This stage ended dramatically with the uprising on Aba Island in March 1970, and its ruthless suppression by the government. From March 1970 up to mid-1971 Numeiri devoted his main efforts to driving out those same leftist forces—among whom the communists were the predominant political power—who had been his allies since the May *coup*. This stage, in which the crucial dates were November 1970 and February 1971, also ended dramatically—by the abortive military *coup d'état* of July 1971, Numeiri's renewed seizure of power and the heavy blow struck against the leadership of the Sudanese Communist Party, which was instrumental in staging the abortive *coup*.

It should be noted that, throughout this first period, the relative weight of civilian circles (Babikr 'Awadallah) in government declined, while the military circle (Khalid Hasan 'Abbas) was on the rise. The abortive *coup* and its aftermath removed another obstacle from the regime's political path, which was now completely free of ideological and practical dependence on leftist (and communist) elements. Indeed, from July 1971 onwards, a consistent attempt was made to create a new political system with a dual role: to fill the vacuum created by the suppression of the traditional-religious and the leftist elements, and to create the tools that would permit those changes that appeared essential to the regime in realizing the ideology of the revolution and consolidating a popular base for the continuation of the regime.

In the year 1967, the Sudan was at the height of a stage in the development of its politics—domestically, on the inter-Arab scene and internationally. In terms of its international orientation, the Sudan was still identified as tending to the West. At the inter-Arab level, the war of June 1967 did have some impact, but it was both indirect and insignificant. In both these spheres the Sudan was very cautious not to take steps or to adopt positions that would implicate it in a clear commitment. Due to a political tradition that had taken shape since independence in 1956, severe internal problems, fear of damage to the consolidation of independence, and fear of unbalancing the equilibrium between Arab and African identity—the Sudan tried hard to be as active as possible with as little involvement as feasible.

Domestically, the Sudan of 1967 was troubled by the same economic, social and political problems that had beset it since independence, and which were the basic cause of the instability of its regimes. Two political blocs were active during the second period of parliamentary rule, which had begun in 1964. In spite of the deep differences between them, all the traditional political forces—which in part relied on very influential religious circles—belonged to one bloc. This bloc was composed of the Umma Party—backed by the Ansar and the Mahdi's family; the People's Democratic Party (PDP)—whose main support was derived from the Khatmiyya; the National Unionist Party (NUP)—whose main support came from urban intelligentsia and officials, but also members of the Khatmiyya; and the Muslim Brethren—mainly supported by students and the religious intelligentsia. The second bloc consisted of new political forces, mostly of leftist tendencies and ideas, and of the communists whose primary power base rested with the trade unions, and the student, women's and youth organizations.

These political forces, whose internal cohesiveness and relative power differed from each other, faced several key problems during the whole period of the second parliamentary regime: how to maintain a coalition system that would permit government stability; how to institutionalize the weak ruling institution by means of a constitution acceptable to the widest possible circles; how to solve two major problems that troubled every regime in Sudan—on the eve of independence and certainly afterwards: the militant separatism in the South, and the lack of economic resources which, quite apart from stifling development, threatened severe hardship. It was the first parliamentary regime's failure to face up to these problems that had created the impetus for 'Abbud's military regime in 1958. At first, 'Abbud raised high hopes in the Sudan, but these ended in bitter disappointment which, together with his inability to undermine the political forces that he wished to replace, resulted in his removal by the civilian *coup* of October 1964.

While the second parliamentary regime (1964–1969) was similar to its predecessor in its external facets, it was much more complex than the one which prevailed in the Sudan immediately after independence. Not unlike the first parliamentary regime, the second was also preoccupied with the composition and the threat of the dissolution of coalitions. To the rise and fall of governments, which reflected factional disputes and personal competition among the traditional Sudanese political forces, was now added a new dimension: the common front of these forces against the threat posed by new political entities, primarily the communists. The latter had achieved prominence in the 1964 civilian *coup*, and thus in the transition government that followed it, and in the April 1965 elections. To the traditional elements, the main problem appeared to be that of removing the leftists from government by parliamentary means. Indeed, Numeiri's military *coup* occurred during a serious parliamentary crisis, deriving from a realignment of the traditional parties[1] and their endeavor to find a *modus videndi* that would alleviate the governmental crisis.

The Numeiri *coup* interrupted the attempts of the Umma Party and the Democratic Unionist Party to redeploy and remove the leftist elements from partnership in government, and elevated to power new civilian and military groups that were moved to take over political power by the fear that intelligent political maneuvering by the reunited Umma might remove them totally from the stage for a long time to come. At first, Numeiri's regime based itself on an alliance between leftist civilian, and radical military elements. This temporary constellation gave the veterans of the Sudanese Communist Party an influence which was out of proportion to the actual size of their power base (not unlike the situation following the civilian revolt of October 1964). Indeed, this advantage of the party and other leftist elements was reflected in the political program which Numeiri presented immediately after the coup,[2] and in the distribution of political power positions that began to crystallize subsequently.

When Numeiri and his comrades seized power in the Sudan, they faced problems similar to those that troubled previous regimes during the preceding fourteen years of independence. Apart from the sectarian political structure (the Khatmiyya and the Ansar), the country was deep in economic trouble—a critical shortage of foreign currency, a declining standard of living, and preponderant dependence on cotton as the main source of income. The problem of the South continued to drain the government's resources, and to threaten its very foundations. The revolutionaries immediately declared the state a democratic republic in which sovereignty was vested in the people as represented by the Revolutionary Command Council (RCC). The declared policy of the RCC was that the new regime would work for the attainment of the following goals: encouragement of national capital, the removal of foreign capital and the expansion of the public sector; a solution to the problem of the South on the basis of regional autonomy within a united Sudan; establishment of one party which would unite the ranks of the workers, peasants, the national bourgeoisie and the progressive intelligentsia. The declarations of the new regime contained, on the one hand, a revolutionary self-image and, on the other, a desire to create a foundation for cooperation with leftist circles and with the communists. However, the tensions within the regime, and between it and its adversaries, coupled with the immediate and supreme need to consolidate power, prevented any meaningful progress in the implementation of the declared policy throughout the entire first period of Numeiri's rule—up to July 1971.

From the very beginning, Numeiri emphasized that the special socialist path chosen by the Sudan was anchored in the values of Arabism and Islam, as well as in the specific requirements of Sudanese tradition and society. As a result of many delays, emanating in part from ideological and practical differences of opinion between Numeiri and the communists, the first steps toward the promulgation of a National Covenant and the formation of a Sudanese Socialist Party were taken only at the end of 1970. It was only after the abortive *coup* of July 1971 that the Covenant was ratified and the SSU set up. The only significant economic step taken before July 1971 was the nationalization of a number of banks and foreign companies in May 1970, and the simultaneous announcement of a "Five Year Development Plan"[3] but no practical measures were taken to implement that plan. The announcement of the reorganization of local government—always a touchy subject in the Sudan—also remained on paper until July 1971. Contrary to Numeiri's promises, and certainly against his best interests, tension in the South also escalated. Shortly after the 1969 *coup* the government of the Sudan created a special ministry for Southern affairs[4] and, during the first two years of Numeiri's rule, attempts were made to negotiate with the rebel leaders.[5] These attempts were either not decisive enough, or the situation was not ripe to facilitate the achievement of pacification. Rather, up to mid-1971 there were a number of armed clashes between the army and the Southern rebel forces.[6]

The failure of the July 1971 *coup d'état* symbolized the end of the first period of Numeiri's rule in that he completed one phase in the elimination of his opponents begun after his own *coup*. It also marked the beginning of the phase that has continued through to this day. In October 1971 Collin Legum wrote that "in its two and a half years of power, the RCC failed to produce a workable political or economic system; and in the year before the *coup* of July 1971 the Sudan was clearly in a state of malaise. The RCC and Numeiri do not lack vigor or vision; yet they failed to generate real support."[7] Immediately after July 1971, however, Numeiri began a government reorganization and accelerated the creation of tools for a new "public order" aimed at providing legitimacy for the regime, a "national consensus" and a broad base of support.

The first step was in the direction of "civilianization" of the regime. As early as 13 August, 1971, a provisional constitution proclaimed, *inter alia*, that the Sudan was a democratic-socialist state founded on an alliance of the popular working forces headed by a president whose term of office is six years, and who is *ex officio* Commander-in-Chief. Upon the swearing-in of the President and his government, the Revolutionary Command Council would be dissolved.[8] On 15 September a referendum was held to elect the President of the Republic, with Numeiri as the sole candidate. Elected by a 98.6% majority,[9] he was proclaimed President on 12 October. The following day, reorganizational decrees were published, the Revolutionary Command Council was dissolved, and a new government was formed with its key positions given to RCC members. The number of Southern representatives in the government was increased from two to three.[10] This reorganization completed a series of actions, some of which had begun early in 1971, and others only after the abortive coup (e.g., the dissolution of various trade unions and their reorganization, and purges in the army and civil administration).[11]

Thus, an effort had been made within a short time to break up the power centers of the left and of the Communist Party, and (early in August 1971) even such communist figures as Foreign Minister Faruk Abu 'Isa and Labor Minister Mu'awiya Ibrahim were removed from the government—even though they belonged to a communist faction that had cooperated with Numeiri ever since he seized power in 1969. The communist opposition to the setting up of a single party organization—similar to that of the Arab Socialist Union in Egypt—having vanished, the first Congess of the Sudanese Socialist Union took place in January 1972. Numeiri was at the head of its "Central Executive Committee," and both the National Covenant and the draft permanent constitution were approved.[12] Between 22 September and 4 October, 1972, elections were held to the first People's Assembly,[13] one of the purposes of which was to prepare and ratify the permanent Constitution of the Sudanese Republic. Following the opening of the People's Assembly, on 12 October, 1972,[14] the establishment of the central organs of the Sudanese Socialist Union was completed by mid-November. The permanent Constitution was first ratified in May 1973, and it recognized Islam as the religion of the majority and Christianity as the religion "of a considerable number of citizens" of the Sudan.[15]

The single-party system was recognized as the only legitimate framework for political activity, and self-government was approved for the Southern provinces. The separate presentation of the process of political institutionalization—with its accompanying constitutional measures, and the clash of political forces which was an integral part of that process—is, of course, artifical. Throughout the whole period, the fundamental issues of national integration were undoubtedly in the background of the struggle of political forces. On the other hand, the achievements of Numeiri's regime—even if not yet permanent—are not likely to be of inconsequential influence on the continued crystallization of new national forces. A comparison of the political texture of the Sudan at the end of 1973 with that of 1967 would show that the country was still composed of basically the same social, religious and tribal groups that had shaped its political image in the previous two decades—and that they continued, as in the past, to form the power centers that were likely to endanger the regime under certain circumstances and constellations. However, it should be noted that disturbances organized by students at the end of August 1973—apparently on the initiative of past leaders from the Umma Party and the Muslim Brethren—did cause a two-week long state of emergency, yet caused no real reverberations in the public at large.[16] It would seem that the Sudanese Socialist Union, after its establishment, became the central political body active in the mobilization of popular support for the regime. According to the information at present available, this organization has gradually drawn into its ranks circles previously identified as communist, socialist, radical or pan-Arab as well as groups numbered among the traditional political forces. In contrast to 'Abbud's regime—which largely rested on the traditional political system (though it ruled with the help of the army)—Numeiri was the first Sudanese leader to attempt to give all strata and groupings of society the feeling that their basic interests would be not only protected within the superstructure of national unity but might even be furthered. In fact, the process of institutionalization and constitutionalization described above created the tools necessary for a dialogue between these diverse elements.

Another element that has contributed to the feeling of progress along the road to an all-Sudanese national integration is the considerable achievement with regard to the South—one which has been maintained for more than two years now. Numeiri prepared the ground for the Addis Ababa Agreement—signed on 27 March, 1972—by stages. At first by declarations and demonstrative actions (such as the appointment of Southerners to ministerial positions in the government) and later, particularly after July 1971, by a series of tangible deeds. At first he mended fences with the Sudan's African neighbors—Ethiopia and Uganda—where there were concentrations of Southern political exiles, rebels and refugees. The preparation of the ground for *rapprochement*, the abandonment of the idea of joining the tripartite federation with Egypt and Libya, and the drafting of the temporary Constitution—all helped Numeiri, on the one hand, to isolate Southerners from their supporters, and on the other, strengthened his image as a man of peace. Haile Selassie's help eventually enabled him to achieve an agreement with the Southern rebels. The three Southern provinces were granted extensive authority to run their own affairs, while foreign, military and security matters remained in the hands of the central government. Some two weeks after the signature of the agreement, a cease-fire was proclaimed, and a process of rehabilitating refugees and integrating the rebel forces (the "Anya Nya") into the regular Sudanese army commenced. A process of institutionalization of the political system, similar to that which had been implemented in the North, now began in the South. A transition government for the South was established in April 1972,[17] and it continued in office until an elected People's Assembly of the Southern Provinces convened in December 1973. A permanent government—called the "Supreme Executive Council of the Southern Region"—then took office.[18] The choice of President of that Council was Abel Alier, who had served as minister in Numeiri's first government, and who has served as Deputy President of the Republic since August 1971.

After July 1971 a change also took place in the basic economic objectives as declared following the *coup* in May 1969. The regime now began to rehabilitate the private sector, alongside with the public sector, and to encourage foreign investment—without which the Sudan could not consolidate its economic infrastructure. For this purpose the Sudan also endeavored to strengthen its links with the West as well as with the oil-rich Arab countries—particularly Saudi Arabia and the Persian Gulf Emirates. New investment laws were promulgated, granting tax relief and guarantees against nationalization—and steps were taken to denationalize various enterprises.[19] It is therefore not surprising that Numeiri's policies were subjected to many attacks leveled mostly by adherents of the Communist Party, which had succeeded in reorganizing itself after the heavy blow it sustained in July 1971. They accused Numeiri of reliance on traditional forces, pro-Western tendencies, his improved relationship with "reactionary regimes" in Africa—and of dictatorship.[20]

Any attempt to sum up the second period of Numeiri's rule, which is still under way, must clearly indicate the fact that at the end of 1973 Numeiri was still confronting the same basic domestic problems that he faced shortly after he came to power. At the end of 1973 the main question was to what degree the instruments created meanwhile by Numeiri had succeeded in filling the vacuum, in reducing the tensions resulting from the shock to the old frameworks which had characterized the period of May 1969–July 1971, and transferring the loyalties of traditional forces away from previous power centers to the new regime. The accelerated political activities that followed July 1971, which were accompanied by a retreat from rigid, dogmatic ideology and the consistent attempt by the regime to compromise with the prevailing socio-political reality, are important phenomena in the internal life of the Sudan that have taken place over the last three years. Numeiri's primary efforts have been directed to internal affairs, and in this there is a clear continuation from previous regimes. It is difficult to determine whether the concentration on internal affairs derives from the multiplicity of critical problems that have been threatening the very existence of the regime and have prevented Numeiri from looking at more distant fields; or whether its source is in the outlook of the ruling group—or whether it is, perhaps, a combination of both factors.

The Sudan's geopolitical location, socio-cultural tradtion and special problems have not permitted the country, since independence, to play a role that might involve it in any defined obligation to any particular party within the inter-Arab and international systems. Up to July 1971 Numeiri's foreign policy and his toughness toward the West, were an exception to this rule, emanating from internal political confrontations in the Sudan at that time. It is no coincidence that, since July 1971, Numeiri's foreign policy—both Arab and international—have reverted to "low profile" and traditional Sudanese neutrality.

THE INTERNAL POLITICAL SITUATION IN LIBYA

For Libya, like the Sudan, the year 1967 is not an appropriate starting point for the analysis of political continuity and change. A survey of the contemporary history of Libya can commence at any of the following three points: in 1951, when Libya attained independence; in 1963, when Libya changed from a federal union of Cyrenaica, Tripolitania and Fezzan to a unitary state; or in 1969—the year of revolution, removal of the monarchy and the rise of Qadhafi and Jallud to power.

As far as the years 1963-1969 are concerned, note must be taken of the cumulative effect of the discovery of oil (in the early 1960s) and its exploitation, coupled with two critical poinmts in the political life: the year 1964—a year of a severe government crisis which, *inter alia*, was expressed in the King's offer to abdicate; and the second half of 1967—again a year of government crisis. The years 1969-1973 can be divided, from the viewpoint of political activities of the ruling group, into three periods: from September to the end of 1969—a short but stormy period of the consolidation of the new regime. This phase came to an end with the plot of two lieutenant-colonels, Minister of Defense Adam al-Hawwaz and Minister of the Interior Musa Ahmad, who were ousted from the government in December. The second period, from

January 1970 to July 1971, was one in which the Revolutionary Command Council took control over the civil aspects of the regime, namely, the government. From August 1971, and up to the present day this process has been reversed: the members of the military junta have been withdrawing from government, though they have carefully preserved their supremacy in the hierarchy of power. There have also been attempts in this period to strengthen the ideological dimension of the Libyan revolution, as has been particularly evident in the attempt to institutionalize the Arab Socialist Union (ASU) and to carry out the "popular revolution" (April 1973).

On 1 September, 1969, a military *coup d'état* brought to power a junta of junior and unknown officers. Qadhafi—who as a result of the *coup* became the leader of Libya—was a 27-year-old captain. The *coup d'état*, which put an end to the regime of King Idris as-Sanussi, established since independence in 1951, was a somewhat surprising step even though the old regime's end was almost a certainty because of the King's advanced age (79) and the absence of an heir with suitable leadership qualities. Notwithstanding the basic weakness of his regime, the King did—by his personality and past—represent the power of government, the legitimacy of rule and a sense of Libyan unity. His strength was anchored in the very longevity of his reign, and in his actions during the Italian colonial rule prior to independence, which turned him into a national figure.

The relative political stability achieved by the King up to April 1963, when he abrogated the federative structure of three provinces in favor of a unitary state, was a result of his ability to maneuver government so that the delicate balance of conflicting internal political interests would not be upset. The King fulfilled this role effectively as long as the political forces involved were limited in scope and offset each other, and as long as the monarchy was the supreme representative mechanism and the only factor capable of compromise. The King was intolerant of any political organization, and tried to prevent any constitutional and institutional development that might permit new socio-political elements to share the practical aspects of his rule. The main significance of this policy lay in the alienation of these political forces, which were crystallizing as a result of the social and economic change in Libya especially after the discovery of oil and the beginning of its exploitation in 1955–1960.[21]

The internal tensions of the years 1963–1969[22] found expression in two parallel developments: on the one hand, increased expectation and as a result, a rise in the demands of workers, intelligentsia, salary earners, etc.; on the other hand, a strengthening of the existent pan-Arab ideas (in part under Nasserist influence), which were no longer limited to an external orientation but began to appear as an alternative to the existing regime. These developments caused shocks at the govermental level (six changes of government between 1963 and 1969) and severe political crises in 1964 and 1967. It should be stressed that, in spite of their internal nature, both crises were stimulated by external events in the Arab world and connected with the Arab–Israeli conflict (the first Arab Summit Conference in January 1964; Nasser's call in January 1964, in the midst of student demonstrations in Libya, to evacuate the foreign bases there; and the June War in 1967). Here then was a warning that the Libyan regime was shaky, and that external circumstances might provide internal political opposition there with a pretext to present extremist nationalist demands not only in foreign affairs but also in domestic issues. In response to the stormy tempers of the second half of 1967, the old King took action both on the domestic and external planes: continued police action—that is, trials of political prisoners (which continued into 1968); and a futile attempt at economic and social reform, and—to a lesser degree—some initiative in foreign affairs in which he made a demand in June 1967 that Britain and the United States should evacuate their bases in Libya, and ordered a stoppage of the oil flow to the West for a month. Both were aimed a placating pan-Arab sensitivities. The King's conservatism, caution and suspiciousness, however, more or less ruled out any expectations for radical change in his domestic and external policies.

Within a political system that was both corrupt and frustrated, the army was the only element that contained any potential for change, whether because it was an organized force, or because of public support following the events of June 1967—or because of the revolutionary fervor of groups of junior officers, who did not belong to the royalist establishment and were therefore far more aware of the expectations and demands of the political public in Libya. It took several years for this new force to organize and to work out a plan for a *coup d'état*. The timing of revolution was influenced by the King's measures to dismiss and exile a group of officers. The King's absence in Turkey for medical treatment provided the revolutionaries with an opportunity to carry out a military *coup* which was aptly described by *Time* as a "textbook coup."[23]

At the outbreak of the revolution, the identity of the young revolutionaries was a mystery.[24] From the beginning it was clear that their aspiration in foreign affairs would be integration into the "eastern" Arab circle, rather than that of the Maghrib. Their first proclamation spoke of three guiding principles of revolution: *freedom* of the state from the foreign yoke, and of the citizen and the Arab from degradation, oppression and ignorance; *socialism* founded on Islam; and *national unity* of each of the Arab countries and of the Arab world, as well as the liberation of Palestine.[25]

The problem that faced the revolutionaries at the end of 1969 could be classified under two headings. The first consisted of those continuous fundamental problems that derived from the Libyan socio-political structure—such as the constant tension between heterogenous tribal groups and the settled population, or the lack of a clear historic-geographic identity at the national level (e.g., the rivalry between Cyrenaica and Tripolitania), which had been aggravated by the royalist policy that impeded free political play. The second group of problems included economic and social issues which had gradually emerged, yet remained unsolved by the royalist regime. Of these, the major issues were an economy founded on rich oil resources, but unable to exploit them fully, insufficient developmental planning, mass migration to the cities and an abandonment of rural areas, a severe lack of cadres suitable for governmental work, the decisive weight of foreigners in the economy, and strong internal pressures for a change of foreign policy in the inter-Arab and international spheres.

The revolution's immediate success in gaining control of the country proved *post factum* just how easy it was for a small but well-organized group to achieve control in the absence of developed political power centers. The only effective force that could put forward any meaningful opposition to the revolution was the Cyrenaican Defense Force, established by the King and based on his Sanussi loyalists, but this force was neutralized by the revolutionaries in the first few days. Other potential adversaries of the new regime were various tribes in Cyrenaica (the main stronghold of King Idris), in Fezzan (the Nasr ad-Din family) and in Tripolitania itself. However, these tribes were dispersed over wide areas, they lacked any unifying factor and had insufficient military might to face the army. On the other hand, the revolution could expect support from urban circles, particularly in Tripolitania, as well as from the echelons of the army, the young intelligentsia, the new working class and the petite bourgeoisie.

Despite the spate of newspaper coverage of Libya since the revolution, little is known about the political events inside the country since 1969. The available sources are sufficient for a survey of the power struggles within the ruling group, but only in its external and declarative aspects. A thorough follow-up of governmental changes, and of Qadhafi's attempts to resign, could, however, indicate certain trends. Two ruling institutions were established after the revolution: the Revolutionary Command Council and the government—with a well-defined link between them. Generally speaking it was the Council which determined policy, while the government was responsible for its implementation.[26] The government formed in September 1969 was civilian and composed of various Pan-Arab, Nasserist and nationalistic elements, including personalities such as the PM Dr. Maghribi and the Foreign Minister Salah Buwaysir, who had in the past expressed opposition to the royalist regime. There were only two army officers in that government: Defense Minister Adan al-Hawwaz and Interior Minister Musa Ahmak—both Cyrenaicans of higher military rank than that of the members of the junta, to which they did not belong. Their important porfolios in government was indicative of their influence in their own province and in the army. Both were accused of plotting the downfall of the regime and, were dismissed in December 1969.

It is evident that the (then) anonymous Revolutionary Command Council tried to use this government in order to reach as wide a circle as possible of the Libyan population, and enlist their support, while preserving the Council's own supremacy. The governmental reshuffle of 16 January, 1970, and Qadhafi's appointment as Prime Minister and Defense Minister, reflected the beginning of a takeover by the Council, first of the government and later of all key economic and political bodies which were set up after the *coup*. They also reflected as did the later personnel changes, the tension between the civilian government and the Council over the initial definition of roles, and perhaps even practical ideological differences in the approach to the solution of problems. In September 1970 there were further changes as more Council members joined the government. Eight out of 13 portfolios were now held by army officers.

By the end of 1970 a reversal of the process became evident. The number of Revolutionary Command Council officers in government now began to decline. Finance Minister 'Umar 'Abdallah al-Muhayshi and Interior Minister 'Abd al-Mun'im al-Huni resigned in October 1970. In December, Foreign Minister Muhammad Najm also resigned. After the government reshuffles of August 1971 the current handling of domestic affairs was concentrated more and more in the hands of technocrats, while the members of the Council concentrated on the making of policy and its direction. From time to time, rumors spread about deep and even unbridgeable differences of opinion within the Council. These rumors usually derived from personnel changes and announcements of changes in the powers of Qadhafi and Jallud—but they were consistently denied by the regime, and Qadhafi himself emphasized, in July 1972 that:

> There is no power conflict in the pro-unity bases in the Libyan Arab Republic....Here there are honest people leading a genuine revolution....The command of the Libyan Arab Republic is not interested in power, nor does it like seats of authority. There is no game of musical chairs....In the Libyan Arab Republic Revolutionary Command there is a tendency to avoid authority and power competition.[27]

It is to be assumed that this statement of denial did, in fact, reflect differences of opinion. In any event—even after the exposure of rifts in the Revolutionary Command Council at a later stage—it was difficult to assess their meaning. The only clear aspect was that they revolved around the right domestic policy for the realization of the revolutionary principles in social and economic matters, as well as the democratization of the regime and the place of Islam in daily life. In external affairs, the bones of contention were changes of emphasis in inter-Arab and international orientations. Whatever the case, the military junta consistently made every effort to maintain an image of unity.[28]

After August 1971, there were two peaks in top echelon reshuffling: in July 1972 and April 1974. Apparently, the first reflected the beginning of a realignment of forces, as the government became a body of civilian technocrats, headed by Jallud instead of Qadhafi, who had held the premiership together with the chairmanship of the Revolutionary Command Council since January 1970. In the new government, only one additional member of the Council—Mun'im al-Huni—held office (the important post of Minister of the Interior). The Defense Ministry was taken from Qadhafi (who had held it since January 1970) while the Foreign Affairs portfolio—not assigned since Muhammad Najm's resignation in December 1970—was given to the head of Libya's mission to the United Nations, Mansur Rashid al-Kahia. On the surface, Qadhafi had thus been relieved of his governmental authority; yet he continued to be the undisputed leader of Libya, who had delegated his powers to Jallud so that he could devote himself to the ideology of the revolution.

This process reached its peak in April 1974. In accordance with a decree of the Revolutionary Command Council, Qadhafi was to devote himself to "organizational and ideological action, and to the organizing of the masses," for which purpose he was released from the handling of political and administrative matters, and from all ceremonies and receptions—without detracting from his office as Chairman of the Revolutionary Command Council and as Commander-in-Chief of the Armed Forces.[29]

Information about the opposition in Libya is no less speculative, and no more founded on accurate data than is that which refers to the balance of power among the ruling elite. Yet there is no doubt that latent opposition of various kinds did exist throughout the period under review. These include tribal elements which, despite their weakening as a result of the socio-economic changes, have retained their importance as power centers; the oligarchy composed of the members of the *ancien regime*, such as the ash-Shalhi family, who held considerable power in the past and attracted supporters both from the tribes and the petit bourgeois; and young civilian and military circles of political opinions differing from those of the members of the Revolutionary Command Council. Thus far, the various elements of opposition have not afforded proof of suffcient cohesion to present a serious threat to the regime. The leaders of the plot uncovered in December 1969 (Adam al-Hawwaz and Musa Ahmad) and the Nasr ad-Din family of Fezzan who headed a plot uncovered in July 1970—did not succeed in gathering together a sufficiently effective force, and were apparently planning to rely on foreign mercenaries. There has been some information about disquiet among the tribes, but they also posed no threat to the regime. The revolutionary regime apparently succeeded in satisfying the urban elements (primarily in Tripolitania) which had been troublesome in royalist times—through its militant Islamic and pan-Arab ideologies, and the availability of a high income.

The social and political structure which hamper the creation of centers of opposition to the regime in Libya, coupled with the regime's firm supervision of its potential opponents, enabled the regime to maintain its military character, while strengthening the army and the police as the central instrument of control. Bodies such as the Popular Resistance Movement (September 1970), the Arab Socialist Union (June 1971), the Council for National Guidance (September 1972) were established—but in all of them members of the Council were the motivating and guiding spirit. When asked at the opening of the Arab Socialist Union Congress in March 1972 about the setting up of a "People's Assembly" and the drafting of a permanent Constitution, Qadhafi replied that he accepted the idea, but he felt that the time was not yet ripe for the widening of the basis of democracy in the revolution.[30]

As long as the regime felt that the time was not ripe for democratization it used a well-trodden path to legitimacy—the direct touch with people at large. Already during its first year of rule the regime took steps in the direction of Libyanization, Arabization, and the methodical introduction of Islamic law into daily life. A law for the nationalization of banks and foreign companies was promulgated as early as November 1969, and was implemented through 1970. In March and June 1970 the British and American military bases were evacuated. In July 1970 the property of Italians and Jews was confiscated. From a very early stage, the new regime decreed that Arabic was to be the only language in teaching, signposts, passports and other documentation. All these steps were aimed at acquiring public support and increasing national identification; yet they did not seem to derive from opportunism or pure pragmatism. Qadhafi, at least, sincerely believed in this as the correct revolutionary path. To him Islamic socialism was "the third doctrine" while Marxism was out of place and capitalism was dead. Qadhafi dedicated most of his thinking to the elaboration of the theory of Islamic socialism.[31]

It is only in the wider conceptual context of an Arab mission which, undoubtedly, motivates Qadhafi (who has been defined by a journalist as a latter-day Saladin with a modern sword), that one can understand a phenomenon such as the "popular revolution" of April 1973. This revolution—though limited in duration—was an outburst of revolutionary sentiment blended with Islamic fundamentalism, which has been characteristic of Qadhafi's ideological thinking ever since his rise to power. From many viewpoints—and despite the use of revolutionary terminology of a kind accepted in the Middle East during the last generation—the conceptual infrastructure of Qadhafi's regime is to a large extent anachronistic. It might persist for a relatively long time as a result of the combination of immense financial resources available to the regime and the non-existence, internally, of any serious body of opposition. However, part of the ruling group are probably aware that the "fireworks" which have escorted them since the revolution could hardly compensate the various sectors of the population in the long run. It is in this light that one would view the power struggles described above, which reflect an oscillation between greater involvement in inter-Arab affairs and the fundamental problems of the Libyan state.

NOTES

1. A union of the NUP and PDP—called "The Democratic Unionist Party"—was completed in December 1967, and resulted in victory to the DUP at the April–May 1968 elections. This union and its results gave a new impetus to a reunification of the two Umma Party factions in April 1969. On the eve of Numeiri's *coup*, the question of a new constitution for the Sudan became a major issue in discussions between these two united parties.

2. See Numeiri's speech, *R. Omdurman (RO)*, 25 May—*Daily Report (DR)*, 26 May, 1969.

3. *RO*, 25 May—*DR*, 26 May, 1969: *Middle East News Agency (MENA)*, 14 June—*DR*, 15 June, 1970.

4. *RO*, 19 June—*DR*, 20 June, 1969.

5. Thus for example, a meeting between Joseph Garang, Minister of State for Southern Affairs, and Southerners during a tour of the Southern provinces: *RO*, 19 July—*DR*, 27 July, 1969; a visit by Garang to Uganda in August 1969, *AFP*, 7 August—*DR*, 8 August, 1969.

6. For example, incidents in September 1969: *al-Ayyam, Time*, 15 September, 1969; in April 1970: *al-Ahram*, 20 April, 1970; in July 1970: *Observer*, 30 August, 1970.

7. *Africa Report*, vol. 16, No. 7, October 1971.

8. *RO*, 13 August—*BBC*, 17 August, 1971.

9. *MENA*, 3 September, 13 October—*IMB*, 6 September, 13 October, 1971.

10. *RO*, 14 October—*BBC*, 16 October, 1971; *Ruz al-Yusuf*, 18 October, 1971.

11. *RO*, 2, 3 August—*DR*, 3, 4 August, 1971; *MENA*, 13, 22 August—*IMTP*, 13, 22 August, 1971.

12. *MENA*, 2, 11 January—*QY*, 5, 14 January, 1972.

13. *RO*, 19 September—*BBC*, 21 September, 1972.

14. *MENA*, 12 October—*IMTP*, 12 October, 1972.

15. *Al-Anwar*, 22 April, 1973.

16. *RO*, 30 August, 5 September—*DR*, 31 August, 5 September, 1973; *Africa Confidential*, vol. 14, no. 8, 21 September, 1973.

17. *MENA*, 5 April—*IMTP*, 5 April, 1972; *RO*, 6 April—*BBC*, 8 April, 1972.

18. *RO*, 15 December—*BBC*, 18 December, 1973; *Guardian*, 24 December, 1973.

19. *Washington Post*, 21 August, 1972; *RO*, 31 August—*BBC*, 5 September, 1972; *Commerce Today*, 4 March, 1974.

20. *Al-Nida'*, 12 August, 1971; *al-Nahar*, 1 October, 1971, 14 January, 1972.

21. The main growth of new socio-political strata began on the eve of independence and took place in urban centers, and primarily in Tripolitania. These included 'Umar al-Mukhtar and the National Congress Party, whose activities were prohibited in 1952. The discovery of oil accelerated this growth in that it brought large-scale migration to the cities and an increase in the urban working circles, the intelligentsia, the clerical professions and the business community.

22. See Jacques Roumani, "Libya and the Military Revolution," in W. I. Zartman (ed.), *Man, State and Society in the Contemporary Maghrib*, New York, 1973, pp. 344–60.

23. *Time*, 12 September, 1969.

24. The name of the Chairman of the Revolutionary Command Council was disclosed only two weeks after the *coup d'état*. A full list of members was not published until January 1970.

25. *Al-Ahram*, 2 September, 1969; *R. Bayda'*, 16 September—*DR*, 17 September, 1969; *al-Hawadith*, 10 October, 1969.

26. See the first policy statement of the Revolutionary Command Council of 1 September, 1969 and the Temporary Constitution of 11 December, 1969. *R. Libya*, 1 September, 11 December—*BBC*, 3 September, 13 December, 1969.

27. *R. Bayda'*, 23 July—*BBC*, 25 July, 1972.

28. In August 1975, 'Umar al-Muhayshi fled from Libya after an attempt to remove Qadhafi. He was given political asylum in Egypt where he gave a series

of interviews to *al-Ahram* in March–April 1976, which threw light on the differences of opinion witnin the RCC.

29. *INA*, 7 April—*QY*, 13 September, 1972.

30. *MENA*, 11 September—*QY*, 13 September, 1972.

31. In January 1976, he published the "Green Book" which elaborates the "Third Theory."

Iran
and the
Gulf

Iran and the Middle East
The Primacy of the Persian Gulf

Rouhollah J. Ramazani

This paper advances two major and interrelated propsitions. One is that Iran's Middle Eastern policy between 1967 and 1973 was primarily a reflection of its policy in the Persian Gulf. That is, that Iranian interests, objectives and policies in the Persian Gulf were not only intimately interlocked with its concerns in the Middle East, but that its Middle Eastern policies were influenced primarily by its concerns in the Persian Gulf. The other proposition is that although the Persian Gulf became the focal point of Iran's Middle Eastern policy within the 1967-1973 period, the processes of recurrent interaction between the dynamics of domestic, regional and global politics had begun to make the Persian Gulf the center of Iranian foreign policy thinking, calculation and formulation as early as the 1950s.

1953–1967: IRAN'S INCREASING CONCERN
WITH THE PERSIAN GULF AREA

The illustration of the latter proposition at the outset will serve as a useful backdrop to the exploration of the first proposition. It will, therefore, be of use initially to portray in broad strokes the basic thrust, patterns and problems of Iran's Middle Eastern policy from 1953 through 1967.

The year 1953 marked the rise of the Shah to a new pinnacle of power following the downfall of the Mosaddeq Government. Once the Shah's regime had settled the twin problems of diplomatic rupture with Britain and the oil nationalization dispute, it plotted its foreign policy on the basic premise that it was in Iran's national interest to support the Western, particularly American, sponsorship of the formation of a military coalition in the Middle East. The Shah's alliance policy of "positive nationalism" was counterpoised against the policy of "positive neutralism" pursued by self-styled "revolutionary" Arab states led by Egypt. The Arab cold war between the so-called "progressive" and "conservative" states was paralleled by the rising Arab-Iranian cold war which fluctuated with the nuances of the Soviet-American rivalry in the Middle East. Iran's accession to the Baghdad Pact, its endorsement of the Eisenhower Doctrine, and its support of the American intervention in Lebanon were vehemently denounced by both Cairo and Damascus. Throughout the post-Mosaddeq 1950s Iranian policies clashed irreconcilably with those of Egypt, even during the Suez crisis, which some observers mistakenly regarded as an exception. Although Iran did not challenge Egypt's right to nationalize the Suez Canal Company, and joined the United States and the Soviet Union in the Security Council, over the protests of France and Britain, to call for an emergency session of the General Assembly to forestall military action in Egypt, it held to the firm view throughout the crisis that Egypt was responsible (under the Constantinople Convention of 1888) for the maintenance of freedom of navigation through the Canal. Furthermore, Iran invoked the Security Council Resolution of 1 September, 1951, which called on Egypt to terminate restrictions on the passage of ships through the canal. Iran argued that in 1955 alone 73% of its imports and 76% of its exports were transported through the Suez Canal, a fact that inclined the Iranian Foreign Minister to characterize uninterrupted navigation through the Canal as of vital importance to Iran.

Abdel Nasser's characterization of the Baghdad Pact as a "Zionist Plot" was an attempt to link his conflict with Israel with his antagonism toward the Shah's regime. The Egyptian President's displeasure with the Iranian attitude toward Israel found its final expression in Cairo's sudden rupture of diplomatic relations with Iran in 1960. The break was explained as a reaction to the Shah's statement to a foreign correspondent that Iran had recognized Israel years before. Abdel Nasser's denunciation of the Iranian leaders as "colleagues of colonialists," and his attempt to bring about the rupture of other Arab states' diplomatic relations with Iran, culminated in an appeal by the rector of al-Azhar University to the Shah to reconsider his decision to recognize Israel, presumably for the purpose of Muslim unity. The Shah in his reply to Shaykh Shaltut, the Iranian Foreign Ministry in its explanations to Egypt and other Arab countries, and the Iranian press all stated that Iran had recognized Israel in 1950; that the recognition had been *de facto* and had not been withdrawn during the Mosaddeq regime; and that no new decision had been taken to extend *de jure* recognition to Israel. Whatever Abdel Nasser's motivation in breaking Egypt's diplomatic relations with Iran, the important point is that the rupture resulted in a new and significant extension of the acrimonious antagonism between Cairo and Tehran into the Persian Gulf area.

The Trucial States in this region were the focal point of the Egyptian challenge to Iran. The Arab League was chosen as the principal instrument of Egyptian policy in the area. Egypt's campaign agianst the Shah and Britain was launched in 1964—1965. Iran and Britain were painted with the same anti-colonialist brush. They were portrayed as the enemies of the Arab nation and as friends of the Zionist state. Cairo claimed that Iran sold Israeli fresh and dried fruits to the Gulf Shaykhdoms; it charged that Iran planted immigrants in Arab lands of the Gulf for colonialization; and it characterized Iranian policies in the Gulf as inimical to both Arabism and Islam. More peturbing to Tehran than these Egyptian charges was the Syrian propaganda offensive in the region. A vital part of Iranian territory on the Persian Gulf, the rich province of Khuzistan, was made the object of an Arab claim. The fate of the Arabic-speaking inhabitants of this province was likened to that of the Palestinian Arabs, also allegedly living under colonialist rule, this time Zionist occupation. The Ba'th regime in Syria went so far as to declare Khuzistan "an integral part of the Arab Homeland" in 1965. In protest, Iran recalled its ambassador to Syria and closed its embassy in Damascus.

As seen from Tehran, the challenge of radical Arab states to Iranian vital interests in the Persian Gulf took a turn for the worse after the Iraqi revolution of 1958. Until then the challenge from Cairo and Damascus had seemed relatively distant, but after the bloody destruction of the monarchy in Iraq, radical Arab antagonism was brought to the very doorstep of Iran. The existence of the monarchy in Iraq, and Iraq's membership of the Baghdad Pact, had mitigated somewhat the ancient differences between Baghdad and Tehran and had constituted a kind of buffer between Tehran and the radical Arab states, but the emergence of the Qassem regime, its flirtation with the Communists in Iraq and, particularly, its growing *rapprochement* with Moscow appeared to Tehran to spell a far-reaching challenge to Iranian Middle Eastern policy in two major ways: on the one hand, the Soviet power in the Middle East seemed strengthened. The rise of linkage between Arab radicalism and increasing Soviet influence had been first signalled in 1955 in the Soviet arms deal with Egypt. In the meantime British influence, which had suffered during the Suez crisis, received a further blow as a result of the Iraqi revolution and the rise of radicalism in the Gulf area. It seemed from Tehran that, as a result of the revolution in Iraq, a Soviet coalition with radical Arab states was for the first time brought to Iran's southwestern frontiers and the Persian Gulf.

Historically Iran had perceived the Russian threat as emanating primarily from the north along its extensive and vulnerable border with Russia, but now for the first time Iran began to feel an indirect Russian menace emanating from the south as well. Iran thus sought a bilateral American commitment against any kind of aggression, whether originating in the Soviet Union or the radical Arab states. Principally for the same reason, Iran simultaneously entered into negotiations with the Soviet Union aimed at a long-term non-aggression treaty. The commonly held notion that Iran entered discussions with the Soviets simply in order to extract new defense commitments from the United States should be challenged. The principal reason for Iran's desire to discuss a non-aggression treaty with the Soviet Union was to minimize its concern with the Soviet threat from the north, in order to be able to concentrate attention more fully in the Gulf area where its vital interest in coastal and offshore oil, in the freedom of navigation through the Shatt al-'Arab and in the defense of its borders seemed threatened. The breakdown of the Irano–Soviet negotiations, and the conclusion of the Irano-American bilateral defense agreement in 1959, intensified Soviet hostility toward Iran to such a degree that on two separate occasions Soviet Premier Nikita Khrushchev himself vehemently denounced the Shah personally. To be sure, Iran's 1962 pledge to Moscow that it would not allow its territory to be used for missile or rocket bases against the Soviet Union ushered in an unprecedented era of cooperation in direct economic-technical and commercial relations between the two countries.[1]

It is important to note that the Shah's regime was seeking to increase Soviet economic and commercial stakes in Iran, partly to counterbalance the rapid development of the Soviet *rapprochement* with radical Arab states on the one hand, and to increase the Iranian capacity to neutralize indirect Soviet influence through radical Arab states on the other.

Since these basic elements of Iranian foreign policy were not adequately understood, the Iranian attitude during the Six Day War in 1967 was a source of simplistic speculation. Looking at Egypt's past bitter antagonism toward Iran on the one hand, and early reports of Iranian newspapers of the lightning Israeli victory on the other, one could assume that Iran would have openly welcomed the humiliating defeat of Abdel Nasser's army. But when, on the contrary, the Shah called on the Israelis to evacuate the territories they had occupied, it was quickly assumed that, because the Israelis had defeated Abdel Nasser and had thus removed the Egyptian threat to Iran, Iran no longer needed Israel's friendship. This was too facile an explanation, largely because the emerging primacy of the Persian Gulf interest of Iran in the formulation of its Middle Eastern policy was not fully appreciated. Although the defeat of Abdel Nasser might have been privately welcomed, insofar as it symbolized the Arab defeat, it could not be publicly hailed principally because Iran wished not only to avoid antagonizing friendly and moderate Arab states in general, but also to be able to continue to cultivate the friendship of Gulf states in particular.

1967–1973: THE PRIMACY OF THE PERSIAN GULF

The really important event consummating the process of emergence of the Persian Gulf as the center of Iranian Middle Eastern policy was Britain's decision, announced in 1968, to withdraw its forces from East of Suez by the end of 1971. Although the Iraqi revolution and Baghdad's emerging *rapprochement* with the Soviet Union, together with the attitudes of Cairo and Damascus toward Tehran mentioned previously, had already increased Iran's concern with the Gulf area, the British decision was the ultimate catalyst. For almost 150 years the existence of a *Pax Britannica* had insured the security of the Persian Gulf in spite of the fact that the British presence had irked Iran. So long as Iran lacked the power necessary to ensure Gulf security itself it could tolerate the British presence as consonant with its own interests. However, the prospective British departure demanded that the area's security should be protected by other means. With the Iraqi defection from the Baghdad Pact, and now the anticipated British withdrawal from the Gulf area, the CENTO mechanism seemed inadequate for the requirements of local security. Pakistan and Turkey, the regional members of CENTO, had no serious and immediate interest in the Gulf area. Nor did the congeries of Arab Shaykhdoms or Saudi Arabia seem prepared to undertake the responsibility for Gulf security, either by themselves or in cooperation with Iran, in spite of their obviously important interest. Ideally, Iran wished to see the formation of a regional defense arrangement capable of taking over the necessary security functions from the British, but realistically no such arrangement was on the horizon. Iran therefore committed itself from the outset to the principle that it would defend Gulf security in cooperation with the other Gulf states if it could, and would do so by itself if necessary.

Toward this paramount end Iran intensified its military buildup, with the active support of the United States and Britain. The United States' willingness to aid Iran in meeting its new defense responsibilities was of particular importance against the background of traditional American resistance to the acquisition of modern and sophisticated weapons by Iran. The British decision to withdraw from the Gulf broke down the American resistance as evinced by the initial promise of President Johnson to help build up the Iranian defense system in spite of the United States' own needs at the height of the Vietnam War. America delivered to Iran the long-sought Phantom fighter-bombers through the United States Navy. There is no need to discuss here in detail the well-publicized military buildup in Iran. Suffice it to state that by the time of the British departure in 1971 Iran had already made itself the most powerful state in the Persian Gulf, and was apparently ready and willing to defend the area, either in cooperation with other littoral states or alone.

Greater publicity given by the Western press to the Iranian military buildup tended to leave the impression that Iran relied exclusively on military prowess for the achievement of its objectives. But as a matter of fact Iran's extensive diplomatic efforts paralleled its rapid military buildup. In anticipation of the British withdrawal Iran launched a vigorous campaign to cultivate the friendship of like-minded Gulf states. The Shah's major visits to Saudi Arabia and Kuwait in 1968 were followed by Iran's single most important friendly gesture toward the Arab states in 1969. The Shah announced in New Delhi his decision to relinquish, in effect, Iran's historical claim to Bahrein. The settlement of the Bahrein dispute through the good offices of the Secretary-General of the United Nations in 1970 represented only the first spectacular conciliatory Iranian move toward the Arab states in general. The settlement or near settlement of numerous other disputes with Saudi Arabia, Qatar, Bahrein, Dubay, Abu Dhabi and others, helped Iran extend its diplomatic, economic and commercial relations with a growing number of states within the Gulf area in particular.

The offer to settle the Bahrein dispute peacefully was also used to achieve a far more important objective of Iran in the Gulf in anticipation of the British withdrawal in 1971. Briefly stated, Iran first took the position that it would withhold recognition from any prospective Arab federation in the Gulf area until the Bahrein dispute was settled. Once progress toward its settlement was being made, it became increasingly clear that the real object of Iran was to acquire the three strategic islands of Abu Musa and the two Tunbs which Iran also claimed. The establishment of the Iranian presence on these islands was considered in Tehran vitally important to the security of the Gulf in general and of the strategic Straits of Hormuz in particular. Thus, in essence, the relinquishment of the ancient claim to Bahrein was used as a bargaining chip in negotiations with the British regarding the future of the three islands. As it turned out, however, the Iranian forces landed on the two Tunbs in the face of the opposition of the Shaykh of Ras al-Khayma, who claimed the islands, while the Shaykh of Sharjah reached an agreement with Iran just before the landing of Iranian forces on the island of Abu Musa.

Reactions of the Arab states were universally unfavorable, although by no means uniform. The most moderate stance was adopted by Egypt, although Cairo did call for the withdrawal of Iranian forces from the three islands. The most vehement opposition—expressed within the Arab league, within the United Nations, and through ordinary diplomatic channels—emanated from Libya, Iraq and South Yemen. Iraq broke diplomatic relations with Iran and urged other Arab states to do the same. The reactions of Iraq and South Yemen were of greater concern to Iran than that of Libya. As has already been mentioned, Irano–Iraqi antagonism began to intensify after the Iraqi revolution of 1958, but power rivalry between Baghdad and Tehran began to surface from the time of the announcement of the British withdrawal. The age-old Shatt al-'Arab dispute, and such other traditional controversies as the status of Iranian residents in Iraq and the Kurdish problem, were now permeated by a new bid for influence in the Gulf. Prior to 1968 the hopes for peaceful settlement of traditional issues had been rekindled as the result of the Shah-'Arif summit meeting in Tehran, but with the rise of the Ahmad Hasan al-Bakr regime in Iraq in 1968 on the one hand, and the announcement in the same year of the forthcoming British withdrawal on the other, all chances of settlement seemed to disappear. As a matter of fact, relations between the two countries deteriorated dangerously as evinced by escalation of border clashes, deportation of thousands of Iranians from Iraq, covert Iranian involvement in the

Kurdish struggle and the moral and material aid given by Iraq to the Baluchi uprising in Pakistan.

It may well be that the landing of Iranian forces on the three islands contributed to the conclusion of the Iraqi–Soviet treaty of April 1972. Nevertheless, this treaty was of such a nature that it appeared in Tehran that the Soviets were deliberately casting their lot with the Iraqis, in spite of their professed desire for good neighborly cooperation with Iran. The text of the treaty, the statement of the Soviet Deputy Foreign Minister, and the accompanying communiqué, evinced even to more objective observers that the new *rapprochement* between Baghdad and Moscow clearly amounted to an anti-Western political alliance which cast the Soviet Union in the role of champion of radical anti-Iranian Arab states in the Persian Gulf area. Tehran made no effort to hide its great displeasure with this fresh source of tension between Iran and the Soviet Union.

The strong opposition of South Yemen to the Iranian landing on the three islands was also a manifestation of deeper cleavages between Aden and Tehran. Not only had the South Yemeni regime declared itself openly anti-Iranian from the beginning, but its Persian Gulf policies clashed sharply with those of Iran ever since South Yemen's independence at the end of 1967. Soviet intrusion into the picture by way of supporting the "Popular Front for the Liberation of the Occupied Arab Gulf" (PFLOAG) complicated the situation for Iran. The overthrow of the Sultan of Oman by his son in 1970, and the subsequent reforms launched by the new sultan were welcomed in Tehran as a sign of the rise of a moderate regime in Oman. The new Omani regime did not appear to impress the Soviets, who regarded it as the product of a British maneuver, and a new "Imperialist plot" against the Arab "liberation movement" in the Gulf area. The Front's aim of creating a revolutionary Arab state in Oman, and then spreading the revolution throughout the Gulf area to include Iran, struck at the heart of Iran's Persian Gulf policy. To Tehran, success for the rebels of Dhofar could have spelled disaster for the general security and political stability of the entire Gulf area, including most particularly the strategic Straits of Hormuz at the entrance of the Gulf. For this important reason Iran welcomed Sultan Qabus' invitation to military aid in his struggle against the Dhofari rebels. According to Omani sources, the Sultan's request for aid from Iran was made only after the Arab states had failed to fulfill their promises of aid to Oman.

Apart from the opposition of Iraq and South Yemen, the relatively restrained position of other Gulf states was partly a reflection of the success of Iranian diplomacy prior to the British departure. As has already been mentioned, Iran's relinquishment of its ancient claim to Bahrein had a favorable impact on most Arab states including those of the Gulf area. The Iranian Majlis endorsed the wish of the people of Bahrein for political independence. The Iranian Government sent a goodwill mission to Bahrein and received a Bahreini mission in Tehran, abolished visa requirements between the two countries and signed a continental shelf accord which was considered in both Manama and Tehran as a significant step in the new Bahreini—Iranian relations. In anticipation of the British withdrawal Iran also improved its relations with Qatar, as evinced by the signing of a continental shelf accord in 1969 and the first state visit of the Qatari ruler to Tehran in 1970. Iran recognized Bahreini and Qatari independence barely one hour after they were declared, and before these new Gulf states received recognition from any other country.

The primacy of the Persian Gulf in Iran's Middle Eastern policy between 1967 and 1973 was evident not only in the nature and scope of its relations with the Gulf states, but also with the non-Gulf states of the Middle East as well. Outside the Gulf area, Iran launched an offensive to gain the friendship of the Arab states in anticipation of the British departure and the expectation of the subsequent consolidation of the Iranian position in the Gulf area. Only a few months before the British departure, for example, diplomatic relations with Lebanon—which had been ruptured over the problem of the extradition of the former head of the Iranian security police—were resumed after a visit of former President Chamoun to Tehran.

The single most important example of the primacy of the Persian Gulf in Iran's Middle Eastern policy between 1967 and 1973 is the resumption of diplomatic relations with Egypt after a decade. To be sure, observers at the time advanced various explanations for the sudden change of heart between Tehran and Cairo. One explanation was that the attitude of Iran in the Six Day War of 1967 had helped to heal old wounds between the Shah and Abdel Nasser. In the wake of the war the Shah had called for the restoration of Arab territories.[2] The other explanation was that the resumption of diplomatic relations was a reflection of the conflict between Cairo and Baghdad. Egyptian—Iraqi relations had been deteriorating since the rise of Bakr to power in Iraq, and

President Abdel Nasser's acceptance of the United States ceasefire initiative—the so-called Rogers Initiative of 1970.

While both these explanations would seem to make some sense, the resumption of diplomatic relations with Egypt was decisively influenced by the situation in the Persian Gulf. This move fitted perfectly the pattern of Iran's determined efforts to seek accommodation with as many Middle Eastern states as possible, in anticipation of the departure of the British in 1971 and the subsequent consolidation of the Iranian position first and foremost in the Persian Gulf area. Tehran had always considered Egypt as the principal Arab state and the one whose friendship could serve Iran's best interests. At that juncture Iran's greatest interest was to ensure that if its negotiations with Britain regarding the future of the three islands failed, its planned unilateral military action for regaining the islands would not be roundly condemned by Arab states. The Iranian calculation paid off handsomely. As has already been mentioned, when Iran did land forces on the three islands Egypt evinced a moderately adverse reaction as compared with the radical Arab states.

Finally, the primacy of the Persian Gulf in Iran's Middle Eastern policy was revealed in its attitudes and actions during the October War of 1973. At the time of the fighting Iran called for Israeli withdrawal from occupied territories (which it had also done in the wake of the 1967 war), airlifted medical supplies to Jordan, sent pilots and planes to Saudi Arabia to help with logistical problems, permitted the overflight of some Soviet planes supplying the Arabs, and consented to the resumption of diplomatic relations with Iraq (requested by the latter for the obvious purpose of concentrating efforts in the war against Israel). It refused to permit passage over Iran of volunteers from Australia to fly to Israel. From all this, one might conclude superficially that the Iranian position simply tilted toward the Arab states. Some observers believed during the 1967 war that Iran ignored Israel's interests as soon as its principal enemy of the moment, Egypt, was defeated. In the same simplistic way one might conclude today that Iran had totally endorsed the Arab stand against Israel because the Arabs initially made a relatively good showing of their capabilities in the October War. In other words, one might suppose that in the 1967 war Iran totally neglected Israel's concerns because of its victory, and in the 1973 war did the same because of its initial setback.

THE PRINCIPAL OBJECTIVES OF IRAN'S MIDDLE EASTERN POLICY

If one is to avoid the pitfalls of superficial conclusions, the assessment of any aspect of Iran's Middle Eastern policy between 1967 and 1973, and all the more so today, must perforce take into account the fundamental objectives and strategies of that country's policy in the Persian Gulf. I would like to conclude my remarks, therefore, by identifying the principal objectives of Iran's Middle Eastern policy in the light of the above analysis of its most basic interests and objectives in the Persian Gulf sub-region.

Iran has three primary objectives in the Gulf. These are, firstly, the protection of the Shah's regime and the Pahlavi dynasty against internal subversion, sponsored directly or indirectly by radical Arab states or groups or by a Soviet proxy; secondly, the preservation of free transit through the Straits of Hormuz, the Gulf and the Shatt al-'Arab; and thirdly, the protection of Iranian coastal and offshore oil resources and facilities against deliberate or accidental disruptions. The basic objectives of Iran in the larger region of the Middle East are, in the last analysis, the extension of its sub-regional Gulf objectives. These are also three. First, neutralization and curtailment of Soviet power and influence in the area; second, isolation of radical Arab states and groups and support of the relatively moderate ones; third, preservation of the freedom of navigation in such international waterways as the Straits of Bab al-Mandab and the Suez Canal.

In a real sense, an understanding of these basic objectives can shed light also on the beginnings of Iran's policies in South Asia during the 1967–1973 period as well as its more recent policies in the vast regions of the southeastern Pacific, but a consideration of these aspects of Iranian regional policies is beyond the scope of this discussion.

NOTES

1. The analysis of the complex mixture of internal and external circumstances underlying the Iranian pledge and the associated normalization of relations with the Soviet Union is beyond the scope of this paper.

2. Iran had also dispatched medical and similar aid to Iraq and Jordan through the Red Lion and Sun (the Iranian equivalent of the Red Cross).

Stability and Tension in the Persian Gulf

Aryeh Shmuelevitz

Between 1967 and 1973, there occurred perhaps the most far-reaching developments in the Persian Gulf area, both as regards the region itself and its foreign relations with the other Middle Eastern countries on the one hand, and with the entire world on the other.

MAJOR DEVELOPMENTS

British Withdrawal

One of the most important events was the decision, taken in 1968 by the British Labor Government and finally implemented by the Conservative Government toward the end of 1971, to withdraw the British presence from the Persian Gulf. Bahrein, Qatar, the United Arab Emirates (formerly the Trucial Coast) and Oman, all gained formal independence. It is noteworthy that during 1969–1970, the Conservative Government wavered about carrying through the withdrawal. This hesitation brought about a broad alliance of expediency between those states which wanted the British to implement their decision to withdraw. Iran and Saudi Arabia, in particular, were determined to use this opportunity to keep the Powers out of the Gulf. They were supported by Iraq and some other Arab states. It became clear, however, that several of the smaller principalities in the Gulf would gladly have welcomed a decision by the British to retain their forces in the Gulf, and some of them even offered Britain substantial payments to offset the cost of maintaining those forces. But the small principalities were unable to counter the pressure exerted by states such as Iran and Saudi Arabia. After the withdrawal, the British remained in the Gulf both as instructors and advisers in the various armies that were established there, and also in active service as mercenaries, for example, as pilots in the Abu Dhabi air force.

Expansion of Economic Power

Another momentous development has undoubtedly been the rise of the politico-economic power of the region due to its immense oil wealth. Perhaps the best way to exemplify this development during the period under discussion is to compare the results of the oil embargo imposed in 1967 after the Six Day War, with the effects of the embargo imposed in 1973 during and after the October War. There is no need to enquire whether the embargo itself was justified in fact and whether it was a total success. The salient fact is that the Gulf states became extremely conscious of the power they held, and they exploited this power to apply maximum pressure—not to mention the huge (fourfold) rise in the price of oil which further increased their politico-economic power.

Their increased power—for which the well known saying "whoever pays the piper calls the tune" might well serve as a motto—found expression in both the inter-Arab and international spheres. The threat to the conservative regimes of the Gulf countries by the so-called progressive states led by Egypt gradually receded after 1967, chiefly because of Egypt's dependence on the substantial contributions of the oil-rich states. In the international sphere the Gulf states exerted political pressure and could begin to successfully negotiate cooperation in a wide range of economic fields on their own terms. Even more important, they began to expand their capital investments in major enterprises throughout the world, including investments in the experimentation with new forms of energy. Two implications emanate from this: the Gulf states will have their own new energy reserves when their own oil reserves are depleted, while maintaining their influence on global supplies of energy—in whatever form. Furthermore, during this period new oil strikes led to additional Gulf emirates—such as Abu Dhabi, Oman and Dubay—joining the alignment of oil producing states.

Internal Development

The discoveries of oil, its production, and its subsequent rise in price, brought in their wake another major development, a massive economic-social revolution because the principalities increasingly began to divert their oil revenues into fostering domestic development on the model of Kuwait. Until 1967, it was mainly the Iranians and the Kuwaitis who had channeled their huge oil income toward these goals, but they were now joined by the principalities and also by Saudi Arabia.

We are witness to the phenomenon of these countries being turned into modern welfare states, although they still have a long way to go. Great impetus was given to the development of desert agriculture, vast housing projects were constructed, and several emirates began the process of settling the nomads: Abu Dhabi, for instance, initiated a five year plan to settle its nomads. Most striking of all are the investments made by all these states in the fields of education and health during the period under discussion. Students receive stipendia ($5,000−$8,000) as an inducement to continue their studies, rather than immediately entering the labor market, where the demand for workers is ever-increasing.

This momentum in economic development and social progress has already begun to leave its mark in the form of the rise of an educated affluent elite alongside the traditional tribal tribal ruling elite; the new social elite is beginning to exert pressure in some places for change in the regime, although it is still well integrated within it. This elite will certainly continue to grow and in the future will constitute a strong pressure group which perhaps, may even attempt to seize power.

Political Development

All the regimes are still traditional, vested in traditional rulers. Following the British withdrawal the position of these rulers was strengthened, first by the British themselves, who had learned from the failure of the transfer of power in the Aden Colony and Protectorates (now the People's Democratic Republic of Yemen), but mainly because of their substantial oil revenues and the cooperation among the Gulf states to maintain the *status quo*. But several features of the period do indicate certain developments which could cause alarm to the traditional exclusivist governments.

Firstly, in several emirates and states there has been movement in the direction of more constitutional government, and several so-called parliaments were set up during the period under discussion. The power of these parliaments remained extremely limited—in fact they were merely advisory bodies—but, together with the parliaments, the rulers established modern ministries and granted them considerable operational authority. These ministries began to absorb personnel who, although they were not of the ruling families, nonetheless were given key roles such as directorships of oil ministries or of ministries of the interior, and the like.

Secondly, palace revolts—in which members of the ruling family were involved—occurred with relative frequency. More important and more interesting than the revolts themselves are the reasons cited for them. Generally, the new incumbent claimed that the overthrown ruler was too conservative and too traditional, that he was not suitable for the spirit of the age, that he failed to carry out plans for development and progress, and that he showed no consideration for his subjects. This is an important departure which can lead to a change in the character of such regimes; at first perhaps through the establishment of semi-democratic institutions, as mentioned above, but in the long term also by means of radical change, such as occurred in a state not far from the Gulf—Afghanistan—where, within the framework of a palace revolt, a republican regime was formed with a member of the royal family as president.

Thirdly, underground movements began to form opposition to the traditional regimes, and information was occasionally filtered through to the outside world of explosive charges going off (for instance, near the palace of the ruler of Abu Dhabi or in the palace of the ruler of Sharjah) or of an attempt on the life of this or that ruler (for instance, the ruler of Oman). All this took place simultaneously with underground activity in the larger countries of the Gulf, such as Iran and Saudi Arabia. The most notorious of these underground movements is the Popular Front for the Liberation of the Occupied Arabian Gulf (PFLOAG), which was very active in the Dhofar region of southwest Oman, and whose branches also operated in the other Gulf principalities. Except for the PFLOAG's own declarations, information was meager.

Together with the appearance of new forces and new elites we see the disappearance of long-standing conflicts between various traditional forces. One conspicuous example of this phenomenon has been the gradual extinction of the long-standing conflict between the Sultan and the Imam of Oman. Another example, no less important, is the establishment of the Federation of the Gulf Emirates in spite of the traditional feuds between their rulers and tribes.

Growth of Military Power

Another very important feature of the period under discussion has been the military aggrandizement of the states involved; this phenomena appears alongside the increase in political and economic power and applies to almost all the Gulf states. The stress is on the desire of the states in the region themselves to fill the vacuum created by the British withdrawal. Here, too, the oil revenues are central, in that they provide the funds to purchase vast quantities of the most modern weapons, to train local personnel and to hire experts from abroad. Iran which sees itself as the largest and strongest power in the Gulf, has determined to play the central role in its defense and takes the leading role in this military aggrandizement. Concurrently, the power of the Arab states of Iraq (with Soviet assistance) and Saudi Arabia (with US assistance) is constantly increasing. The smaller emirates too—such as Kuwait, Qatar, Bahrein, Abu Dhabi and Oman—have, in accordance with their financial capability, joined the large states in the race for power.

Their military build-up binds these states to the global powers through arms supply, training and the building of military installations, and enables the latter to maintain a foothold in the Gulf, always with the possibility of increasing their influence in the future. The chief arms suppliers of the Gulf states are the Americans. Moreover, Iran is tied to the United States through a series of agreements for defense and military cooperation, and Bahrein has leased a former British base to the Americans. It is true that in the wake of the October War the Americans were asked to evacuate this base, but they are still maintaining it. The USSR, not content with providing arms and training to the Iraqi army, has also attempted to become a procurer of weapons for other emirates in the area, such as Kuwait. The Soviets are also building a large naval base at Umm Qasr in southern Iraq and consolidating their hold on the Republic of South Yemen not far from the Gulf.

FACTORS FAVORING MAINTENANCE OF STABILITY

The danger of great power involvement in a possible conflict in this extraordinarily rich Gulf, along with internal developments which could perhaps undermine the firm hold of the traditional regimes, led the states in the region, especially Iran and Saudi Arabia, to draw up several basic principles for a common policy of the Gulf states.

The most important and perhaps the most hallowed principle among the states of the region—a principle which the Iranians formulated—is that the region will be defended exclusively by the littoral states. They themselves will guarantee free navigation in the Persian Gulf, the Gulf of Oman, and the Indian Ocean, and will do everything in their power to prevent the area from becoming an arena for great power conflict. This principle stems from the fact that the Gulf is a vital lifeline to these states, as the entire future depends on the free flow of oil; any stoppage of oil from the Gulf could lead to their disintegration. Iran, more than any other country in the Gulf, knows from past experience what a stoppage in the flow of oil entails.

The second principle, related to the first and also accepted by the majority of the states in the Gulf, is that of preserving peace and stability within each state and in their reciprocal relations. In pursuance of this principle several of the states in the region made far-reaching concessions to one another solely in order to maintain the general *status quo*. First and foremost, Iran waived its historic claim to Bahrein in order to remove the main obstacle to closer cooperation between itself and its Arab neighbors. However, the Iranians did not relinquish their claim to Bahrein without compensation, which took the form of control by Iran, as the strongest power in the area, over the entrance to the Persian Gulf. Iran took practical steps to make this a reality through the military occupation of the three islands—the Greater and Lesser Tunbs, and Abu Musa—situated in the mouth of the Persian Gulf, northwest of the Strait of Hormuz, on the only route for tankers bound for and leaving the Persian Gulf. Though considerable tension was created in Iran's relations with the Arab states after the seizure of the islands, it was Saudi Arabia, and along with it some other Arab countries, that finally yielded and agreed to Iranian control over them. Iraq, South Yemen and Libya continued to voice objections. However, this quasi-agreement was facilitated by the fact that a settlement was reached between the Iranians and the emirates of Sharjah and Ras al-Khayma, which previously claimed the islands. In consequence Iran and Saudi Arabia could continue to implement the gentlemen's agreement they had reached following the British decision on the withdrawal, for the division of the Gulf into Iranian and Saudi Arabian spheres of influence.

In order to maintain stability in the Gulf, Iran rendered effective military aid to the Sultan of Oman in his war against the Dhofar rebels, aid clearly intended to preserve the Omani regime as well as to eliminate the rebel movement, which is also striving to undermine the regimes of the other Gulf emirates, and which is supported by the pro-Soviet regime in the Republic of South Yemen. The Iranians also pressured the Chinese into withholding their support and aid from the rebels in Dhofar. Apparently, Iranian pressure achieved its end in no small measure thanks to the pragmatic approach of the Chinese, for whom it is expedient to be on terms of understanding and cooperation with the Gulf states in the hope of preventing the Russians from gaining a stronger foothold in the Gulf.

Furthermore, there is the need to reach a prompt agreement of the division of the Persian Gulf itself between the littoral states, because of the vast quantities of oil beneath the waters of the Gulf. Ownership of these waters must be determined as clearly as possible before the oil can be extracted, and serious friction be avoided.

FACTORS CONTRIBUTING TOWARD TENSION

This last point underlines the fact that between 1967 and 1973 there were still several focal points of tension and conflict which might have threatened the peace and stability of the Gulf states, and might still do so.

One of the clearest foci of discord revolves around Iraq's share in the waters of the Gulf. The Iraqis have a very narrow corridor to the Persian Gulf but they are demanding a larger share of the Gulf coast at the expense of their neighbors on either side—Iran and Kuwait. Furthermore, the dispute betwen Sharjah and Ras al-Khayma concerning their rights in the region of the three islands, mentioned above, has by no means been finally settled.

A second cause of tension is to be found in Iraqi—Kuwaiti relations. After 1961 it appeared that Iraq had finally relinquished its claims on Kuwait, but by the end of the period these claims were introduced anew, which led to a real military threat to the territorial integrity of Kuwait, and to an Iranian warning of a military response.

A third source of tension exists in the sphere of Iranian—Iraqi relations, which occasionally erupt in sharp clashes along their mutual border, as they particularly did after the Iranians unilaterally abrogated the sovereignty agreements on the Shatt al-'Arab in 1969. The dispute between the two countries is well-known; other sources of conflict involving Iraq and Iran during the period include Kurdish—Iraqi tension and Iraqi aid to the Baluchis in southeast Iran.

A fourth source of tension, which cannot be ignored in this framework, is the slogan which calls for the preservation of the Arab character of the Gulf; this slogan is occasionally voiced by those opposed to cooperation with Iran and finds expression in various spheres in the relations of the Arab Gulf states to Iran. There is no need to recall the demand to rename the Persian Gulf the Arabian Gulf, or Arab insistence on Iran breaking off relations with Israel, but it is worth noting, for example, the effort of Saudi Arabia, an ally of Iran, to have the Iranian expeditionary force in Oman replaced by an Arab expeditionary force (of Jordanian and Sudanese) in order to prevent the Iranians from gaining a foothold on the Arabian Peninsula, or the difference of opinion between Saudi Arabia and Iran on oil price policy. Efforts are also being made to prevent several of the emirates in the Gulf, especially those comprising the United Arab Emirates, from forming too close-knit alliances with Iran.

A fifth cause of tension is to be found in the issue of the delineation of the borders between the Gulf emirates. It is true that much effort has been made to relax focal points of tension on the borders, examples of which are the division of the neutral zone between Saudi Arabia and Kuwait and the compromise over the Buraymi Oasis. But from time to time bordermarkers are shifted, or the movement of tribes from one emirate to another involves a local dispute; events which are followed by great efforts at pacification. This applies mainly to the borders between the emirates constituting the United Arab Emirates, but it is noteworthy that, in the period under review, the border between the UAE and Saudi Arabia had not yet been fixed. Nor had sovereignty over the islands between Qatar and Bahrein yet been determined.

Another factor leading to the disruption of internal stability is the attitude of the emirates to the foreign Arabs who have entered their territories to find work. The local governments flagrantly discriminate in various spheres between local-born and foreigners: many positions, especially key appointments, are closed to foreigners; they are not permitted to set up enterprises or open businesses without a locally-born partner; many grants are not given them, etc. Often there are reports of expulsion of foreign Arabs from the emirates, not infrequently on the charge that they are cooperating with local subversive elements. There are also significant numbers of Iranians in the emirates and an increasing immigration of Iranian citizens. This attitude of the rulers toward the foreigners may give Iran an ostensible excuse for intervention.

Subversive and radical elements are, of course, an additional source of tension. It would be difficult to define these elements, but they certainly originate amongst the young, educated, financially-established generation which, more and more, is involved in the larger world. This generation, which is constantly expanding, constitutes a threat to the stability of the region, at least as regards the continuity of the traditional regimes.

A final, though no less important, factor in producing tension is the great power competition in the Gulf region. It is true that during the period under discussion the Gulf states did make efforts to prevent the region from being caught up in the great power conflict; that they also succeeded was largely due to the fact that the Suez Canal was closed during this period, which considerably slowed down the consolidation of the great powers in the Gulf area. But the great powers did begin to entrench themselves in and around the Gulf, mainly in the Indian Ocean. For the USSR, this took the form of strengthening its position in Iraq and the People's Republic of South Yemen on the one side, and in India on the other side (especially in the light of the Indo–Pakistan war of 1971–1972), and of attempts to obtain naval bases and facilities in the Indian Ocean islands of Socotra and Mauritius, and in South Yemen and Somalia. Nor did the British or Americans merely sit back in this period; they too developed naval bases in the Diego Garcia islands of the Indian Ocean. Among the Gulf states, it seems that the Iranians were the only ones to enter the arena of the Indian Ocean, through a rapid development of air and naval bases along the Persian coast of the ocean, and they made strenuous efforts to prevent the great powers, especially the Russians, from further consolidating themselves. For example, the Iranians agreed to give an undisclosed amount of aid to Mauritius in return for Mauritius' undertaking to give the Iranian Navy the right to use its port facilities, and to deny those facilities to the Soviet Navy.

Moreover, since the Indo–Pakistan war had exposed the weakness of CENTO, and the danger inherent in the intervention of the great powers in that conflict, relations between Iran and Pakistan were tightened and the CENTO treaty was renewed in a more binding form, especially as regards the Indian Ocean. Nor did this prevent Iran and India from making the effort to renew their ties and cooperation—India for fear of growing Pakistani influence in the rich Gulf emirates, and Iran with the aim of enlisting India in support of the principle of safeguarding the entire region from great power intervention. The People's Republic of China, which at the outset of the period still supported radical subversive movements, apparently retreated from this line, and toward the end of the period was more concerned that the Russians, their rivals, should not be able to consolidate themselves in the Gulf as a bridgehead to Southeast Asia.

● ● ● ●

The littoral states of the oil-rich Gulf are fully aware of all the factors which contribute to tension. In the years 1967–1973 the Gulf states devoted considerable efforts to removing these and other tensions and to safeguarding the stability of the region so as to preserve it from great power rivalry, while simultaneously increasing their own economic, political, and military power; in their view this policy can only assist them in preserving the peace and in securing their region's independent future.

The Persian Gulf as a Focus for Regional Conflicts[1]

Mordechai Abir

Despite the uninterrupted historical importance of the Persian Gulf, the peoples who inhabit its shores have always been backward and relatively uninfluential. Even the empires which arose in Persia and Mesopotamia were not oriented toward the Gulf and their contribution to its history was minimal. There has been no lack of tension in the Gulf in the past, but with few exceptions it has been local in character and of little consequence in the wider context. The discovery of oil in Iran in the 19th century and in the Gulf itself in the 20th century led the area to become an active, rather than merely a passive, factor in Middle Eastern and international affairs.

Several basic factors have had an impact on the accelerating process of socio-political change which the Gulf has been undergoing in recent years. Firstly, until recent times, the Gulf was among the backwaters of Western (mainly British) influence, although other powers were also interested in the region. The decline of British influence and the growing importance of the region's oil caused the Gulf to rise to prominence in the sphere of international and regional power politics. Secondly, the Gulf is a cultural-ethnic-religious watershed where the Arab (*Sunni*) and Irani (*Shi'i*) spheres overlap, a fact which has caused political tension. Apart from oil, Iran's interests and political aspirations are different from, and to some extent even contrary to those of most Arab countries. Thirdly, there are fundamental asymmetries in the region. This small and backward part of the world controls nearly 60% of the world's proven oil reserves. There is a vast disproportion between the tiny population of most of the Gulf countries and their revenues from oil (see Table A). The majority of Gulf countries are among the most backward in the Middle East, despite their fabulous wealth, and are ruled by the most conservative of regimes. With the exceptions of Iran and Iraq, the Gulf countries have unusually large immigrant communities on which their economies and, in some cases, their administrations depend. Notwithstanding financial resources, eastern Arabia's oil producers lack almost every factor essential for economic development and diversification. Finally, Iran has a population which is larger than that of all other Gulf countries combined and has the potential for diversified economic development.

Two interrelated factors have been directly responsible for the rising importance of the Gulf in connection with the major tension-complexes in the Middle East. The first is Britain's 1968 declaration of intent to evacuate the Gulf by the end of 1971, and the resultant repercussions on local and power politics. The second has been the growing strength and cooperation of the member countries of the "Organization of Petroleum Exporting Countries (OPEC) and the "Organization of Arab Petroleum Exporting Countries" (OAPEC) since the turn of the 1960s. This was mainly the outcome of the United States becoming a net oil importer in about 1970. With OPEC beginning to flex its muscles in 1971, following the Tehran and Tripoli conferences, it was not long before it (and OAPEC) began to dictate terms to the consumers. This paper will attempt, *inter alia*, to establish a correlation between OPEC's ability to force its will on the industrial West, the decline of Western power in the Gulf and Soviet strategy in the region. Three potential conflict-complexes, affected by the Gulf becoming a central focus of tension in the Middle East, will be discussed in this paper: 1. inter-Arab relations; 2. power politics in the Gulf region; and 3. tensions between Arabs and non-Arabs in the Middle East, namely, the Arab–Israeli conflict and Arab–Iranian relations.

INTER–ARAB RELATIONS

For the sake of convenience, scholars tend to classify Arab countries as "progressive," "moderate" or "conservative." No less important as far as this analysis is concerned is the distinction between the "haves" and "have-nots" in relation to oil. Although the most important Arab oil producers could be classified as "conservative," the "have-nots" (including all the "confrontations states") consist of "progressive," "moderate" and even "conservative" regimes. There is, therefore, a marked correlation between the "haves" and "have-nots" classification and the asymmetries existing in the Gulf area.

Undoubtedly, one of the most dramatic changes the Arab world has experienced over the past decade is the position of leadership which Saudi Arabia has achieved. Only a decade ago the Pan-Arabists, led by Abdel Nasser, were still trying to breach the fortress of conservatism in the Arabian Peninsula. Saudi Arabia, however, showed surprising resilience and was, to some extent, instrumental in the downfall of Nasserism. Though continuously challenged by the "progressive" regimes, especially Libya (since 1970), King Faisal succeeded after 1967 in smoothing over his differences with what is now considered the "moderate" camp led by Egypt by, *inter alia*, granting that country and other "confrontation states" financial aid.

King Faisal, who considered the spread of Communism a threat to Islam, was said to be devoted to combating Soviet influence in the Arab countries. For a time, therefore, he became a target of subversion, emanating from the Soviet Union's Arab allies, and of Soviet propaganda which was, suprisingly, limited and mild. Far from suffering however, Saudi Arabia succeeded in enticing the Yemen Arab Republic (YAR) into the "moderate" camp and in forming a *cordon sanitaire* around the People's Democratic Republic of Yemen (PDRY),[2] the Soviet Union's staunchest Arab friend. Since 1967, having improved his relations with the Syrian Ba'th regime, Faisal tried unsuccessfully to drive a wedge between Damascus and the USSR. In cooperation with Iran, Saudi Arabia blocked Iraq's attempts to expand in the direction of the Gulf and to subvert its weak rulers.[3] Faisal's role in the successful exploitation of the "oil weapon" during and after the 1973 October War, and his country's enormous financial resources and control of about a third of the Western world's proven oil reserves, unquestionably established his position of leadership in the Arab camp. More recently, due to Saudi Arabia's growing self-confidence and possibly also to suspicion and jealousy of Iran, she viewed favorably, and even encouraged attempts to "re-Arabize" the PDRY while improving her own relations with Iraq "for the sake of Arab solidarity."[4] Having preserved Arab cooperation and unity, Faisal emerged from the 1974 Rabat summit conference (where he subtly eroded Dr. Kissinger's policy) even stronger than before.

The anomalies which exist today in eastern Arabia are the result of British 19th and early 20th century imperialism, which halted sociopolitical dynamism in the region. Nevertheless Saudi Arabia now looms like a giant among minions in the Arabian Peninsula. When Britain announced its intention to evacuate the Gulf by 1971, Saudi Arabia, Iraq and Iran welcomed this decision. However, the rulers of the eastern Arabian principalities were thrown into panic. The asymmetries discussed above applied most closely to them, and their oil wealth was bound to tempt their stronger neighbors, whether "moderate" or "progressive."

Widely publicized in the 1950s, the conflict between Saudi Arabia, Abu Dhabi and Oman over the area of Buraymi was until recently the cause of constant tension in the region. Due to the realistic policy of Sultan Qabus the Omani–Saudi differences were settled in 1972, leading to close cooperation between the two "conservative" regimes. Thus, not only was the Rub' al-Khali route closed to the Marxist Dhofari rebels, but Oman began to receive financial as well as logistic and military aid (with Jordanian cooperation) from Saudi Arabia.[5] More complicated was the solution of the Saudi conflict with Abu Dhabi because in addition to Buraymi it involved a good part of Abu Dhabi's territory. Moreover, the Saudi claim to Khor Udayd, on the Abu Dhabi coast, implied introducing a wedge between Abu Dhabi and Qatar. This conflict was only resolved in August 1974, as a result of political developments in the Gulf and the pressure exerted on Shaykh Zayid of Abu Dhabi by Western and "moderate" Arab countries. Though it gave up its claim to Buraymi proper, Saudi Arabia gained, *inter alia*, through the annexation of Khor Udayd, and outlet to the "lower Gulf" which is of unquestionable military, political and economic importance. Moreover, the consolidated "conservative" front in eastern Arabia served, in a way, as a mutual protection organization against internal subversion and external intervention, mainly from Iran or Iraq.[6] It was bound to affect Iraq's policy in the Gulf and would hinder any new attempt to annex Kuwait. Anyway Iraq decided to give up, temporarily, its aggressive policy in the Gulf since 1973. By the beginning of 1975 it even signed an agreement with Iran, resolving most outstanding differences between the two countries, mainly in order to preserve OPEC unity. This however did not indicate a basic change in Iraq's revolutionary ideology and the principles guiding its policy in the Gulf.

The annexation of Kuwait is considered a political and strategic necessity by Iraq due to the latter's tiny share of the Gulf coast, and the Kuwaiti islands which block its approaches. Moreover, if Iraq were to control Kuwait, it could become the second largest oil producing country in the world, with revenues approaching those of Saudi Arabia. Iraq's position in the Arab camp and its importance in the world would change dramatically, as would the balance of power in the Gulf. Aware of this potential threat, Saudi Arabia and Iran were determined to prevent such a development.

The West has also been closely watching events in Kuwait, because an Iraqi gain could not only spark off a chain reaction in the region, but would mean an important strategic advantage for the Soviet Union, which has a friendship and defense treaty with Iraq. Claiming rightful ownership, Iraq tried to annex Kuwait in 1961 and was only prevented from doing so by British intervention. The traumatic experience of 1961 led Kuwait's rulers to follow a policy which, with some variation, was later adopted by most east Arabian rulers. A large part of the oil revenues has been channeled to the population through an extensive network of social services and a development fund established to help the economy of "sister" Arab countries. Moreover, together with other Arab oil producers, Kuwait undertook at the Khartoum summit conference of 1967 to subsidize the "confrontation states." These subsidies have been considerably increased since 1967 and include grants to the Palestine Liberation Organization (PLO).[7]

Following its friendship and defense agreement with the Soviet Union in April 1972, Iraq began with Soviet aid to expand the port of Umm Qasr, where facilities were granted to the Soviet navy. This port was, however, strategically handicapped by the proximity of the Irani and Kuwaiti borders and of several Kuwaiti islands. When it became apparent that Iraq's attempts to subvert the Gulf regimes and to exploit socio-economic tensions in Kuwait were unsuccessful, the Iraqi army marched into Kuwait in March 1973. Obviously, Iraq hoped to pressure Kuwait into at least giving up part of its coast, as well as two of the major islands at the head of the Gulf. However, the Iraqis discovered that, although Kuwait refused to sign a defensive agreement with Iran—for both internal and external reasons—and had none with Saudi Arabia, both were prepared to intervene if matters were to get out of hand. Finally, under increasing international and Arab pressure and on Soviet advice, the Iraqis returned to their own territory; but they have not given up their claim to Kuwait and are biding their time.[8]

Kuwait and the other east Arabian "countries" are rapidly building up the power of their armed forces.[9] Still, having to "buy" the goodwill of their sister Arab states, they are substantially increasing allocations to procure arms for the "confrontation states," development funds and economic aid to poorer Arab countries. But the asymmetries discussed above, the rapid social upheaval within their societies, and the steam building up within their large immigrant communities, have made them especially vulnerable to pressure and to a tendency toward extremism in matters connected with Arab solidarity. This is once again most evident in Kuwait (which has made more meaningful progress toward constitutional democracy than Bahrein, where the process began much earlier), partly due to the 1961 Kuwaiti–Iraqi war and to internal pressures. This progress has found expression not only in Kuwait's relatively free press but even more so in its vociferously anti-Western, anti-Irani and somewhat anti-Saudi parliament. Here middle-class nationalists and intellectuals have gradually been gaining power at the expense of the traditional ruling "aristocracy." Together with their leftist comrades and the "proletariat," they are an important factor in Kuwait's extremist policy in OPEC and OAPEC, and in its supprt of the use of the "oil weapon."[10] Undoubtedly, such a policy, as well as the process of "controlled democracy," is influenced in Kuwait by the presence of a huge immigrant community which includes a very large Palestinian element.

The oil boom in eastern Arabia has attracted immigrants from many countries, such as Pakistan, Iran and India, but above all from the poorer Arab countries (noticeably Yemen) and Palestinians. This influx, which is responsible for cultural and political influences, has already threatened the stability of the tiny Arab principalities of the lower Gulf and in some cases, even their "Arab character." In the case of Kuwait, there is already an important community totaling over half a million, with a citizenry of just about 450,000. Although relatively well-paid, until recently the immigrant population—even Arabs—were not allowed any of the privileges and social benefits granted to citizens, and only a chosen few are permitted to become Kuwaiti citizens.[11] Although not monolithic in its composition, the Palestinian immigrant community in Kuwait is probably the largest and the most cohesive element. In fact, of all the immigrants in the Gulf both Arab and non-Arab, the Palestinians, depite their important contribution to the economy, are the most feared.

The number of Palestinians in the Gulf began to grow with the development of the oil industry in the early 1950s, because of their skills and willingness to perform manual labor in this relatively primitive and remote area. The high pay in the oil fields enticed more and more people from the refugee camps and from Jordan. Thus, they number today more than 250,000—about 180,000 of them in Kuwait. Here the PLO was allowed some control over, and even to levy a tax on, the Palestinian community. This is typical of the ambivalence in the Gulf rulers' attitude toward the Palestinians. All pay lip service to their cause, and are helping to finance their struggle against Israel (one of Kuwait's major newspapers is published by Palestinians), but when local or non-Palestinian manpower is available, the Palestinians are the first to lose their jobs or even to be deported for "reasons of security." To some extent this is to be explained by events in Jordan between 1967 and 1970, and later in Lebanon, and by the fact that most of the Gulf's subversive organizations are related to Marxist-oriented Palestinian organizations, or have Palestinians among their members.[12] Apprehensions about the Palestinians and "radicals" in their countries occasionally coerce some Gulf rulers into adopting a more extremist policy than they might wish even in matters not related to Israel. Moreover, fearing the impact of a *coup d'état* in Jordan, which could bring to power a radical government on Saudi Arabia's border, they support and cooperate with King Hussein. The new accord in eastern Arabia coordinated in Riyadh, which contributes to the ability of these regimes to withstand internal and external pressures, is therefore extremely important to them. However, the future of this fragile front will depend on its relations with the "moderate" Arab camp, the policies of the powers and Iran and, above all, on the stability of Saudi Arabia.

Although far from being a revolutionary reformer, Faisal was not unaware of the need for change in the character of his government and regime. During his reign he gradually replaced most of the representatives of the ruling aristocracy in the government with members of the new educated elite and the growing middle class of Saudi Arabia. This mild "white revolution" broadened the base on which the regime rests, yet did not alienate the old "aristocracy" and the "*ulama*." However, there has been some dissatisfaction among the "conservatives" about their loss of power, and among the middle class and technocrats about the anachronistic character of the regime, whereas the limited radical element is still trying to subvert the government. Even the assassination of King Faisal by a member of his family and its aftermath, proves rather than disproves this assertion. The real danger to the regime lies however mainly in the modernization and expansion of the armed forces, which is a by-product of events in the Persian Gulf and developments within the Arab world following the October War.

For nearly half a century the Saudi Goverment has succeeded in maintaining the balance between the "aristocratic" tribal "white army" (national guard), which was the mainstay of the regime, and the regular army which drew its recruits from lesser tribes and urban elements. Lately, Saudi Arabia's position in the Gulf and the Arab world, and the development of the armies of its neighbors, necessitated the expansion of its armed forces and enhanced sophistication of their equipment. Consequently, the Saudi regime has been drawing heavily on elements which have previously never been considered loyal. Indeed, the traditional equilibrium in the armed forces has been upset by the quantitative and qualitative growth of the regular army. In 1974 the Americans sold large quantities of modern and simple-to-operate sophisticated arms to the tribal army, and undertook to train it in order to counter this development. But changes in the character of the "national guard" are also inevitable due to its modernization. Such a process could threaten the very existence of the Saudi regime, especially in the light of a possible struggle for power within the royal family—which was avoided following Faisal's death by rapid negotiations and agreement between the most powerful factions about the sharing of power between them.[13] A change in the Saudi regime could touch off a chain reaction, which would not only bring down all the conservative governments of eastern Arabia, but might change the whole balance of power in the Arab world. In the meantime Saudi Arabia successfully maintains its important position in the Arab leadership by continuing on the path of Faisal's evolutionary reforms, and by walking the tight rope between the "moderate" and "extremist" camps in the Arab world.

Modern Pan-Arabists who dream of a revival of the glory of the Arab peoples have worked for the unification of all Arab countries, stretching from "the (Atlantic) ocean to the (Persian) Gulf." In addition to this vast area of substantial population, the Arabs would control considerable oil revenues and strategic waterways. But even leaders with great vision, such as Gamal Abdel Nasser, did not envisage the amount of power and wealth which oil would bring the Arabs in the 1970s. The euphoria resulting from the successful Arab use of the "oil weapon," and the ability to flex their muscles in the community of nations, added to that vengefulness which derived from the previous humiliation of having been colonized by the West, and led the Arabs—now drunk with power—to lose their sense of proportion.[14] However, retention of control over their oil and power—in the face of Iran's increasing ambition and the hostility provoked in the West, whose economic difficulties they have relished—will depend to a great extent on maintaining Arab unity, the importance of which was manifested during the October War and at the Rabat summit conference in 1974. Hence, ideological differences and traditional rivalries have been largely, and at least temporarily, shelved. What has become extremely important, especially after the Lebanese tragedy, is to impress the world with Arab solidarity, both in connection with the threats occasionally heard from Washington, Iran's policy and the Arab–Israeli conflict. Consequently the Arabs are doing their best to maintain the pragmatic "front of cooperation" which emerged after the Yom Kippur War.

OIL AND POWER POLITICS

Although the closure of the Suez Canal in 1956 caused a shortage of tanker tonnage rather than a real shortage of oil, the West's dependence on Gulf oil was exposed for the first time during that crisis. Between 1956 and 1967 the Soviet Union had refrained from direct involvement in the countries of the Arabian peninsula and had channeled aid to, and coordinated its activities in the region through Egypt. However, following South Yemen's independence in 1967, and the British declaration the following year of their intention to evacuate the entire Gulf area, a small Soviet flotilla has been permanently stationed in the Gulf of Aden. The USSR also began substantial expansion of its strategic infrastructure in the region.[15]

Some scholars claim that Soviet activity in the northwestern Indian Ocean resulted from the development by the Americans of the Polaris A-3 (operational since 1964) and Poseidon missiles. These can be ideally deployed against Russia by nuclear-powered submarines operating from the Arabian Sea. It follows, they maintain, that the Soviet naval presence and other activities in the region are of a defensive character.[16] Due to factors argued elsewhere, however, it would seem that Soviet long-range strategy necessitates their presence in the Indian Ocean.[17] That strategy is motivated by the fact that Persian Gulf oil is essential to Western economy and power rather than just by defensive reasons.

Moreover, the new MIRV missiles (with about twice the range of the Polaris A-3) and DELTA submarines developed by the US in the meantime, and the character of the Soviet Indian Ocean navy, completely refute the argument about the defensive purpose of the USSR's presence in the region.

In anticipation of the reopening of the Suez Canal, and the resultant feasibility of rotating its fleets between different seas, the Soviet Union has been constructing a strategic infrastructure stretching from the Red Sea through the Gulf of Aden and Somalia to island "states" of the Indian Ocean, as far as Chitagong in Bangladesh and Umm Qasr at the head of the Persian Gulf. In the last two years Soviet activities, naval power and facilities in the Indian Ocean and its environs have been substantially expanded, and aircraft carriers of the Kiev class, designed to pass through the Suez Canal for service in this area, are hurriedly being completed (the first will be operational, it is claimed, in the very near future). No less impressive is the Soviet presence (mainly air force) and stockpiling of arms and munitions in Somalia—and to a lesser degree in Iraq—to an extent far beyond their apparent needs.[18]

Without intending to interfere directly with the flow of Gulf oil to the West, the USSR has forced the West to take into consideration the Soviet presence in the region and the creation of a new balance of power there. The nuclear "balance of fear" and the *détente* policy have limited the freedom of action of the superpowers in many fields. This does not inhibit the Soviet Union, however, from interfering indirectly with the Western oil supply through a proxy, or by subverting the authority of rulers "friendly" to the West. The very presence of the Soviet Union in the region has ruled out the possibility that the West would use "gunboat diplomacy" in the Gulf, and has accelerated the process of change in the oil industry.

Soviet attempts to erode the power of the traditional Gulf rulers and to expand Moscow's influence in the area have generally misfired, with the exception of the April 1972 friendship and defense treaty with Iraq. But the Soviet presence in the region was no doubt a factor in OPEC's aggressive price policy and determination between 1971 and 1973 to gain control of the major oil companies.[19] Thus, without lifting a finger, the Soviet Union has managed to achieve a tremendous strategic victory and economic advantages while the West has suffered an enormous strategic and economic blow, the repercussions of which are still being felt. Moreover, the Soviet Union's revenues from the export of oil, though not dramatic, have grown considerably in real terms. Finally, the new prices of oil made the exploitation of western Siberia's fuel resources economical in a period when the Soviet Union's sources in its European region were drying up. Even eastern Siberia's resources, which are technologically difficult and economically prohibitive to exploit, are now attracting the attention of Japan and the United States, which wish to diversify their sources of fuel.[20]

In the last two years the effects of developments in the oil market on the Western economy have caused the United States to reevaluate its policy in the region. During the October War Washington realized how difficult it was to operate effectively in the region with its nearest base in Subic Bay, 7,000 miles away, while local governments refused the United States base facilities. No longer satisfied with merely strengthening its Gulf allies, the United States is trying to establish a presence in the northwestern Indian Ocean and to build a strategic infrastructure in the region. Such plans evolve around the island of Diego Garcia, in the Indian Ocean opposite the Gulf, which is admirably suited to the purpose. It was reported that the Americans are also seeking permission to use other British bases and facilities, such as the island of Masirah, off the coast of Oman.[21] In addition to its value in relation to Soviet activities in the region, Diego Garcia would be useful if the US found itself forced to use military means to ensure the flow of oil to the West. In such an event, it could supplement, or make unnecessary, a massive airlift from the Mediterranean depending on Israeli airfields and the cooperation of Israel in other fields.[22]

The appearance in the Gulf of a massive American task force at the end of 1974, and the allusion by American leaders to the possible use of power against Gulf producers in the case of "economic strangulation," as well as the Soviet activity in the region, probably lends urgency to US plans. Although many believe that military intervention is not the answer to the problem, it is evident to most economists that, if the West is to survive, it cannot afford to pay in real terms more than the present oil price. Altogether, the new American policy has already convinced most Gulf producers of the need for moderation, as was seen in OPEC's meetings during 1975 and 1976.[23]

Obviously if the Arab countries decide to use the "oil weapon" again, or even if the present policy of the oil producers remains unchanged, causing Western economy and power to decline, the West (mainly the United States) may have to use force in the Gulf. In addition to the dangers of a confrontation between the two superpowers, such brinkmanship would have grave repercussions on the superpowers' relations with the Middle East countries. Until now, US influence over Israel and its relations with the Gulf "conservative" regimes seemed to facilitate improvement of its relations with most Arab countries. Soviet willingness to support the Arabs almost unconditionally, and the Arab ability to exploit this fact, on the other hand, gave the United States an important advantage. Still, Western intervention in the Gulf would undoubtedly cause a strong anti-Western backlash, and may be exploited by the Soviet Union to reestablish its waning influence in the Arab world.

Although most of the Gulf producers claim that they fear the influence of communist Russia, they have few qualms about using its presence in the region to further their economic and political interests. Despite their dependence on a protective Western umbrella, they do not hesitate (with the help of the oil companies) to milk the Western economy dry—a process which, they must be aware, may lead to its destruction. Despite constant professions of concern about the state of the Western economy, Saudi Arabia did nothing to bring down the price of oil. On the contrary, when it seemed that a Saudi oil auction might further depress oil prices in mid-1974, it was cancelled and, in the Abu Dhabi conference at the end of 1974, eastern Arabia's oil producers, claiming that they intended to reduce oil prices, merely decided to take a larger share of the huge profits made by the oil companies in the previous year.[24] Because of a saturated market some OPEC members, mainly Saudi Arabia and Kuwait, have been constantly reducing production thus serving as a "shock absorber" for the organization in order to maintain its solidarity and unity. In October 1975 they supported a rise of 10% of the already artificially high price of oil.

In fact, the apprehension in Saudi Arabia of the USSR and its local allies has recently greatly diminished. It is ironic that the US undertaking to train the forces protecting the oil fields, and the huge quantities of arms procured by the Gulf countries from the West, presumably to safeguard themselves against the Soviet Union, are providing the Gulf states with a shield against the West, if it ever tries to take the oil fields by force.[25] An even more fantastic situation is one in which the "conservative" producers, fighting the Western powers with the most sophisticated Western weapons, could be supported at least partially by the Soviet Union. Be that as it may, the Soviet Union, as well as the oil producing countries, at present evidently consider ideological factors and even traditional allegiances as of little importance, since developments are proving beneficial to both sides. The "conservative" producers, it seems, are manipulating the mythical Soviet threat to maintain the high prices of oil, to avert American military intervention, and to acquire sophisticated Western weapon systems. On the other hand, the policy of the producers, whatever the character of their regimes, benefits the USSR because it erodes Western economy and power.

With the growing crisis in the Western economy and leadership, it is doubtful whether the European countries will be able to cooperate concerning the economic and energy crisis. Were the need to arise, it is unlikely that even NATO members would join the United States in a concerted military action in the Gulf. Britain has already announced that, due to economic considerations, it will further reduce its Indian Ocean commitments and, *inter alia*, give up its important staging post on Gan Island (in the Maldive group).[26] In fact, the economic crisis widened the rift between the United States and Western Europe, particularly France. In addition to oil, the United States and all the European countries are competing with each other in the Gulf states for contracts for the sale of arms, technology, services, finished products and the financial reserves which the oil producers are willing to recycle. It is an open question how long Western countries will be able to continue to pay the exorbitant oil prices which are causing the disintegration of their economies and a rise in their unemployment rates. Even the United States in 1975 faced an enormous balance of payments deficit due to the additional cost of oil. Hence, if America's attempts to align the consumers in the International Energy Agency (IEA) fail, and possibly even if they succeed, the West even if it so wishes may not be capable of military intervention in the Gulf.[27]

Since the panic caused by use of the "oil weapon" subsided, it has become evident that the Arab–Israeli conflict has little to do with the global energy and economic crisis. It is now clear that the price of oil rather than its supply is affecting the Western and Third World economies. But whether the West remains apathetic to its own decline or decides to take action, the Arab–Israeli conflict is bound to be affected.

TENSIONS BETWEEN ARABS AND NON-ARABS
IN THE MIDDLE EAST

The Arab–Israeli Conflict, the West and the Gulf

The flow of oil from the Gulf has been stopped on several occasions in the past by different Arab governments, or through the actions of individuals belonging to subversive organizations. But, as none of these stoppages was the result of a concerted action by the Arab producers, the impact of the Gulf countries on the Arab–Israeli conflict remained marginal. The Gulf producers' offer, in the Khartoum summit conference of December 1967, to subsidize the "confrontation states," was made partly in order to avert pressures to use the "oil weapon" while their revenues were still relatively limited and the oil companies and the West were still feared. Consumption of oil in the industrialized countries continued to grow, from the late 1960s, at an average rate of about 8% per year. Since US and some Western non-Arab fuel sources were gradually being exhausted, the balance of the increased demand had to come from Arab producers, mainly in the Gulf region. With the development of a "seller's market" in the early 1970s, OPEC—radicalized by new members such as Libya and by Soviet support—began to flex its muscles.

By its very nature the oil industry attracted a skilled and sophisticated Arab labor force, which was not only nationalist in attitude but in many cases radically socialist in ideology.[28] In addition, the flow of capital into the oil countries caused them to hire a constantly increasing labor force, mainly to perform manual work. This force included many Palestinians. Consequently, Gulf rulers, always willing to adopt extremist attitudes in Pan-Arab matters, became gradually more and more involved, though still indirectly, in the Arab–Israeli conflict.

While OPEC was pressing for higher prices and a change in relationships with the oil companies, it became evident that Arab control of the larger part of the world's proven reserves, and their substantial financial resources, would become increasingly relevant to the Arab struggle against Israel. The first signs of such a development were felt as early as 1971–1972, when the term "oil weapon" (silah al-batrul) was frequently mentioned by the Arab press, and shortly afterward when OAPEC tried to put pressure on consumers to support the Arab policy against Israel.[29]

The energy crisis in the United States at the turn of 1972 was the outcome of oil companies policy, which had led to the lack of suitable refining and other installations in the United States; but it was most significant to producers and consumers alike because of its tremendous psychological effect on America and Europe, and led to a gradual rise in the price of oil. The fact that the price of oil more than quadrupled within 1973 resulted from this crisis and from OPEC's power; its relation to the October War was strictly incidental. This war nevertheless presented OPEC with a perfect opportunity for a further substantial and unilateral price increase. Moreover, Arab use of the "oil weapon" during and after this war was so effective that the industrial West was thrown into unbelievable panic. It was ready to pay any price, and in most cases to accept any condition set by the Arab producers, in order to ensure the supply of oil.

The new developments in the oil industry as well as the war had an immediate and dramatic effect on the Arab–Israeli conflict. Many Third World countries severed their diplomatic relations with Israel. Over and above their refusal to cooperate with the United States in its efforts to supply Israel with war materials during the October War, most European NATO members, following the lead of France, capitulated to Arab pressures and jointly adopted anti-Israeli resolutions. Though Europe's panic subsided after the first months of 1974, when everybody realized that, despite the Arab embargo, the oil market was saturated—the West still fears the Arab ability to wield the "oil weapon." This affects the attitude of most countries, especially in international forums concerning the Arab–Israeli conflict.[30]

Unable to absorb their vast oil revenues, the Gulf oil producing countries (particularly Saudi Arabia, Kuwait and Abu Dhabi, as well as Libya) have in the past two years managed to accumulate currency surpluses which have made them dominant in the field of international finance.[31] Western countries are desperately anxious to get some of the funds which they previously paid for oil recycled into their declining economies. Therefore, in addition to oil, the Arabs are now able to manipulate their surpluses to gain political influence.

Today, nearly every technology is available at a price. Part of the Arab monetary reserve was already utilized during the October War to pay for the arms supplied by the Soviet Union to the "confrontation states."[32] Further substantial sums have been paid to the Soviet Union and to several European countries, mainly France, for sophisticated weapon systems which they now supply to Syria, Iraq, Egypt and Jordan. Western countries, including the United States, are hungry for oil dollars and are competing for contracts for the supply of the vast quantities of armaments sought by Gulf governments.[33] The latter have also been drawn into an arms race to ensure their safety against neighbors and outside intervention. But a close examination of recent arms purchases and orders by the Arab oil producers in the West creates the impression that they are following a master plan, aimed at least at standardizing major systems. These are obviously meant partly for Egypt and Jordan, and generally to be used in a future war against Israel, and could change the balance of power in the region.[34]

The Arab (primarily Saudi) ability to wield the "oil weapon" has already influenced US policy in the Middle East. Although less dependent on Gulf oil, the latter has a responsibility toward its European allies (and Japan), and is already importing oil—and may have to continue to import even more—from Arab countries.[35] It is feared that a new Arab–Israeli war would provoke a renewal of the Arab oil boycott against the West and affect the world economy. The need to prevent such a development, and to preserve the balance of power, further erodes the Soviet position in the Arab countries and strengthens US influence in the Gulf—and was an important factor in the US decision to supply the substantial quantity of sophisticated weaponry which Saudi Arabia and Kuwait wish to purchase.[36] But, tragically, these weapons could also spark off a new war, disrupt the present balance of power in the Middle East and within Saudi Arabia and, in certain circumstances, be used against the West.

Israel fully appreciates the increasing influence of the oil factor and the Arabs' economic and political power on US considerations and policy in the region. Although said to be mitigating the extremist Arab countries' attitudes, Saudi Arabia systematically exploited the oil companies' oil pricing and its relations with the United States to erode the latter's relations with Israel, and to obtain sophisticated Western weaponry for the Arabs. It is generally agreed that the price of oil, the most important single factor contributing to the West's economic crisis, has nothing to do with the Arab–Israeli conflict. But a renewed oil boycott could still cause great hardship to the West, and put it to the test of whether to sacrifice Israel or to use military force against the Arab producers. In fact, a leading West German weekly—examining such a possibility—suggested that if the fate of the industrial West was at stake, Europe might have to face a difficult choice, and therefore should examine the possibilities for a "humane" solution for Israel's Jews.[37] But, although it is unlikely that the United States would adopt such a cynical attitude, President Ford constantly reiterated his fears of the impact of a new round of Arab–Israeli war which would induce the Arab producers to use once again the "oil weapon."

Israel has become painfully aware of the increasingly important role already played by the Gulf Arab oil producers in changing the balance of power in the Arab–Israeli conflict, and the possibility that forces from the Gulf countries would participate in a new war against it. Israel is, therefore, gradually expanding its strategic considerations beyond the immediate circle of "confrontation states" to the Gulf, so as not to find itself in an intolerable situation in the near future.[38] Sadly, the unlimited supply of weaponry to the Gulf states by the West and a waning in US support for Israel could be the causes of such escalation.

Iran and the Arab States

Relations between Iran and Arab nationalists have been at best merely correct. Whereas Iran has had historical claims to parts of eastern Arabia and islands in the Gulf (especially Bahrein with its large Shi'i–Irani minority), Arab nationalists lay claim to Khuzistan (termed "Arabistan") with its largely "Arab" population, and to other parts of western Iran. The modern Pan-Arabists, who describe the borders of the envisaged Arab union as being from the "ocean to the Gulf," never specify which side of the Gulf. They insist, moreover, that rather than the historical name "Persian Gulf," the name "Arab Gulf" be universally used.

Relations between Iran and Abdel Nasser's Egypt deteriorated throughout the 1950s up until the mid-1960s. In addition to territorial claims, this was mainly the outcome of Iran's policy and participation in Western-oriented defense alliances, above all the Baghdad Pact. Classified, therefore, as "reactionary," Iran's regime was also criticized by the "progressive" Arab regimes for its relations with Israel, but this criticism remained of secondary importance until 1967.

Iran's relations with Iraq rapidly deteriorated after the Qassem revolution in 1958. But, with the decline of Nasserism since the mid-1960s, Iraq became Iran's main antagonist in the Arab camp. Egypt's defeat in the 1967 Six Day War caused Iran to reorient its policy in the

Middle East completely and focus it on the Gulf. Agreements forced on Iran by the British after World War I surrendered important Irani interests to Iraq, and were a source of constant friction between the two countries. By far the most irritating to Iran was the 1937 agreement by which its border along the Shatt al-'Arab ran along the Irani coast of this waterway, rather than down its center as is customary when a river separates countries (*Talweg*). Thus, navigation in the Shatt was left under Iraqi control, affecting Iran's oil industry then centered around Abadan (on the Shatt al-'Arab), and through it Iran's economy. Moreover, both the fact that the most important Shi'i shrines are in Iraq, and that Shi'is constitute the largest population group in this Sunni Arab-dominated state, also contributed to the tension between the two countries. As relations beteen them worsened, Iran covertly supported the Kurdish rebels, while Iraq reciprocated in kind and supported subversive radical elements in Iran.

In 1969, no longer willing to tolerate the situation on the Shatt al-'Arab, Iran forcefully and unilaterally broke the 1937 agreement. Under normal circumstances, such high-handed action might have brought down on Iran the wrath of the Arab countries, but Iraq's extremist Ba'th regime was at this time generally considered the pariah of the Arab world. In the Gulf, Saudi Arabia and its smaller neighbors were gravely concerned over Iraqi intentions following the British withdrawal in 1971, and were willing to cooperate with Iran. The "confrontation states" led by Egypt—preoccupied at the time with the War of Attrition—viewed positively Iran's role in safeguarding stability in the Gulf together with Saudi Arabia. Dependent on subsidies from "conservative" Arab oil producers, Egypt had a stake in the preservation of this stability and did not wish Arab attention to be diverted from its conflict with Israel to the Gulf. In fact, even before Nasser's death in 1970, but especially after Sadat had come to power, Egypt gradually improved its relations with Iran. Moreover, in 1971 Iran gave up its claim to Bahrein and further ingratiated itself with the Arabs by supporting OPEC's hard line policy. At the end of 1971, Iran captured the three islands, Tunb and Abu Musa, in the Straits of Hormuz (which it claimed, and which were controlled by Ras al-Khayma and Sharja respectively). The strong reaction of the "progressive" Arab countries was to be expected. But, with the exception of Libya, criticism of Iran in other Arab countries was surprisingly mild, and there are indications that hte whole matter was previously coordinated with the "moderates" including Egypt.[39]

For more than a decade Iran has been investing a substantial part of its oil revenue in building up its military power, with American help. When Britain declared its intention to evacuate the Gulf, Iran determined to replace it and maintain stability in the region, preferably in cooperation with Saudi Arabia. Consequently the expansion and modernization of Iran's armed forces were accelerated. By the end of 1972 Iran's military power was already inspiring awe and apprehension among all its Arab neighbors. Its size, and the number of its nationals flocking to the Gulf countries, awakened old fears and concern for the "Arab character" of the Gulf. The matter of the three islands occupied by Iran was also not forgotten, as it was good propaganda for the "progressive" Arab regimes and Libya, which accused Iran of supplying oil to Israel as well as "plotting" with that country and "American imperialism" against the Arabs.[40]

As Saudi Arabia failed to live up to the expectation of its allies, Iran abandoned its low profile policy in the Gulf and the Shah announced, and occasionally reiterated, his intention to intervene in eastern Arabia in the eventuality of a radical upheaval there. Such declarations irritated even local "moderate" Arab rulers, and especially King Faisal. Any doubt about the Shah's credibility disappeared when a small Irani task force was sent to Oman to fight the Marxist Dhofari rebels at the end of 1972 and was substantially reinforced after the October War, in late 1973. Iran's activity in Oman in 1974 caused grave concern in the "progressive" Arab camp as well as in several "moderate" Arab states, including Kuwait and Saudi Arabia.[41] The latter resent Iran's special relations with Oman, and along with other Arab Gulf states are even more concerned about the systematic strengthening of Irani power and its stranglehold on the Gulf through its established control on both sides of the Straits of Hormuz.

Taking its role as the Gulf's policeman and local mini-superpower seriously, Iran has been developing an impressive strategic infrastructure for its armed forces in the Gulf and in the Indian Ocean. Especially after the October War and the blockade of Bab al-Mandab, Iran accelerated the construction of airfields capable of handling Phantom jets on its side of the Straits of Hormuz, on Abu Musa and Omani soil. Iran's growing navy has bases along its Gulf and Indian Ocean coasts and facilities in Oman, Indian Ocean island states, and even in South Africa. Eventually, an agreement was reached with Sultan Qabus concerning the use of Ra's Musandam and the mutual control of the Straits of

Hormuz.[42] Thus there is no question of Iran's determination and ability to guarantee its freedom of navigation through the Straits of Hormuz. But in following this policy it also established its option of control over navigation and freedom of passage of the Arab Gulf oil producers. Moreover, whereas Iran has in fact another outlet to the Indian Ocean, the Straits of Hormuz are practically the only outlet for most of the Gulf countries. Apprehensive of the Shah's policy and power, most Arab countries, including some "conservatives," became more hostile toward Iran during 1974. The eastern Arabian states closed their ranks under Faisal's leadership and have, at least superficially, even bridged their differences and begun to cooperate in the military field with their "progressive" brethren, especially Iraq. Though clearly aimed against Iran, this policy has been carried out prudently in order not to create an immediate open split with Tehran, or to afford the Soviet Union and its local radical allies an opportunity to exploit such a situation.[43] This pragmatic approach as well as the need to conserve the unity of OPEC paved the way for the new Irani–Iraqi accord of March 1975, although the motivation of the two sides and of Iraq's allies is temporary and dubious. Despite the supposed *rapprochement* with Iran, steps are now being taken by Saudi Arabia and all its neighbors to build up their military power in order to be in a position to challenge the arbitrary responsibilities that Iran has taken on itself.

Since the late 1960s Iran's policy and strategic planning have been oriented to ensure its position of power in the Gulf, especially as its relations with the Soviet Union improved rapidly after 1969. Hence, Iran's strategy is more concerned with the Soviet presence in Iraq and the Indian Ocean than with countering danger from the direction of its northern borders.[44] Although the USSR maintains a formal policy of scrupulous neutrality in the Iraqi–Irani conflict, vast quantities of sophisticated weaponry, including MiG-23s and SCUD surface-to-surface missiles have been supplied to Iraq. Iran thus has no illusions concerning the Soviet attitude should a common anti-Iranian front emerge among the Arab states.[45] The growing Arab hostility toward Iran was probably a major reason for the much-publicized erosion of Iran's relations with Israel after the October War and its substantial aid to several "confrontation states" especially Egypt. However, this process had already begun after the Six Day War, and is now chiefly exploited as a smoke screen for Iran's continued high-handed activity in the Gulf and the Indian Ocean.[46]

Though influenced by the fact that it is a Muslim state, Iran's relations with Israel are motivated mainly by *realpolitik* and not by sentiment. Iran considers Israel as its first line of defense—as drawing the bulk of Arab hostility away from itself. Being cynically interested in the continuation of a low profile Arab–Israeli conflict, it is also interested in Israel's survival and ability to withstand pressure. Israel's victory in 1967 was counter-productive with respect to Israeli–Irani relations because it diminished Iran's apprehension of the power of an Arab coalition and especially of Egypt. Between 1967 and 1973, Iran's formal attitude toward Israel became increasingly critical. During the October War, Iran even rendered logistic support to Saudi Arabia, allowed Soviet cargo planes to overfly its airspace, and enabled Iraq to withdraw from their mutual front two divisions which were sent to the battlefield in Syria. The obvious ambivalence in Iran's attitude is easily explained by the reasons stated above. Naturally, Iran supports Dr. Kissinger's peace-by-stages policy which, in addition to eroding Soviet influence, temporarily prevents another outbreak of war between Israel and the Arabs, though it does not resolve their differences. An Arab–Israeli war would undoubtedly cause a renewal of the Arab oil boycott, and could lead to Western intervention, or even escalate beyond that to Soviet intervention in the Gulf or against Iran. However, in the expectation that Dr. Kissinger will succeed, Iran must strengthen its relations with the "moderate" Arabs in order to avert the possibility that, once free from the Israeli trauma, the Arabs will unite and turn against Iran itself. Egypt is, of course, the cornerstone of this policy. Hence the substantial increase of aid to Egypt and Iran's firm support of its stand concerning the return by Israel of the occupied Arab territories.[47]

No doubt Iran has a common interest with Egypt, in that both fear developments which could divert attention from the Arab–Israeli conflict to the Gulf. Both countries may also have grounds for further cooperation because of possible rivalry in the future between the Arab "have-nots" (chiefly Egypt) and Saudi Arabia. It is unlikely that the "have-nots" will tolerate the present *status quo* in inter-Arab relations indefinitely. The constant decline in Egypt's economic situation and the fact that, despite its being the largest and strongest Arab country, it depends on political nonentities, may bring it back to revolutionary Pan-Arabism or to social radicalism. In both cases it would revive an aggressive foreign policy. Despite American efforts it is also unlikely that the present Saudi regime, the cornerstone of the "conservative" block, will not be affected by developments in the Gulf and the Arab world. At best Saudi Arabia would simply undergo a "white revolution" and be taken over by the newly emergent nationalistic bourgeoisie. It could, however, be overthrown by a military revolution which might adopt the Ba'th ideology and turn to the USSR. Be that as it may, relations between Iran and Saudi Arabia continue to deteriorate. Iran, it seems, considers the character of the present Saudi regime and its policy in the region a danger to the Gulf's stability, and a challenge to Iran's hegemony in the region. It is indicative that an Iranian scholar, who obviously represents the Shah's opinion, classifies Arab regimes as "corrupt," "democratic-nationalist" and "extremist." In relation to possible Iranian intervention in eastern Arabia he differentiates between "Arab nationalist-inspired revolutions," which should not be opposed by Iran, and "Soviet-inspired Marxist" ones.[48] But, to break the emerging Saudi-sponsored "Arab front" in the Gulf, the Shah was even willing to sign a new friendship agreement with Iraq in March 1975, demonstrating once again how allegiances and ideologies are easily forgotten in the intricate game presently being played in the Gulf.

CONCLUSION

Persian Gulf oil has become the fountainhead of Arab power and pride and the hope for development for the Arabs and Iran. On the other hand, it is essential to the existence of the industrial West and, indeed, for the Third World as well, and an increasingly significant threat to the survival of Israel. Until substitutes for Gulf oil are found, or OPEC's ability to dictate terms is curtailed, the Gulf is bound to grow as the focus of local and international tensions. Already resembling an arsenal of the most sophisticated weaponry, with more on order, the region's startling asymmetries are highly conducive to the eruption of violence.

The October War indicated, *inter alia*, that quantity could, to some extent and in certain circumstances, substitute for quality. Financial resources are now used to accelerate the qualitative as well as the quantitative growth of Arab power. With the "oil weapon," these financial surpluses are being translated into political power and influence. As such capabilities increase with time, Israel cannot afford to disregard the Persian Gulf even in its short-range considerations and strategic planning. Despite its temporary military superiority, the time factor seems to be on the Arab side. Hence, if the US will not maintain the power ratio between Israel and the Arabs, and unless Israel can negotiate a meaningful peace agreement with the Arab states, which will guarantee its security—the likelihood of which is remote—another round of war in the Middle East may be inevitable; this time it is very likely that it will involve and affect the Gulf as well. Violence may erupt in the Gulf anyway, as the outcome of a local conflict, most likely between the Arab states and Iran, or through the use of power by the West, induced by "economic strangulation."

In a recently published book (*Oil, Power and Politics*) the present author wrote that "because deep emotional and psychological factors are involved, the conflicts between Arab countries and non-Arab countries seem at present to be potentially far more dangerous than inter-Arab issues. A marginal case, that of Ethiopia, succeeded in rallying a number of Arab countries..."[49] In reality, developments in Ethiopia prove that the depth of Arab support for the Eritrean rebels (whose "Arabism" is questionable) was grossly underestimated, but the statement considering the impact of conflicts between Arab and non-Arab countries is obviously more than correct.

Iran will always remain suspect to the Arab countries because of its different culture, political interests, allegiances and aspirations. The Arabs cannot forget the fact that while they manipulated the "oil weapon," Iran exploited the situation to increase its production—and the Shah openly reiterates that he will do so again if Arab producers boycott the West in the future. More important than its common interest with the West, Iran's oil policy, which may seem shortsighted, is motivated by relatively short-term needs dictated by its ability and determination to diversify its economy through rapid exploitation of its oil resources, while they still fetch high prices. If Iran's future economic development is guaranteed, many Arabs argue that it would cooperate with the West, and probably "betray" OPEC,[50] or if its oil resources are depleted, it may revive its historical claims to some parts of Eastern Arabia. For the time being, because the Gulf is so important for the revival of their power and their pride,[51] the Arab countries cannot remain indifferent to Iran's hegemony in the area, its ability to control approaches to the Gulf and its growing military power.

The Shah's new Middle East policy derives from the assumption that most of the "moderate" Arab countries are inhibited from taking direct action against Iran, either because they fear its power or because of the possibility that the Soviets would exploit any such conflict to penetrate the Gulf, whereas the "confrontation states" are more preoccupied with the Arab–Israeli conflict, or are jealous of their conservative oil-rich brethren. Iran's calculations, which necessitate a limited Arab–Israeli conflict and financial and strong verbal support to certain "moderate" Arab countries, may seem reasonable, but could actually prove to be a mistake. There is no guarantee that a "limited conflict" can be contained, especially with the vast quantities of arms expected to reach the Gulf in the near future. Moreover, whether the Arab–Israeli conflict is solved or not, the tension building up in the Gulf (and above all the growing anti-Iranian feeling in the region) which is covertly encouraged by the USSR, in certain circumstances may become even more intense and overshadow the Arab–Israeli conflict. The cooperation between "conservatives" and "progressives" which is becoming more evident in the Gulf region should serve as the "writing on the wall" for Iran. Above all, should the West or Iran decide to intervene militarily in the Gulf, the latter may find itself in very difficult circumstances, not only in relation to the Arab countries and the West, but because of possible Soviet intervention on her northern borders to mollify the Arabs, among other reasons. Moreover, it has become evident that the US has begun to favor the Saudis and their allies and are becoming far less friendly to Iran.

The United States, and other Western countries, have come to realize that they cannot remain apathetic to the impact of oil prices on their economies and the concomitant ability of—in some cases miniscule—states to erode their power. They are also aware of the effect of the decline of the Western economy on the international balance of power, and of the service rendered by the oil producers to the Soviet Union. Gradually some cooperation is emerging between the United States and other Western industrial countries. Recycling petro-dollars, which for a time seemed a solution, is proving disappointing and, to some extent, dangerous. In fact, some Western countries have already taken steps to protect their economies, or at least their essential industries, from being controlled by the oil producers. For Dr. Kissinger's policy, time has become the most essential factor, because he believes in the ability of the IEA to stand up to OPEC in the future, or that events may bring OPEC's disintegration in the meantime. Consequently, it seems that to buy time, and to strengthen America's Arab "allies," he has been even ready to sacrifice some of Israel's interests, although this could prove most detrimental both to Israel and to the West in the future. Such a policy might, however not only fail, but could prove counterproductive and dangerous to the West as well as for the countries of the region.

Evidently, the Soviet Union has been building a strategic infrastructure in the Red Sea, the Gulf of Aden and the Indian Ocean for a reason. With the reopening of the Suez Canal there is bound to be an escalation in the superpower rivalry in the Indian Ocean and the Gulf, although the Soviet Union is prudently trying to maintain a low profile in the region for the time being. Such a development has no doubt been expected for some time by the United States and is the reason for its accelerated activity in the Gulf and its environs. However, despite a certain amount of Western brinkmanship, the Soviet leadership is well aware that Gulf oil and the question of its price are crucial to the West, while they are at present simply a lever for Soviet strategy. The Kremlin, though dogmatic as ever concerning ideology and goals, is more pragmatic concerning tactics. Soviet activity in the Gulf region, except for national security, is part of the general aim of eroding Western power and economy. Once convinced of Western determination, unless its own national interest is at stake or its own oil resources will be depleted, Russia is unlikely to intervene in the Gulf and—especially if allowed to save face—may merely try to exploit the situation to its advantage.[52]

Even so, the near future is likely to prove a most crucial period in the Middle East and in the Gulf in particular.

Persian Gulf—Population and Oil

	Population (000,000s)			Oil Extraction 1974–75 (m$b per day)			
Country	Incl. Immigrants	Emigrants Incl. Communities	1974–75	Revenues IX '74 ($ bill.)	III '75[1]	Oil Reserves (000 m/b)	Currency Reserves ($ bill.)
S. Arabia	5.0–6.0	1.25	29.4	8.3	6.5	140.7	18.5
Kuwait	0.95	0.55	11.9	3.2	2.3	72.7	6.0–7.0
Abu Dhabi	0.1	0.05	4.8	1.4	1.15	24.0	1.0
Qatar	0.15–0.2	0.65	1.4	0.6	0.43	6.5	
Iraq	10.1		5.9	2.0	2.1	31.5	2.9
Iran	31.9		18.0	5.9(1973)	5.5	60.0	6.3
Oman	0.6–0.8		0.95	0.8	0.31	1.0	
Dubay	0.11	0.04	0.3	0.27	0.22		
Bahrein	0.30	0.10	0.05	0.068	0.06		
N. Yemen	9.0–10.0						
PDRY	1.7						

Sources: *Financial Times*, 30 January, 23 March, 5 June, 6 June, 1974 (oil extraction in 1973 in Iran), 26 February, 23 May, 1975 on new population census; *Al-Anwar*, 12 April, 1975; *Ha'aretz*, 3 November, 1974 (currency reserves); *Business Week*, 13 January, 1975; M. Abir, *Oil, Power and Politics*, London and New York, 1974, pp. 10-11, *as-Siyasa al-Dawliya*, 26 May, 1975; *The Oil and Gas Journal*, 26 May, 1975.

* Extraction was further reduced after March 1975.

NOTES

1. The author wishes to acknowledge his indebtedness to The Leonard Davis Institute for International Relations, Hebrew University, Jerusalem, for its help.

2. M. Abir, *Oil, Power and Politics*, (London 1974), p. 106. On Saudi influence in YAR see *Jerusalem Post (JP)*, 17 January 1975; *Ha'aretz*, 30 January, 1975.

3. *Le Monde Diplomatique (MD)*, 16 September, 1974; R. Riyadh, *Foreign Broadcasting Information Service Middle East (FBIS)*, 4 December, 1974; *Ma'ariv*, 6 December, 1974 (on the Saudi military infrastructure built near Iraq's border). On Faisal's visit to Syria, see *Ha'aretz*, 2 January, 1975.

4. On the re-Arabization of the PDRY and Saudi attempts to maintain Arab solidarity, see *al-Ahram* (21 March, 20 September, 1974; *Al-Jadid*, 20 September, 1974; *al-Sayyad*, 22 August, 2 November, 1974; *al-Usbu' al-'Arabi*, 4 November, 1974; *Afro–Asian Affairs* (London), 15 January, 1975; *Financial Times (FT)*, 29 January, 1975. For a rare Soviet attack on the Saudi regime and a discussion of this phenomenon, see *JP*, 17 December, 1974. Another indication of this development is the PDRY's willingness to establish relations with the Gulf countries and the change of name of the Popular Front for the Liberation of Oman and the Arab Gulf (PFLOAG) to the more modest Popular Front for the Liberation of Oman: *al-Anwar*, 10 February, 1975.

5. M. Abir, *Oil, op. cit*, p. 106.

6. *Ar-Ra'y al-'Amm*, 24 January, 1974; *al-Hawadith*, 23 June, 1974; *al-Hadaf*, 29 June 1974; *Middle East Economic Digest (MEED)*, 2 August, 1974; *Ha'aretz*, 22 August, 1974; *as-Sayyad*, 22 August, 19 September, 1974 (on the agreement and the importance of the outlet to the sea). Egypt was named as having been instrumental in bringing about the reconciliation: *as-Sayyad*, 22 August, 1974.

7. *Ruz al-Yusuf*, 29 May, 1972; *Al-Ra'y al-'Amm*, 19 April, 1974; *as-Siyasa* (Kuwait), 3, 25 May, 11 June, 1974; *Ma'ariv*, 16 September, 1974.

8. *Ma'ariv*, *JP*, 22 March, *FT*, 30 March, 1973; *Ha'aretz*, 1 April, 1973 (on Saudi division moved to Kuwaiti border); *as-Sayyad*, 5 April, 1973 (Iraqi foreign minister claims Kuwait's territory), December, 1974 ("Is Iraq a Gulf country?"). For the strategic importance of the Kuwaiti Islands, see *Ma'ariv*, 8 April, 1973. On Iran's uncompromising attitude to Iraqi expansionism, see *FT*, 31 May, 1973 ("Iran and the Gulf States"); On Iraq's infringement on Kuwait's territory and the latter's attempt to use its contributions to "confrontation

states" to ease the pressure, see *International Herald Tribune (IHT)*, 3 December, 1974.

9. *FT*, 31 May, 1973; International Institute of Strategic Studies, *The Military Balance 1976–1977* (London, 1975); *ar-Ra'y al-'Amm*, 28 March, 19 April, 1974; *Yediyot Aharonot*, 16 January, 1975.

10. *Ruz al-Yusuf*, 29 May, 1972; *FT*, 14 June, 1973, 12 February, 1975; *as-Siyasa*, 13 May, 1974; *MD*, 16 June, 1974; *al-Hadaf*, 30 November, 1974; *Ma'ariv*, 13 January, 1975 (on opposition in Kuwaiti parliament); *JP*, 27, 30 January, 1975 (on new elections to the parliament and its composition). Exploiting developments in Lebanon the regime in Kuwait completely reversed its liberal policy after a similar development in Bahrein.

11. John Duke Anthony, *Political Dynamics of the Lower Persian Gulf States* (Washington, 1973) [draft], pp. 28-31; al-Hasan Bilal, *Al-Falastiniyun fi al-Kuwait*, (PLO Information Research Center, Beirut, 1974). On the Palestinian community in Kuwait, its size, occupation and history, see *Falastin ath-Thawra*, 19 June, 1974. On the Kuwaiti policy not to allow Palestinians citizenship, see *JP*, 24 May, 1972; *Ha'aretz*, 25 September, 1974; *Yediyot Aharonot*, 16 January, 1975. On the status of the PLO, see *al-Siyasa*, 21 March, 1974. On 30,000 Palestinians in Saudi Arabia, see *FT*, 5 March, 1973.

12. *FT*, 5 March, 1973, 29 January, 1975 (on Saudi pressure on PLO to purge radical elements); *al-Muharrir*, 8 September, 1973; *MD*, 4 October, 1973; *as-Siyasa*, 3 February, 4 March, 22 May, 1974; *as-Sayyad*, 21 February, 29 August, 1974; *Shu'un Falastiniya*, July 1974, pp. 126-29; *Newsweek*, 21 October, 1974; *al-Hadaf*, 30 November, 1974; *Ha'aretz*, 8 December, 1974; *al-Hawadith*, 1 February, 1975. On attempts to sabotage Saudi Arabia's oil fields, see *Ma'ariv*, 6 February, 1975; J.L. Price, *Oman, Conflict Studies*, No. 53, January 1975, p.7. Palestinians were also accused of being involved in disturbances in Bahrein in August 1975. Palestinians were the first to be affected by the change in Kuwait's internal policies since the last months of 1976 and the suppression of the partial "democracy" there.

13. William Rough, "Emergence of a New Middle Class in Saudi Arabia," *Middle East Journal*, Vol. XXVII, 1973, pp. 7-21; On the tension within the royal family, see *Ma'ariv*, 10 May, 1973; *Newsweek*, 1 July, 1974; *Ha'aretz*, 2 December,1974; *Afro-Asian Affairs*, 15 January, 1975; Abir, *Oil, op. cit.*, pp. 43-62. On the modernization of the tribal army, see R. Riyadh, 14 April—*FBIS*, 15 April, 1974; *MEED*, 19 April, 1974, p. 456; *FT*, 31 January, 1975 (arms sales to the Middle East). On the Saudi Arabian armed forces, see *al-Usbu' al-'Arabi*, 23 December, 1974. On US company training Saudi Arabian national guard, see *JP*, 9, 14 February, 1975; *FT*, 29 January, 10 February, 1975; *Iraqi News Agency (INA)*, 22 October, 1974; *FBIS*, 23 October, 1974.

14. B. Lewis, "The Palestinians and the PLO," *Commentary*, January 1975, p. 42; *Ha'aretz* (weekly supplement), 24 January, 1975.

15. M. Abir, "Red Sea Politics," *Adelphi Paper*, (IISS, London), No. 93, December 1972, pp. 25-37, and "Power rivalry in the Indian Ocean," chapter in *The Arab–Israeli Conflict: Risks and Opportunities*, ed. A. Levi, (Stratis, Tel Aviv, 1975) pp.87-100.

16. G. Jukes, "The Indian Ocean in Soviet Naval Policy," *Adelphi Paper*, No. 87, May 1972; *The Defense Monitor*, (Center for Defense Information, Washington), Vol. iii, No.3, April 1974; S. Karnaw, "Confrontation in the Gulf," *New Republic*, 4, May 1974.

17. See M. Abir, *Adelphi Paper*, No. 93, December 1972, pp.35-37; Abir, *Oil*, *op. cit.*, pp. 124–29; M. Abir, "The Strategic Impact of the Opening of the Suez Canal," *Ma'arakhot*, May 1974, pp.5-11 (Heb.); M. Abir, "Power Rivalry in the Indian Ocean"; UN Document A/AC 159/1, 3 May, 1974 (report to the Scretary General); "The Indian Ocean: A Zone of Peace?" *Swiss Review of World Affairs*, September 1974. On a Soviet delegation, including the commander-in-chief of the navy, in Somalia: *R. Mogadishu*, 16 December—*FBIS*, (Sub-Saharan Africa), 17 December, 1974. Later this visit led to a new Soviet-Somali treaty.

18. In addition to naval facilities the Soviets have in Iraq, it is claimed, a squadron of TU-22s ("Blinder") capable of carrying long-range air-to-surface missiles, several squadrons of SU-20, MiG-23s and 25s, all flown by Soviet pilots: see *New York Times (NYT)*, 3 October, 1973; *Swiss Review*, September, 1974; *Kayhan International*, 3 April, 1974; *IHT*, 7 October, 1974. On stockpiles in Iraq and Russians in MiG-23s overflying Iran and the Gulf states, see *NYT*, 22 January, 1975. The Soviet presence, stockpiling and activity in the Somalia Republic was extensively covered by Western media as well as by the US Office of Defense in 1975.

19. See, for instance, *Falastin ath-Thawra*, 14 August, 1974.

20. On east Siberia's oil, see *JP*, 26 January, 1975 (according to Reuter in Moscow, Russia will become world's biggest oil producer); *JP*, 30 January, 1975, (Japan to help Soviets drill for oil).

21. *FT*, 21 January, 1975; *IHT*, 21 January, 1975. On the US seeking a base in Pakistan, see *FT*, 19 February, 1975.

22. Such a scenario is outlined in an article published in *Harper's Magazine*, March 1975, written under a pseudonym by "an important scholar in US government service."

23. Jens Friedmann, *Die Zeit*, 24 January, 1975. See also, *Christian Science Monitor*, 26 November, 1974; *Washington Post*, 30 December, 1974 ("The

Price of Oil: Achilles Heel''); *Business Week*, 3 January, 1975; *IHT*, 4-5 January, 1975; *Ha'aretz* (weekly supplement), 24 January, 1975. *FT*, 3 February,1975 (Kuwait demands a new price increase in view of decline of US dollar). How aware of the West's economic dilemma Riyadh is can be seen from its policy to prevent a 10% increase in the price of oil in OPEC's meeting in Qatar at the end of 1976.

24. *Washington Post*, 9 January, 1975 ("The Oil Lobby: Image of Vast Power"): *Ha'aretz* (weekly supplement), 24 January, 1975. For promises given to Dr. Kissinger in Riyadh concerning a reduction in the price of oil, see *FT*, 18-19 February, 1975.

25. On an arms deal to the value of nearly $ 20 billion with Iran and with Saudi Arabia, nearly 2 billion with Kuwait and a similar sum with Abu Dhabi, see D.R. Tathinen, *Arms in the Persian Gulf*, (Washington 1974); *The Military Balance 1976–1977*; *MEED*, 12 April, 5 July, 1974; *Akhbar al-Yawm*, 11 May, 1974; *MD*, 17 June, 1974 ("L'Intervention des forces Iranniennes"); *Newsweek*, 12 January, 1975; *FT*, 31 January, 1975. On Saudi Arabia: *Ha'aretz*, 15 March, 1974 (navy), 10 January, 1975; *al-Usbu' al-'Arabi*, 18 November, 1974; *Ma'ariv*, 5 December, 1974; *FT*, 31 January, 1975. On Kuwait: *as-Siyasa*, 28 March, 1974; *ar-Ra'y al-'Amm*, 28 March, 19 April, 1974; *Ma'ariv*, 17 April, 1974; *FT*, 31 January, 1975. On Abu Dhabi: *Le Monde*, 25 April, 1974; *JP*, 13 December, 1974; The Shah discussing the possibility that the Soviet Union may exploit this opportunity to invade his country and on possibility that Western produced arms will be used against their makers, see; *Der Spiegel*, 27 January, 1975.

26. *FT*, 21 January, 1975. On the possibility that the Soviets would take over this base, see *Ma'ariv, 5 February, 1975*.

27. *Der Spiegel*, 27 January, 1975.

28. *Al-Tali'a* (Beirut), October 1972; *MD*, 17 May, 1973, 16 June, 1974; *FT*, 31 May, 1973 ("Iran and the Gulf States").

29. *Ha'aretz*, 5 July, 1972; *JP*, 4, 8 December, 1972; *Arab Report and Record*, 16-30 June, 1973, p.282; *FT*, 22 March, 1974 ("How the Arabs Took Stock"); *Business Week*, 13 January, 1975 ("OPEC").

30. On the declaration of members of the European Economic Community on 6 November, 1973, see *Ma'ariv*, 19 November, 1974.

31. World Bank sources had claimed that Arab producers may accumulate by 1985 US $1,000 billion. See *JP*, 30 July, 1974; *IHT*, 2 December, 1974, 15 January, 1975; *Ha'aretz*, 10 January, 1975. In the meantime the projection of accumulating reserves was greatly reduced. On US $47 billion invested by producers in ten months, see *JP*, 25 December, 1974. On the use of financial

power by Arabs against Jewish-owned banks in Europe, see *FT*, 8-11 February, 1975. An extensive five-year development plan (1975–80) of Saudi Arabia involving an investment of US $142 billion, *FT*, 23 May, 1975.

32. *Ha'aretz*, 18 January, 1974 ($2 billion dollars paid to the Soviet Union during the war); *Ma'ariv*, 3 October, 5 December, 1974; *FT*, 5, 17 December, 1974, 30 January, 31 January, 1975; 1 February, 3 February, 1975. *Le Monde*, 29 January, 1975.

33. *FT*, 17 April, 16 December 1975; *Ma'ariv*, 2 September, 1975; *Christian Science Monitor*, 23 December, 1975. Report of Committee on International Relations, US House of Representatives, 19 December, 1975 (US Arms sales to the Persian Gulf); E. Kennedy: "The Persian Gulf—Arms Race or Arms Control," *Foreign Affairs*, October, 1975, pp. 14-35.

34. See, e.g., the acquisition of Mirage fighter bombers: *ar-Ra'y al-'Amm*, 17 April, 1974; *MEED*, 19 April, 25 October, 1974; *FT*, 17 July, 5 December, 1974, 31 January, 1975. The Kuwaiti defense minister on coordination of arms purchases: *as-Siyasa*, 17 April, 1974. See also *Christian Science Monitor*, 23 December, 1974; *Ha'aretz*, 20 February, 1975).

35. *FT*, 21 January, 1975.

36. *FT*, 10, 31 January, 1975; *Ha'aretz*, 10, 12, 14 January, 20 February, 1975.

37. *Ha'aretz*, 13-20 January, 1975 (quoting *Der Spiegel*).

38. In a speech following the US–Saudi Arabian arms deal, Israel's CoS, General Gur, stated that Israel would have to take into consideration Saudi threats, *Ha'aretz*, *Ma'ariv*, 10 January, 1975. On Israeli protests concerning the flow of US arms to Saudi Arabia and Kuwait, see *Ha'aretz*, 20 February, 1975. Saudi forces stationed in Syria and Jordan were withdrawn in 1976.

39. Abir, *Oil*, *op. cit.*, p. 20.

40. *Ma'ariv*, 17 December, 1970; *ar-Risala*, 21 June, 1972; *JP*, 7 December, 1973 (on reports in the Arab press on Iran's inimical actions against the Arabs in cooperation with the American fleet and Israel during the October War); *al-Muharrir*, 18 September, 1974; Abir, *Oil*, *op. cit.*, pp. 109, 118 (n. 89).

41. *FT*, 31 May, 1973 ("Iran and the Gulf states"); *ar-Ra'y al-'Amm*, 23 February, 1974 (editorial); *MD*, 18 June, 1974; S. Chubin "Iran between the Arab West and the Asian East," *Survival*, (IISS, London, July–August 1974, pp. 180-181. On the expansion of Irani activity in Dhofar, see *al-Hawadith*, 23 November 1973, Price: Oman, p. 9: *Ma'ariv*, (W.P. Jim Hoagland) 2 May, 1975; *JP*, 24 May, 1975. For an Arab League investigation committee concerning complaints of the PDRY's intervention in the Dhofar rebellion and

counter-accusations of Irani–Western–Omani intervention and plot against the Arabs, see *ar-Ra'y al-'Amm*, 8 January, 1974; *as-Siyasa*, 8 January, 12 February, 7 April, 16 May, 1974; *INA*, 11 June—*FBIS*, 12 June, 1974, *Voice of Palestine*, R. Baghdad, 24 June—*FBIS*, 25 June, 1974. The control of the Hormuz Straits became essential for Iran after the blockade of Bab al-Mandab. See *ar-Ra'y al-'Amm*, 8 January, 1974.

42. *JP*, 9 January, 1973 (on Shah-Bahar); *Newsweek*, 21 May, 1973. On military infrastructure on both sides of the Gulf, see *MD*, 4 October, 1973; 16 June, 1974. On the control of Hormuz, see *FT*, 30 May, 1973; *Washington Post*, 25 June, 1973, 31 January, 1975. On an Omani–Irani secret agreement concerning bases and Ra's Musandam, see *as-Sayyad*, 22 August, 1974, pp. 26-27. On the Irani navy, see *Military Balance 1975–1976*; Tathinen, *op. cit.*, p. 14; *Newsweek*, 14 May, 1973, 12 January, 1975; *South African Digest*, 15, 29 November, 1974; On the question of Iran's control of the Straits of Hormuz and its impact, see *as-Siyasa*, 12 February, 1974; *South African Digest*, 1 November, 1974.

43. *FT*, 31 May, 1973 (on the question of Saudi and Kuwaiti decisions to strengthen their armed forces due to fear of Iran's policy, see also *ar-Ra'y al-'Amm*, 24 January, 23 February, 1974; Chubin, p. 180; *al-Muharrir*, 18 September, 1974; *al-Anba'*, 3 October, 1974 (on this inevitability of a clash between Iranian and Arab nationalism if Iran continues its political and economic tactics in the Arab Gulf). On the growing dislike and suspicion of Iran in Saudi Arabia, see *MD*, 4 October, 1973, 17 June, 1974; *Ma'ariv*, 13 June, 1974; *FT*, 8 January, 1975; *NYT*, 2 February, 1975. On a Gulf countries' front aimed against Iran's expansionism led by Saudi Arabia, see *as-Sayyad*, 22 August, 1974; *Afro–Asian Affairs*, 15 January, 1975. *R. Riyad*, 3 December—*FBIS*, 4 December, 1974; *Washington Post*, 23 February, 1975 (a suggested Saudi–Iraqi alliance to preserve "the Arab character" of the Gulf).

44. Chubin, p. 181; *al-Nahar*, 23 December, 1974; *Christian Science Monitor*, 23 December, 1974; *FT*, 24 December, 1974; *NYT*, 22 January, 1975; *Der Spiegel*, No. 4, January, 1975 (interview with the Shah).

45. *JP*, 10 January, 1975, according to UP. On recent Irani activities to consolidate its control over the Gulf and the Straits of Hormuz: *Washington Post*, 3 January, 1975; *FT*, 4 January, 1975; *Le Monde*, 4 February, 1975, on intensification of Irani activity in Dhofar. Also: note 40 above.

46. Chubin, pp. 172-174.

47. Chubin, p. 174; *FT*, 8 January, 1975 ("End of an Estrangement"), 23 January, 1975 ("Sadat's Military Tightrope"). Egypt has been the recipient of substantial Iranian economic support since the beginning of 1974. See *al-Ahram*, 26 April, 1974; *as-Siyasa*, 27 May, 1974 (US $850 million), 5 June,

1974 (projects in the field of oil); *FT*, 29 November, 1974 (US $640 million Irani aid program to Egypt), 8 January, 1975. Chubin, p.174, makes the point that a new escalation in Arab–Israeli relations may also accelerate the process of radicalization which has already begun in some of the Gulf states.

48. Chubin, pp. 173-174. Dr. Sharam Chubin is a member of the Iranian Institute for International, Economic and Political Studies and, together with its Acting Director, Dr. Abbas Amirie, visited several Arab countries before writing his article, in order to compile a report on the Middle East following the October War. It is evident from Chubin's article that Iran's sympathy is with the democratic-nationalist Arab regimes. He also recommends, on p. 181, that Iran should not oppose nationalist-oriented revolutions in the Arabian Peninsula: Also Sharam Chubin and Mohammad Fard-Saidi; *Recent Trends in Middle East Politics and Iran's Foreign Policy*, (Tehran, 1975) pp. 1-106; *Ma'ariv*, 16 February, 1975, Qadhafi's interview to *Vienna Daily Courier* accuses Iran of meddling in Arab Affairs.

49. Abir, *Oil, op. cit.*, p. 208.

50. Chubin, pp. 173-174; *FT*, 23 January, 1975. On the Shah's reiteration that he would not take part in future Arab oil embargo, see *JP*, 3 February, 1975; *FT*, 3 February, 1975. Iran's per capita income is still US $800, compared to Kuwait's $7,000: see *Fortune*, October 1974, pp. 146-147. Iran temporarily withdrew its ambassadors from the Gulf Arab countries at the beginning of 1976 when the latter decided to use the term "Arab Gulf" when founding a news agency (the name was duly changed). In a sense this was also a protest against the growing hostility to Iran and the undermining of its oil price policy by some Arab producers.

51. Lewis, p. 74.

52. See, e.g., *Ha'aretz*, 24 January, 1975 (a *Der Spiegel* correspondent interviewing a Soviet official in the UN).

Index

Index

Aba Island, 326
Abadan, 386
'Abbas, Khalid Hasan, 326
'Abbud, Ibrahim, 325-6, 328, 332
Abdallah, 242
Abdel Nasser, Jamal, *See Nasser*
Abu Ageila, 100
Abu Dhabi, 149, 152, 352, 359-63, 372, 380, 383, 393
Abu 'Isa, Faruk, 331
Abu 'Ita, Nikula, 280
Abu Mayzar, 'Abd al-Muhsin, 272, 284
Abu Musa, 353, 364, 386, 387
Abu Shilbaya, Muhammad, 271, 279, 290n.
Aden, 295, 300-1, 303-4, 306, 361, 377-8, 393
Adenauer, Konrad, 53-54
Afghanistan, 362
'Aflaq, Michel, 319
Africa, 323, 327, 332-3
Afro-Asian World, 194, 209, 211
Ahmad, Musa, 335, 338, 340
Ahmar, 'Abdallah al-, 299, 305,
'Ajlun, 237
al-'Alami, Musa, 274, 277
'Alawis, 219, 224
Alexandria, 31, 35, 181
ALF, 252
Algeria, *See also Arab Summit Con-ferences*, 33, 58, 60, 164, 167-8, 181
Algiers Agreement, 318-9
'Ali, Muhammad, 325
Alier, Abel, 333
Amer, 'Abd al-Hakim, 157-8, 206
Amman, 236-7, 241, 277, 279
Amman Agreement, 238
'Ammash, Salih Mahdi, 313
Ansar, 326-7, 329
Anya Nya, 333

Arab League, 53, 147, 157, 165, 173, 185, 280, 349, 353
Arab Republic of Egypt, 210
Arab Socialist Union, *See Egypt*
Arab Summit Conferences, 336
  Algeria, 182
  Khartoum, 5, 140, 142, 146, 160, 168, 185, 191, 209, 226, 373, 382
  Rabat, 10, 143, 160, 209, 226, 245, 253, 256, 287-9, 371, 377
"Arabian Gulf," 365, 385
Arabian Peninsula, 163, 231, 295, 297, 302, 305, 366, 370-5, 377, 380, 385, 387-8, 390-1, 400n.
Arabism, 95, 210, 329, 349, 391
"Arabistan," 385
Arafat, Yasir, 33, 35, 41, 256, 261n., 263n. 266n., 277
'Arif, 'Abd ar-Rahman, 309, 312, 353, al-'Arish, 218n.
'Arqub, 250
Asad, Hafiz al-, 43, 158-9, 179-80, 201, 219-24, 226-7, 228n., 319
ASU, *See Egypt*
Aswan High Dam, 89, 128-9, 196, 211
Atlantic Ocean, 165, 376
Australia, 356
'Awadallah, Babikr, 326
'Awwad, 'Arabi, 284
Al-Azhar, 348

Bab al-Mandab, 306, 357, 387
Baghdad, *See also Iraq*, 320n.
Baghdad Pact, 211, 348-9, 385
Bahrein, 352-3, 355, 359, 363-4, 366, 374, 385-6, 393
Bakr, Ahmad Hasan al-, 309-11, 313-7, 320-321, 353, 355
Bakr, Ibrahim, 272
Bangladesh, 378

List of
Participants
in the
Colloquium

List of Participants
in the Colloquium

PROFESSOR MORDECHAI ABIR
Institute of Asian and African Studies. Hebrew University of Jerusalem.

DR. SHLOMO AHRONSON
Dept. of Political Science, Hebrew University of Jerusalem.

MR. YIGAL ALLON
Deputy Prime Minister and Minister of Foreign Affairs.

PROFESSOR SEADIA AMIEL
Ministry of Defense and Israel Atomic Energy Commission, Tel Aviv.

MR. MEIR AMIT
Tel Aviv.

PROFESSOR GABRIEL BAER
Institute of Asian and African Studies, Hebrew University of Jerusalem.

DR. GABRIEL BEN-DOR
Institute for Research on the Middle East, Dept. of Political Science, Haifa University.

PROFESSOR HAIM BEN-SHACHAR

President of Tel Aviv University.

MRS. VARDA BEN-ZVI
The Shiloah Center for Middle Eastern and African Studies. Tel Aviv University.

MR. MOSHE BITAN
Director, Paz-Oil Co. Ltd., Tel Aviv.

PROFESSOR W. Z. BRINER
Dept. of Near Eastern Studies, Berkeley.

DR. RAINER BÜREN
Deutsches Orient Institut, Hamburg.

PROFESSOR JOSEPH CHURBA
Arlington, Virginia.

MR. GABRIEL COHEN
Dept. of History, Tel Aviv University.

PROFESSOR URIEL DANN
Dept. of Middle Eastern and African History and The Shiloah
Center for Middle Eastern and African Studies, Tel Aviv
University.

MR. DANIEL DISHON
The Shiloah Center for Middle Eastern and African Studies, Tel
Aviv University.

MR. AMOS ERAN
Director-General, Prime Minister's Office.

DR. ODED ERAN
The Russian and East European Research Center, Tel Aviv
University.

DR. YAIR EVRON
The Leonard Davis Institute for International Relations and
Activities, Hebrew University of Jerusalem.

MR. LARRY L. FABIAN
Middle East Program, Carnegie Endowment for International
Peace, Washington D.C.

MR. JOSEPH GEVA
Director, Super-Sol Ltd., Tel Aviv

DR. BARUCH GORWITZ
The Russian and East European Research Center, Tel Aviv
University.

DR. ARNON GOTFELD
Dept. of History, Tel Aviv University.

PROFESSOR Y. HARKABI
Hebrew University of Jerusalem.

MR. HAIM HERZOG
Israel Ambassador to the UN.

MR. YAIR HIRSHFELD
Dept. of Middle Eastern and African History, Tel Aviv University.

PROFESSOR ELIYAHU KANOVSKY
Dept. of Economics, Bar Ilan University and The Shiloah Center
for Middle Eastern and African Studies, Tel Aviv University.

PROFESSOR GEOFFREY KEMP
The Fletcher School of Law and Diplomacy, Tufts University,
Massachusetts.

DR. JOEL KRAEMER
Dept. of Middle Eastern and African History, Tel Aviv University.

PROFESSOR MOSHE MAOZ
The Harry S. Truman Research Institute, Hebrew University of
Jerusalem.

PROFESSOR HAROLD MARCUS
Michigan State University.

DR. MATI MAYZEL
The Russian and East European Research Center and the Center
for Strategic Studies, Tel Aviv University.

PROFESSOR LINDA B. MILLER
Wellesley College, Wellesley, Mass.

DR. GUR OFER
Dept. of Economics and The Soviet and East European Research
Center, Hebrew University of Jerusalem.

DR. MATTITYAHU PELED
Dept. of Arabic, Tel Aviv University.

DR. BEN-CION PINCHUK
The Russian and East European Research Center, Tel Aviv
University.

DR. YEHOSHUA PORAT
Institute of Asian and African Studies, Hebrew University of
Jerusalem.

PROFESSOR WILLIAM B. QUANDT
Dept. of Political Science, University of Pennsylvania, Philadelphia and National Security Council/Near East, Washington.

DR. ITAMAR RABINOVICH
Dept. of Middle Eastern and African History and The Shiloah Center for Middle Eastern and African Studies, Tel Aviv University.

PROFESSOR ROUHOLLAH K. RAMAZANI
Edward R. Stettinius Jr., Woodrow Wilson Dept. of Government and Foreign Affairs, University of Virginia.

MR. ELIE REKHESS
The Shiloah Center for Middle Eastern and African Studies, Tel Aviv University.

DR. YAACOV RO'I
The Russian and East European Research Center, Tel Aviv University.

PROFESSOR ALVIN Z. RUBINSTEIN
Dept. of Political Science, University of Pennsylvania, Philadelphia.

DR. AMNON SELA
Dept. of International Relations and Dept. of Russian and Slavic Studies, Hebrew University of Jerusalem.

PROFESSOR HAIM SHAKED
The Shiloah Center for Middle Eastern and African Studies, Department of Middle Eastern and African History, Tel Aviv University.

PROFESSOR SHIMON SHAMIR
The Shiloah Center for Middle Eastern and African Studies, Department of Middle Eastern and African History. Tel Aviv University.

DR. ELIEZER SHEFFER
Bank of Israel, Jerusalem.

DR. GABRIEL SHEFFER
The Van Leer Foundation, Jerusalem.

MR. ARYEH SHMUELEVITZ
Dept. of Middle Eastern and African History and The Shiloah Center for Middle Eastern and African Studies, Tel Aviv University.

PROFESSOR BENJAMIN SHWADRAN
Dept. of Middle Eastern and African History, Tel Aviv University.

PROFESSOR MAX SINGER
World Institute, Jerusalem.

MR. ASHER SUSSER
The Shiloah Center for Middle Eastern and African Studies, Tel Aviv University.

DRᵢ DALE R. TAHTINEN
The American Enterprise Institute, Washington D.C.

MR. ISRAEL TAL
Ministry of Defense.

PROFESSOR DAVID VITAL
Dept. of Political Science, Haifa University.

PROFESSOR YEHUDA WALLACH
The Aranne School of History, Tel Aviv University.

PROFESSOR GABRIEL WARBURG
Dept. of Middle Eastern and African Studies, Haifa University.

MRS. ESTHER (SOUERY) WEBMAN
The Shiloah Center for Middle Eastern and African Studies, Tel Aviv University.

MRS. TAMAR YEGNESS
The Shiloah Center for Middle Eastern and African Studies, Tel Aviv University.